45,00

D1547947

COLLECTED POETRY AND PROSE

Dante Gabriel Rossetti

Collected Poetry and Prose

EDITED BY JEROME MCGANN

Yale University Press / New Haven & London

Designed by Nancy Ovedovitz and set in Galliard Old Style
type by Integrated Publishing Solutions, Grand Rapids,
Michigan. Printed in the United States of America by
Vail-Ballou Press, Binghamton, New York.

Library of Congress Cataloging-in-Publication Data
Rossetti, Dante Gabriel, 1828–1882.
[Selections. 2003]
Collected poetry and prose / Dante Gabriel Rossetti ; edited
by Jerome McGann.
p. cm.
Includes bibliographical references and indexes.
ISBN 0-300-09801-4 (cloth : alk. paper)—ISBN 0-300-09802-2
(pbk. : alk. paper)
I. McGann, Jerome J. II. Title.

PR5242.M38 2003
821'.8—dc21   2002191017

A catalogue record for this book is available from the
British Library.

The paper in this book meets the guidelines for permanence
and durability of the Committee on Production Guidelines
for Book Longevity of the Council on Library Resources.

10 9 8 7 6 5 4 3 2 1

CONTENTS

Part Three • Sonnets for Pictures and Other Sonnets
(1850, 1870, 1881)

Part Six • Other Translations

THE LIFE

Dante Gabriel Rossetti was born in London on 12 May 1828 and died on Easter Day, 9 April 1882. He spent nearly his entire working life in the city of his birth. Indeed, he only left Great Britain three times, and in each case but the first quite briefly. Though his work is steeped in Italian traditions (both poetical and pictorial), Rossetti never visited Italy. He is first and always an English — more, a London — writer and artist.

His father was the celebrated (and controversial) Dante scholar and Italian political exile Gabriele Rossetti (1783–1854). His mother, Frances (1800–1886), much younger than her husband, was Anglo-Italian — Polidori on her father's side. (Her brother, Dr. John Polidori, was Byron's doctor and companion during the first part of his exile from England in 1816.) Rossetti had three siblings, two younger than himself. All were remarkable. His sister Christina (1830–1894) became as distinguished a poet as her brother. His brother, William Michael (1829–1919), a writer himself, edited his brother's work after the latter's death and served as the first archivist and historian of the Pre-Raphaelite movement. His other sister, Maria Francesca (1827–1876), was the oldest sibling; she published a commentary on Dante and became an Anglican nun.

Rossetti's interests in writing and painting appeared early, encouraged by his immediate family life as well as by the literary interests of his grandfather Polidori. All four siblings were writing from a very early age, and drawings by Rossetti survive from the mid-1830s. He went to Sass's drawing school in 1841, and in 1845 moved to the Antique School of the Royal Academy. He did not work well under academic tutelage, however, and in 1848 he dropped away from school altogether.

The departure from school proved a crucial event in Rossetti's life. He initially apprenticed himself to Ford Madox Brown (1821–1893), whose work he had first seen and admired in 1844. At the 1848 Royal Academy Exhibition he saw William Holman Hunt's (1827–1910) *Eve of St. Agnes* and was so taken with it that he sought out the young painter. The two quickly became friends. Soon Rossetti moved in with Hunt and, under his friend's critical eye, tried to develop more disciplined work habits. It was under Hunt's supervision that Rossetti executed his first important painting, *The Girlhood of Mary Virgin*, begun in the summer of 1848. At the same time, he was working on or finishing a series of remarkable writings (among them, "The Blessed Damozel" and most of the translations that eventually appeared as the *Early Italian Poets* in 1861), which he shared with Hunt and his other new friends, including the young prodigy John Everett Millais (1829–1896). It was in this year that the core set of Rossetti's artistic and poetical touchstones began to coalesce in a practical way. Thus, 1848 marks not only a European watershed, it is equally the year of Rossetti's emergence as a serious — indeed, an epochal — figure in British art and poetry.

In the same year, Rossetti's extraordinary range of talents and interests, combined with his energy and enthusiasm, made him the central figure in the formation of a group of writers and artists who were to name themselves the Pre-Raphaelite Brotherhood (PRB). Hunt's express hostility to academy art gave the movement its initial polemical and theoretical focus. He was particularly inspired by the first two volumes of Ruskin's *Modern Painters* (1843–1846) and introduced the others to Ruskin's ideas, which proved fruitful to so many in and associated with the Pre-Raphaelite movement and its aftermath. But it was Rossetti whose cultural vision and force of character magnetized the group, just as it was Rossetti's work which was to have the longest and most significant impact on poetry and the visual arts.

The movement's founding is customarily dated to an evening in October 1848, when Hunt, Millais, and Rossetti were studying Carlo Lasinio's engravings after the Campo Santo frescoes in Pisa. Their admiration for these pictures impelled them to form a group devoted to bringing about a revolution in artistic practice and cultural sensibilities. The three men soon gathered together a number of artists and writers who met monthly to discuss topics of mutual interest. They included Rossetti's brother, William Michael, the young sculptor Thomas Woolner (1825–1892), James Collinson (1825?–1881; a painter engaged to Rossetti's sister Christina), and F. G. Stephens (1828–1907), who would later become an influential art critic.

The PRB made its debut early in 1849 when Hunt and Millais put up works at the Royal Academy Exhibition and Rossetti at the Free Exhibition at Hyde Park Corner. Despite the "PRB" signatures on their works — the initials would soon become a focus of critical attack — their works were reasonably well received. In the fall of 1849 Hunt and Rossetti left for a brief trip to Belgium and Paris, where they studied and enthused over the works of various painters whom they regarded as their spiritual precursors. Upon their return, the group began to lay plans for publishing a journal that would carry the ideas of the PRB to a larger audience. This was the famous periodical *The Germ* (subtitled "Thoughts towards Nature in Poetry, Literature, and Art"). Begun early in 1850, it ran for only four issues. Despite its lack of initial success, however, the publication would prove an important venture.

In contrast to the response in 1849, the exhibition of the work of Rossetti and the other PRBs in 1850 produced a firestorm of hostile criticism. The event brought

Ruskin to the defense of the young painters — a signal moment in their history. Ruskin defined the members of the PRB as "serious artists," and his authority in effect established the movement's cultural position. Rossetti and Ruskin became close friends for a time, but they grew apart when Rossetti grew tired of playing the role of Ruskin's pupil.

1850 brought another crucial change to Rossetti's life: He met the beautiful Elizabeth Siddal (1829–1862), the daughter of a cutler. He painted and drew "Lizzie" — as everyone knew her — obsessively. At first, it was the poverty of their circumstances that prevented their marriage. Later in the 50s, though, other beautiful women began to invade Rossetti's imagination, including Fanny Cornforth (1835?–1905) and Jane Burden (1839–1914), who would eventually marry Rossetti's friend William Morris. Nonetheless, though their relationship grew increasingly troubled, Rossetti's devotion to Elizabeth never really failed, and they finally married in 1860. Two years later Elizabeth — whose health had been uncertain for a number of years — died of an overdose of laudanum.

Through the 1850s Rossetti worked mainly on his painting. The initial intense period of his imaginative writing all but ceased for a time after 1852. Rossetti poured himself into his art, where he seemed — by his own judgment — unable to express himself exactly as he wanted. He gave up oil painting for a time and turned to watercolor, the medium in which he would produce some of his greatest works.

In terms of his public career, the central event of this period was the so-called Jovial Campaign, Rossetti's 1857 commission to paint the walls of the Debating Hall of the Union Society in Oxford. As it turned out, Rossetti and his friends did execute the murals, but the work almost immediately faded and disappeared because the group of artists did not know how to prepare the walls properly for the paintings. Despite this disaster, the project attracted great attention to Rossetti and his friends — in this case, largely a new cast of friends including Edward Jones (later Burne-Jones) and William Morris.

The Jovial Campaign ought to be seen as the culminant event in the years 1856–57, when Rossetti and the PRB finally gained a position of recognized cultural authority. Two other projects of these years were also important. In 1856 William Morris and his friends launched the *Oxford and Cambridge Magazine*. A sequel to the *Germ*, and in certain obvious ways a much superior production, it too perished after a short run — this time after a year. But the magazine brought Rossetti a new set of attachments that would prove fateful for all concerned. The other event was the publication of Moxon's illustrated edition of Tennyson's selected poetry, which appeared early in 1857. The book carried illustrations by various artists of the day. Rossetti's contributions, which illustrated "The Palace of Art" and several other poems, were stunning. His appearance in this book defined him as an artist of established position.

The death of Elizabeth early in 1862 put a (temporary) end to some elaborate publishing plans that Rossetti had set in train. In 1861 he assembled the poetical translations of medieval Italian poetry that he had been doing in the 1840s. He finished the work and brought out, at the end of the year, the important volume *The Early Italian Poets* (later revised and reissued in 1874 as *Dante and His Circle*). His plan was to publish an accompanying volume of original poetry to be called *Dante at Verona and Other Poems*. Though advertised as forthcoming in his book of translations, the volume was never issued. In one of the two most celebrated acts of his life, Rossetti buried the manuscript in the coffin with his wife. (The second was his recovery of the volume, in 1869, from Elizabeth's grave.)

During the 1860s Rossetti wrote little poetry but returned to oils and produced a great deal of work as a painter. This was the period when his reputation as an artist grew and he began to command remarkable prices for his pictures. The Arthurian and Dantean subjects that had been his main preoccupation for several years were now succeeded by a series of erotic female portraits. Fanny Cornforth was Rossetti's principal model for the earliest of these works, but later the face of Jane Morris dominated his pictures.

After the death of his wife he began to experience onsets of depression and hypochondria. He moved to 16 Cheyne Walk and after a few years began to close himself into its precincts. He slowly narrowed his social circle, stopped exhibiting, and began to take spirits and drugs. In 1867 his mental and physical condition deteriorated precipitously when he began to fear he would go blind. It was at this point that he began to take chloral, to which he became addicted.

For the remainder of his life he would be surrounded by accumulating darknesses — guilts, depressions, illnesses — and he would gradually break with some of his closest and most loyal friends. But out of the nightmare world that gradually arose in the midst of his growing public success and suffocating middle class luxury, Rossetti created a series of literary and pictorial works of great power and significance.

In 1866 and 1867 he wrote two sonnets for recent pictures — the poems now known as "Soul's Beauty" and "Body's Beauty," which appeared in print in 1868, along with another sonnet for a picture, "Venus Verticordia." The poems restored him to a sense of the importance of his poetry, which he began to take up again in earnest. The activity stimulated his old desire to see his original writings in print. His eye problems further induced him to shift his principal creative activity from art to literature. Since much of this poetry had been buried with Elizabeth, and since Rossetti kept no copies of some of his most important works, the grisly scheme to exhume the volume was set in motion. In the end the book was recovered for Rossetti by some friends. In 1869 he began recopying and revising these older works and adding new poems to them. He had these works printed up in a series of proofs and so-called trial books marked "for private circulation," and eventually he gathered the lot together and published his 1870 volume, *Poems*.

The book was a stunning success. Its publication was also the occasion of one of the most famous literary controversies of the century when it was reviewed in 1871 by Robert Buchanan in the pseudonymous essay "The Fleshly School of Poetry — Mr. D. G. Rossetti" in the *Contemporary Review*. Buchanan's main charge, that Rossetti's volume was full of indecencies, started a furious series of further attacks, defenses, counterattacks, and general public clamour. Rossetti himself entered the fray with an essay of self-defense, "The Stealthy School of Criticism," which he published in the *Athenæum* in December. None of this did any serious damage to Rossetti's celebrity, and indeed Buchanan would, after Rossetti's death, all but recant his original position.

The 1870 poems had been put together, and many new ones written, after Rossetti had moved from London to Barbara Bodichon's country house, Scalands, near Robertsbridge, Hastings. He moved there in March 1870 to escape his claustrophobic London existence. Soon Jane and William Morris came to visit him, with Jane staying on for nearly the entire period of his sojourn, which ended on May 9. In those two months she would stamp his new book with her presence. From a biographical point of view, the volume is dominated by Rossetti's two great love obsessions — his old love, Elizabeth, now dead and enshrined to an imaginative heaven; and the new love, Jane Morris, whose very earthly existence seemed to bring Rossetti back to life.

Between 1871 and 1874 the relationship between Rossetti and Jane Morris achieved an extreme intensity. Rossetti spent much of the time at the Morrises' house at Kelmscott, and much of that time William was not at home. The poetry Rossetti wrote largely focuses on his love for Jane Morris. But in the end the romantic idyl began to dissipate, and finally Jane left Kelmscott with her family in July 1874.

With that separation the final phase of Rossetti's life was inaugurated. It was a period during which Rossetti's eccentricities, manias, and hallucinations began to dominate his existence. Although he continued to paint, and in fact produced some astonishing works, he often seemed to be filling up — or out — his time. In 1880–81 he experienced a renewed burst of poetical work as he prepared to issue a new and augmented edition of his 1870 volume. This was to include a new version of his masterwork "The House of Life," now twice the size of the 1870 version. He also wrote some new, long ballads and returned to a number of important works written or begun earlier, like the impressive fragment "The Bride's Prelude." The body of work proved so large, in fact, that he eventually decided two volumes should be published. These were *Ballads and Sonnets* and the augmented "new edition" of *Poems*. Both appeared in 1881.

Rossetti's devoted brother William Michael called this last phase of Rossetti's life "the chloralized years." With his mind continually transacted by various guilts and regrets, Rossetti's health slowly deteriorated. After the last two volumes were published he made two vain efforts to restore his health. He went to the Lake District in the fall of 1881 and later, on his doctor's advice, went to stay with a friend at his country house in Birchington. There he died.

THE WORKS

The point of departure for reading Rossetti has to be Walter Pater's essay on the poetry, which he published in 1883 shortly after Rossetti's death. The strongest as well as the subtlest literary-critical intelligence of the period in England, Pater saw "poetic originality" as the defining quality of Rossetti's work. The writing features an "almost grotesque materialising of abstractions" and stylistic "particularisation." Pater's essay explores the paradox of a writer seen as both limpid and abstruse. On one hand Rossetti covets a "transparency in language" devoted to "the imaginative creation of things that are ideal from their very birth." On the other he is "always personal and even recondite, in a certain sense learned and casuistical, sometimes complex or obscure."

Like Pope, when Rossetti came into his own as a writer he was quite young, in his teens; and although some of the work from his later years is arguably stronger or more profound, the prose and poetry composed between his fifteenth and twentieth years is already mature, and he is in full possession of his distinctive poetic resources. Coleridge, Keats, Tennyson, Poe, and Browning: these are the English-language writers who stand behind his work and lead him to that "originality" Pater recognized. Almost equally important, of course, are the writers Rossetti himself named "Dante and his circle." Indeed, Dante is probably Rossetti's single most important precursor, partly because he supplied Rossetti with a powerful myth of the poet's life, and partly because, in seeking to reconstruct that myth through his translations, Rossetti was led to fashion an English style that has been materially marked by Italian linguistic and poetical resources.

> Beatrice is gone up into high Heaven,
> The kingdom where the angels are at peace
> . . . .
> Wonderfully out of the beautiful form
> Soared her clear spirit
>
> Who is she coming, whom all gaze upon
> Who makes the air all tremulous with light,
> And at whose side is Love himself? That none
> Dare speak, but each man's sighs are infinite?

In the first two passages, which open the second and third stanzas of his translation of Dante's famous canzone "Gli occhi dolente," Rossetti fashions remarkable English equivalents for Dante's hendecasyllabic rhythms. The third passage is his translation of the opening of Cavalcanti's sonnet "Chi e questa che vien," and it nicely exhibits a number of stylistic features that Rossetti will later incorporate into his English verse. Notable are the synaesthesia, the sharp rendering of abstractions, the resort to sequences of brief words that subtly highlight key longer words ("coming," "tremulous," "himself," "infinite"), the careful rhythmic arrangement of the latter, and finally, the slightly off rhymes. The rhyming resources of Italian will draw Rossetti to develop many unusual rhymes and rhyming rhythms, some of them shocking, even outrageous.

The combination of Rossetti's favorite English poets and his Italian verse inheritance lies behind that astonishing signature work of Rossetti's late teens, "The Blessed Damozel," with its paradoxical combinations — rhythmical as well as figurative.

> It lies in Heaven, across the flood
> Of ether, as a bridge.
> Beneath, the tides of day and night
> With flame and darkness ridge
> The void, as low as where this earth
> Spins like a fretful midge
> . . . .
> The sun was gone now; the curled moon
> Was like a little feather
> Fluttering far down the gulf; and now
> She spoke through the still weather.
> Her voice was like the voice the stars
> Had when they sang together.

In this writing Rossetti is not just materializing spiritual realities and abstract ideas. He is rather *literalizing* that range of perceived and unperceived phenomena, turning it into a new kind of reality, purely linguistic. The effect inevitably recalls Coleridge's commentary on "Kubla Khan" as a vision in which "all the images rose up before [him] as things." Here we would be inclined to say "all the images *and* all the rhythms."

Rossetti's characteristic style is well suited to his most famous pair of subjects, Art and Love, where "matter and spirit . . . play inextricably into each other." Though Pater does not pursue that thought, both subjects are best taken up as activities, in performative and, finally, in interactive ways. The blending of the material and the spiritual, of soul and body, of idea and act, defines Rossetti's pictorial work as much as it does his verse. A pair of famous lines summarizes Rossetti's position: "Thy soul I know not from thy body, nor / Thee from myself, neither our love from God." Despite the resolute "fleshliness" of the poetry, Pater astutely calls it "sacramental" because it displays this performative quality. Its extreme idealizations emerge in and through acts of writing, much as prayer represents an instantiated act of devotion.

One other general characteristic of Rossetti's work is important: his commitment to what he called "fundamental brainwork." Unlike his greatly gifted but undemonstrative sister, Dante Gabriel is driven by programmatic ideas and conceptual goals, as his contemporaries well knew. "Exhaustless invention" is how Ruskin described his pictorial work, which he learned to admire but came to deplore as it kept plunging through its Faustian pursuits. Rossetti holds our attention as we are held by the restless and brilliant Stephen Dedalus, who was — as Stephen tells Mr. Deasy in *Ulysses* — "A learner rather" than a teacher. So to read or look at Rossetti's work — actions required by both the texts and the pictures — is to enter a demanding intellectual space. Rossetti broke with Ruskin in the mid-1860s over a disagreement about how to manage the inheritance of Venetian art. But he remained to the end primarily Ruskinian (rather than Paterian) in treating art and writing more as a scene of intellectual action rather than reflection.

Rossetti began his career by catalyzing the formation of the Pre-Raphaelite Brotherhood through the force of his ideas and personality, which no one at the time — not even those who were teaching him how to paint, like Madox Brown and Holman Hunt — could stay or resist. *The Germ* was his brainchild, and he placed in its first number one of the signal aesthetic documents of the period, his artistic manifesto "Hand and Soul." Modest though it seems, "Hand and Soul" undertakes to overhaul the entire edifice of art history as it was formulated by Vasari and handed down to Rossetti's day and even to our own. The argument with Vasari concentrates on the idea — for Rossetti, the illusion — of progress in the arts. Primitive Italian art undergoes a revisionary reading in the history of Rossetti's narrator, Chiaro, who refuses the promise of the coming glories of the Renaissance. A modern incarnation of what Trotsky would later call "the privilege of historical backwardness," Chiaro represents an imaginative resource for the nineteenth century precisely because of his primitive aesthetic commitments — all those stylistic features that would come to be judged crude and incompetent by later art historians, with their enlightened and progressivist myths of art.

Crucially important is the fact that Rossetti casts his argument in an imaginative rather than an expository form. His point is that the most incisive explanation of an artistic practice ought to be performative — as it is, for example, in Horace's *Ars Poetica,* in Pope, in Blake's *Marriage of Heaven and Hell,* or in Wilde's dialogues. In this programmatic context three topics emerge as indispensable areas of critical attention. Each is closely related to the others. They are, first, Rossetti's theory and practice of translation; second, his exploration of the "double work of art"; and third, his remarkable understanding of what he called "an inner standing-point" as one of the "motive powers of art."

Rossetti set out his ideas about translation in the preface to his first published book, *The Early Italian Poets* (1861), where he calls it the "most direct form of commentary" and exegesis. It is thus paradigmatic of a performative act of literary criticism. Furthermore, the translator's obligation is to pursue "fidelity" rather than "literality" as his translational goal. So Rossetti's translations tend to be relatively free with respect to semantic literality and relatively strict with respect to metrical imitation. For Rossetti, a prose translation of poetry is no translation at all. A final "fidelity" is measured by this explicit rule: "a good poem shall not be turned into a bad one." The rule follows from Rossetti's basic thought that "the only true motive for putting poetry into a fresh language must be to endow a fresh nation, as far as possible, with one more possession of beauty."

Rossetti sees Dante's *La Vita Nuova* as a prophetic annunciation of these ideas, and when he translates that work as "The New Life" the translation incarnates the emergence of a new artistic life in the nineteenth century. Rossetti literally becomes "Dante Rossetti," the resurrected figure of the great Florentine and, as such, the living sign of the deathless character of art. This dynamic is what "Art for Art's sake" signifies for Rossetti. As Dante Alighieri's avatar, he is called to his comprehensive work of translation because, in his view, Dante's writings are the gravitational center of the literary rebirth that took place between the emergence of the Sicilian School and the appearance of Boccaccio and Petrarch.

But Rossetti's aesthetic program was not only a literary one. Perhaps his most important aesthetic contribution was that remarkable generic form known as "the double work of art." This form is an amalgam of literary and pictorial works on a single subject — two at a minimum, but the number of objects can be and often are multiple: for example, the various constellations of pictures and texts named "The Blessed Damozel," "Proserpina," " Fazio's Mistress," "La Bella Mano," and so forth. Rossetti's first important double work, *The Girlhood of Mary Virgin,* exhibits the form's typical dynamic structure. That is to say, Rossetti usually "doubles" a pictorial work with a text or a set of texts. The picture may be his own or someone else's. In 1849, for example, he wrote a series of outstanding poems, "Sonnets for Pictures," that responded to various paintings he saw on the trip he and Holman Hunt made to Belgium and Paris. The doubling may also proceed in the other direction, however, as when Rossetti "illustrates" his own texts or texts from Poe, Tennyson, or other writers. Rossetti's earliest double works are of this last kind and they clearly derive from the illustrated book tradition.

These double works are translational forms — "direct forms of commentary" and exegesis. The dialectic of the forms is once again performative rather than conceptual. One might judge from this process that Rossetti is pursuing an unmediated form of knowing, but the truth is otherwise. What the artist wants to avoid with these double works is precisely the transformation of artistic acts into ideated terms, as if thinking were an abstract process of reflection. For Rossetti, on the contrary, the practice of art is a practice of thought more penetrating than expository explanation. The Ideal forms of thinking are not abstract, they are enfleshed, aesthetic: total body experiences, as it were. Knowing by (re)doing.

This kind of imaginative work leads Rossetti to his theory of "the inner standing-point" as one of the "motive powers of art." The key text is Rossetti's discussion of his dramatic monologue "Jenny" in "The Stealthy School of Criticism," his 1871 critical response to Buchanan's attack on his poetry. Like Ruskin earlier, Buchanan was offended and troubled by "Jenny." The subject — prostitution — was problematic to a degree, but worse was the way Rossetti's poem draws a close relation between prostitution and the practice of art. Would "a treatment from without" — for instance, a prose essay on the subject — have been preferable? Rossetti says no. The more difficult the material, the more one needs an imaginative rather than an expository approach, for "the motive powers of art reverse the requirement of science, and demand first of all an inner standing-point. The heart of such a mystery as this must be plucked from the very world in which it beats or bleeds."

Rossetti had introduced the theory of the inner standing-point some years before, in an unpublished note to his pastiche poem "Ave," one of his early "Songs of the Art Catholic." The idea of art at an inner standing-point is a clear theoretical reflection on the dramatic monologue, especially on Robert Browning's use of the form, which Rossetti much admired. Rossetti's thoughts on this genre, however, are quite different from Browning's—both in 1847–1848, when he wrote "Ave" and in 1859 and 1871, when his focus of attention was on "Jenny." Rossetti's 1871 comment is arguing that an inner standing-point is not simply a feature of a particular genre or poetic form, it is a foundational requirement of "art." Not just writing, not just poetry, but "art" in general.

It helps to reconsider briefly Rossetti's thinking in 1847–1848. Like those other two urban artists Poe and Baudelaire, Rossetti at the time was much involved with projects that cultivated escaping from the contemporary world. "Ave" and the "Songs of the Art Catholic" were magical texts written to open a passage whereby Rossetti could plunge into a lost land of his heart's desire. To manage this feat he elaborated various kinds of inner standing-point procedures. He composed pastiche works like "Ave" and "Mary's Girlhood," quasi-pastiche works like "The Blessed Damozel," conjuring prose tales like "Hand and Soul" and "St. Agnes of Intercession," and the ventriloquizing translations from Dante and other early Italian poets. In none of these cases did the crucial move abstract Rossetti away from his texts, which was Browning's object and great achievement. Rather, it drew Rossetti into his own poem's dramatic action. "Ave" is a special kind of dramatic monologue where an inner standing-point is constructed and then occupied simultaneously by the writing/composing Victorian poet, Rossetti, and his imaginary Catholic antitype from the fourteenth century. Rossetti's innovation on Browning was to reintroduce the action of the subjective artist (and poet) into the critical space of the work.

When a poetics of the inner standing-point is undertaken in a poem of contemporary life, such as "Jenny," the results are very different from those gained when Rossetti wrote "Ave." The world of "Jenny" is no lost spiritual dreamland, it is an all-too-present nightmare. Readers to this day argue about whether the "young and thoughtful man of the world" (as Rossetti called him) is offered for our judgment or our sympathy, and about Rossetti's relation to his imaginative figure. But the poem incarnates a structure of doubtfulness by troubling every effort to reach a normative or stable judgment on the characters or the situation. Biographically inflected readings of the poem — and they are common — underscore this difficulty. The more explicit of these readings range between praise for Rossetti's enlightened or brave undertaking in the poem to sharp criticism of his sexist and pornographic illusions.

Rossetti's theory of the inner standing-point involves a major rewriting of the sympathetic contract poetry and art make with both their subjects and their readers. Romantic sympathy in its most authoritative cultural form displays — as Keats famously put the matter — "the holiness of the heart's affections." In this view, because the artist is imagined to have clearest access to that holy place, the artistic act becomes a moral and spiritual standard. Arnold would authorize this set of attitudes when he argued that poetry would replace religion for persons living in the modern world. His sonnet "Shakespeare" represents this set of ideas about the transcendental status of poetry:

> Other abide our question. Thou art free.
> We ask and ask, thou smilest and art still,
> Outtopping knowledge.

That is the romance — really, the romanticism — of an art conceived as some still point of a turning world. Rossetti's aesthetic move called such a view into radical question. Or perhaps one should say, Rossetti exposed the bad faith on which it had come to rest, for the authority of Arnold's sonnet is pure illusion, as Arnold himself showed in other of his poems, especially a devastating work like "The Buried Life." In Rossetti's story "Hand and Soul" the exposure comes when Chiaro, Rossetti's surrogate, poses this question for himself and his art: "May one be a devil without knowing it?" If the heart and its affections are that problematic, the ground of sympathy will only be gained through what Tennyson called, in one of his wittiest and wickedest moments, "honest doubt."

So in reading "Jenny" we want to see that the poet sympathizes with his bohemian artist-hero precisely in that young man's contradictions. Furthermore, when Rossetti takes up his subject at an inner standing-point, the move puts the reader in an equivalently equivocal position. The poem's sympathetic contract, written in ambivalent characters, must be entered on those uncertain terms. In this idea of art, the only understanding of value is a questionable understanding, the only feelings to be trusted are doubtful and uncertain. To enter the poem is to enter a space for studying problems, of which the reader's problems with the poem's moral import are among the most pertinent.

Not without cause, then, do readers follow Ruskin and Buchanan in recoiling from the poem. Its space is treacherous, as we see with special clarity in the marvelous line "Ah Jenny, yes, we know your dreams." Readers will scarcely miss the folly exposed here in the young man's facile judgment, and if we also see Rossetti reflected in the poem — as we often do — we may be led to rethink that line, as if it might also have said: "Ah Rossetti, yes, we know your dreams." But Rossetti is not alone engulfed in this cunning text. That first-person plural pronoun snares the reader as well. If Jenny has dreams, readers make representations of those dreams. What "we" in fact know are nothing more than representations of representations. Although criticism and critics regularly covet definitive judgment and understanding, Rossetti's poetic method undermines that obscure object of desire. A poem like "Jenny" is a dangerous critical mirror that turns the readers' eyes back on themselves.

So Rossetti is a difficult writer for several related reasons. Like Baudelaire and Swinburne, Rossetti is a learned poet who covets a highly finished surface. That surface is a careful and self-conscious structure of nuanced language games — ambiguous and aquarian pronouns, strange words that seem more physical than cognitive, wordplays that are less puns than elusively suggestive and "worked" language, as when he torques the word "draw" to such splendid effect at various times and places. This kind of writing typically spins out texts that can snare the reader with the sense that they have entered some kind of labyrinth. (The title of one of Rossetti's most important poems, "Troy Town," is an old colloquial expression meaning a maze.) But unlike Baudelaire and Swinburne, Rossetti is a more guarded and secretive writer, as if he knows how much of the reader's fear and hypocrisy he shares. The inner standing-point controls Rossetti's work even at the level of its style. He is incapable of writing poems like "Les Litanies de Satan" or "L'Aube Spirituelle," "Anactoria" or "The Leper."

But when we read Rossetti we really must not think of them, for Rossetti has his music too. "Recondite . . . casuistical . . . obscure": Pater's shrewd terms define a poet whose access to psychic recesses is acute precisely because he writes about them from an inner standing-point and because he is so assiduous in his explorations. Rossetti's obsessive corrections and revisions carry him into deep waters, nor does it matter if his brainwork continues to mask or to unmask his process of thought. Either way we get uncommon revelations, for the writing is, in the end, a reciprocal play of both.

THE TEXT

Until the initial appearance, in 2000, of *The Rossetti Archive* (i.e., my electronic edition *The Complete Writings and Pictures of Dante Gabriel Rossetti: A Hypermedia Research Archive*), the standard edition of Rossetti's works was William Michael Rossetti's 1911 collection, *The Works of Dante Gabriel Rossetti*. The latter was the culmination of a series of excellent editions that William Michael brought out, beginning in 1886. None of William Michael's editions are critical (in the scholarly sense) or complete.

The texts in this edition are prepared from the scholarly texts of *The Rossetti Archive*, meaning that I have here chosen texts that in my judgment are the best "reading texts" from those made available in the archive. The chosen text is indicated in the editorial notes here supplied for each work. Since *The Rossetti Archive* makes available all documentary states of all of Rossetti's works, as well as multiple copies of many, the reader of this edition should know that the present texts are those designated in *The Rossetti Archive* as "Reading Text." This designation, in *The Rossetti Archive,* was determined by exhaustive comparison of all available and relevant documents. Readers interested in assessing these choices can consult the editorial materials in *The Rossetti Archive*.

This is a reader's edition, then. It is also, like William Michael's editions, a "collected" rather than a "complete" edition of the works. For the latter, one may consult *The Rossetti Archive*. The present edition contains what I judge to be the core body of Rossetti's most interesting and important writings. As such, it prints works not published in William Michael's editions and excludes works that they include. My object here has been much more akin to Paull Baum's when he published his fine edition of what he saw as the most important of Rossetti's works: *Poems Ballads and Sonnets* (Doubleday, Doran and Co., 1937). The present edition has many more of Rossetti's works than can be found in Baum's edition, but — once again — some that he chose are not included here.

Editor's notes are signalled by line number for the poetry; for the prose, they are signalled by page and line number.

SUGGESTED FURTHER READING

D. M. R. Bentley, "Rossetti's 'Ave' and Related Pictures," *Victorian Poetry* 15 (1977): 21–35.

——, "Rossetti's 'Hand and Soul'," *English Studies in Canada* 3 (1977): 445–457.

Oswald Doughty, *A Victorian Romantic. Dante Gabriel Rossetti,* 2nd ed. Oxford University Press: London, 1960.

Henry Currie Marillier, *Dante Gabriel Rossetti: An Illustrated Memorial of His Life and Art*. Bell: London, 1899.

Jan Marsh, ed., *Dante Gabriel Rossetti. Collected Writings*. Dent: London, 1999.

——, *Dante Gabriel Rossetti. Painter and Poet*. Weidenfeld and Nicholson: London, 1999.

Jerome McGann, *The Complete Writings and Pictures of Dante Gabriel Rossetti: A Hypermedia Research Archive* (http://jefferson.village.virginia.edu/rossetti).

——, *Dante Gabriel Rossetti and the Game that Must Be Lost*. Yale University Press: New Haven, Conn., 2000.

Walter Pater, *Appreciations*. Macmillan: London, 1889.

Joan Rees, *The Poetry of Dante Gabriel Rossetti: Modes of Self-Expression*. Cambridge University Press: Cambridge, 1981.

David Riede, ed., *Critical Essays on Dante Gabriel Rossetti*. Hall: New York, 1992.

——, *Dante Gabriel Rossetti Revisited*. Twayne: New York, 1992.

Richard L. Stein, *The Ritual of Interpretation: The Fine Arts as Literature in Ruskin, Rossetti, and Pater*. Harvard University Press: Cambridge, Mass., 1975.

Virginia Surtees, *The Paintings and Drawings of Dante Gabriel Rossetti 1828–1882. A Catalogue Raisonné*. 2 vols. Clarendon Press: Oxford, 1971.

PART ONE

Poems (1870, 1881)

The Blessed Damozel

The blessed damozel leaned out
   From the gold bar of Heaven;
Her eyes were deeper than the depth
   Of waters stilled at even;
She had three lilies in her hand,   5
   And the stars in her hair were seven.

Her robe, ungirt from clasp to hem,
   No wrought flowers did adorn,
But a white rose of Mary's gift,
   For service meetly worn;   10
Her hair that lay along her back
   Was yellow like ripe corn.

Herseemed she scarce had been a day
   One of God's choristers;
The wonder was not yet quite gone   15
   From that still look of hers;
Albeit, to them she left, her day
   Had counted as ten years.

(To one, it is ten years of years.
   . . . Yet now, and in this place,   20
Surely she leaned o'er me — her hair
   Fell all about my face. . . .
Nothing: the autumn-fall of leaves.
   The whole year sets apace.)

It was the rampart of God's house   25
   That she was standing on;
By God built over the sheer depth
   The which is Space begun;
So high, that looking downward thence
   She scarce could see the sun.   30

It lies in Heaven, across the flood
   Of ether, as a bridge.
Beneath, the tides of day and night
   With flame and darkness ridge
The void, as low as where this earth   35
   Spins like a fretful midge.

Around her, lovers, newly met
   'Mid deathless love's acclaims,
Spoke evermore among themselves
   Their heart-remembered names;   40
And the souls mounting up to God
   Went by her like thin flames.

And still she bowed herself and stooped
   Out of the circling charm;
Until her bosom must have made   45
   The bar she leaned on warm,
And the lilies lay as if asleep
   Along her bended arm.

From the fixed place of Heaven she saw
   Time like a pulse shake fierce   50
Through all the worlds. Her gaze still strove
   Within the gulf to pierce
Its path; and now she spoke as when
   The stars sang in their spheres.

The sun was gone now; the curled moon   55
   Was like a little feather
Fluttering far down the gulf; and now
   She spoke through the still weather.
Her voice was like the voice the stars
   Had when they sang together.   60

(Ah sweet! Even now, in that bird's song,
   Strove not her accents there,
Fain to be hearkened? When those bells
   Possessed the mid-day air,
Strove not her steps to reach my side   65
   Down all the echoing stair?)

"I wish that he were come to me,
   For he will come," she said.
"Have I not prayed in Heaven? — on earth,
   Lord, Lord, has he not pray'd?   70

Are not two prayers a perfect strength?
    And shall I feel afraid?

"When round his head the aureole clings,
    And he is clothed in white,
I'll take his hand and go with him   75
    To the deep wells of light;
As unto a stream we will step down,
    And bathe there in God's sight.

"We two will stand beside that shrine,
    Occult, withheld, untrod,   80
Whose lamps are stirred continually
    With prayer sent up to God;
And see our old prayers, granted, melt
    Each like a little cloud.

"We two will lie i' the shadow of   85
    That living mystic tree
Within whose secret growth the Dove
    Is sometimes felt to be,
While every leaf that His plumes touch
    Saith His Name audibly.   90

"And I myself will teach to him,
    I myself, lying so,
The songs I sing here; which his voice
    Shall pause in, hushed and slow,
And find some knowledge at each pause,   95
    Or some new thing to know."

(Alas! We two, we two, thou say'st!
    Yea, one wast thou with me
That once of old. But shall God lift
    To endless unity   100
The soul whose likeness with thy soul
    Was but its love for thee?)

"We two," she said, "will seek the groves
    Where the lady Mary is,
With her five handmaidens, whose names   105
    Are five sweet symphonies,
Cecily, Gertrude, Magdalen,
    Margaret and Rosalys.

"Circlewise sit they, with bound locks
    And foreheads garlanded;   110

Into the fine cloth white like flame
    Weaving the golden thread,
To fashion the birth-robes for them
    Who are just born, being dead.

"He shall fear, haply, and be dumb: 115
    Then will I lay my cheek
To his, and tell about our love,
    Not once abashed or weak:
And the dear Mother will approve
    My pride, and let me speak.   120

"Herself shall bring us, hand in hand,
    To him round whom all souls
Kneel, the clear-ranged unnumbered heads
    Bowed with their aureoles:
And angels meeting us shall sing   125
    To their citherns and citoles.

"There will I ask of Christ the Lord
    Thus much for him and me: —
Only to live as once on earth
    With Love, — only to be,   130
As then awhile, for ever now
    Together, I and he."

She gazed and listened and then said,
    Less sad of speech than mild, —
"All this is when he comes." She ceased.   135
    The light thrilled towards her, fill'd
With angels in strong level flight.
    Her eyes prayed, and she smil'd.

(I saw her smile.) But soon their path
    Was vague in distant spheres: 140
And then she cast her arms along
    The golden barriers,
And laid her face between her hands,
    And wept. (I heard her tears.)

Sister Helen

"Why did you melt your waxen man,
     Sister Helen?
To-day is the third since you began."

"The time was long, yet the time ran,
    Little brother."   5
  (O Mother, Mary Mother,
Three days to-day, between Hell and Heaven!)

"But if you have done your work aright,
    Sister Helen,
You'll let me play, for you said I might."   10
"Be very still in your play to-night,
    Little brother."
  (O Mother, Mary Mother,
Third night, to-night, between Hell and Heaven!)

"You said it must melt ere vesper-bell,   15
    Sister Helen;
If now it be molten, all is well."
"Even so, — nay, peace! you cannot tell,
    Little brother."
  (O Mother, Mary Mother,   20
O what is this, between Hell and Heaven?)

"Oh the waxen knave was plump to-day,
    Sister Helen;
How like dead folk he has dropped away!"
"Nay now, of the dead what can you say,   25
    Little brother?"
  (O Mother, Mary Mother,
What of the dead, between Hell and Heaven?)

"See, see, the sunken pile of wood,
    Sister Helen,   30
Shines through the thinned wax red as blood!"
"Nay now, when looked you yet on blood,
    Little brother?"
  (O Mother, Mary Mother,
How pale she is, between Hell and Heaven!)   35

"Now close your eyes, for they're sick and sore,
    Sister Helen,
And I'll play without the gallery door."
"Aye, let me rest, — I'll lie on the floor,
    Little brother."   40
  (O Mother, Mary Mother,
What rest to-night, between Hell and Heaven?)

"Here high up in the balcony,
    Sister Helen,

The moon flies face to face with me." 45
"Aye, look and say whatever you see,
    Little brother."
  (O Mother, Mary Mother,
What sight to-night, between Hell and Heaven?)

"Outside it's merry in the wind's wake, 50
    Sister Helen;
In the shaken trees the chill stars shake."
"Hush, heard you a horse-tread as you spake,
    Little brother?"
  (O Mother, Mary Mother, 55
What sound to-night, between Hell and Heaven?)

"I hear a horse-tread, and I see,
    Sister Helen,
Three horsemen that ride terribly."
"Little brother, whence come the three, 60
    Little brother?"
  (O Mother, Mary Mother,
Whence should they come, between Hell and Heaven?)

"They come by the hill-verge from Boyne Bar,
    Sister Helen, 65
And one draws nigh, but two are afar."
"Look, look, do you know them who they are,
    Little brother?"
  (O Mother, Mary Mother,
Who should they be, between Hell and Heaven?) 70

"Oh, it's Keith of Eastholm rides so fast,
    Sister Helen,
For I know the white mane on the blast."
"The hour has come, has come at last,
    Little brother!" 75
  (O Mother, Mary Mother,
Her hour at last, between Hell and Heaven!)

"He has made a sign and called Halloo!
    Sister Helen,
And he says that he would speak with you." 80
"Oh tell him I fear the frozen dew,
    Little brother."
  (O Mother, Mary Mother,
Why laughs she thus, between Hell and Heaven?)

"The wind is loud, but I hear him cry,
    Sister Helen,
That Keith of Ewern's like to die."
"And he and thou, and thou and I,
    Little brother."
    (O Mother, Mary Mother,
And they and we, between Hell and Heaven!)

"Three days ago, on his marriage-morn,
    Sister Helen,
He sickened, and lies since then forlorn."
"For bridegroom's side is the bride a thorn,
    Little brother?"
    (O Mother, Mary Mother,
Cold bridal cheer, between Hell and Heaven!)

"Three days and nights he has lain abed,
    Sister Helen,
And he prays in torment to be dead."
"The thing may chance, if he have prayed,
    Little brother!"
    (O Mother, Mary Mother,
If he have prayed, between Hell and Heaven!)

"But he has not ceased to cry to-day,
    Sister Helen,
That you should take your curse away."
"My prayer was heard, — he need but pray,
    Little brother!"
    (O Mother, Mary Mother,
Shall God not hear, between Hell and Heaven?)

"But he says, till you take back your ban,
    Sister Helen,
His soul would pass, yet never can."
"Nay then, shall I slay a living man,
    Little brother?"
    (O Mother, Mary Mother,
A living soul, between Hell and Heaven!)

"But he calls for ever on your name,
    Sister Helen,
And says that he melts before a flame."
"My heart for his pleasure fared the same,
    Little brother."

(O Mother, Mary Mother, 125
Fire at the heart, between Hell and Heaven!)

"Here's Keith of Westholm riding fast,
    Sister Helen,
For I know the white plume on the blast."
"The hour, the sweet hour I forecast, 130
    Little brother!"
    (O Mother, Mary Mother,
Is the hour sweet, between Hell and Heaven?)

"He stops to speak, and he stills his horse,
    Sister Helen; 135
But his words are drowned in the wind's course."
"Nay hear, nay hear, you must hear perforce,
    Little brother!"
    (O Mother, Mary Mother,
What word now heard, between Hell and Heaven?) 140

"Oh he says that Keith of Ewern's cry,
    Sister Helen,
Is ever to see you ere he die."
"In all that his soul sees, there am I,
    Little brother!" 145
    (O Mother, Mary Mother,
The soul's one sight, between Hell and Heaven!)

"He sends a ring and a broken coin,
    Sister Helen,
And bids you mind the banks of Boyne." 150
"What else he broke will he ever join,
    Little brother?"
    (O Mother, Mary Mother,
No, never joined, between Hell and Heaven!)

"He yields you these and craves full fain, 155
    Sister Helen,
You pardon him in his mortal pain."
"What else he took will he give again,
    Little brother?"
    (O Mother, Mary Mother, 160
Not twice to give, between Hell and Heaven!)

"He calls your name in an agony,
    Sister Helen,

That even dead Love must weep to see."
"Hate, born of Love, is blind as he,
    Little brother!"   165
   (O Mother, Mary Mother,
Love turned to hate, between Hell and Heaven!)

"Oh it's Keith of Keith now that rides fast,
    Sister Helen,   170
For I know the white hair on the blast."
"The short short hour will soon be past,
    Little brother!"
   (O Mother, Mary Mother,
Will soon be past, between Hell and Heaven!)   175

"He looks at me and he tries to speak,
    Sister Helen,
But oh! his voice is sad and weak!"
"What here should the mighty Baron seek,
    Little brother?"   180
   (O Mother, Mary Mother,
Is this the end, between Hell and Heaven?)

"Oh his son still cries, if you forgive,
    Sister Helen,
The body dies but the soul shall live."   185
"Fire shall forgive me as I forgive,
    Little brother!"
   (O Mother, Mary Mother,
As she forgives, between Hell and Heaven!)

"Oh he prays you, as his heart would rive,   190
    Sister Helen,
To save his dear son's soul alive."
"Fire cannot slay it, it shall thrive,
    Little brother!"
   (O Mother, Mary Mother,   195
Alas, alas, between Hell and Heaven!)

"He cries to you, kneeling in the road,
    Sister Helen,
To go with him for the love of God!"
"The way is long to his son's abode,   200
    Little brother."
   (O Mother, Mary Mother,
The way is long, between Hell and Heaven!)

"A lady's here, by a dark steed brought,
    Sister Helen,
So darkly clad, I saw her not."
"See her now or never see aught,
    Little brother!"
    (O Mother, Mary Mother,
What more to see, between Hell and Heaven?)

"Her hood falls back, and the moon shines fair,
    Sister Helen,
On the Lady of Ewern's golden hair."
"Blest hour of my power and her despair,
    Little brother!"
    (O Mother, Mary Mother,
Hour blest and bann'd, between Hell and Heaven!)

"Pale, pale her cheeks, that in pride did glow,
    Sister Helen,
'Neath the bridal-wreath three days ago."
"One morn for pride and three days for woe,
    Little brother!"
    (O Mother, Mary Mother,
Three days, three nights, between Hell and Heaven!)

"Her clasped hands stretch from her bending head,
    Sister Helen;
With the loud wind's wail her sobs are wed."
"What wedding-strains hath her bridal-bed,
    Little brother?"
    (O Mother, Mary Mother,
What strain but death's, between Hell and Heaven?)

"She may not speak, she sinks in a swoon,
    Sister Helen, —
She lifts her lips and gasps on the moon."
"Oh! might I but hear her soul's blithe tune,
    Little brother!"
    (O Mother, Mary Mother,
Her woe's dumb cry, between Hell and Heaven!)

"They've caught her to Westholm's saddle-bow,
    Sister Helen,
And her moonlit hair gleams white in its flow."
"Let it turn whiter than winter snow,
    Little brother!"

(O Mother, Mary Mother,
Woe-withered gold, between Hell and Heaven!) 245

"O Sister Helen, you heard the bell,
 Sister Helen!
More loud than the vesper-chime it fell."
"No vesper-chime, but a dying knell,
 Little brother!" 250
 (O Mother, Mary Mother,
His dying knell, between Hell and Heaven!)

"Alas! but I fear the heavy sound,
 Sister Helen;
Is it in the sky or in the ground?" 255
"Say, have they turned their horses round,
 Little brother?"
 (O Mother, Mary Mother,
What would she more, between Hell and Heaven?)

"They have raised the old man from his knee, 260
 Sister Helen,
And they ride in silence hastily."
"More fast the naked soul doth flee,
 Little brother!"
 (O Mother, Mary Mother, 265
The naked soul, between Hell and Heaven!)

"Flank to flank are the three steeds gone,
 Sister Helen,
But the lady's dark steed goes alone."
"And lonely her bridegroom's soul hath flown, 270
 Little brother."
 (O Mother, Mary Mother,
The lonely ghost, between Hell and Heaven!)

"Oh the wind is sad in the iron chill,
 Sister Helen, 275
And weary sad they look by the hill."
"But he and I are sadder still,
 Little brother!"
 (O Mother, Mary Mother,
Most sad of all, between Hell and Heaven!) 280

"See, see, the wax has dropped from its place,
 Sister Helen,
And the flames are winning up apace!"

"Yet here they burn but for a space,
    Little brother!"   285
  (O Mother, Mary Mother,
Here for a space, between Hell and Heaven!)

"Ah! what white thing at the door has cross'd,
    Sister Helen?
Ah! what is this that sighs in the frost?"   290
"A soul that's lost as mine is lost,
    Little brother!"
  (O Mother, Mary Mother,
Lost, lost, all lost, between Hell and Heaven!)

Stratton Water

"O have you seen the Stratton flood
    That's great with rain to-day?
It runs beneath your wall, Lord Sands,
    Full of the new-mown hay.

"I led your hounds to Hutton bank   5
    To bathe at early morn:
They got their bath by Borrowbrake
    Above the standing corn."

Out from the castle-stair Lord Sands
    Looked up the western lea;   10
The rook was grieving on her nest,
    The flood was round her tree.

Over the castle-wall Lord Sands
    Looked down the eastern hill:
The stakes swam free among the boats,   15
    The flood was rising still.

"What's yonder far below that lies
    So white against the slope?"
"O it's a sail o' your bonny barks
    The waters have washed up."   20

"But I have never a sail so white,
    And the water's not yet there."
"O it's the swans o' your bonny lake
    The rising flood doth scare."

"The swans they would not hold so still,
    So high they would not win."
"O it's Joyce my wife has spread her smock
    And fears to fetch it in."

"Nay, knave, it's neither sail nor swans,
    Nor aught that you can say;
For though your wife might leave her smock,
    Herself she'd bring away."

Lord Sands has passed the turret-stair,
    The court, and yard, and all;
The kine were in the byre that day,
    The nags were in the stall.

Lord Sands has won the weltering slope
    Whereon the white shape lay:
The clouds were still above the hill,
    And the shape was still as they.

Oh pleasant is the gaze of life
    And sad is death's blind head;
But awful are the living eyes
    In the face of one thought dead!

"In God's name, Janet, is it me
    Thy ghost has come to seek?"
"Nay, wait another hour, Lord Sands, —
    Be sure my ghost shall speak."

A moment stood he as a stone,
    Then grovelled to his knee.
"O Janet, O my love, my love,
    Rise up and come with me!"
"O once before you bade me come,
    And it's here you have brought me!

"O many's the sweet word, Lord Sands,
    You've spoken oft to me;
But all that I have from you to-day
    Is the rain on my body.

"And many's the good gift, Lord Sands,
    You've promised oft to me;
But the gift of yours I keep to-day
    Is the babe in my body.

"O it's not in any earthly bed
 That first my babe I'll see;
For I have brought my body here   65
 That the flood may cover me."

His face was close against her face,
 His hands of hers were fain:
O her wet cheeks were hot with tears,
 Her wet hands cold with rain.   70

"They told me you were dead, Janet, —
 How could I guess the lie?"
"They told me you were false, Lord Sands, —
 What could I do but die?"

"Now keep you well, my brother Giles, —   75
 Through you I deemed her dead!
As wan as your towers seem to-day,
 To-morrow they'll be red.

"Look down, look down, my false mother,
 That bade me not to grieve: 80
You'll look up when our marriage fires
 Are lit to-morrow eve.

"O more than one and more than two
 The sorrow of this shall see:
But it's to-morrow, love, for them, —   85
 To-day's for thee and me."

He's drawn her face between his hands
 And her pale mouth to his:
No bird that was so still that day
 Chirps sweeter than his kiss.   90

The flood was creeping round their feet.
 "O Janet, come away!
The hall is warm for the marriage-rite,
 The bed for the birthday."

"Nay, but I hear your mother cry,   95
 'Go bring this bride to bed!
And would she christen her babe unborn
 So wet she comes to wed?'

"I'll be your wife to cross your door
 And meet your mother's e'e.   100

We plighted troth to wed i' the kirk,
    And it's there you'll wed with me."

He's ta'en her by the short girdle
    And by the dripping sleeve:
"Go fetch Sir Jock my mother's priest, —   105
    You'll ask of him no leave.

"O it's one half-hour to reach the kirk
    And one for the marriage-rite;
And kirk and castle and castle-lands
    Shall be our babe's to-night."   110

"The flood's in the kirkyard, Lord Sands,
    And round the belfry-stair."
"I bade you fetch the priest," he said,
    "Myself shall bring him there.

"It's for the lilt of wedding bells   115
    We'll have the hail to pour,
And for the clink of bridle-reins
    The plashing of the oar."

Beneath them on the nether hill
    A boat was floating wide: 120
Lord Sands swam out and caught the oars
    And rowed to the hill-side.

He's wrapped her in a green mantle
    And set her softly in;
Her hair was wet upon her face,   125
    Her face was grey and thin;
And "Oh!" she said, "lie still, my babe,
    It's out you must not win!"

But woe's my heart for Father John
    As hard as he might pray,   130
There seemed no help but Noah's ark
    Or Jonah's fish that day.

The first strokes that the oars struck
    Were over the broad leas;
The next strokes that the oars struck   135
    They pushed beneath the trees;

The last stroke that the oars struck,
    The good boat's head was met,

And there the gate of the kirkyard
   Stood like a ferry-gate. 140

He's set his hand upon the bar
   And lightly leaped within:
He's lifted her to his left shoulder,
   Her knees beside his chin.

The graves lay deep beneath the flood 145
   Under the rain alone;
And when the foot-stone made him slip,
   He held by the head-stone.

The empty boat thrawed i' the wind,
   Against the postern tied. 150
"Hold still, you've brought my love with me,
   You shall take back my bride."

But woe's my heart for Father John
   And the saints he clamoured to!
There's never a saint but Christopher 155
   Might hale such buttocks through!

And "Oh!" she said, "on men's shoulders
   I well had thought to wend,
And well to travel with a priest,
   But not to have cared or ken'd. 160

"And oh!" she said, "it's well this way
   That I thought to have fared, —
Not to have lighted at the kirk
   But stopped in the kirkyard.

"For it's oh and oh I prayed to God, 165
   Whose rest I hoped to win,
That when to-night at your board-head
   You'd bid the feast begin,
This water past your window-sill
   Might bear my body in." 170

Now make the white bed warm and soft
   And greet the merry morn.
The night the mother should have died,
   The young son shall be born.

The Staff and the Scrip

"Who rules these lands?" the Pilgrim said.
  "'Stranger, Queen Blanchelys."
"And who has thus harried them?" he said.
  "It was Duke Luke did this:
    God's ban be his!"   5

The Pilgrim said: "Where is your house?
  I'll rest there, with your will."
"You've but to climb these blackened boughs
  And you'll see it over the hill,
    For it burns still."   10

"Which road, to seek your Queen?" said he.
  "Nay, nay, but with some wound
You'll fly back hither, it may be,
  And by your blood i' the ground
    My place be found."   15

"Friend, stay in peace. God keep your head,
  And mine, where I will go;
For He is here and there," he said.
  He passed the hill-side, slow,
    And stood below.   20

The Queen sat idle by her loom:
  She heard the arras stir,
And looked up sadly: through the room
  The sweetness sickened her
    Of musk and myrrh.   25

Her women, standing two and two,
  In silence combed the fleece.
The Pilgrim said, "Peace be with you,
  Lady;" and bent his knees.
    She answered, "Peace."   30

Her eyes were like the wave within;
  Like water-reeds the poise
Of her soft body, dainty thin;
  And like the water's noise
    Her plaintive voice.   35

For him, the stream had never well'd
  In desert tracts malign

So sweet; nor had he ever felt
　　So faint in the sunshine
　　　　Of Palestine.　　　　　　　　　40

Right so, he knew that he saw weep
　　Each night through every dream
The Queen's own face, confused in sleep
　　With visages supreme
　　　　Not known to him.　　　　　　45

"Lady," he said, "your lands lie burnt
　　And waste: to meet your foe
All fear: this I have seen and learnt.
　　Say that it shall be so,
　　　　And I will go."　　　　　　　50

She gazed at him. "Your cause is just,
　　For I have heard the same:"
He said: "God's strength shall be my trust.
　　Fall it to good or grame,
　　　　'Tis in His name."　　　　　　55

"Sir, you are thanked. My cause is dead.
　　Why should you toil to break
A grave, and fall therein?" she said.
　　He did not pause but spake:
　　　　"For my vow's sake."　　　　　60

"Can such vows be, Sir — to God's ear,
　　Not to God's will?" "My vow
Remains: God heard me there as here,"
　　He said with reverent brow,
　　　　"Both then and now."　　　　　65

They gazed together, he and she,
　　The minute while he spoke;
And when he ceased, she suddenly
　　Looked round upon her folk
　　　　As though she woke.　　　　　70

"Fight, Sir," she said; "my prayers in pain
　　Shall be your fellowship."
He whispered one among her train, —
　　"To-morrow bid her keep
　　　　This staff and scrip."　　　　　75

She sent him a sharp sword, whose belt
　　About his body there

As sweet as her own arms he felt.
　　He kissed its blade, all bare,
　　　　Instead of her.　　　　　　　　　　　　　　80

She sent him a green banner wrought
　　With one white lily stem,
To bind his lance with when he fought.
　　He writ upon the same
　　　　And kissed her name.　　　　　　　　　85

She sent him a white shield, whereon
　　She bade that he should trace
His will. He blent fair hues that shone,
　　And in a golden space
　　　　He kissed her face.　　　　　　　　　90

Born of the day that died, that eve
　　Now dying sank to rest;
As he, in likewise taking leave,
　　Once with a heaving breast
　　　　Looked to the west.　　　　　　　　　95

And there the sunset skies unseal'd,
　　Like lands he never knew,
Beyond to-morrow's battle-field
　　Lay open out of view
　　　　To ride into.　　　　　　　　　　　　100

Next day till dark the women pray'd:
　　Nor any might know there
How the fight went: the Queen has bade
　　That there do come to her
　　　　No messenger.　　　　　　　　　　105

The Queen is pale, her maidens ail;
　　And to the organ-tones
They sing but faintly, who sang well
　　The matin-orisons,
　　　　The lauds and nones.　　　　　　　110

Lo, Father, is thine ear inclin'd,
　　And hath thine angel pass'd?
For these thy watchers now are blind
　　With vigil, and at last
　　　　Dizzy with fast.　　　　　　　　　115

Weak now to them the voice o' the priest
　　As any trance affords;

And when each anthem failed and ceas'd,
   It seemed that the last chords
     Still sang the words.   120

"Oh what is the light that shines so red?
   'Tis long since the sun set;"
Quoth the youngest to the eldest maid:
   "'Twas dim but now, and yet
     The light is great."   125

Quoth the other: "'Tis our sight is dazed
   That we see flame i' the air."
But the Queen held her brows and gazed,
   And said, "It is the glare
     Of torches there."   130

"Oh what are the sounds that rise and spread?
   All day it was so still;"
Quoth the youngest to the eldest maid;
   "Unto the furthest hill
     The air they fill."   135

Quoth the other; "'Tis our sense is blurr'd
   With all the chants gone by."
But the Queen held her breath and heard,
   And said, "It is the cry
     Of Victory."   140

The first of all the rout was sound,
   The next were dust and flame,
And then the horses shook the ground:
   And in the thick of them
     A still band came.   145

"Oh what do ye bring out of the fight,
   Thus hid beneath these boughs?"
"Thy conquering guest returns to-night,
   And yet shall not carouse,
     Queen, in thy house."   150

"Uncover ye his face," she said.
   "O changed in little space!"
She cried, "O pale that was so red!
   O God, O God of grace!
     Cover his face."   155

His sword was broken in his hand
   Where he had kissed the blade.

"O soft steel that could not withstand!
  O my hard heart unstayed,
    That prayed and prayed!" 160

His bloodied banner crossed his mouth
  Where he had kissed her name.
"O east, and west, and north, and south,
  Fair flew my web, for shame,
    To guide Death's aim!" 165

The tints were shredded from his shield
  Where he had kissed her face.
"Oh, of all gifts that I could yield,
  Death only keeps its place,
    My gift and grace!" 170

Then stepped a damsel to her side,
  And spoke, and needs must weep:
"For his sake, lady, if he died,
  He prayed of thee to keep
    This staff and scrip." 175

That night they hung above her bed,
  Till morning wet with tears.
Year after year above her head
  Her bed his token wears,
    Five years, ten years. 180

That night the passion of her grief
  Shook them as there they hung.
Each year the wind that shed the leaf
  Shook them and in its tongue
    A message flung. 185

And once she woke with a clear mind
  That letters writ to calm
Her soul lay in the scrip; to find
  Only a torpid balm
    And dust of palm. 190

They shook far off with palace sport
  When joust and dance were rife;
And the hunt shook them from the court;
  For hers, in peace or strife,
    Was a Queen's life. 195

A Queen's death now: as now they shake
  To gusts in chapel dim, —

Hung where she sleeps, not seen to wake,
  (Carved lovely white and slim),
    With them by him.   200

Stand up to-day, still armed, with her,
  Good knight, before His brow
Who then as now was here and there,
  Who had in mind thy vow
    Then even as now.   205

The lists are set in Heaven to-day,
  The bright pavilions shine;
Fair hangs thy shield, and none gainsay;
  The trumpets sound in sign
    That she is thine.   210

Not tithed with days' and years' decease
  He pays thy wage He owed,
But with imperishable peace
  Here in His own abode,
    Thy jealous God.   215

Ave

  Mother of the Fair Delight,
Thou handmaid perfect in God's sight,
Now sitting fourth beside the Three,
Thyself a woman-Trinity, —
Being a daughter borne to God,   5
Mother of Christ from stall to rood,
And wife unto the Holy Ghost: —
Oh when our need is uttermost,
Think that to such as death may strike
Thou once wert sister sisterlike!   10
Thou headstone of humanity,
Groundstone of the great Mystery,
Fashioned like us, yet more than we!

  Mind'st thou not (when June's heavy breath
Warmed the long days in Nazareth,)   15
That eve thou didst go forth to give
Thy flowers some drink that they might live
One faint night more amid the sands?
Far off the trees were as pale wands

Against the fervid sky: the sea 20
Sighed further off eternally
As human sorrow sighs in sleep.
Then suddenly the awe grew deep,
As of a day to which all days
Were footsteps in God's secret ways: 25
Until a folding sense, like prayer,
Which is, as God is, everywhere,
Gathered about thee; and a voice
Spake to thee without any noise,
Being of the silence: — "Hail," it said, 30
"Thou that art highly favourèd;
The Lord is with thee here and now;
Blessed among all women thou."

Ah! knew'st thou of the end, when first
That Babe was on thy bosom nurs'd? — 35
Or when He tottered round thy knee
Did thy great sorrow dawn on thee? —
And through His boyhood, year by year
Eating with Him the Passover,
Didst thou discern confusedly 40
That holier sacrament, when He,
The bitter cup about to quaff,
Should break the bread and eat thereof? —
Or came not yet the knowledge, even
Till on some day forecast in Heaven 45
His feet passed through thy door to press
Upon His Father's business? —
Or still was God's high secret kept?

Nay, but I think the whisper crept
Like growth through childhood. Work and play, 50
Things common to the course of day,
Awed thee with meanings unfulfill'd;
And all through girlhood, something still'd
Thy senses like the birth of light,
When thou hast trimmed thy lamp at night 55
Or washed thy garments in the stream;
To whose white bed had come the dream
That He was thine and thou wast His
Who feeds among the field-lilies.
O solemn shadow of the end 60
In that wise spirit long contain'd!

O awful end! and those unsaid
Long years when It was Finishèd!

   Mind'st thou not (when the twilight gone
Left darkness in the house of John,)   65
Between the naked window-bars
That spacious vigil of the stars? —
For thou, a watcher even as they,
Wouldst rise from where throughout the day
Thou wroughtest raiment for His poor;   70
And, finding the fixed terms endure
Of day and night which never brought
Sounds of His coming chariot,
Wouldst lift through cloud-waste unexplor'd
Those eyes which said, "How long, O Lord?"   75
Then that disciple whom He loved,
Well heeding, haply would be moved
To ask thy blessing in His name;
And that one thought in both, the same
Though silent, then would clasp ye round   80
To weep together, — tears long bound,
Sick tears of patience, dumb and slow.
Yet, "Surely I come quickly," — so
He said, from life and death gone home.
Amen: even so, Lord Jesus, come!   85

   But oh! what human tongue can speak
That day when Michael came* to break
From the tir'd spirit, like a veil,
Its covenant with Gabriel
Endured at length unto the end?   90
What human thought can apprehend
That mystery of motherhood
When thy Beloved at length renew'd
The sweet communion severéd, —
His left hand underneath thine head   95
And His right hand embracing thee? —
Lo! He was thine, and this is He!

   Soul, is it Faith, or Love, or Hope,
That lets me see her standing up
Where the light of the Throne is bright?   100

*A Church legend of the Blessed Virgin's death.

Unto the left, unto the right,
The cherubim, succinct, conjoint,
Float inward to a golden point,
And from between the seraphim
The glory issues for a hymn. 105
O Mary Mother, be not loth
To listen, — thou whom the stars clothe,
Who seëst and mayst not be seen!
Hear us at last, O Mary Queen!
Into our shadow bend thy face, 110
Bowing thee from the secret place,
O Mary Virgin, full of grace!

Dante at Verona

"Yea, thou shalt learn how salt his food who fares
Upon another's bread, — how steep his path
Who treadeth up and down another's stairs."
(Div. Com. Parad. *xvii.*)

"Behold, even I, even I am Beatrice."
(Div. Com. Purg. *xxx.*)

Of Florence and of Beatrice
    Servant and singer from of old,
    O'er Dante's heart in youth had toll'd
The knell that gave his Lady peace;
    And now in manhood flew the dart 5
    Wherewith his City pierced his heart.

Yet if his Lady's home above
    Was Heaven, on earth she filled his soul;
    And if his City held control
To cast the body forth to rove, 10
    The soul could soar from earth's vain throng,
    And Heaven and Hell fulfil the song.

Follow his feet's appointed way; —
    But little light we find that clears
    The darkness of the exiled years. 15
Follow his spirit's journey: — nay,
    What fires are blent, what winds are blown
    On paths his feet may tread alone?

Yet of the twofold life he led
　　In chainless thought and fettered will
　　Some glimpses reach us, — somewhat still
Of the steep stairs and bitter bread, —
　　Of the soul's quest whose stern avow
　　For years had made him haggard now.

Alas! the Sacred Song whereto
　　Both heaven and earth had set their hand
　　Not only at Fame's gate did stand
Knocking to claim the passage through,
　　But toiled to ope that heavier door
　　Which Florence shut for evermore.

Shall not his birth's baptismal Town
　　One last high presage yet fulfil,
　　And at that font in Florence still
His forehead take the laurel-crown?
　　O God! or shall dead souls deny
　　The undying soul its prophecy?

Aye, 'tis their hour. Not yet forgot
　　The bitter words he spoke that day
　　When for some great charge far away
Her rulers his acceptance sought.
　　"And if I go, who stays?" — so rose
　　His scorn: — "and if I stay, who goes?"

"Lo! thou art gone now, and we stay:"
　　(The curled lips mutter): "and no star
　　Is from thy mortal path so far
As streets where childhood knew the way.
　　To Heaven and Hell thy feet may win,
　　But thine own house they come not in."

Therefore, the loftier rose the song
　　To touch the secret things of God,
　　The deeper pierced the hate that trod
On base men's track who wrought the wrong;
　　Till the soul's effluence came to be
　　Its own exceeding agony.

Arriving only to depart,
　　From court to court, from land to land,
　　Like flame within the naked hand

20

25

30

35

40

45

50

55

His body bore his burning heart
    That still on Florence strove to bring
    God's fire for a burnt offering. 60

Even such was Dante's mood, when now,
    Mocked for long years with Fortune's sport,
    He dwelt at yet another court,
There where Verona's knee did bow
    And her voice hailed with all acclaim 65
    Can Grande della Scala's name.

As that lord's kingly guest awhile
    His life we follow; through the days
    Which walked in exile's barren ways, —
The nights which still beneath one smile 70
    Heard through all spheres one song increase, —
    "Even I, even I am Beatrice."

At Can La Scala's court, no doubt,
    Due reverence did his steps attend;
    The ushers on his path would bend 75
At ingoing as at going out;
    The penmen waited on his call
    At council-board, the grooms in hall.

And pages hushed their laughter down,
    And gay squires stilled the merry stir, 80
    When he passed up the dais-chamber
With set brows lordlier than a frown;
    And tire-maids hidden among these
    Drew close their loosened bodices.

Perhaps the priests, (exact to span 85
    All God's circumference,) if at whiles
    They found him wandering in their aisles,
Grudged ghostly greeting to the man
    By whom, though not of ghostly guild,
    With Heaven and Hell men's hearts were fill'd. 90

And the court-poets (he, forsooth,
    A whole world's poet strayed to court!)
    Had for his scorn their hate's retort.
He'd meet them flushed with easy youth,
    Hot on their errands. Like noon-flies 95
    They vexed him in the ears and eyes.

But at this court, peace still must wrench
  Her chaplet from the teeth of war:
  By day they held high watch afar,
At night they cried across the trench;   100
  And still, in Dante's path, the fierce
  Gaunt soldiers wrangled o'er their spears.

But vain seemed all the strength to him,
  As golden convoys sunk at sea
  Whose wealth might root out penury: 105
Because it was not, limb with limb,
  Knit like his heart strings round the wall
  Of Florence, that ill pride might fall.

Yet in the tiltyard, when the dust
  Cleared from the sundered press of knights   110
  Ere yet again it swoops and smites,
He almost deemed his longing must
  Find force to yield that multitude
  And hurl that strength the way he would.

How should he move them, — fame and gain   115
  On all hands calling them at strife?
  He still might find but his one life
To give, by Florence counted vain;
  One heart the false hearts made her doubt,
  One voice she heard once and cast out.   120

Oh! if his Florence could but come,
  A lily-sceptred damsel fair,
  As her own Giotto painted her
On many shields and gates at home, —
  A lady crowned, at a soft pace   125
  Riding the lists round to the dais:

Till where Can Grande rules the lists,
  As young as Truth, as calm as Force,
  She draws her rein now, while her horse
Bows at the turn of the white wrists;   130
  And when each knight within his stall
  Gives ear, she speaks and tells them all:

All the foul tale, — truth sworn untrue
  And falsehood's triumph. All the tale?
  Great God! and must she not prevail   135

To fire them ere they heard it through, —
    And hand achieve ere heart could rest
    That high adventure of her quest?

How would his Florence lead them forth,
    Her bridle ringing as she went;   140
    And at the last within her tent,
'Neath golden lilies worship-worth,
    How queenly would she bend the while
    And thank the victors with her smile!

Also her lips should turn his way   145
    And murmur: "O thou tried and true,
    With whom I wept the long years through!
What shall it profit if I say,
    Thee I remember? Nay, through thee
    All ages shall remember me."   150

Peace, Dante, peace! The task is long,
    The time wears short to compass it.
    Within thine heart such hopes may flit
And find a voice in deathless song:
    But lo! as children of man's earth,   155
    Those hopes are dead before their birth.

Fame tells us that Verona's court
    Was a fair place. The feet might still
    Wander for ever at their will
In many ways of sweet resort;   160
    And still in many a heart around
    The Poet's name due honour found.

Watch we his steps. He comes upon
    The women at their palm-playing.
    The conduits round the gardens sing   165
And meet in scoops of milk-white stone,
    Where wearied damsels rest and hold
    Their hands in the wet spurt of gold.

One of whom, knowing well that he,
    By some found stern, was mild with them,   170
    Would run and pluck his garment's hem,
Saying, "Messer Dante, pardon me," —
    Praying that they might hear the song
    Which first of all he made, when young.

"Donne che avete"* . . . Thereunto   175
 Thus would he murmur, having first
 Drawn near the fountain, while she nurs'd
His hand against her side: a few
 Sweet words, and scarcely those, half said:
 Then turned, and changed, and bowed his head.   180

For then the voice said in his heart,
 "Even I, even I am Beatrice;"
 And his whole life would yearn to cease:
Till having reached his room, apart
 Beyond vast lengths of palace-floor,   185
 He drew the arras round his door.

At such times, Dante, thou hast set
 Thy forehead to the painted pane
 Full oft, I know; and if the rain
Smote it outside, her fingers met   190
 Thy brow; and if the sun fell there,
 Her breath was on thy face and hair.

Then, weeping, I think certainly
 Thou hast beheld, past sight of eyne, —
 Within another room of thine   195
Where now thy body may not be
 But where in thought thou still remain'st, —
 A window often wept against:

The window thou, a youth, hast sought,
 Flushed in the limpid eventime,   200
 Ending with daylight the day's rhyme
Of her; where oftenwhiles her thought
 Held thee — the lamp untrimmed to write —
 In joy through the blue lapse of night.

At Can La Scala's court, no doubt,   205
 Guests seldom wept. It was brave sport,
 No doubt, at Can La Scala's court,
Within the palace and without;
 Where music, set to madrigals,
 Loitered all day through groves and halls.   210

Because Can Grande of his life
 Had not had six-and-twenty years

*"Donne che avete intelletto d'amore:" — the first canzone of the "Vita Nuova."

As yet. And when the chroniclers
Tell you of that Vicenza strife
    And of strifes elsewhere, — you must not
    Conceive for church-sooth he had got

Just nothing in his wits but war:
    Though doubtless 'twas the young man's joy
    (Grown with his growth from a mere boy,)
To mark his "Viva Cane!" scare
    The foe's shut front, till it would reel
    All blind with shaken points of steel.

But there were places — held too sweet
    For eyes that had not the due veil
    Of lashes and clear lids — as well
In favour as his saddle-seat:
    Breath of low speech he scorned not there
    Nor light cool fingers in his hair.

Yet if the child whom the sire's plan
    Made free of a deep treasure-chest
    Scoffed it with ill-conditioned jest, —
We may be sure too that the man
    Was not mere thews, nor all content
    With lewdness swathed in sentiment.

So you may read and marvel not
    That such a man as Dante — one
    Who, while Can Grande's deeds were done,
Had drawn his robe round him and thought —
    Now at the same guest-table far'd
    Where keen Uguccio wiped his beard.*

Through leaves and trellis-work the sun
    Left the wine cool within the glass, —
    They feasting where no sun could pass:
And when the women, all as one,
    Rose up with brightened cheeks to go,
    It was a comely thing, we know.

But Dante recked not of the wine;
    Whether the women stayed or went,
    His visage held one stern intent:

  215

  220

  225

  230

  235

  240

  245

*Uguccione della Faggiuola, Dante's former protector, was now his fellow-guest at Verona.

And when the music had its sign   250
    To breathe upon them for more ease,
    Sometimes he turned and bade it cease.

And as he spared not to rebuke
    The mirth, so oft in council he
    To bitter truth bore testimony: 255
And when the crafty balance shook
    Well poised to make the wrong prevail,
    Then Dante's hand would turn the scale.

And if some envoy from afar
    Sailed to Verona's sovereign port   260
    For aid or peace, and all the court
Fawned on its lord, "the Mars of war,
    Sole arbiter of life and death," —
    Be sure that Dante saved his breath.

And Can La Scala marked askance   265
    These things, accepting them for shame
    And scorn, till Dante's guestship came
To be a peevish sufferance:
    His host sought ways to make his days
    Hateful; and such have many ways.   270

There was a Jester, a foul lout
    Whom the court loved for graceless arts;
    Sworn scholiast of the bestial parts
Of speech; a ribald mouth to shout
    In Folly's horny tympanum   275
    Such things as make the wise man dumb.

Much loved, him Dante loathed. And so,
    One day when Dante felt perplex'd
    If any day that could come next
Were worth the waiting for or no,   280
    And mute he sat amid their din, —
    Can Grande called the Jester in.

Rank words, with such, are wit's best wealth.
    Lords mouthed approval; ladies kept
    Twittering with clustered heads, except   285
Some few that took their trains by stealth
    And went. Can Grande shook his hair
    And smote his thighs and laughed i' the air.

Then, facing on his guest, he cried, —
  "Say, Messer Dante, how it is
  I get out of a clown like this
More than your wisdom can provide."
  And Dante: "'Tis man's ancient whim
  That still his like seems good to him."

Also a tale is told, how once,
  At clearing tables after meat,
  Piled for a jest at Dante's feet
Were found the dinner's well-picked bones;
  So laid, to please the banquet's lord,
  By one who crouched beneath the board.

Then smiled Can Grande to the rest: —
  "Our Dante's tuneful mouth indeed
  Lacks not the gift on flesh to feed!"
"Fair host of mine," replied the guest,
  "So many bones you'd not descry
  If so it chanced the dog were I."*

But wherefore should we turn the grout
  In a drained cup, or be at strife
  From the worn garment of a life
To rip the twisted ravel out?
  Good needs expounding; but of ill
  Each hath enough to guess his fill.

They named him Justicer-at-Law:
  Each month to bear the tale in mind
  Of hues a wench might wear unfin'd
And of the load an ox might draw;
  To cavil in the weight of bread
  And to see purse-thieves gibbeted.

And when his spirit wove the spell
  (From under even to over-noon
  In converse with itself alone,)
As high as Heaven, as low as Hell, —
  He would be summoned and must go:
  For had not Gian stabbed Giacomo?

290

295

300

305

310

315

320

---

*"*Messere, voi nonvedreste tant 'ossa se cane io fossi.*" The point of the reproach is difficult to render, depending as it does on the literal meaning of the name *Cane*.

Therefore the bread he had to eat 325
  Seemed brackish, less like corn than tares;
  And the rush-strown accustomed stairs
Each day were steeper to his feet;
  And when the night-vigil was done,
  His brows would ache to feel the sun. 330

Nevertheless, when from his kin
  There came the tidings how at last
  In Florence a decree was pass'd
Whereby all banished folk might win
  Free pardon, so a fine were paid 335
  And act of public penance made, —

This Dante writ in answer thus,
  Words such as these: "That clearly they
  In Florence must not have to say, —
The man abode aloof from us 340
  Nigh fifteen years, yet lastly skulk'd
  Hither to candleshrift and mulct.

"That he was one the Heavens forbid
  To traffic in God's justice sold
  By market-weight of earthly gold, 345
Or to bow down over the lid
  Of steaming censers, and so be
  Made clean of manhood's obloquy.

"That since no gate led, by God's will,
  To Florence, but the one whereat 350
  The priests and money-changers sat,
He still would wander; for that still,
  Even through the body's prison-bars,
  His soul possessed the sun and stars."

Such were his words. It is indeed 355
  For ever well our singers should
  Utter good words and know them good
Not through song only; with close heed
  Lest, having spent for the work's sake
  Six days, the man be left to make. 360

Months o'er Verona, till the feast
  Was come for Florence the Free Town:
  And at the shrine of Baptist John

The exiles, girt with many a priest
   And carrying candles as they went,
   Were held to mercy of the saint.

On the high seats in sober state, —
   Gold neck-chains range o'er range below
   Gold screen-work where the lilies grow, —
The Heads of the Republic sate,
   Marking the humbled face go by
   Each one of his house-enemy.

And as each proscript rose and stood
   From kneeling in the ashen dust
   On the shrine-steps, some magnate thrust
A beard into the velvet hood
   Of his front colleague's gown, to see
   The cinders stuck in the bare knee.

Tosinghi passed, Manelli passed,
   Rinucci passed, each in his place;
   But not an Alighieri's face
Went by that day from first to last
   In the Republic's triumph; nor
   A foot came home to Dante's door.

(RESPUBLICA — a public thing:
   A shameful shameless prostitute,
   Whose lust with one lord may not suit,
So takes by turns its reveling
   A night with each, till each at morn
   Is stripped and beaten forth forlorn,

And leaves her, cursing her. If she,
   Indeed, have not some spice-draught, hid
   In scent under a silver lid,
To drench his open throat with — he
   Once hard asleep; and thrust him not
   At dawn beneath the stairs to rot.

Such this Republic! — not the Maid
   He yearned for; she who yet should stand
   With Heaven's accepted hand in hand,
Invulnerable and unbetray'd:
   To whom, even as to God, should be
   Obeisance one with Liberty.)

Years filled out their twelve moons, and ceased
  One in another; and always
  There were the whole twelve hours each day 405
And each night as the years increased;
  And rising moon and setting sun
  Beheld that Dante's work was done.

What of his work for Florence? Well
  It was, he knew, and well must be. 410
  Yet evermore her hate's decree
Dwelt in his thought intolerable: —
  His body to be burned,* — his soul
  To beat its wings at hope's vain goal.

What of his work for Beatrice? 415
  Now well-nigh was the third song writ, —
  The stars a third time sealing it
With sudden music of pure peace:
  For echoing thrice the threefold song,
  The unnumbered stars the tone prolong.† 420

Each hour, as then the Vision pass'd,
  He heard the utter harmony
  Of the nine trembling spheres, till she
Bowed her eyes towards him in the last,
  So that all ended with her eyes, 425
  Hell, Purgatory, Paradise.

"It is my trust, as the years fall,
  To write more worthily of her
  Who now, being made God's minister,
Looks on His visage and knows all." 430
  Such was the hope that love dar'd blend
  With grief's slow fires, to make an end

Of the "New Life," his youth's dear book:
  Adding thereunto: "In such trust
  I labour, and believe I must 435
Accomplish this which my soul took
  In charge, if God, my Lord and hers,
  Leave my life with me a few years."

---

*Such was the last sentence passed by Florence against Dante, as a recalcitrant exile.
  †"E quindi uscimmo a riveder le*stelle*." — INFERNO
"Puro e disposto a salire alle*stelle*." — PURGATORIO
"L'amor che muove il sole e l'altre*stelle*." — PARADISO

The trust which he had borne in youth
  Was all at length accomplished. He 440
  At length had written worthily —
Yea even of her; no rhymes uncouth
  'Twixt tongue and tongue; but by God's aid
  The first words Italy had said.

Ah! haply now the heavenly guide 445
  Was not the last form seen by him:
  But there that Beatrice stood slim
And bowed in passing at his side,
  For whom in youth his heart made moan
  Then when the city sat alone.* 450

Clearly herself; the same whom he
  Met, not past girlhood, in the street,
  Low-bosomed and with hidden feet;
And then as woman perfectly,
  In years that followed, many an once, — 455
  And now at last among the suns

In that high vision. But indeed
  It may be memory might recall
  Last to him then the first of all, —
The child his boyhood bore in heed 460
  Nine years. At length the voice brought peace, —
  "Even I, even I am Beatrice."

All this, being there, we had not seen.
  Seen only was the shadow wrought
  On the strong features bound in thought; 465
The vagueness gaining gait and mien;
  The white streaks gathering clear to view
  In the burnt beard the women knew.

For a tale tells that on his track,
  As through Verona's streets he went, 470
  This saying certain women sent: —
"Lo, he that strolls to Hell and back
  At will! Behold him, how Hell's reek
  Has crisped his beard and singed his cheek."

*"*Quomodo sedet sola civitas!*" — The words quoted by Dante in the "Vita Nuova" when he speaks of the death of Beatrice.

"Whereat" (Boccaccio's words) "he smil'd   475
  For pride in fame." It might be so:
  Nevertheless we cannot know
If haply he were not beguil'd
  To bitterer mirth, who scarce could tell
  If he indeed were back from Hell.   480

So the day came, after a space,
  When Dante felt assured that there
  The sunshine must lie sicklier
Even than in any other place,
  Save only Florence. When that day   485
  Had come, he rose and went his way.

He went and turned out. From his shoes
  It may be that he shook the dust,
  As every righteous dealer must
Once and again ere life can close: 490
  And unaccomplished destiny
  Struck cold his forehead, it may be.

No book keeps record how the Prince
  Sunned himself out of Dante's reach,
  Nor how the Jester stank in speech: 495
While courtiers, used to cringe and wince,
  Poets and harlots, all the throng,
  Let loose their scandal and their song.

No book keeps record if the seat
  Which Dante held at his host's board   500
  Were sat in next by clerk or lord, —
If leman lolled with dainty feet
  At ease, or hostage brooded there,
  Or priest lacked silence for his prayer.

Eat and wash hands, Can Grande; — scarce   505
  We know their deeds now: hands which fed
  Our Dante with that bitter bread;
And thou the watch-dog of those stairs
  Which, of all paths his feet knew well,
  Were steeper found than Heaven or Hell.   510

Troy Town

Heavenborn Helen, Sparta's queen,
   (O Troy Town!)
Had two breasts of heavenly sheen,
The sun and moon of the heart's desire:
All Love's lordship lay between.   5
   (O Troy's down,
   Tall Troy's on fire!)

Helen knelt at Venus' shrine,
   (O Troy Town!)
Saying, "A little gift is mine,   10
A little gift for a heart's desire.
Hear me speak and make me a sign!
   (O Troy's down,
   Tall Troy's on fire!)

"Look, I bring thee a carven cup;   15
   (O Troy Town!)
See it here as I hold it up, —
Shaped it is to the heart's desire,
Fit to fill when the gods would sup.
   (O Troy's down,   20
   Tall Troy's on fire!)

"It was moulded like my breast;
   (O Troy Town!)
He that sees it may not rest,
Rest at all for his heart's desire.   25
O give ear to my heart's behest!
   (O Troy's down,
   Tall Troy's on fire!)

"See my breast, how like it is;
   (O Troy Town!)   30
See it bare for the air to kiss!
Is the cup to thy heart's desire?
O for the breast, O make it his!
   (O Troy's down,
   Tall Troy's on fire!)   35

"Yea, for my bosom here I sue;
   (O Troy Town!)
Thou must give it where 'tis due,

Give it there to the heart's desire.
Whom do I give my bosom to? 40
(O Troy's down,
Tall Troy's on fire!)

"Each twin breast is an apple sweet.
(O Troy Town!)
Once an apple stirred the beat 45
Of thy heart with the heart's desire: —
Say, who brought it then to thy feet?
(O Troy's down,
Tall Troy's on fire!)

"They that claimed it then were three: 50
(O Troy Town!)
For thy sake two hearts did he
Make forlorn of the heart's desire.
Do for him as he did for thee!
(O Troy's down, 55
Tall Troy's on fire!)

"Mine are apples grown to the south,
(O Troy Town!)
Grown to taste in the days of drouth,
Taste and waste to the heart's desire: 60
Mine are apples meet for his mouth."
(O Troy's down,
Tall Troy's on fire!)

Venus looked on Helen's gift,
(O Troy Town!) 65
Looked and smiled with subtle drift,
Saw the work of her heart's desire: —
"There thou kneel'st for Love to lift!"
(O Troy's down,
Tall Troy's on fire!) 70

Venus looked in Helen's face,
(O Troy Town!)
Knew far off an hour and place,
And fire lit from the heart's desire;
Laughed and said, "Thy gift hath grace!" 75
(O Troy's down,
Tall Troy's on fire!)

Cupid looked on Helen's breast,
    (O Troy Town!)
Saw the heart within its nest,   80
Saw the flame of the heart's desire, —
Marked his arrow's burning crest.
    (O Troy's down,
    Tall Troy's on fire!)

Cupid took another dart,   85
    (O Troy Town!)
Fledged it for another heart,
Winged the shaft with the heart's desire,
Drew the string and said, "Depart!"
    (O Troy's down,   90
    Tall Troy's on fire!)

Paris turned upon his bed,
    (O Troy Town!)
Turned upon his bed and said,
Dead at heart with the heart's desire, —   95
"Oh to clasp her golden head!"
    (O Troy's down,
    Tall Troy's on fire!)

Eden Bower

It was Lilith the wife of Adam:
    (Sing Eden Bower!)
Not a drop of her blood was human,
But she was made like a soft sweet woman.

Lilith stood on the skirts of Eden;   5
    (Alas the hour!)
She was the first that thence was driven;
With her was hell and with Eve was heaven.

In the ear of the Snake said Lilith: —
    (Sing Eden Bower!)   10
"To thee I come when the rest is over;
A snake was I when thou wast my lover.

"I was the fairest snake in Eden:
    (Alas the hour!)

By the earth's will, new form and feature 15
Made me a wife for the earth's new creature.

"Take me thou as I come from Adam:
  (Sing Eden Bower!)
Once again shall my love subdue thee;
The past is past and I am come to thee. 20

"O but Adam was thrall to Lilith!
  (Alas the hour!)
All the threads of my hair are golden,
And there in a net his heart was holden.

"O and Lilith was queen of Adam! 25
  (Sing Eden Bower!)
All the day and the night together
My breath could shake his soul like a feather.

"What great joys had Adam and Lilith! —
  (Alas the hour!) 30
Sweet close rings of the serpent's twining,
As heart in heart lay sighing and pining.

"What bright babes had Lilith and Adam! —
  (Sing Eden Bower!)
Shapes that coiled in the woods and waters, 35
Glittering sons and radiant daughters.

"O thou God, the Lord God of Eden!
  (Alas the hour!)
Say, was this fair body for no man,
That of Adam's flesh thou mak'st him a woman? 40

"O thou Snake, the King-snake of Eden!
  (Sing Eden Bower!)
God's strong will our necks are under,
But thou and I may cleave it in sunder.

"Help, sweet Snake, sweet lover of Lilith! 45
  (Alas the hour!)
And let God learn how I loved and hated
Man in the image of God created.

"Help me once against Eve and Adam!
  (Sing Eden Bower!) 50
Help me once for this one endeavour,
And then my love shall be thine for ever!

"Strong is God, the fell foe of Lilith:
   (Alas the hour!)
Nought in heaven or earth may affright him;   55
But join thou with me and we will smite him.

"Strong is God, the great God of Eden:
   (Sing Eden Bower!)
Over all He made He hath power;
But lend me thou thy shape for an hour!   60

"Lend thy shape for the love of Lilith!
   (Alas the hour!)
Look, my mouth and my cheek are ruddy,
And thou art cold, and fire is my body.

"Lend thy shape for the hate of Adam!   65
   (Sing Eden Bower!)
That he may wail my joy that forsook him,
And curse the day when the bride-sleep took him.

"Lend thy shape for the shame of Eden!
   (Alas the hour!)   70
Is not the foe-God weak as the foeman
When love grows hate in the heart of a woman?

"Would'st thou know the heart's hope of Lilith?
   (Sing Eden Bower!)
Then bring thou close thine head till it glisten   75
Along my breast, and lip me and listen.

"Am I sweet, O sweet Snake of Eden?
   (Alas the hour!)
Then ope thine ear to my warm mouth's cooing
And learn what deed remains for our doing.   80

"Thou didst hear when God said to Adam: —
   (Sing Eden Bower!)
'Of all this wealth I have made thee warden;
Thou'rt free to eat of the trees of the garden:

"'Only of one tree eat not in Eden;   85
   (Alas the hour!)
All save one I give to thy freewill, —
The Tree of the Knowledge of Good and Evil.'

"O my love, come nearer to Lilith!
   (Sing Eden Bower!)   90

In thy sweet folds bind me and bend me,
And let me feel the shape thou shalt lend me!

"In thy shape I'll go back to Eden;
   (Alas the hour!)
In these coils that Tree will I grapple,   95
And stretch this crowned head forth by the apple.

"Lo, Eve bends to the breath of Lilith!
   (Sing Eden Bower!)
O how then shall my heart desire
All her blood as food to its fire!   100

"Lo, Eve bends to the words of Lilith! —
   (Alas the hour!)
'Nay, this Tree's fruit, — why should ye hate it,
Or Death be born the day that ye ate it?

"'Nay, but on that great day in Eden,   105
   (Sing Eden Bower!)
By the help that in this wise Tree is,
God knows well ye shall be as He is.'

"Then Eve shall eat and give unto Adam;
   (Alas the hour!)   110
And then they both shall know they are naked,
And their hearts ache as my heart hath achèd.

"Aye, let them hide 'mid the trees of Eden,
   (Sing Eden Bower!)
As in the cool of the day in the garden   115
God shall walk without pity or pardon.

"Hear, thou Eve, the man's heart in Adam!
   (Alas the hour!)
Of his brave words hark to the bravest: —
'This the woman gave that thou gavest.'   120

"Hear Eve speak, yea list to her, Lilith!
   (Sing Eden Bower!)
Feast thine heart with words that shall sate it —
'This the serpent gave and I ate it.'

"O proud Eve, cling close to thine Adam,   125
   (Alas the hour!)
Driven forth as the beasts of his naming
By the sword that for ever is flaming.

"Know, thy path is known unto Lilith!
    (Sing Eden Bower!)
While the blithe birds sang at thy wedding,
There her tears grew thorns for thy treading.

"O my love, thou Love-snake of Eden!
    (Alas the hour!)
O to-day and the day to come after!
Loose me, love, — give breath to my laughter.

"O bright Snake, the Death-worm of Adam!
    (Sing Eden Bower!)
Wreathe thy neck with my hair's bright tether,
And wear my gold and thy gold together!

"On that day on the skirts of Eden,
    (Alas the hour!)
In thy shape shall I glide back to thee,
And in my shape for an instant view thee.

"But when thou'rt thou and Lilith is Lilith,
    (Sing Eden Bower!)
In what bliss past hearing or seeing
Shall each one drink of the other's being!

"With cries of 'Eve!' and 'Eden!' and 'Adam!'
    (Alas the hour!)
How shall we mingle our love's caresses,
I in thy coils, and thou in my tresses!

"With those names, ye echoes of Eden,
    (Sing Eden Bower!)
Fire shall cry from my heart that burneth, —
'Dust he is and to dust returneth!'

"Yet to-day, thou master of Lilith, —
    (Alas the hour!)
Wrap me round in the form I'll borrow
And let me tell thee of sweet to-morrow.

"In the planted garden eastward in Eden,
    (Sing Eden Bower!)
Where the river goes forth to water the garden,
The springs shall dry and the soil shall harden.

"Yea, where the bride-sleep fell upon Adam,
    (Alas the hour!)

130

135

140

145

150

155

160

165

None shall hear when the storm-wind whistles
Through roses choked among thorns and thistles.

"Yea, beside the east-gate of Eden,
   (Sing Eden Bower!)   170
Where God joined them and none might sever,
The sword turns this way and that for ever.

"What of Adam cast out of Eden?
   (Alas the hour!)
Lo! with care like a shadow shaken,   175
He tills the hard earth whence he was taken.

"What of Eve too, cast out of Eden?
   (Sing Eden Bower!)
Nay, but she, the bride of God's giving,
Must yet be mother of all men living.   180

"Lo, God's grace, by the grace of Lilith!
   (Alas the hour!)
To Eve's womb, from our sweet to-morrow,
God shall greatly multiply sorrow.

"Fold me fast, O God-snake of Eden!   185
   (Sing Eden Bower!)
What more prize than love to impel thee?
Grip and lip my limbs as I tell thee!

"Lo! two babes for Eve and for Adam!
   (Alas the hour!)   190
Lo! sweet Snake, the travail and treasure, —
Two men-children born for their pleasure!

"The first is Cain and the second Abel:
   (Sing Eden Bower!)
The soul of one shall be made thy brother,   195
And thy tongue shall lap the blood of the other."
   (Alas the hour!)

The Card-Dealer

Could you not drink her gaze like wine?
   Yet though its splendour swoon
Into the silence languidly
   As a tune into a tune,

Those eyes unravel the coiled night
    And know the stars at noon.

The gold that's heaped beside her hand,
    In truth rich prize it were;
And rich the dreams that wreathe her brows
    With magic stillness there;
And he were rich who should unwind
    That woven golden hair.

Around her, where she sits, the dance
    Now breathes its eager heat;
And not more lightly or more true
    Fall there the dancers' feet
Than fall her cards on the bright board
    As 'twere an heart that beat.

Her fingers let them softly through,
    Smooth polished silent things;
And each one as it falls reflects
    In swift light-shadowings,
Blood-red and purple, green and blue,
    The great eyes of her rings.

Whom plays she with? With thee, who lov'st
    Those gems upon her hand;
With me, who search her secret brows;
    With all men, bless'd or bann'd.
We play together, she and we,
    Within a vain strange land:

A land without any order, —
    Day even as night, (one saith,) —
Where who lieth down ariseth not
    Nor the sleeper awakeneth;
A land of darkness as darkness itself
    And of the shadow of death.

What be her cards, you ask? Even these: —
    The heart, that doth but crave
More, having fed; the diamond,
    Skilled to make base seem brave;
The club, for smiting in the dark;
    The spade, to dig a grave.

And do you ask what game she plays?
    With me 'tis lost or won;

With thee it is playing still; with him 45
   It is not well begun;
But 'tis a game she plays with all
   Beneath the sway o' the sun.

Thou seest the card that falls, — she knows
   The card that followeth: 50
Her game in thy tongue is called Life,
   As ebbs thy daily breath:
When she shall speak, thou'lt learn her tongue
   And know she calls it Death.

Love's Nocturne

Master of the murmuring courts
   Where the shapes of sleep convene! —
Lo! my spirit here exhorts
   All the powers of thy demesne
   For their aid to woo my queen. 5
     What reports
   Yield thy jealous courts unseen?

Vaporous, unaccountable,
   Dreamworld lies forlorn of light,
Hollow like a breathing shell. 10
   Ah! that from all dreams I might
   Choose one dream and guide its flight!
     I know well
   What her sleep should tell to-night.

There the dreams are multitudes: 15
   Some that will not wait for sleep,
Deep within the August woods;
   Some that hum while rest may steep
   Weary labour laid a-heap;
     Interludes, 20
   Some, of grievous moods that weep.

Poets' fancies all are there:
   There the elf-girls flood with wings
Valleys full of plaintive air;
   There breathe perfumes; there in rings 25

Whirl the foam-bewildered springs;
    Siren there
Winds her dizzy hair and sings.

Thence the one dream mutually
    Dreamed in bridal unison,   30
Less than waking ecstasy;
    Half-formed visions that make moan
    In the house of birth alone;
        And what we
    At death's wicket see, unknown.   35

But for mine own sleep, it lies
    In one gracious form's control,
Fair with honourable eyes,
    Lamps of a translucent soul:
    O their glance is loftiest dole,   40
        Sweet and wise,
    Wherein Love descries his goal.

Reft of her, my dreams are all
    Clammy trance that fears the sky:
Changing footpaths shift and fall;   45
    From polluted coverts nigh,
    Miserable phantoms sigh;
        Quakes the pall,
    And the funeral goes by.

Master, is it soothly said   50
    That, as echoes of man's speech
Far in secret clefts are made,
    So do all men's bodies reach
    Shadows o'er thy sunken beach, —
        Shape or shade   55
    In those halls pourtrayed of each?

Ah! might I, by thy good grace
    Groping in the windy stair,
(Darkness and the breath of space
    Like loud waters everywhere,)   60
    Meeting mine own image there
        Face to face,
    Send it from that place to her!

Nay, not I; but oh! Do thou,
    Master, from thy shadowkind   65

Call my body's phantom now:
  Bid it bear its face declin'd
  Till its flight her slumbers find,
    And her brow
  Feel its presence bow like wind.   70

Where in groves the gracile Spring
  Trembles, with mute orison
Confidently strengthening,
  Water's voice and wind's as one
  Shed an echo in the sun.   75
    Soft as Spring,
  Master, bid it sing and moan.

Song shall tell how glad and strong
  Is the night she soothes alway;
Moan shall grieve with that parched tongue   80
  Of the brazen hours of day:
  Sounds as of the springtide they,
    Moan and song,
  While the chill months long for May.

Not the prayers which with all leave   85
  The world's fluent woes prefer, —
Not the praise the world doth give,
  Dulcet fulsome whisperer; —
  Let it yield my love to her,
    And achieve   90
  Strength that shall not grieve or err.

Wheresoe'er my dreams befall,
  Both at night-watch, (let it say,)
And where round the sundial
  The reluctant hours of day,   95
  Heartless, hopeless of their way,
    Rest and call; —
  There her glance doth fall and stay.

Suddenly her face is there:
  So do mounting vapours wreathe   100
Subtle-scented transports where
  The black firwood sets its teeth.
  Part the boughs and look beneath, —
    Lilies share
  Secret waters there, and breathe.   105

Master, bid my shadow bend
   Whispering thus till birth of light,
Lest new shapes that sleep may send
   Scatter all its work to flight; —
   Master, master of the night,   110
     Bid it spend
   Speech, song, prayer, and end aright.

Yet, ah me! if at her head
   There another phantom lean
Murmuring o'er the fragrant bed, —   115
   Ah! and if my spirit's queen
   Smile those alien prayers between, —
     Ah! poor shade!
   Shall it strive, or fade unseen?

How should love's own messenger   120
   Strive with love and be love's foe?
Master, nay! If thus, in her,
   Sleep a wedded heart should show, —
   Silent let mine image go,
     Its old share   125
   Of thy spell-bound air to know.

Like a vapour wan and mute,
   Like a flame, so let it pass;
One low sigh across her lute,
   One dull breath against her glass;   130
   And to my sad soul, alas!
     One salute
   Cold as when death's foot shall pass.

Then, too, let all hopes of mine,
   All vain hopes by night and day,   135
Slowly at thy summoning sign
   Rise up pallid and obey.
   Dreams, if this is thus, were they: —
     Be they thine,
   And to dreamworld pine away.   140

Yet from old time, life, not death,
   Master, in thy rule is rife:
Lo! through thee, with mingling breath,
   Adam woke beside his wife.
   O Love bring me so, for strife,   145

Force and faith,
  Bring me so not death but life!

Yea, to Love himself is pour'd
  This frail song of hope and fear.
Thou art Love, of one accord   150
  With kind Sleep to bring her near,
  Still-eyed, deep-eyed, ah how dear!
    Master, Lord,
  In her name implor'd, O hear!

The Stream's Secret

    What thing unto mine ear
  Wouldst thou convey, — what secret thing,
O wandering water ever whispering?
  Surely thy speech shall be of her.
Thou water, O thou whispering wanderer,   5
    What message dost thou bring?

    Say, hath not Love leaned low
  This hour beside thy far well-head,
And there through jealous hollowed fingers said
  The thing that most I long to know, —   10
Murmuring with curls all dabbled in thy flow
    And washed lips rosy red?

    He told it to thee there
  Where thy voice hath a louder tone;
But where it welters to this little moan   15
  His will decrees that I should hear.
Now speak: for with the silence is no fear,
    And I am all alone.

    Shall Time not still endow
  One hour with life, and I and she   20
Slake in one kiss the thirst of memory?
  Say, stream; lest Love should disavow
Thy service, and the bird upon the bough
    Sing first to tell it me.

    What whisperest thou? Nay, why   25
  Name the dead hours? I mind them well:
Their ghosts in many darkened doorways dwell

With desolate eyes to know them by.
The hour that must be born ere it can die, —
   Of that I'd have thee tell.   30

   But hear, before thou speak!
   Withhold, I pray, the vain behest
That while the maze hath still its bower for quest
   My burning heart should cease to seek.
Be sure that Love ordained for souls more meek   35
   His roadside dells of rest.

   Stream, when this silver thread
   In flood-time is a torrent brown
May any bulwark bind thy foaming crown?
   Shall not the waters surge and spread   40
And to the crannied boulders of their bed
   Still shoot the dead drift down?

   Let no rebuke find place
   In speech of thine: or it shall prove
That thou dost ill expound the words of Love,   45
   Even as thine eddy's rippling race
Would blur the perfect image of his face.
   I will have none thereof.

   O learn and understand
   That 'gainst the wrongs himself did wreak   50
Love sought her aid; until her shadowy cheek
   And eyes beseeching gave command;
And compassed in her close compassionate hand
   My heart must burn and speak.

   For then at last we spoke   55
   What eyes so oft had told to eyes
Through that long-lingering silence whose half-sighs
   Alone the buried secret broke,
Which with snatched hands and lips' reverberate stroke
   Then from the heart did rise.   60

   But she is far away
   Now; nor the hours of night grown hoar
Bring yet to me, long gazing from the door,
   The wind-stirred robe of roseate grey
And rose-crown of the hour that leads the day   65
   When we shall meet once more.

Dark as thy blinded wave
  When brimming midnight floods the glen, —
Bright as the laughter of thy runnels when
  The dawn yields all the light they crave;   70
Even so these hours to wound and that to save
    Are sisters in Love's ken.

  Oh sweet her bending grace
  Then when I kneel beside her feet;
And sweet her eyes' o'erhanging heaven; and sweet   75
  The gathering folds of her embrace;
And her fall'n hair at last shed round my face
    When breaths and tears shall meet.

  Beneath her sheltering hair,
  In the warm silence near her breast,   80
Our kisses and our sobs shall sink to rest;
  As in some still trance made aware
That day and night have wrought to fulness there
    And Love has built our nest.

  And as in the dim grove,   85
  When the rains cease that hushed them long,
'Mid glistening boughs the song-birds wake to song, —
  So from our hearts deep-shrined in love,
While the leaves throb beneath, around, above,
    The quivering notes shall throng.   90

  Till tenderest words found vain
  Draw back to wonder mute and deep,
And closed lips in closed arms a silence keep,
  Subdued by memory's circling strain, —
The wind-rapt sound that the wind brings again   95
    While all the willows weep.

  Then by her summoning art
  Shall memory conjure back the sere
Autumnal Springs, from many a dying year
  Born dead; and, bitter to the heart,   100
The very ways where now we walk apart
    Who then shall cling so near.

  And with each thought new-grown,
  Some sweet caress or some sweet name
Low-breathed shall let me know her thought the same;   105

Making me rich with every tone
And touch of the dear heaven so long unknown
  That filled my dreams with flame.

  Pity and love shall burn
In her pressed cheek and cherishing hands;   110
And from the living spirit of love that stands
  Between her lips to soothe and yearn,
Each separate breath shall clasp me round in turn
  And loose my spirit's bands.

  Oh passing sweet and dear,   115
Then when the worshipped form and face
Are felt at length in darkling close embrace;
  Round which so oft the sun shone clear,
With mocking light and pitiless atmosphere,
  In many an hour and place.   120

  Ah me! with what proud growth
Shall that hour's thirsting race be run;
While, for each several sweetness still begun
  Afresh, endures love's endless drouth:
Sweet hands, sweet hair, sweet cheeks, sweet eyes, sweet mouth   125
  Each singly wooed and won.

  Yet most with the sweet soul
Shall love's espousals then be knit;
For very passion of peace shall breathe from it
  O'er tremulous wings that touch the goal,   130
As on the unmeasured height of Love's control
  The lustral fires are lit.

  Therefore, when breast and cheek
Now part, from long embraces free, —
Each on the other gazing shall but see   135
  A self that has no need to speak:
All things unsought, yet nothing more to seek, —
  One love in unity.

  O water wandering past, —
Albeit to thee I speak this thing,   140
O water, thou that wanderest whispering,
  Thou keep'st thy counsel to the last.
What spell upon thy bosom should Love cast,
  His message thence to wring?

Nay, must thou hear the tale   145
    Of the past days, — the heavy debt
Of life that obdurate time withholds, — ere yet
    To win thine ear these prayers prevail,
And by thy voice Love's self with high All-hail
    Yield up the love-secret?   150

    How should all this be told? —
    All the sad sum of wayworn days; —
Heart's anguish in the impenetrable maze;
    And on the waste uncoloured wold
The visible burthen of the sun grown cold   155
    And the moon's labouring gaze?

    Alas! shall hope be nurs'd
    On life's all-succouring breast in vain,
And made so perfect only to be slain?
    Or shall not rather the sweet thirst   160
Even yet rejoice the heart with warmth dispers'd
    And strength grown fair again?

    Stands it not by the door —
    Love's Hour — till she and I shall meet;
With bodiless form and unapparent feet   165
    That cast no shadow yet before,
Though round its head the dawn begins to pour
    The breath that makes day sweet?

    Its eyes invisible
    Watch till the dial's thin-thrown shade   170
Be born, — yea, till the journeying line be laid
    Upon the point that wakes the spell,
And there in lovelier light than tongue can tell
    Its presence stand array'd.

    Its soul remembers yet   175
    Those sunless hours that passed it by;
And still it hears the night's disconsolate cry,
    And feels the branches wringing wet
Cast on its brow, that may not once forget,
    Dumb tears from the blind sky.   180

    But oh! when now her foot
    Draws near, for whose sake night and day
Were long in weary longing sighed away, —
    The Hour of Love, 'mid airs grown mute,

Shall sing beside the door, and Love's own lute
    Thrill to the passionate lay.

    Thou know'st, for Love has told
  Within thine ear, O stream, how soon
That song shall lift its sweet appointed tune.
    O tell me, for my lips are cold,
And in my veins the blood is waxing old
    Even while I beg the boon.

    So, in that hour of sighs
  Assuaged, shall we beside this stone
Yield thanks for grace; while in thy mirror shown
    The twofold image softly lies,
Until we kiss, and each in other's eyes
    Is imaged all alone.

    Still silent? Can no art
  Of Love's then move thy pity? Nay,
To thee let nothing come that owns his sway:
    Let happy lovers have no part
With thee; nor even so sad and poor a heart
    As thou hast spurned to-day.

    To-day? Lo! night is here.
  The glen grows heavy with some veil
Risen from the earth or fall'n to make earth pale;
    And all stands hushed to eye and ear,
Until the night-wind shake the shade like fear
    And every covert quail.

    Ah! by a colder wave
  On deathlier airs the hour must come
Which to thy heart, my love, shall call me home.
    Between the lips of the low cave
Against that night the lapping waters lave,
    And the dark lips are dumb.

    But there Love's self doth stand,
  And with Life's weary wings far-flown,
And with Death's eyes that make the water moan,
    Gathers the water in his hand:
And they that drink know nought of sky or land
    But only love alone.

    O soul-sequestered face
Far off, — O were that night but now!

So even beside that stream even I and thou   225
   Through thirsting lips should draw Love's grace,
And in the zone of that supreme embrace
    Bind aching breast and brow.

   O water whispering
   Still through the dark into mine ears, —   230
As with mine eyes, is it not now with hers? —
   Mine eyes that add to thy cold spring,
Wan water, wandering water weltering,
    This hidden tide of tears.

Jenny

"Vengeance of Jenny's case! Fie on her!
Never name her, child"
(Mrs. Quickly.)

Lazy laughing languid Jenny,
Fond of a kiss and fond of a guinea,
Whose head upon my knee to-night
Rests for a while, as if grown light
With all our dances and the sound   5
To which the wild tunes spun you round:
Fair Jenny mine, the thoughtless queen
Of kisses which the blush between
Could hardly make much daintier;
Whose eyes are as blue skies, whose hair   10
Is countless gold incomparable:
Fresh flower, scarce touched with signs that tell
Of Love's exuberant hotbed: — Nay,
Poor flower left torn since yesterday
Until to-morrow leave you bare;   15
Poor handful of bright spring-water
Flung in the whirlpool's shrieking face;
Poor shameful Jenny, full of grace
Thus with your head upon my knee; —
Whose person or whose purse may be   20
The lodestar of your reverie?

   This room of yours, my Jenny, looks
A change from mine so full of books,
Whose serried ranks hold fast, forsooth,
So many captive hours of youth, —   25

The hours they thieve from day and night
To make one's cherished work come right,
And leave it wrong for all their theft,
Even as to-night my work was left:
Until I vowed that since my brain   30
And eyes of dancing seemed so fain,
My feet should have some dancing too: —
And thus it was I met with you.
Well, I suppose 'twas hard to part,
For here I am. And now, sweetheart,   35
You seem too tired to get to bed.

   It was a careless life I led
When rooms like this were scarce so strange
Not long ago. What breeds the change, —
The many aims or the few years?   40
Because to-night it all appears
Something I do not know again.

   The cloud's not danced out of my brain, —
The cloud that made it turn and swim
While hour by hour the books grew dim.   45
Why, Jenny, as I watch you there, —
For all your wealth of loosened hair,
Your silk ungirdled and unlac'd
And warm sweets open to the waist,
All golden in the lamplight's gleam, —   50
You know not what a book you seem,
Half-read by lightning in a dream!
How should you know, my Jenny? Nay,
And I should be ashamed to say: —
Poor beauty, so well worth a kiss!   55
But while my thought runs on like this
With wasteful whims more than enough,
I wonder what you're thinking of.

   If of myself you think at all,
What is the thought? — conjectural   60
On sorry matters best unsolved? —
Or inly is each grace revolved
To fit me with a lure? — or (sad
To think!) perhaps you're merely glad
That I'm not drunk or ruffianly   65
And let you rest upon my knee.

For sometimes, were the truth confess'd,
You're thankful for a little rest, —
Glad from the crush to rest within,
From the heart-sickness and the din   70
Where envy's voice at virtue's pitch
Mocks you because your gown is rich;
And from the pale girl's dumb rebuke,
Whose ill-clad grace and toil-worn look
Proclaim the strength that keeps her weak   75
And other nights than yours bespeak;
And from the wise unchildish elf,
To schoolmate lesser than himself
Pointing you out, what thing you are: —
Yes, from the daily jeer and jar,   80
From shame and shame's outbraving too,
Is rest not sometimes sweet to you? —
But most from the hatefulness of man
Who spares not to end what he began,
Whose acts are ill and his speech ill,   85
Who, having used you at his will,
Thrusts you aside, as when I dine
I serve the dishes and the wine.

Well, handsome Jenny mine, sit up,
I've filled our glasses, let us sup,   90
And do not let me think of you,
Lest shame of yours suffice for two.
What, still so tired? Well, well then, keep
Your head there, so you do not sleep;
But that the weariness may pass   95
And leave you merry, take this glass.
Ah! lazy lily hand, more bless'd
If ne'er in rings it had been dress'd
Nor ever by a glove conceal'd!

Behold the lilies of the field,   100
They toil not neither do they spin;
(So doth the ancient text begin, —
Not of such rest as one of these
Can share.) Another rest and ease
Along each summer-sated path   105
From its new lord the garden hath,
Than that whose spring in blessings ran
Which praised the bounteous husbandman,

Ere yet, in days of hankering breath,
The lilies sickened unto death.   110

    What, Jenny, are your lilies dead?
Aye, and the snow-white leaves are spread
Like winter on the garden-bed.
But you had roses left in May, —
They were not gone too. Jenny, nay,   115
But must your roses die, and those
Their purfled buds that should unclose?
Even so; the leaves are curled apart,
Still red as from the broken heart,
And here's the naked stem of thorns.   120

    Nay, nay, mere words. Here nothing warns
As yet of winter. Sickness here
Or want alone could waken fear, —
Nothing but passion wrings a tear.
Except when there may rise unsought   125
Haply at times a passing thought
Of the old days which seem to be
Much older than any history
That is written in any book;
When she would lie in fields and look   130
Along the ground through the blown grass,
And wonder where the city was,
Far out of sight, whose broil and bale
They told her then for a child's tale.

    Jenny, you know the city now.   135
A child can tell the tale there, how
Some things which are not yet enroll'd
In market-lists are bought and sold
Even till the early Sunday light,
When Saturday night is market-night   140
Everywhere, be it dry or wet,
And market-night in the Haymarket.
Our learned London children know,
Poor Jenny, all your pride and woe;
Have seen your lifted silken skirt   145
Advertise dainties through the dirt;
Have seen your coach-wheels splash rebuke
On virtue; and have learned your look
When, wealth and health slipped past, you stare
Along the streets alone, and there,   150

Round the long park, across the bridge,
The cold lamps at the pavement's edge
Wind on together and apart,
A fiery serpent for your heart.

Let the thoughts pass, an empty cloud!   155
Suppose I were to think aloud, —
What if to her all this were said?
Why, as a volume seldom read
Being opened halfway shuts again,
So might the pages of her brain   160
Be parted at such words, and thence
Close back upon the dusty sense.
For is there hue or shape defin'd
In Jenny's desecrated mind,
Where all contagious currents meet,   165
A Lethe of the middle street?
Nay, it reflects not any face,
Nor sound is in its sluggish pace,
But as they coil those eddies clot,
And night and day remember not.   170

Why, Jenny, you're asleep at last! —
Asleep, poor Jenny, hard and fast, —
So young and soft and tired; so fair,
With chin thus nestled in your hair,
Mouth quiet, eyelids almost blue   175
As if some sky of dreams shone through!

Just as another woman sleeps!
Enough to throw one's thoughts in heaps
Of doubt and horror, — what to say
Or think, — this awful secret sway,   180
The potter's power over the clay!
Of the same lump (it has been said)
For honour and dishonour made,
Two sister vessels. Here is one.

My cousin Nell is fond of fun,   185
And fond of dress, and change, and praise,
So mere a woman in her ways:
And if her sweet eyes rich in youth
Are like her lips that tell the truth,
My cousin Nell is fond of love.   190
And she's the girl I'm proudest of.

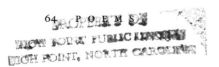

Who does not prize her, guard her well?
The love of change, in cousin Nell,
Shall find the best and hold it dear:
The unconquered mirth turn quieter   195
Not through her own, through others' woe:
The conscious pride of beauty glow
Beside another's pride in her,
One little part of all they share.
For Love himself shall ripen these   200
In a kind soil to just increase
Through years of fertilizing peace.

   Of the same lump (as it is said)
For honour and dishonour made,
Two sister vessels. Here is one.   205

   It makes a goblin of the sun.

   So pure, — so fall'n! How dare to think
Of the first common kindred link?
Yet, Jenny, till the world shall burn
It seems that all things take their turn;   210
And who shall say but this fair tree
May need, in changes that may be,
Your children's children's charity?
Scorned then, no doubt, as you are scorn'd!
Shall no man hold his pride forewarn'd   215
Till in the end, the Day of Days,
At Judgment, one of his own race,
As frail and lost as you, shall rise, —
His daughter, with his mother's eyes?

   How Jenny's clock ticks on the shelf!   220
Might not the dial scorn itself
That has such hours to register?
Yet as to me, even so to her
Are golden sun and silver moon,
In daily largesse of earth's boon,   225
Counted for life-coins to one tune.
And if, as blindfold fates are toss'd,
Through some one man this life be lost,
Shall soul not somehow pay for soul?

   Fair shines the gilded aureole   230
In which our highest painters place
Some living woman's simple face.

And the stilled features thus descried
As Jenny's long throat droops aside, —
The shadows where the cheeks are thin,   235
And pure wide curve from ear to chin, —
With Raffael's, Leonardo's hand
To show them to men's souls, might stand,
Whole ages long, the whole world through,
For preachings of what God can do.   240
What has man done here? How atone,
Great God, for this which man has done?
And for the body and soul which by
Man's pitiless doom must now comply
With lifelong hell, what lullaby   245
Of sweet forgetful second birth
Remains? All dark. No sign on earth
What measure of God's rest endows
The many mansions of his house.

   If but a woman's heart might see   250
Such erring heart unerringly
For once! But that can never be.

   Like a rose shut in a book
In which pure women may not look,
For its base pages claim control   255
To crush the flower within the soul;
Where through each dead rose-leaf that clings,
Pale as transparent psyche-wings,
To the vile text, are traced such things
As might make lady's cheek indeed   260
More than a living rose to read;
So nought save foolish foulness may
Watch with hard eyes the sure decay;
And so the life-blood of this rose,
Puddled with shameful knowledge, flows   265
Through leaves no chaste hand may unclose:
Yet still it keeps such faded show
Of when 'twas gathered long ago,
That the crushed petals' lovely grain,
The sweetness of the sanguine stain,   270
Seen of a woman's eyes, must make
Her pitiful heart, so prone to ache,
Love roses better for its sake: —
Only that this can never be: —
Even so unto her sex is she.   275

Yet, Jenny, looking long at you,
The woman almost fades from view.
A cipher of man's changeless sum
Of lust, past, present, and to come,
Is left. A riddle that one shrinks   280
To challenge from the scornful sphinx.

Like a toad within a stone
Seated while Time crumbles on;
Which sits there since the earth was curs'd
For Man's transgression at the first;   285
Which, living through all centuries,
Not once has seen the sun arise;
Whose life, to its cold circle charmed,
The earth's whole summers have not warmed;
Which always — whitherso the stone   290
Be flung — sits there, deaf, blind, alone; —
Aye, and shall not be driven out
Till that which shuts him round about
Break at the very Master's stroke,
And the dust thereof vanish as smoke,   295
And the seed of Man vanish as dust: —
Even so within this world is Lust.

Come, come, what use in thoughts like this?
Poor little Jenny, good to kiss, —
You'd not believe by what strange roads   300
Thought travels, when your beauty goads
A man to-night to think of toads!
Jenny, wake up. . . . Why, there's the dawn!

And there's an early waggon drawn
To market, and some sheep that jog   305
Bleating before a barking dog;
And the old streets come peering through
Another night that London knew;
And all as ghostlike as the lamps.

So on the wings of day decamps   310
My last night's frolic. Glooms begin
To shiver off as lights creep in
Past the gauze curtains half drawn-to,
And the lamp's doubled shade grows blue, —
Your lamp, my Jenny, kept alight,   315
Like a wise virgin's, all one night!
And in the alcove coolly spread

Glimmers with dawn your empty bed;
And yonder your fair face I see
Reflected lying on my knee,   320
Where teems with first foreshadowings
Your pier-glass scrawled with diamond rings:
And on your bosom all night worn
Yesterday's rose now droops forlorn
But dies not yet this summer morn.   325

   And now without, as if some word
Had called upon them that they heard,
The London sparrows far and nigh
Clamour together suddenly;
And Jenny's cage-bird grown awake   330
Here in their song his part must take,
Because here too the day doth break.

   And somehow in myself the dawn
Among stirred clouds and veils withdrawn
Strikes greyly on her. Let her sleep.   335
But will it wake her if I heap
These cushions thus beneath her head
Where my knee was? No, — there's your bed,
My Jenny, while you dream. And there
I lay among your golden hair   340
Perhaps the subject of your dreams,
These golden coins.

     For still one deems
That Jenny's flattering sleep confers
New magic on the magic purse, —
Grim web, how clogged with shrivelled flies!   345
Between the threads fine fumes arise
And shape their pictures in the brain.
There roll no streets in glare and rain,
Nor flagrant man-swine whets his tusk;
But delicately sighs in musk   350
The homage of the dim boudoir;
Or like a palpitating star
Thrilled into song, the opera-night
Breathes faint in the quick pulse of light;
Or at the carriage-window shine   355
Rich wares for choice; or, free to dine,
Whirls through its hour of health (divine
For her) the concourse of the Park.

And though in the discounted dark
Her functions there and here are one,   360
Beneath the lamps and in the sun
There reigns at least the acknowledged belle
Apparelled beyond parallel.
Ah Jenny, yes, we know your dreams.

 For even the Paphian Venus seems   365
A goddess o'er the realms of love,
When silver-shrined in shadowy grove:
Aye, or let offerings nicely plac'd
But hide Priapus to the waist,
And whoso looks on him shall see   370
An eligible deity.

 Why, Jenny, waking here alone
May help you to remember one,
Though all the memory's long outworn
Of many a double-pillowed morn.   375
I think I see you when you wake,
And rub your eyes for me, and shake
My gold, in rising, from your hair,
A Danaë for a moment there.

 Jenny, my love rang true! for still   380
Love at first sight is vague, until
That tinkling makes him audible.

 And must I mock you to the last,
Ashamed of my own shame, — aghast
Because some thoughts not born amiss   385
Rose at a poor fair face like this?
Well, of such thoughts so much I know:
In my life, as in hers, they show,
By a far gleam which I may near,
A dark path I can strive to clear.   390

 Only one kiss. Goodbye, my dear.

The Portrait

This is her picture as she was:
 It seems a thing to wonder on,
As though mine image in the glass
 Should tarry when myself am gone.

I gaze until she seems to stir, —   5
Until mine eyes almost aver
    That now, even now, the sweet lips part
    To breathe the words of the sweet heart: —
And yet the earth is over her.

Alas! even such the thin-drawn ray   10
    That makes the prison-depths more rude, —
The drip of water night and day
    Giving a tongue to solitude.
Yet only this, of love's whole prize,
Remains; save what in mournful guise   15
    Takes counsel with my soul alone, —
    Save what is secret and unknown,
Below the earth, above the skies.

In painting her I shrined her face
    Mid mystic trees, where light falls in   20
Hardly at all; a covert place
    Where you might think to find a din
Of doubtful talk, and a live flame
Wandering, and many a shape whose name
    Not itself knoweth, and old dew,   25
    And your own footsteps meeting you,
And all things going as they came.

A deep dim wood; and there she stands
    As in that wood that day: for so
Was the still movement of her hands   30
    And such the pure line's gracious flow.
And passing fair the type must seem,
Unknown the presence and the dream.
    'Tis she: though of herself, alas!
    Less than her shadow on the grass   35
Or than her image in the stream.

That day we met there, I and she
    One with the other all alone;
And we were blithe; yet memory
    Saddens those hours, as when the moon   40
Looks upon daylight. And with her
I stooped to drink the spring-water,
    Athirst where other waters sprang;
    And where the echo is, she sang, —
My soul another echo there.   45

But when that hour my soul won strength
   For words whose silence wastes and kills,
Dull raindrops smote us, and at length
   Thundered the heat within the hills.
That eve I spoke those words again   50
Beside the pelted window-pane;
   And there she hearkened what I said,
   With under-glances that surveyed
The empty pastures blind with rain.

Next day the memories of these things,   55
   Like leaves through which a bird has flown,
Still vibrated with Love's warm wings;
   Till I must make them all my own
And paint this picture. So, 'twixt ease
Of talk and sweet long silences,   60
   She stood among the plants in bloom
   At windows of a summer room,
To feign the shadow of the trees.

And as I wrought, while all above
   And all around was fragrant air,   65
In the sick burthen of my love
   It seemed each sun-thrilled blossom there
Beat like a heart among the leaves.
O heart that never beats nor heaves,
   In that one darkness lying still,   70
   What now to thee my love's great will
Or the fine web the sunshine weaves?

For now doth daylight disavow
   Those days, — nought left to see or hear.
Only in solemn whispers now   75
   At night-time these things reach mine ear;
When the leaf-shadows at a breath
Shrink in the road, and all the heath,
   Forest and water, far and wide,
   In limpid starlight glorified,   80
Lie like the mystery of death.

Last night at last I could have slept,
   And yet delayed my sleep till dawn,
Still wandering. Then it was I wept:
   For unawares I came upon   85
Those glades where once she walked with me:

And as I stood there suddenly,
　　All wan with traversing the night,
　　Upon the desolate verge of light
Yearned loud the iron-bosomed sea.　　　　　　　　90

Even so, where Heaven holds breath and hears
　　The beating heart of Love's own breast, —
Where round the secret of all spheres
　　All angels lay their wings to rest, —
How shall my soul stand rapt and awed,　　　　　　95
When, by the new birth borne abroad
　　Throughout the music of the suns,
　　It enters in her soul at once
And knows the silence there for God!

Here with her face doth memory sit　　　　　　　　100
　　Meanwhile, and wait the day's decline,
Till other eyes shall look from it,
　　Eyes of the spirit's Palestine,
Even than the old gaze tenderer:
While hopes and aims long lost with her　　　　　　105
　　Stand round her image side by side,
　　Like tombs of pilgrims that have died
About the Holy Sepulchre.

My Sister's Sleep

She fell asleep on Christmas Eve:
　　At length the long-ungranted shade
　　Of weary eyelids overweigh'd
The pain nought else might yet relieve.

Our mother, who had leaned all day　　　　　　　　5
　　Over the bed from chime to chime,
　　Then raised herself for the first time,
And as she sat her down, did pray.

Her little work-table was spread
　　With work to finish. For the glare　　　　　　　10
　　Made by her candle, she had care
To work some distance from the bed.

Without, there was a cold moon up,
　　Of winter radiance sheer and thin;

The hollow halo it was in $\quad\quad\quad\quad\quad\quad\quad$ 15
Was like an icy crystal cup.

Through the small room, with subtle sound
   Of flame, by vents the fireshine drove
   And reddened. In its dim alcove
The mirror shed a clearness round. $\quad\quad\quad\quad\quad\quad\quad$ 20

I had been sitting up some nights,
   And my tired mind felt weak and blank;
   Like a sharp strengthening wine it drank
The stillness and the broken lights.

Twelve struck. That sound, by dwindling years $\quad\quad\quad$ 25
   Heard in each hour, crept off; and then
   The ruffled silence spread again,
Like water that a pebble stirs.

Our mother rose from where she sat:
   Her needles, as she laid them down, $\quad\quad\quad\quad$ 30
   Met lightly, and her silken gown
Settled: no other noise than that.

"Glory unto the Newly Born!"
   So, as said angels, she did say;
   Because we were in Christmas Day, $\quad\quad\quad\quad$ 35
Though it would still be long till morn.

Just then in the room over us
   There was a pushing back of chairs,
   As some who had sat unawares
So late, now heard the hour, and rose. $\quad\quad\quad\quad$ 40

With anxious softly-stepping haste
   Our mother went where Margaret lay,
   Fearing the sounds o'erhead — should they
Have broken her long watched-for rest!

She stopped an instant, calm, and turned; $\quad\quad\quad$ 45
   But suddenly turned back again;
   And all her features seemed in pain
With woe, and her eyes gazed and yearned.

For my part, I but hid my face,
   And held my breath, and spoke no word: $\quad\quad\quad$ 50
   There was none spoken; but I heard
The silence for a little space.

Our mother bowed herself and wept:
   And both my arms fell, and I said,
   "God knows I knew that she was dead."   55
And there, all white, my sister slept.

Then kneeling, upon Christmas morn
   A little after twelve o'clock
   We said, ere the first quarter struck,
"Christ's blessing on the newly born!"   60

A Last Confession. (Regno Lombardo-Veneto , 1848.)

Our Lombard country-girls along the coast
Wear daggers in their garters; for they know
That they might hate another girl to death
Or meet a German lover. Such a knife
I bought her, with a hilt of horn and pearl.   5

   Father, you cannot know of all my thoughts
That day in going to meet her, — that last day
For the last time, she said; — of all the love
And all the hopeless hope that she might change
And go back with me. Ah! and everywhere,   10
At places we both knew along the road,
Some fresh shape of herself as once she was
Grew present at my side; until it seemed —
So close they gathered round me — they would all
Be with me when I reached the spot at last,   15
To plead my cause with her against herself
So changed. O Father, if you knew all this
You cannot know, then you would know too, Father,
And only then, if God can pardon me.
What can be told I'll tell, if you will hear.   20

   I passed a village-fair upon my road,
And thought, being empty-handed, I would take
Some little present: such might prove, I said,
Either a pledge between us, or (God help me!)
A parting gift. And there it was I bought   25
The knife I spoke of, such as women wear.

   That day, some three hours afterwards, I found
For certain, it must be a parting gift.
And, standing silent now at last, I looked

Into her scornful face; and heard the sea   30
Still trying hard to din into my ears
Some speech it knew which still might change her heart,
If only it could make me understand.
One moment thus. Another, and her face
Seemed further off than the last line of sea,   35
So that I thought, if now she were to speak
I could not hear her. Then again I knew
All, as we stood together on the sand
At Iglio, in the first thin shade o' the hills.

   "Take it," I said, and held it out to her,   40
While the hilt glanced within my trembling hold;
"Take it and keep it for my sake," I said.
Her neck unbent not, neither did her eyes
Move, nor her foot left beating of the sand;
Only she put it by from her and laughed.   45

   Father, you hear my speech and not her laugh;
But God heard that. Will God remember all?

   It was another laugh than the sweet sound
Which rose from her sweet childish heart, that day
Eleven years before, when first I found her   50
Alone upon the hill-side; and her curls
Shook down in the warm grass as she looked up
Out of her curls in my eyes bent to hers.
She might have served a painter to pourtray
That heavenly child which in the latter days   55
Shall walk between the lion and the lamb.
I had been for nights in hiding, worn and sick
And hardly fed; and so her words at first
Seemed fitful like the talking of the trees
And voices in the air that knew my name.   60
And I remember that I sat me down
Upon the slope with her, and thought the world
Must be all over or had never been,
We seemed there so alone. And soon she told me
Her parents both were gone away from her.   65
I thought perhaps she meant that they had died;
But when I asked her this, she looked again
Into my face, and said that yestereve
They kissed her long, and wept and made her weep,
And gave her all the bread they had with them,   70

And then had gone together up the hill
Where we were sitting now, and had walked on
Into the great red light; "and so," she said,
"I have come up here too; and when this evening
They step out of the light as they stepped in,   75
I shall be here to kiss them." And she laughed.

   Then I bethought me suddenly of the famine;
And how the church-steps throughout all the town,
When last I had been there a month ago,
Swarmed with starved folk; and how the bread was weighed   80
By Austrians armed; and women that I knew
For wives and mothers walked the public street,
Saying aloud that if their husbands feared
To snatch the children's food, themselves would stay
Till they had earned it there. So then this child   85
Was piteous to me; for all told me then
Her parents must have left her to God's chance,
To man's or to the Church's charity,
Because of the great famine, rather than
To watch her growing thin between their knees.   90
With that, God took my mother's voice and spoke,
And sights and sounds came back and things long since,
And all my childhood found me on the hills;
And so I took her with me.

                    I was young,
Scarce man then, Father; but the cause which gave   95
The wounds I die of now had brought me then
Some wounds already; and I lived alone,
As any hiding hunted man must live.
It was no easy thing to keep a child
In safety; for herself it was not safe,   100
And doubled my own danger: but I knew
That God would help me.

                  Yet a little while
Pardon me, Father, if I pause. I think
I have been speaking to you of some matters
There was no need to speak of, have I not?   105
You do not know how clearly those things stood
Within my mind, which I have spoken of,
Nor how they strove for utterance. Life all past
Is like the sky when the sun sets in it,
Clearest where furthest off.   110

I told you how
She scorned my parting gift and laughed. And yet
A woman's laugh's another thing sometimes:
I think they laugh in Heaven. I know last night
I dreamed I saw into the garden of God,
Where women walked whose painted images   115
I have seen with candles round them in the church.
They bent this way and that, one to another,
Playing: and over the long golden hair
Of each there floated like a ring of fire
Which when she stooped stooped with her, and when she rose 120
Rose with her. Then a breeze flew in among them,
As if a window had been opened in heaven
For God to give His blessing from, before
This world of ours should set; (for in my dream
I thought our world was setting, and the sun   125
Flared, a spent taper;) and beneath that gust
The rings of light quivered like forest-leaves.
Then all the blessed maidens who were there
Stood up together, as it were a voice
That called them; and they threw their tresses back,   130
And smote their palms, and all laughed up at once,
For the strong heavenly joy they had in them
To hear God bless the world. Wherewith I woke:
And looking round, I saw as usual
That she was standing there with her long locks   135
Pressed to her side; and her laugh ended theirs.

For always when I see her now, she laughs.
And yet her childish laughter haunts me too,
The life of this dead terror; as in days
When she, a child, dwelt with me. I must tell   140
Something of those days yet before the end.

I brought her from the city — one such day
When she was still a merry loving child, —
The earliest gift I mind my giving her;
A little image of a flying Love   145
Made of our coloured glass-ware, in his hands
A dart of gilded metal and a torch.
And him she kissed and me, and fain would know
Why were his poor eyes blindfold, why the wings
And why the arrow. What I knew I told   150
Of Venus and of Cupid, — strange old tales.

And when she heard that he could rule the loves
Of men and women, still she shook her head
And wondered; and, "Nay, nay," she murmured still,
"So strong, and he a younger child than I!"   155
And then she'd have me fix him on the wall
Fronting her little bed; and then again
She needs must fix him there herself, because
I gave him to her and she loved him so,
And he should make her love me better yet,   160
If women loved the more, the more they grew.
But the fit place upon the wall was high
For her, and so I held her in my arms:
And each time that the heavy pruning-hook
I gave her for a hammer slipped away   165
As it would often, still she laughed and laughed
And kissed and kissed me. But amid her mirth,
Just as she hung the image on the nail,
It slipped and all its fragments strewed the ground:
And as it fell she screamed, for in her hand   170
The dart had entered deeply and drawn blood.
And so her laughter turned to tears: and "Oh!"
I said, the while I bandaged the small hand, —
"That I should be the first to make you bleed,
Who love and love and love you!" — kissing still   175
The fingers till I got her safe to bed.
And still she sobbed, — "not for the pain at all,"
She said, "but for the Love, the poor good Love
You gave me." So she cried herself to sleep.

    Another later thing comes back to me.   180
'Twas in those hardest foulest days of all,
When still from his shut palace, sitting clean
Above the splash of blood, old Metternich
(May his soul die, and never-dying worms
Feast on its pain for ever!) used to thin   185
His year's doomed hundreds daintily, each month
Thirties and fifties. This time, as I think,
Was when his thrift forbad the poor to take
That evil brackish salt which the dry rocks
Keep all through winter when the sea draws in.   190
The first I heard of it was a chance shot
In the street here and there, and on the stones
A stumbling clatter as of horse hemmed round.

Then, when she saw me hurry out of doors,
My gun slung at my shoulder and my knife   195
Stuck in my girdle, she smoothed down my hair
And laughed to see me look so brave, and leaped
Up to my neck and kissed me. She was still
A child; and yet that kiss was on my lips
So hot all day where the smoke shut us in.   200

  For now, being always with her, the first love
I had — the father's, brother's love — was changed,
I think, in somewise; like a holy thought
Which is a prayer before one knows of it.
The first time I perceived this, I remember,   205
Was once when after hunting I came home
Weary, and she brought food and fruit for me,
And sat down at my feet upon the floor
Leaning against my side. But when I felt
Her sweet head reach from that low seat of hers   210
So high as to be laid upon my heart,
I turned and looked upon my darling there
And marked for the first time how tall she was;
And my heart beat with so much violence
Under her cheek, I thought she could not choose   215
But wonder at it soon and ask me why;
And so I bade her rise and eat with me.
And when, remembering all and counting back
The time, I made out fourteen years for her
And told her so, she gazed at me with eyes   220
As of the sky and sea on a grey day,
And drew her long hands through her hair, and asked me
If she was not a woman; and then laughed:
And as she stooped in laughing, I could see
Beneath the growing throat the breasts half-globed   225
Like folded lilies deepset in the stream.

  Yes, let me think of her as then; for so
Her image, Father, is not like the sights
Which come when you are gone. She had a mouth
Made to bring death to life, — the underlip   230
Sucked in, as if it strove to kiss itself.
Her face was pearly pale, as when one stoops
Over wan water; and the dark crisped hair
And the hair's shadow made it paler still: —
Deep-serried locks, the dimness of the cloud   235

Where the moon's gaze is set in eddying gloom.
Her body bore her neck as the tree's stem
Bears the top branch; and as the branch sustains
The flower of the year's pride, her high neck bore
That face made wonderful with night and day.   240
Her voice was swift, yet ever the last words
Fell lingeringly; and rounded finger-tips
She had, that clung a little where they touched
And then were gone o' the instant. Her great eyes,
That sometimes turned half dizzily beneath   245
The passionate lids, as faint, when she would speak,
Had also in them hidden springs of mirth,
Which under the dark lashes evermore
Shook to her laugh, as when a bird flies low
Between the water and the willow-leaves,   250
And the shade quivers till he wins the light.

   I was a moody comrade to her then,
For all the love I bore her. Italy,
The weeping desolate mother, long has claimed
Her sons' strong arms to lean on, and their hands   255
To lop the poisonous thicket from her path,
Cleaving her way to light. And from her need
Had grown the fashion of my whole poor life
Which I was proud to yield her, as my father
Had yielded his. And this had come to be   260
A game to play, a love to clasp, a hate
To wreak, all things together that a man
Needs for his blood to ripen; till at times
All else seemed shadows, and I wondered still
To see such life pass muster and be deemed   265
Time's bodily substance. In those hours, no doubt,
To the young girl my eyes were like my soul, —
Dark wells of death-in-life that yearned for day.
And though she ruled me always, I remember
That once when I was thus and she still kept   270
Leaping about the place and laughing, I
Did almost chide her; whereupon she knelt
And putting her two hands into my breast
Sang me a song. Are these tears in my eyes?
'Tis long since I have wept for anything.   275
I thought that song forgotten out of mind;
And now, just as I spoke of it, it came

All back. It is but a rude thing, ill rhymed,
Such as a blind man chaunts and his dog hears
Holding the platter, when the children run   280
To merrier sport and leave him. Thus it goes: —

    La bella donna*
    Piangendo disse:
    "Come son fisse
    Le stelle in cielo!   285
    Quel fiato anelo
    Dello stanco sole,
    Quanto m' assonna!
    E la luna, macchiata
    Come uno specchio   290
    Logoro e vecchio, —
    Faccia affannata,
    Che cosa vuole?

    "Chà stelle, luna, e sole,
    Ciascun m' annoja   295
    E m' annojano insieme;
    Non me ne preme
    Nà ci prendo gioja.
    E veramente,
    Che le spalle sien franche   300
    E la braccia bianche
    E il seno caldo e tondo,
    Non mi fa niente.
    Chà cosa al mondo
    Posso più far di questi   305
Se non piacciono a te, come dicesti?"

---

    * She wept, sweet lady,
And said in weeping:
"What spell is keeping
The stars so steady?
Why does the power   5
Of the sun's noon-hour
To sleep so move me?
And the moon in heaven,
Stained where she passes
As a worn-out glass is, —   10
Wearily driven,
Why walks she above me?

    "Stars, moon, and sun too,
I'm tired of either
And all together!   15
Whom speak they unto
That I should listen?
For very surely,
Though my arms and shoulders
Dazzle beholders,   20
And my eyes glisten,
All's nothing purely!
What are words said for
At all about them,
If he they are made for   25
Can do without them?"

La donna rise
E riprese ridendo: —
"Questa mano che prendo
E dunque mia?   310
Tu m' ami dunque?
Dimmelo ancora,
Non in modo qualunque,
Ma le parole
Belle e precise   315
Che dicesti pria.

"Siccome suole
La state talora
(Dicesti) un qualche istante
Tornare innanzi inverno,   320
Così tu fai ch' io scerno
Le foglie tutte quante,
Ben ch' io certo tenessi
Per passato l' autunno.

"Eccolo il mio alunno!   325
Io debbo insegnargli
Quei cari detti istessi
Ch' ei mi disse una volta!
Oimà! Che cosa dargli,"
(Ma ridea piano piano   330
Dei baci in sulla mano,)
"Ch' ei non m'abbia da lungo tempo tolta?"

She laughed, sweet lady,
And said in laughing:
"His hand clings half in
My own already!   30
Oh! do you love me?
Oh! speak of passion
In no new fashion,
No loud inveighings,
But the old sayings   35
You once said of me.

"You said: 'As summer,
Through boughs grown brittle,
Comes back a little
Ere frosts benumb her, —   40
So bring'st thou to me
All leaves and flowers,

Though autumn's gloomy
To-day in the bowers.'

"Oh! does he love me,   45
When my voice teaches
The very speeches
He then spoke of me?
Alas! what flavour
Still with me lingers?"   50
(But she laughed as my kisses
Glowed in her fingers
With love's old blisses.)
"Oh! what one favour
Remains to woo him,   55
Whose whole poor savour
Belongs not to him?"

That I should sing upon this bed! — with you
To listen, and such words still left to say!
Yet was it I that sang? The voice seemed hers,   335
As on the very day she sang to me;
When, having done, she took out of my hand
Something that I had played with all the while
And laid it down beyond my reach; and so
Turning my face round till it fronted hers, —   340
"Weeping or laughing, which was best?" she said.

But these are foolish tales. How should I show
The heart that glowed then with love's heat, each day
More and more brightly? — when for long years now
The very flame that flew about the heart,   345
And gave it fiery wings, has come to be
The lapping blaze of hell's environment
Whose tongues all bid the molten heart despair.

Yet one more thing comes back on me to-night
Which I may tell you: for it bore my soul   350
Dread firstlings of the brood that rend it now.
It chanced that in our last year's wanderings
We dwelt at Monza, far away from home,
If home we had: and in the Duomo there
I sometimes entered with her when she prayed.   355
An image of Our Lady stands there, wrought
In marble by some great Italian hand
In the great days when she and Italy
Sat on one throne together: and to her
And to none else my loved one told her heart.   360
She was a woman then; and as she knelt, —
Her sweet brow in the sweet brow's shadow there, —
They seemed two kindred forms whereby our land
(Whose work still serves the world for miracle)
Made manifest herself in womanhood.   365
Father, the day I speak of was the first
For weeks that I had borne her company
Into the Duomo; and those weeks had been
Much troubled, for then first the glimpses came
Of some impenetrable restlessness   370
Growing in her to make her changed and cold.
And as we entered there that day, I bent
My eyes on the fair Image, and I said
Within my heart, "Oh turn her heart to me!"

And so I left her to her prayers, and went 375
To gaze upon the pride of Monza's shrine,
Where in the sacristy the light still falls
Upon the Iron Crown of Italy,
On whose crowned heads the day has closed, nor yet
The daybreak gilds another head to crown. 380
But coming back, I wondered when I saw
That the sweet Lady of her prayers now stood
Alone without her; until further off,
Before some new Madonna gaily decked,
Tinselled and gewgawed, a slight German toy, 385
I saw her kneel, still praying. At my step
She rose, and side by side we left the church.
I was much moved, and sharply questioned her
Of her transferred devotion; but she seemed
Stubborn and heedless; till she lightly laughed 390
And said: "The old Madonna? Aye indeed,
She had my old thoughts, — this one has my new."
Then silent to the soul I held my way:
And from the fountains of the public place
Unto the pigeon-haunted pinnacles, 395
Bright wings and water winnowed the bright air;
And stately with her laugh's subsiding smile
She went, with clear-swayed waist and towering neck
And hands held light before her; and the face
Which long had made a day in my life's night 400
Was night in day to me; as all men's eyes
Turned on her beauty, and she seemed to tread
Beyond my heart to the world made for her.

Ah there! my wounds will snatch my sense again:
The pain comes billowing on like a full cloud 405
Of thunder, and the flash that breaks from it
Leaves my brain burning. That's the wound he gave
The Austrian whose white coat I still made match
With his white face, only the two grew red
As suits his trade. The devil makes them wear 410
White for a livery, that the blood may show
Braver that brings them to him. So he looks
Sheer o'er the field and knows his own at once.

Give me a draught of water in that cup;
My voice feels thick; perhaps you do not hear; 415
But you must hear. If you mistake my words

And so absolve me, I am sure the blessing
Will burn my soul. If you mistake my words
And so absolve me, Father, the great sin
Is yours, not mine: mark this: your soul shall burn   420
With mine for it. I have seen pictures where
Souls burned with Latin shriekings in their mouths:
Shall my end be as theirs? Nay, but I know
'Tis you shall shriek in Latin. Some bell rings,
Rings through my brain: it strikes the hour in hell.   425

   You see I cannot, Father; I have tried,
But cannot, as you see. These twenty times
Beginning, I have come to the same point
And stopped. Beyond, there are but broken words
Which will not let you understand my tale.   430
It is that then we have her with us here,
As when she wrung her hair out in my dream
To-night, till all the darkness reeked of it.
Her hair is always wet, for she has kept
Its tresses wrapped about her side for years;   435
And when she wrung them round over the floor,
I heard the blood between her fingers hiss;
So that I sat up in my bed and screamed
Once and again; and once to once, she laughed.
Look that you turn not now, — she's at your back: 440
Gather your robe up, Father, and keep close,
Or she'll sit down on it and send you mad.

   At Iglio in the first thin shade o' the hills
The sand is black and red. The black was black
When what was spilt that day sank into it,   445
And the red scarcely darkened. There I stood
This night with her, and saw the sand the same.

   What would you have me tell you? Father, father,
How shall I make you know? You have not known
The dreadful soul of woman, who one day   450
Forgets the old and takes the new to heart,
Forgets what man remembers, and therewith
Forgets the man. Nor can I clearly tell
How the change happened between her and me.
Her eyes looked on me from an emptied heart   455
When most my heart was full of her; and still
In every corner of myself I sought
To find what service failed her; and no less

Than in the good time past, there all was hers.
What do you love? Your Heaven? Conceive it spread 460
For one first year of all eternity
All round you with all joys and gifts of God;
And then when most your soul is blent with it
And all yields song together, — then it stands
O' the sudden like a pool that once gave back 465
Your image, but now drowns it and is clear
Again, — or like a sun bewitched, that burns
Your shadow from you, and still shines in sight.
How could you bear it? Would you not cry out,
Among those eyes grown blind to you, those ears 470
That hear no more your voice you hear the same, —
"God! what is left but hell for company,
But hell, hell, hell?" — until the name so breathed
Whirled with hot wind and sucked you down in fire?
Even so I stood the day her empty heart 475
Left her place empty in our home, while yet
I knew not why she went nor where she went
Nor how to reach her: so I stood the day
When to my prayers at last one sight of her
Was granted, and I looked on heaven made pale 480
With scorn, and heard heaven mock me in that laugh.

O sweet, long sweet! Was that some ghost of you,
Even as your ghost that haunts me now, — twin shapes
Of fear and hatred? May I find you yet
Mine when death wakes? Ah! be it even in flame, 485
We may have sweetness yet, if you but say
As once in childish sorrow: "Not my pain,
My pain was nothing: oh your poor poor love,
Your broken love!"

My Father, have I not
Yet told you the last things of that last day 490
On which I went to meet her by the sea?
O God, O God! But I must tell you all.

Midway upon my journey, when I stopped
To buy the dagger at the village fair,
I saw two cursed rats about the place 495
I knew for spies — blood-sellers both. That day
Was not yet over; for three hours to come
I prized my life: and so I looked around

For safety. A poor painted mountebank
Was playing tricks and shouting in a crowd.   500
I knew he must have heard my name, so I
Pushed past and whispered to him who I was,
And of my danger. Straight he hustled me
Into his booth, as it were in the trick,
And brought me out next minute with my face   505
All smeared in patches and a zany's gown;
And there I handed him his cups and balls
And swung the sand-bags round to clear the ring
For half an hour. The spies came once and looked;
And while they stopped, and made all sights and sounds   510
Sharp to my startled senses, I remember
A woman laughed above me. I looked up
And saw where a brown-shouldered harlot leaned
Half through a tavern window thick with vine.
Some man had come behind her in the room   515
And caught her by her arms, and she had turned
With that coarse empty laugh on him, as now
He munched her neck with kisses, while the vine
Crawled in her back.

    And three hours afterwards,
When she that I had run all risks to meet   520
Laughed as I told you, my life burned to death
Within me, for I thought it like the laugh
Heard at the fair. She had not left me long;
But all she might have changed to, or might change to,
(I know nought since — she never speaks a word —)   525
Seemed in that laugh. Have I not told you yet,
Not told you all this time what happened, Father,
When I had offered her the little knife,
And bade her keep it for my sake that loved her,
And she had laughed? Have I not told you yet?   530

  "Take it," I said to her the second time,
"Take it and keep it." And then came a fire
That burnt my hand; and then the fire was blood,
And sea and sky were blood and fire, and all
The day was one red blindness; till it seemed,   535
Within the whirling brain's eclipse, that she
Or I or all things bled or burned to death.
And then I found her laid against my feet
And knew that I had stabbed her, and saw still

Her look in falling. For she took the knife
Deep in her heart, even as I bade her then,
And fell; and her stiff bodice scooped the sand
Into her bosom.

And she keeps it, see,
Do you not see she keeps it? — there, beneath
Wet fingers and wet tresses, in her heart.
For look you, when she stirs her hand, it shows
The little hilt of horn and pearl, — even such
A dagger as our women of the coast
Twist in their garters.

        Father, I have done:
And from her side now she unwinds the thick
Dark hair; all round her side it is wet through,
But, like the sand at Iglio, does not change.
Now you may see the dagger clearly. Father,
I have told all: tell me at once what hope
Can reach me still. For now she draws it out
Slowly, and only smiles as yet: look, Father,
She scarcely smiles: but I shall hear her laugh
Soon, when she shows the crimson steel to God.

540

545

550

555

The Burden of Nineveh

In our Museum galleries
To-day I lingered o'er the prize
Dead Greece vouchsafes to living eyes, —
Her Art for ever in fresh wise
    From hour to hour rejoicing me.
Sighing I turned at last to win
Once more the London dirt and din;
And as I made the swing-door spin
And issued, they were hoisting in
    A wingèd beast from Nineveh.

A human face the creature wore,
And hoofs behind and hoofs before,
And flanks with dark runes fretted o'er.
'Twas bull, 'twas mitred Minotaur,
    A dead disbowelled mystery:
The mummy of a buried faith

5

10

15

88   P O E M S

Stark from the charnel without scathe,
Its wings stood for the light to bathe, —
Such fossil cerements as might swathe
   The very corpse of Nineveh.   20

The print of its first rush-wrapping,
Wound ere it dried, still ribbed the thing.
What song did the brown maidens sing,
From purple mouths alternating,
   When that was woven languidly?   25
What vows, what rites, what prayers preferr'd,
What songs has the strange image heard?
In what blind vigil stood interr'd
For ages, till an English word
   Broke silence first at Nineveh?   30

Oh when upon each sculptured court,
Where even the wind might not resort, —
O'er which Time passed, of like import
With the wild Arab boys at sport, —
   A living face looked in to see: —   35
O seemed it not — the spell once broke —
As though the carven warriors woke,
As though the shaft the string forsook,
The cymbals clashed, the chariots shook,
   And there was life in Nineveh?   40

On London stones our sun anew
The beast's recovered shadow threw.
(No shade that plague of darkness knew,
No light, no shade, while older grew
   By ages the old earth and sea.)   45
Lo thou! could all thy priests have shown
Such proof to make thy godhead known?
From their dead Past thou liv'st alone;
And still thy shadow is thine own,
   Even as of yore in Nineveh.   50

That day whereof we keep record,
When near thy city-gates the Lord
Sheltered His Jonah with a gourd,
This sun, (I said) here present, pour'd
   Even thus this shadow that I see.   55
This shadow has been shed the same
From sun and moon, — from lamps which came

For prayer, — from fifteen days of flame,
The last, while smouldered to a name
  Sardanapalus' Nineveh.   60

Within thy shadow, haply, once
Sennacherib has knelt, whose sons
Smote him between the altar-stones:
Or pale Semiramis her zones
  Of gold, her incense brought to thee,   65
In love for grace, in war for aid: . . .
Ay, and who else? . . . till 'neath thy shade
Within his trenches newly made
Last year the Christian knelt and pray'd —
  Not to thy strength — in Nineveh.*   70

Now, thou poor god, within this hall
Where the blank windows blind the wall
From pedestal to pedestal,
The kind of light shall on thee fall
  Which London takes the day to be: 75
While school-foundations in the act
Of holiday, three files compact,
Shall learn to view thee as a fact
Connected with that zealous tract:
  "ROME, — Babylon and Nineveh."   80

Deemed they of this, those worshippers,
When, in some mythic chain of verse
Which man shall not again rehearse,
The faces of thy ministers
  Yearned pale with bitter ecstasy?   85
Greece, Egypt, Rome, — did any god
Before whose feet men knelt unshod
Deem that in this unblest abode
Another scarce more unknown god
  Should house with him, from Nineveh?   90

Ah! in what quarries lay the stone
From which this pillared pile has grown,
Unto man's need how long unknown,
Since those thy temples, court and cone,
  Rose far in desert history?   95

*During the excavations, the Tiyari workmen held their services in the shadow of the
great bulls. — (*Layard's "Nineveh,"* ch. ix.)

Ah! what is here that does not lie
All strange to thine awakened eye?
Ah! what is here can testify
(Save that dumb presence of the sky)
  Unto thy day and Nineveh?   100

Why, of those mummies in the room
Above, there might indeed have come
One out of Egypt to thy home,
An alien. Nay, but were not some
  Of these thine own "antiquity?"   105
And now, — they and their gods and thou
All relics here together, — now
Whose profit? whether bull or cow,
Isis or Ibis, who or how,
  Whether of Thebes or Nineveh?   110

The consecrated metals found,
And ivory tablets, underground,
Winged teraphim and creatures crown'd,
When air and daylight filled the mound,
  Fell into dust immediately.   115
And even as these, the images
Of awe and worship, — even as these, —
So, smitten with the sun's increase,
Her glory mouldered and did cease
  From immemorial Nineveh.   120

The day her builders made their halt,
Those cities of the lake of salt
Stood firmly 'stablished without fault,
Made proud with pillars of basalt,
  With sardonyx and porphyry.   125
The day that Jonah bore abroad
To Nineveh the voice of God,
A brackish lake lay in his road,
Where erst Pride fixed her sure abode,
  As then in royal Nineveh.   130

The day when he, Pride's lord and Man's,
Showed all the kingdoms at a glance
To Him before whose countenance
The years recede, the years advance,
  And said, Fall down and worship me: —   135
'Mid all the pomp beneath that look,

Then stirred there, haply, some rebuke,
Where to the wind the Salt Pools shook,
And in those tracts, of life forsook,
    That knew thee not, O Nineveh! 140

Delicate harlot! On thy throne
Thou with a world beneath thee prone
In state for ages sat'st alone;
And needs were years and lustres flown
    Ere strength of man could vanquish thee: 145
Whom even thy victor foes must bring,
Still royal, among maids that sing
As with doves' voices, taboring
Upon their breasts, unto the King, —
    A kingly conquest, Nineveh! 150

. . . Here woke my thought. The wind's slow sway
Had waxed; and like the human play
Of scorn that smiling spreads away,
The sunshine shivered off the day:
    The callous wind, it seemed to me, 155
Swept up the shadow from the ground:
And pale as whom the Fates astound,
The god forlorn stood winged and crown'd:
Within I knew the cry lay bound
    Of the dumb soul of Nineveh. 160

And as I turned, my sense half shut
Still saw the crowds of kerb and rut
Go past as marshalled to the strut
Of ranks in gypsum quaintly cut.
    It seemed in one same pageantry 165
They followed forms which had been erst;
To pass, till on my sight should burst
That future of the best or worst
When some may question which was first,
    Of London or of Nineveh. 170

For as that Bull-god once did stand
And watched the burial-clouds of sand,
Till these at last without a hand
Rose o'er his eyes, another land,
    And blinded him with destiny: — 175
So may he stand again; till now,
In ships of unknown sail and prow,

Some tribe of the Australian plough
Bear him afar, — a relic now
   Of London, not of Nineveh! 180

Or it may chance indeed that when
Man's age is hoary among men, —
His centuries threescore and ten, —
His furthest childhood shall seem then
   More clear than later times may be: 185
Who, finding in this desert place
This form, shall hold us for some race
That walked not in Christ's lowly ways,
But bowed its pride and vowed its praise
   Unto the God of Nineveh. 190

The smile rose first, — anon drew nigh
The thought: . . . Those heavy wings spread high
So sure of flight, which do not fly;
That set gaze never on the sky;
   Those scriptured flanks it cannot see; 195
Its crown, a brow-contracting load;
Its planted feet which trust the sod: . . .
(So grew the image as I trod:)
O Nineveh, was this thy God, —
   Thine also, mighty Nineveh? 200

An Old Song Ended

"How should I your true love know
   From another one?"
"By his cockle-hat and staff
   And his sandal-shoon."

"And what signs have told you now 5
   That he hastens home?"
"Lo! the spring is nearly gone,
   He is nearly come."

"For a token is there nought,
   Say, that he should bring?" 10
"He will bear a ring I gave
   And another ring."

"How may I, when he shall ask,
   Tell him who lies there?"

"Nay, but leave my face unveiled   15
  And unbound my hair."

"Can you say to me some word
  I shall say to him?"
"Say I'm looking in his eyes
  Though my eyes are dim."   20

Aspecta Medusa
(For a Picture)

Andromeda, by Perseus saved and wed,
Hankered each day to see the Gorgon's head:
Till o'er a fount he held it, bade her lean,
And mirrored in the wave was safely seen
That death she lived by.

                Let not thine eyes know   5
Any forbidden thing itself, although
It once should save as well as kill: but be
Its shadow upon life enough for thee.

The Bride's Prelude

"Sister," said busy Amelotte
  To listless Aloÿse;
"Along your wedding-road the wheat
Bends as to hear your horse's feet,
And the noonday stands still for heat."   5

Amelotte laughed into the air
  With eyes that sought the sun:
But where the walls in long brocade
Were screened, as one who is afraid
Sat Aloÿse within the shade.   10

And even in shade was gleam enough
  To shut out full repose
From the bride's 'tiring-chamber, which
Was like the inner altar-niche
Whose dimness worship has made rich.   15

Within the window's heaped recess
  The light was counterchanged

In blent reflexes manifold
From perfume-caskets of wrought gold
And gems the bride's hair could not hold   20

All thrust together: and with these
    A slim-curved lute, which now,
At Amelotte's sudden passing there,
Was swept in somewise unaware,
And shook to music the close air.   25

Against the haloed lattice-panes
    The bridesmaid sunned her breast
Then to the glass turned tall and free,
And braced and shifted daintily
Her loin-belt through her côte-hardie.   30

The belt was silver, and the clasp
    Of lozenged arm-bearings;
A world of mirrored tints minute
The rippling sunshine wrought into 't,
That flushed her hand and warmed her foot.   35

At least an hour had Aloÿse, —
    Her jewels in her hair, —
Her white gown, as became a bride,
Quartered in silver at each side, —
Sat thus aloof, as if to hide.   40

Over her bosom, that lay still,
    The vest was rich in grain,
With close pearls wholly overset:
Around her throat the fastenings met
Of chevesayle and mantelet.   45

Her arms were laid along her lap
    With the hands open: life
Itself did seem at fault in her:
Beneath the drooping brows, the stir
Of thought made noonday heavier.   50

Long sat she silent; and then raised
    Her head, with such a gasp
As while she summoned breath to speak
Fanned high that furnace in the cheek
But sucked the heart-pulse cold and weak.   55

(Oh gather round her now, all ye
    Past seasons of her fear, —

Sick springs, and summers deadly cold!
To flight your hovering wings unfold,
For now your secret shall be told.

Ye many sunlights, barbed with darts
 Of dread detecting flame, —
Gaunt moonlights that like sentinels
Went past with iron clank of bells, —
Draw round and render up your spells!)

"Sister," said Aloÿse, "I had
 A thing to tell thee of
Long since, and could not. But do thou
Kneel first in prayer awhile, and bow
Thine heart, and I will tell thee now."

Amelotte wondered with her eyes;
 But her heart said in her:
"Dear Aloÿse would have me pray
Because the awe she feels to-day
Must need more prayers than she can say."

So Amelotte put by the folds
 That covered up her feet,
And knelt, — beyond the arras'd gloom
And the hot window's dull perfume, —
Where day was stillest in the room.

"Queen Mary, hear," she said, "and say
 To Jesus the Lord Christ,
This bride's new joy, which He confers,
New joy to many ministers,
And many griefs are bound in hers."

The bride turned in her chair, and hid
 Her face against the back,
And took her pearl-girt elbows in
Her hands, and could not yet begin,
But shuddering, uttered, "Urscelyn!"

Most weak she was; for as she pressed
 Her hand against her throat,
Along the arras she let trail
Her face, as if all heart did fail,
And sat with shut eyes, dumb and pale.

Amelotte still was on her knees
 As she had kneeled to pray.

Deeming her sister swooned, she thought,
At first, some succour to have brought;
But Aloÿse rocked, as one distraught.   100

She would have pushed the lattice wide
    To gain what breeze might be;
But marking that no leaf once beat
The outside casement, it seemed meet
Not to bring in more scent and heat.   105

So she said only: "Aloÿse,
    Sister, when happened it
At any time that the bride came
To ill, or spoke in fear of shame,
When speaking first the bridegroom's name?"   110

A bird had out its song and ceased
    Ere the bride spoke. At length
She said: "The name is as the thing: —
Sin hath no second christening,
And shame is all that shame can bring.   115

"In divers places many an while
    I would have told thee this;
But faintness took me, or a fit
Like fever. God would not permit
That I should change thine eyes with it.   120

"Yet once I spoke, hadst thou but heard: —
    That time we wandered out
All the sun's hours, but missed our way
When evening darkened, and so lay
The whole night covered up in hay.   125

"At last my face was hidden: so,
    Having God's hint, I paused
Not long; but drew myself more near
Where thou wast laid, and shook off fear,
And whispered quick into thine ear   130

"Something of the whole tale. At first
    I lay and bit my hair
For the sore silence thou didst keep:
Till, as thy breath came long and deep,
I knew that thou hadst been asleep.   135

"The moon was covered, but the stars
    Lasted till morning broke.

Awake, thou told'st me that thy dream
Had been of me, — that all did seem
At jar, — but that it was a dream. 140

"I knew God's hand and might not speak.
   After that night I kept
Silence and let the record swell:
Till now there is much more to tell
Which must be told out ill or well." 145

She paused then, weary, with dry lips
   Apart. From the outside
By fits there boomed a dull report
From where i' the hanging tennis-court
The bridegroom's retinue made sport. 150

The room lay still in dusty glare,
   Having no sound through it
Except the chirp of a caged bird
That came and ceased: and if she stirred,
Amelotte's raiment could be heard. 155

Quoth Amelotte: "The night this chanced
   Was a late summer night
Last year! What secret, for Christ's love,
Keep'st thou since then? Mary above!
What thing is this thou speakest of? 160

"Mary and Christ! Lest when 'tis told
   I should be prone to wrath, —
This prayer beforehand! How she errs
Soe'er, take count of grief like hers,
Whereof the days are turned to years!" 165

She bowed her neck, and having said,
   Kept on her knees to hear;
And then, because strained thought demands
Quiet before it understands,
Darkened her eyesight with her hands. 170

So when at last her sister spoke,
   She did not see the pain
O' the mouth nor the ashaméd eyes,
But marked the breath that came in sighs
And the half-pausing for replies. 175

This was the bride's sad prelude-strain: —
   "I' the convent where a girl

I dwelt till near my womanhood,
I had but preachings of the rood
And Aves told in solitude   180

"To spend my heart on: and my hand
   Had but the weary skill
To eke out upon silken cloth
Christ's visage, or the long bright growth
Of Mary's hair, or Satan wroth.   185

"So when at last I went, and thou,
   A child not known before,
Didst come to take the place I left, —
My limbs, after such lifelong theft
Of life, could be but little deft   190

"In all that ministers delight
   To noble women: I
Had learned no word of youth's discourse,
Nor gazed on games of warriors,
Nor trained a hound, nor ruled a horse.   195

"Besides, the daily life i' the sun
   Made me at first hold back.
To thee this came at once; to me
It crept with pauses timidly;
I am not blithe and strong like thee.   200

"Yet my feet liked the dances well,
   The songs went to my voice,
The music made me shake and weep;
And often, all night long, my sleep
Gave dreams I had been fain to keep.   205

"But though I loved not holy things,
   To hear them scorned brought pain, —
They were my childhood; and these dames
Were merely perjured in saints' names
And fixed upon saints' days for games.   210

"And sometimes when my father rode
   To hunt with his loud friends,
I dared not bring him to be quaff'd,
As my wont was, his stirrup-draught,
Because they jested so and laugh'd.   215

"At last one day my brothers said,
   'The girl must not grow thus, —

Bring her a jennet, — she shall ride.'
They helped my mounting, and I tried
To laugh with them and keep their side.   220

"But brakes were rough and bents were steep
     Upon our path that day:
My palfrey threw me; and I went
Upon men's shoulders home, sore spent,
While the chase followed up the scent.   225

"Our shrift-father (and he alone
     Of all the household there
Had skill in leechcraft,) was away
When I reached home. I tossed, and lay
Sullen with anguish the whole day.   230

"For the day passed ere some one brought
     To mind that in the hunt
Rode a young lord she named, long bred
Among the priests, whose art (she said)
Might chance to stand me in much stead.   235

"I bade them seek and summon him:
     But long ere this, the chase
Had scattered, and he was not found.
I lay in the same weary stound,
Therefore, until the night came round.   240

"It was dead night and near on twelve
     When the horse-tramp at length
Beat up the echoes of the court:
By then, my feverish breath was short
With pain the sense could scarce support.   245

"My fond nurse sitting near my feet
     Rose softly, — her lamp's flame
Held in her hand, lest it should make
My heated lids, in passing, ache;
And she passed softly, for my sake.   250

"Returning soon, she brought the youth
     They spoke of. Meek he seemed,
But good knights held him of stout heart.
He was akin to us in part,
And bore our shield, but barred athwart.   255

"I now remembered to have seen
     His face, and heard him praised

For letter-lore and medicine,
Seeing his youth was nurtured in
Priests' knowledge, as mine own had been." 260

The bride's voice did not weaken here,
    Yet by her sudden pause
She seemed to look for questioning;
Or else (small need though) 'twas to bring
Well to her mind the bygone thing. 265

Her thought, long stagnant, stirred by speech,
    Gave her a sick recoil;
As, dip thy fingers through the green
That masks a pool, — where they have been
The naked depth is black between. 270

Amelotte kept her knees; her face
    Was shut within her hands,
As it had been throughout the tale;
Her forehead's whiteness might avail
Nothing to say if she were pale. 275

Although the lattice had dropped loose,
    There was no wind; the heat
Being so at rest that Amelotte
Heard far beneath the plunge and float
Of a hound swimming in the moat. 280

Some minutes since, two rooks had toiled
    Home to the nests that crowned
Ancestral ash-trees. Through the glare
Beating again, they seemed to tear
With that thick caw the woof o' the air. 285

But else, 'twas at the dead of noon
    Absolute silence; all,
From the raised bridge and guarded sconce
To green-clad places of pleasaùnce
Where the long lake was white with swans. 290

Amelotte spoke not any word
    Nor moved she once; but felt
Between her hands in narrow space
Her own hot breath upon her face,
And kept in silence the same place. 295

Aloÿse did not hear at all
    The sounds without. She heard

The inward voice (past help obey'd)
Which might not slacken nor be stay'd,
But urged her till the whole were said.   300

Therefore she spoke again: "That night
   But little could be done:
My foot, held in my nurse's hands,
He swathed up heedfully in bands,
And for my rest gave close commands.   305

"I slept till noon, but an ill sleep
   Of dreams: through all that day
My side was stiff and caught the breath;
Next day, such pain as sickeneth
Took me, and I was nigh to death.   310

"Life strove, Death claimed me for his own
   Through days and nights: but now
'Twas the good father tended me,
Having returned. Still, I did see
The youth I spoke of constantly.   315

"For he would with my brothers come
   To stay beside my couch,
And fix my eyes against his own,
Noting my pulse; or else alone,
To sit at gaze while I made moan.   320

"(Some nights I knew he kept the watch,
   Because my women laid
The rushes thick for his steel shoes.)
Through many days this pain did use
The life God would not let me lose.   325

"At length, with my good nurse to aid,
   I could walk forth again:
And still, as one who broods or grieves,
At noons I'd meet him and at eves,
With idle feet that drove the leaves.   330

"The day when I first walked alone
   Was thinned in grass and leaf,
And yet a goodly day o' the year:
The last bird's cry upon mine ear
Left my brain weak, it was so clear.   335

"The tears were sharp within mine eyes;
   I sat down, being glad,

And wept; but stayed the sudden flow
Anon, for footsteps that fell slow;
'Twas that youth passed me, bowing low. 340

"He passed me without speech; but when,
    At least an hour gone by,
Rethreading the same covert, he
Saw I was still beneath the tree,
He spoke and sat him down with me. 345

"Little we said; nor one heart heard
    Even what was said within;
And, faltering some farewell, I soon
Rose up; but then i' the autumn noon
My feeble brain whirled like a swoon. 350

"He made me sit. 'Cousin, I grieve
    Your sickness stays by you.'
'I would,' said I, 'that you did err
So grieving. I am wearier
Than death, of the sickening dying year.' 355

"He answered: 'If your weariness
    Accepts a remedy,
I hold one and can give it you.'
I gazed: 'What ministers thereto,
Be sure,' I said, 'that I will do.' 360

"He went on quickly: — 'Twas a cure
    He had not ever named
Unto our kin, lest they should stint
Their favour, for some foolish hint
Of wizardry or magic in't: 365

"But that if he were let to come
    Within my bower that night,
(My women still attending me,
He said, while he remain'd there,) he
Could teach me the cure privily. 370

"I bade him come that night. He came;
    But little in his speech
Was cure or sickness spoken of,
Only a passionate fierce love
That clamoured upon God above. 375

"My women wondered, leaning close
    Aloof. At mine own heart

I think great wonder was not stirr'd.
I dared not listen, yet I heard
His tangled speech, word within word.   380

"He craved my pardon first, — all else
    Wild tumult. In the end
He remained silent at my feet
Fumbling the rushes. Strange quick heat
Made all the blood of my life meet.   385

"And lo! I loved him. I but said,
    If he would leave me then,
His hope some future might forecast.
His hot lips stung my hand: at last
My damsels led him forth in haste."   390

The bride took breath to pause; and turned
    Her gaze where Amelotte
Knelt, — the gold hair upon her back
Quite still in all its threads, — the track
Of her still shadow sharp and black.   395

That listening without sight had grown
    To stealthy dread; and now
That the one sound she had to mark
Left her alone too, she was stark
Afraid, as children in the dark.   400

Her fingers felt her temples beat;
    Then came that brain-sickness
Which thinks to scream, and murmureth;
And pent between her hands, the breath
Was damp against her face like death.   405

Her arms both fell at once; but when
    She gasped upon the light,
Her sense returned. She would have pray'd
To change whatever words still stay'd
Behind, but felt there was no aid.   410

So she rose up, and having gone
    Within the window's arch
Once more, she sat there, all intent
On torturing doubts, and once more bent
To hear, in mute bewilderment.   415

But Aloÿse still paused. Thereon
    Amelotte gathered voice

In somewise from the torpid fear
Coiled round her spirit. Low but clear
She said: "Speak, sister; for I hear." 420

But Aloÿse threw up her neck
    And called the name of God: —
"Judge, God, 'twixt her and me to-day!
She knows how hard this is to say,
Yet will not have one word away." 425

Her sister was quite silent. Then
    Afresh: — "Not she, dear Lord!
Thou be my judge, on Thee I call!"
She ceased, — her forehead smote the wall:
"Is there a God," she said, "at all?" 430

Amelotte shuddered at the soul,
    But did not speak. The pause
Was long this time. At length the bride
Pressed her hand hard against her side,
And trembling between shame and pride 435

Said by fierce effort: "From that night
    Often at nights we met:
That night, his passion could but rave:
The next, what grace his lips did crave
I knew not, but I know I gave." 440

Where Amelotte was sitting, all
    The light and warmth of day
Were so upon her without shade,
That the thing seemed by sunshine made
Most foul and wanton to be said. 445

She would have questioned more, and known
    The whole truth at its worst,
But held her silent, in mere shame
Of day. 'Twas only these words came: —
"Sister, thou hast not said his name." 450

"Sister," quoth Aloÿse, "thou know'st
    His name. I said that he
Was in a manner of our kin.
Waiting the title he might win,
They called him the Lord Urscelyn." 455

The bridegroom's name, to Amelotte
    Daily familiar, — heard

Thus in this dreadful history, —
Was dreadful to her; as might be
Thine own voice speaking unto thee.   460

The day's mid-hour was almost full;
    Upon the dial-plate
The angel's sword stood near at One.
An hour's remaining yet; the sun
Will not decrease till all be done.   465

Through the bride's lattice there crept in
    At whiles (from where the train
Of minstrels, till the marriage-call,
Loitered at windows of the wall,)
Stray lute-notes, sweet and musical.   470

They clung in the green growths and moss
    Against the outside stone;
Low like dirge-wail or requiem
They murmured, lost 'twixt leaf and stem:
There was no wind to carry them.   475

Amelotte gathered herself back
    Into the wide recess
That the sun flooded: it o'erspread
Like flame the hair upon her head
And fringed her face with burning red.   480

All things seemed shaken and at change:
    A silent place o' the hills
She knew, into her spirit came:
Within herself she said its name
And wondered was it still the same.   485

The bride (whom silence goaded) now
    Said strongly, — her despair
By stubborn will kept underneath: —
"Sister, 'twere well thou didst not breathe
That curse of thine. Give me my wreath."   490

"Sister," said Amelotte, "abide
    In peace. Be God thy judge,
As thou hast said — not I. For me,
I merely will thank God that he
Whom thou hast lovèd loveth thee."   495

Then Aloÿse lay back, and laughed
    With wan lips bitterly,

Saying, "Nay, thank thou God for this, —
That never any soul like his
Shall have its portion where love is."   500

Weary of wonder, Amelotte
   Sat silent: she would ask
No more, though all was unexplained:
She was too weak; the ache still pained
Her eyes, — her forehead's pulse remained.   505

The silence lengthened. Aloÿse
   Was fain to turn her face
Apart, to where the arras told
Two Testaments, the New and Old,
In shapes and meanings manifold.   510

One solace that was gained, she hid.
   Her sister, from whose curse
Her heart recoiled, had blessed instead:
Yet would not her pride have it said
How much the blessing comforted.   515

Only, on looking round again
   After some while, the face
Which from the arras turned away
Was more at peace and less at bay
With shame than it had been that day.   520

She spoke right on, as if no pause
   Had come between her speech:
"That year from warmth grew bleak and pass'd;"
She said: "the days from first to last
How slow, — woe's me! the nights how fast!"   525

"From first to last it was not known:
   My nurse, and of my train
Some four or five, alone could tell
What terror kept inscrutable:
There was good need to guard it well.   530

"Not the guilt only made the shame,
   But he was without land
And born amiss. He had but come
To train his youth here at our home
And, being man, depart therefrom.   535

"Of the whole time each single day
   Brought fear and great unrest:

It seemed that all would not avail
Some once, — that my close watch would fail,
And some sign, somehow, tell the tale.   540

"The noble maidens that I knew,
    My fellows, oftentimes
Midway in talk or sport, would look
A wonder which my fears mistook,
To see how I turned faint and shook.   545

"They had a game of cards, where each
    By painted arms might find
What knight she should be given to.
Ever with trembling hand I threw
Lest I should learn the thing I knew.   550

"And once it came. And Aure d'Honvaulx
    Held up the bended shield
And laughed: 'Gramercy for our share! —
If to our bridal we but fare
To smutch the blazon that we bear!'   555

"But proud Denise de Villenbois
    Kissed me, and gave her wench
The card, and said: 'If in these bowers
You women play at paramours,
You must not mix your game with ours.'   560

"And one upcast it from her hand:
    'Lo! see how high he'll soar!'
But then their laugh was bitterest;
For the wind veered at fate's behest
And blew it back into my breast.   565

"Oh! if I met him in the day
    Or heard his voice, — at meals
Or at the Mass or through the hall, —
A look turned towards me would appal
My heart by seeming to know all.   570

"Yet I grew curious of my shame,
    And sometimes in the church,
On hearing such a sin rebuked,
Have held my girdle-glass unhooked
To see how such a woman looked.   575

"But if at night he did not come,
    I lay all deadly cold

To think they might have smitten sore
And slain him, and as the night wore,
His corpse be lying at my door. 580

"And entering or going forth,
  Our proud shield o'er the gate
Seemed to arraign my shrinking eyes.
With tremors and unspoken lies
The year went past me in this wise. 585

"About the spring of the next year
  An ailing fell on me;
(I had been stronger till the spring;)
'Twas mine old sickness gathering,
I thought; but 'twas another thing. 590

"I had such yearnings as brought tears,
  And a wan dizziness:
Motion, like feeling, grew intense;
Sight was a haunting evidence
And sound a pang that snatched the sense. 595

"It now was hard on that great ill
  Which lost our wealth from us
And all our lands. Accursed be
The peevish fools of liberty
Who will not let themselves be free! 600

"The Prince was fled into the west:
  A price was on his blood,
But he was safe. To us his friends
He left that ruin which attends
The strife against God's secret ends. 605

"The league dropped all asunder, — lord,
  Gentle and serf. Our house
Was marked to fall. And a day came
When half the wealth that propped our name
Went from us in a wind of flame. 610

"Six hours I lay upon the wall
  And saw it burn. But when
It clogged the day in a black bed
Of louring vapour, I was led
Down to the postern, and we fled. 615

"But ere we fled, there was a voice
  Which I heard speak, and say

That many of our friends, to shun
Our fate, had left us and were gone,
And that Lord Urscelyn was one.   620

"That name, as was its wont, made sight
   And hearing whirl. I gave
No heed but only to the name
I held my senses, dreading them,
And was at strife to look the same.   625

"We rode and rode. As the speed grew,
   The growth of some vague curse
Swarmed in my brain. It seemed to me
Numbed by the swiftness, but would be —
That still — clear knowledge certainly.   630

"Night lapsed. At dawn the sea was there
   And the sea-wind: afar
The ravening surge was hoarse and loud,
And underneath the dim dawn-cloud
Each stalking wave shook like a shroud.   635

"From my drawn litter I looked out
   Unto the swarthy sea,
And knew. That voice, which late had cross'd
Mine ears, seemed with the foam uptoss'd:
I knew that Urscelyn was lost.   640

"Then I spake all: I turned on one
   And on the other, and spake:
My curse laughed in me to behold
Their eyes: I sat up, stricken cold,
Mad of my voice till all was told.   645

"Oh! of my brothers, Hugues was mute,
   And Gilles was wild and loud,
And Raoul strained abroad his face,
As if his gnashing wrath could trace
Even there the prey that it must chase.   650

"And round me murmured all our train,
   Hoarse as the hoarse-tongued sea;
Till Hugues from silence louring woke,
And cried: 'What ails the foolish folk?
Know ye not frenzy's lightning-stroke?'   655

"But my stern father came to them
   And quelled them with his look,

Silent and deadly pale. Anon
I knew that we were hastening on,
My litter closed and the light gone.   660

"And I remember all that day
   The barren bitter wind
Without, and the sea's moaning there
That I first moaned with unaware,
And when I knew, shook down my hair.   665

"Few followed us or faced our flight:
   Once only I could hear,
Far in the front, loud scornful words,
And cries I knew of hostile lords,
And crash of spears and grind of swords.   670

"It was soon ended. On that day
   Before the light had changed
We reached our refuge; miles of rock
Bulwarked for war; whose strength might mock
Sky, sea, or man, to storm or shock.   675

"Listless and feebly conscious, I
   Lay far within the night
Awake. The many pains incurred
That day, — the whole, said, seen or heard, —
Stayed by in me as things deferred.   680

"Not long. At dawn I slept. In dreams
   All was passed through afresh
From end to end. As the morn heaved
Towards noon, I, waking sore aggrieved,
That I might die, cursed God, and lived.   685

"Many days went, and I saw none
   Except my women. They
Calmed their wan faces, loving me;
And when they wept, lest I should see,
Would chaunt a desolate melody.   690

"Panic unthreatened shook my blood
   Each sunset, all the slow
Subsiding of the turbid light.
I would rise, sister, as I might,
And bathe my forehead through the night   695

"To elude madness. The stark walls
   Made chill the mirk: and when

We oped our curtains, to resume
Sun-sickness after long sick gloom,
The withering sea-wind walked the room.   700

Through the gaunt windows the great gales
   Bore in the tattered clumps
Of waif-weed and the tamarisk-boughs;
And sea-mews, 'mid the storm's carouse,
Were flung, wild-clamouring, in the house.   705

"My hounds I had not; and my hawk,
   Which they had saved for me,
Wanting the sun and rain to beat
His wings, soon lay with gathered feet;
And my flowers faded, lacking heat.   710

"Such still were griefs: for grief was still
   A separate sense, untouched
Of that despair which had become
My life. Great anguish could benumb
My soul, — my heart was quarrelsome.   715

"Time crept. Upon a day at length
   My kinsfolk sat with me:
That which they asked was bare and plain:
I answered: the whole bitter strain
Was again said, and heard again.   720

"Fierce Raoul snatched his sword, and turned
   The point against my breast.
I bared it, smiling: 'To the heart
Strike home,' I said; 'another dart
Wreaks hourly there a deadlier smart.'   725

"'Twas then my sire struck down the sword,
   And said with shaken lips:
'She from whom all of you receive
Your life, so smiled; and I forgive.'
Thus, for my mother's sake, I live.   730

"But I, a mother even as she,
   Turned shuddering to the wall:
For I said: 'Great God! and what would I do,
When to the sword, with the thing I knew,
I offered not one life but two!'   735

"Then I fell back from them, and lay
   Outwearied. My tired sense

Soon filmed and settled, and like stone
I slept; till something made me moan,
And I woke up at night alone.   740

"I woke at midnight, cold and dazed;
  Because I found myself
Seated upright, with bosom bare,
Upon my bed, combing my hair,
Ready to go, I knew not where.   745

"It dawned light day, — the last of those
  Long months of longing days.
That noon, the change was wrought on me
In somewise, — nought to hear or see, —
Only a trance and agony."   750

The bride's voice failed her, from no will
  To pause. The bridesmaid leaned,
And where the window-panes were white,
Looked for the day: she knew not quite
If there were either day or night.   755

It seemed to Aloÿse that the whole
  Day's weight lay back on her
Like lead. The hours that did remain
Beat their dry wings upon her brain
Once in mid-flight, and passed again.   760

There hung a cage of burnt perfumes
  In the recess: but these,
For some hours, weak against the sun,
Had simmered in white ash. From One
The second quarter was begun.   765

They had not heard the stroke. The air,
  Though altered with no wind,
Breathed now by pauses, so to say:
Each breath was time that went away, —
Each pause a minute of the day.   770

I' the almonry, the almoner,
  Hard by, had just dispensed
Church-dole and march-dole. High and wide
Now rose the shout of thanks, which cried
On God that He should bless the bride.   775

Its echo thrilled within their feet,
  And in the furthest rooms

Was heard, where maidens flushed and gay
Wove with stooped necks the wreaths alway
Fair for the virgin's marriage-day. 780

The mother leaned along, in thought
    After her child; till tears,
Bitter, not like a wedded girl's,
Fell down her breast along her curls,
And ran in the close work of pearls. 785

The speech ached at her heart. She said:
    "Sweet Mary, do thou plead
This hour with thy most blessed Son
To let these shameful words atone,
That I may die when I have done." 790

The thought ached at her soul. Yet now: —
    "Itself — that life" (she said,)
"Out of my weary life — when sense
Unclosed, was gone. What evil men's
Most evil hands had borne it thence 795

"I knew, and cursed them. Still in sleep
    I have my child; and pray
To know if it indeed appear
As in my dream's perpetual sphere,
That I — death reached — may seek it there. 800

"Sleeping, I wept; though until dark
    A fever dried mine eyes
Kept open; save when a tear might
Be forced from the mere ache of sight.
And I nursed hatred day and night. 805

"Aye, and I sought revenge by spells;
    And vainly many a time
Have laid my face into the lap
Of a wise woman, and heard clap
Her thunder, the fiend's juggling trap. 810

"At length I feared to curse them, lest
    From evil lips the curse
Should be a blessing; and would sit
Rocking myself and stifling it
With babbled jargon of no wit. 815

"But this was not at first: the days
    And weeks made frenzied months

Before this came. My curses, pil'd
Then with each hour unreconcil'd,
Still wait for those who took my child."

She stopped, grown fainter. "Amelotte,
    Surely," she said, "this sun
Sheds judgment-fire from the fierce south:
It does not let me breathe: the drouth
Is like sand spread within my mouth."

The bridesmaid rose. I' the outer glare
    Gleamed her pale cheeks, and eyes
Sore troubled; and aweary weigh'd
Her brows just lifted out of shade;
And the light jarred within her head.

'Mid flowers fair-heaped there stood a bowl
    With water. She therein
Through eddying bubbles slid a cup,
And offered it, being risen up,
Close to her sister's mouth, to sup.

The freshness dwelt upon her sense,
    Yet did not the bride drink;
But she dipped in her hand anon
And cooled her temples; and all wan
With lids that held their ache, went on.

"Through those dark watches of my woe,
    Time, an ill plant, had waxed
Apace. That year was finished. Dumb
And blind, life's wheel with earth's had come
Whirled round: and we might seek our home.

"Our wealth was rendered back, with wealth
    Snatched from our foes. The house
Had more than its old strength and fame:
But still 'neath the fair outward claim
I rankled, — a fierce core of shame.

"It chilled me from their eyes and lips
    Upon a night of those
First days of triumph, as I gazed
Listless and sick, or scarcely raised
My face to mark the sports they praised.

"The endless changes of the dance
    Bewildered me: the tones

820

825

830

835

840

845

850

855

Of lute and cithern struggled tow'rds
Some sense; and still in the last chords
The music seemed to sing wild words.   860

"My shame possessed me in the light
    And pageant, till I swooned.
But from that hour I put my shame
From me, and cast it over them
By God's command and in God's name   865

"For my child's bitter sake. O thou
    Once felt against my heart
With longing of the eyes, — a pain
Since to my heart for ever, — then
Beheld not, and not felt again!"   870

She scarcely paused, continuing: —
    "That year drooped weak in March;
And April, finding the streams dry,
Choked, with no rain, in dust: the sky
Shall not be fainter this July.   875

"Men sickened; beasts lay without strength;
    The year died in the land.
But I, already desolate,
Said merely, sitting down to wait, —
'The seasons change and Time wears late.'   880

"For I had my hard secret told,
    In secret, to a priest;
With him I communed; and he said
The world's soul, for its sins, was sped,
And the sun's courses numberéd.   885

"The year slid like a corpse afloat:
    None trafficked, — who had bread
Did eat. That year our legions, come
Thinned from the place of war, at home
Found busier death, more burdensome.   890

"Tidings and rumours came with them,
    The first for months. The chiefs
Sat daily at our board, and in
Their speech were names of friend and kin:
One day they spoke of Urscelyn.   895

"The words were light, among the rest:
    Quick glance my brothers sent
To sift the speech; and I, struck through,
Sat sick and giddy in full view:
Yet did none gaze, so many knew.   900

"Because in the beginning, much
    Had caught abroad, through them
That heard my clamour on the coast:
But two were hanged; and then the most
Held silence wisdom, as thou know'st.   905

"That year the convent yielded thee
    Back to our home; and thou
Then knew'st not how I shuddered cold
To kiss thee, seeming to enfold
To my changed heart myself of old.   910

"Then there was showing thee the house,
    So many rooms and doors;
Thinking the while how thou would'st start
If once I flung the doors apart
Of one dull chamber in my heart.   915

"And yet I longed to open it;
    And often in that year
Of plague and want, when side by side
We've knelt to pray with them that died,
My prayer was, 'Show her what I hide!'"   920

END OF PART I.

A New-Year's Burden

Along the grass sweet airs are blown
    Our way this day in Spring.
Of all the songs that we have known
    Now which one shall we sing?
        Not that, my love, ah no! —   5
        Not this, my love? why, so! —
Yet both were ours, but hours will come and go.

The grove is all a pale frail mist,
    The new year sucks the sun.

Of all the kisses that we kissed   10
   Now which shall be the one?
     Not that, my love, ah no! —
     Not this, my love? — heigh-ho
For all the sweets that all the winds can blow!

The branches cross above our eyes,   15
   The skies are in a net:
And what's the thing beneath the skies
   We two would most forget?
     Not birth, my love, no, no, —
     Not death, my love, no, no, —   20
The love once ours, but ours long hours ago.

Even So

   So it is, my dear
All such things touch secret strings
   For heavy hearts to hear.
   So it is, my dear.

   Very like indeed: 5
Sea and sky, afar, on high,
   Sand and strewn seaweed, —
   Very like indeed.

   But the sea stands spread
As one wall with the flat skies,   10
Where the lean black craft like flies
   Seem well-nigh stagnated,
   Soon to drop off dead.

   Seemed it so to us
When I was thine and thou wast mine,   15
   And all these things were thus,
   But all our world in us?

   Could we be so now?
Not if all beneath heaven's pall
   Lay dead but I and thou,   20
   Could we be so now!

A Ballad of Dead Ladies

Tell me now in what hidden way is
   Lady Flora the lovely Roman?
Where's Hipparchia, and where is Thais,
   Neither of them the fairer woman?
   Where is Echo, beheld of no man,   5
Only heard on river and mere, —
   She whose beauty was more than human? . . .
But where are the snows of yester-year?

Where's Héloise, the learned nun,
   For whose sake Abeillard, I ween,   10
Lost manhood and put priesthood on?
   (From Love he won such dule and teen!)
   And where, I pray you, is the Queen
Who willed that Buridan should steer
   Sewed in a sack's mouth down the Seine? . . .   15
But where are the snows of yester-year?

White Queen Blanche, like a queen of lilies,
   With a voice like any mermaiden, —
Bertha Broadfoot, Beatrice, Alice,
   And Ermengarde the lady of Maine, —   20
   And that good Joan whom Englishmen
At Rouen doomed and burned her there, —
   Mother of God, where are they then? . . .
But where are the snows of yester-year?

Nay, never ask this week, fair lord,   25
   Where they are gone, nor yet this year,
Save with thus much for an overword, —
   But where are the snows of yester-year?

To Death, of His Lady

Death, of thee do I make my moan,
   Who hadst my lady away from me,
   Nor wilt assuage thine enmity
Till with her life thou hast mine own;

For since that hour my strength has flown. 5
   Lo! what wrong was her life to thee,
      Death?

Two we were, and the heart was one;
   Which now being dead, dead I must be,
   Or seem alive as lifelessly 10
As in the choir the painted stone,
      Death!

His Mother's Service to Our Lady

Lady of Heaven and earth, and therewithal
   Crowned Empress of the nether clefts of Hell, —
I, thy poor Christian, on thy name do call,
   Commending me to thee, with thee to dwell,
   Albeit in nought I be commendable. 5
But all mine undeserving may not mar
Such mercies as thy sovereign mercies are;
   Without the which (as true words testify)
No soul can reach thy Heaven so fair and far.
   Even in this faith I choose to live and die. 10

Unto thy Son say thou that I am His,
   And to me graceless make Him gracious.
Sad Mary of Egypt lacked not of that bliss,
   Nor yet the sorrowful clerk Theophilus,
   Whose bitter sins were set aside even thus 15
Though to the Fiend his bounden service was.
Oh help me, lest in vain for me should pass
   (Sweet Virgin that shalt have no loss thereby!)
The blessed Host and sacring of the Mass.
   Even in this faith I choose to live and die. 20

A pitiful poor woman, shrunk and old,
   I am, and nothing learn'd in letter-lore.
Within my parish-cloister I behold
   A painted Heaven where harps and lutes adore,
   And eke an Hell whose damned folk seethe full sore: 25
One bringeth fear, the other joy to me.
That joy, great Goddess, make thou mine to be, —
   Thou of whom all must ask it even as I;
And that which faith desires, that let it see.
   For in this faith I choose to live and die. 30

O excellent Virgin Princess! thou didst bear
King Jesus, the most excellent comforter,
Who even of this our weakness craved a share
   And for our sake stooped to us from on high,
Offering to death His young life sweet and fair.   35
Such as He is, Our Lord, I Him declare,
   And in this faith I choose to live and die.

John of Tours. Old French

John of Tours is back with peace,
But he comes home ill at ease.

"Good-morrow, mother." "Good-morrow, son;
Your wife has borne you a little one."

"Go now, mother, go before,   5
Make me a bed upon the floor;

"Very low your foot must fall,
That my wife hear not at all."

As it neared the midnight toll,
John of Tours gave up his soul.   10

"Tell me now, my mother my dear,
What's the crying that I hear?"

"Daughter, it's the children wake,
Crying with their teeth that ache."

"Tell me though, my mother my dear,   15
What's the knocking that I hear?"

"Daughter, it's the carpenter
Mending planks upon the stair."

"Tell me too, my mother my dear,
What's the singing that I hear?"   20

"Daughter, it's the priests in rows
Going round about our house."

"Tell me then, my mother my dear,
What's the dress that I should wear?"

"Daughter, any reds or blues,
But the black is most in use."

"Nay, but say, my mother my dear,
Why do you fall weeping here?"

"Oh! the truth must be said, —
It's that John of Tours is dead."

"Mother, let the sexton know
That the grave must be for two;

"Aye, and still have room to spare,
For you must shut the baby there."

25

30

My Father's Close. Old French

Inside my father's close,
  (Fly away O my heart away!)
Sweet apple-blossom blows
  So sweet.

Three kings' daughters fair,
  (Fly away O my heart away!)
They lie below it there
  So sweet.

"Ah!" says the eldest one,
  (Fly away O my heart away!)
"I think the day's begun
  So sweet."

"Ah!" says the second one,
  (Fly away O my heart away!)
"Far off I hear the drum
  So sweet."

"Ah!" says the youngest one,
  (Fly away O my heart away!)
"It's my true love, my own,
  So sweet.

"Oh! if he fight and win,"
  (Fly away O my heart away!)
"I keep my love for him,
  So sweet:
Oh! let him lose or win,
    He hath it still complete."

5

10

15

20

25

Beauty (A Combination from Sappho)

I.
Like the sweet apple which reddens upon the topmost bough,
A-top on the topmost twig, — which the pluckers forgot, somehow, —
Forgot it not, nay, but got it not, for none could get it till now.

II.
Like the wild hyacinth flower which on the hills is found,
Which the passing feet of the shepherds for ever tear and wound,   5
Until the purple blossom is trodden into the ground.

PART TWO

The House of Life (1870, 1881)

THE SONNETS (1881)

[Sonnet on the Sonnet]

A Sonnet is a moment's monument, —
  Memorial from the Soul's eternity
  To one dead deathless hour. Look that it be,
Whether for lustral rite or dire portent,
Of its own arduous fulness reverent: 5
  Carve it in ivory or in ebony,
  As Day or Night may rule; and let Time see
Its flowering crest impearled and orient.

A Sonnet is a coin: its face reveals
  The soul, — its converse, to what Power 'tis due: —   10
Whether for tribute to the august appeals
  Of Life, or dower in Love's high retinue,
It serve; or, 'mid the dark wharf's cavernous breath,
In Charon's palm it pay the toll to Death.

PART I. YOUTH AND CHANGE

Sonnet I. Love Enthroned

I marked all kindred Powers the heart finds fair: —
  Truth, with awed lips; and Hope, with eyes up-cast;
  And Fame, whose loud wings fan the ashen Past
To signal-fires, Oblivion's flight to scare;
And Youth, with still some single golden hair   5
  Unto his shoulder clinging, since the last
  Embrace wherein two sweet arms held him fast;
And Life, still wreathing flowers for Death to wear.

Love's throne was not with these; but far above
  All passionate wind of welcome and farewell   10

He sat in breathless bowers they dream not of;
   Though Truth foreknow Love's heart, and Hope foretell,
   And Fame be for Love's sake desirable,
And Youth be dear, and Life be sweet to Love.

Sonnet II. Bridal Birth

As when desire, long darkling, dawns, and first
   The mother looks upon the newborn child,
   Even so my Lady stood at gaze and smiled
When her soul knew at length the Love it nurs'd.
Born with her life, creature of poignant thirst   5
   And exquisite hunger, at her heart Love lay
   Quickening in darkness, till a voice that day
Cried on him, and the bonds of birth were burst.

Now, shadowed by his wings, our faces yearn
   Together, as his fullgrown feet now range   10
      The grove, and his warm hands our couch prepare:
Till to his song our bodiless souls in turn
   Be born his children, when Death's nuptial change
      Leaves us for light the halo of his hair.
(1870)

Sonnet III. Love's Testament

O thou who at Love's hour ecstatically
   Unto my heart dost evermore present,
   Clothed with his fire, thy heart his testament;
Whom I have neared and felt thy breath to be
The inmost incense of his sanctuary;   5
   Who without speech hast owned him, and, intent
   Upon his will, thy life with mine hast blent,
And murmured, "I am thine, thou'rt one with me!"

O what from thee the grace, to me the prize,
   And what to Love the glory, — when the whole   10
   Of the deep stair thou tread'st to the dim shoal
And weary water of the place of sighs,
And there dost work deliverance, as thine eyes
   Draw up my prisoned spirit to thy soul!
(1870)

Sonnet IV. Lovesight

When do I see thee most, beloved one?
   When in the light the spirits of mine eyes
   Before thy face, their altar, solemnize
The worship of that Love through thee made known?
Or when in the dusk hours, (we two alone,)   5
   Close-kissed and eloquent of still replies
   Thy twilight-hidden glimmering visage lies,
And my soul only sees thy soul its own?

O love, my love! if I no more should see
Thyself, nor on the earth the shadow of thee,   10
   Nor image of thine eyes in any spring, —
How then should sound upon Life's darkening slope
The ground-whirl of the perished leaves of Hope,
   The wind of Death's imperishable wing?
(1870)

Sonnet V. Heart's Hope

By what word's power, the key of paths untrod,
   Shall I the difficult deeps of Love explore,
   Till parted waves of Song yield up the shore
Even as that sea which Israel crossed dryshod?
For lo! in some poor rhythmic period,   5
   Lady, I fain would tell how evermore
   Thy soul I know not from thy body, nor
Thee from myself, neither our love from God.

Yea, in God's name, and Love's, and thine, would I
   Draw from one loving heart such evidence   10
As to all hearts all things shall signify;
   Tender as dawn's first hill-fire, and intense
   As instantaneous penetrating sense,
In Spring's birth-hour, of other Springs gone by.

Sonnet VI. The Kiss

What smouldering senses in death's sick delay
   Or seizure of malign vicissitude
   Can rob this body of honour, or denude
This soul of wedding-raiment worn to-day?

For lo! even now my lady's lips did play   5
   With these my lips such consonant interlude
   As laurelled Orpheus longed for when he wooed
The half-drawn hungering face with that last lay.

I was a child beneath her touch, — a man
   When breast to breast we clung, even I and she, —   10
   A spirit when her spirit looked through me, —
A god when all our life-breath met to fan
Our life-blood, till love's emulous ardours ran,
   Fire within fire, desire in deity.
(1870)

Sonnet VIa. Nuptial Sleep

At length their long kiss severed, with sweet smart:
   And as the last slow sudden drops are shed
   From sparkling eaves when all the storm has fled,
So singly flagged the pulses of each heart.
Their bosoms sundered, with the opening start   5
   Of married flowers to either side outspread
   From the knit stem; yet still their mouths, burnt red,
Fawned on each other where they lay apart.

Sleep sank them lower than the tide of dreams,
   And their dreams watched them sink, and slid away.   10
Slowly their souls swam up again, through gleams
   Of watered light and dull drowned waifs of day;
Till from some wonder of new woods and streams
   He woke, and wondered more: for there she lay.
(1870)

Sonnet VII. Supreme Surrender

To all the spirits of Love that wander by
   Along his love-sown harvest-field of sleep
   My lady lies apparent; and the deep
Calls to the deep; and no man sees but I.
The bliss so long afar, at length so nigh,   5
   Rests there attained. Methinks proud Love must weep
   When Fate's control doth from his harvest reap
The sacred hour for which the years did sigh.

First touched, the hand now warm around my neck
   Taught memory long to mock desire: and lo!
   Across my breast the abandoned hair doth flow,
Where one shorn tress long stirred the longing ache:
And next the heart that trembled for its sake
   Lies the queen-heart in sovereign overthrow.
(1870)

Sonnet VIII. Love's Lovers

Some ladies love the jewels in Love's zone
   And gold-tipped darts he hath for painless play
   In idle scornful hours he flings away;
And some that listen to his lute's soft tone
Do love to vaunt the silver praise their own;5
   Some prize his blindfold sight; and there be they
   Who kissed his wings which brought him yesterday
And thank his wings to-day that he is flown.

My lady only loves the heart of Love:
   Therefore Love's heart, my lady, hath for thee10
   His bower of unimagined flower and tree:
There kneels he now, and all-anhungered of
Thine eyes grey-lit in shadowing hair above,
   Seals with thy mouth his immortality.

Sonnet IX. Passion and Worship

One flame-winged brought a white-winged harp-player
   Even where my lady and I lay all alone;
   Saying: "Behold, this minstrel is unknown;
Bid him depart, for I am minstrel here:
Only my strains are to Love's dear ones dear."5
   Then said I: "Through thine hautboy's rapturous tone
   Unto my lady still this harp makes moan,
And still she deems the cadence deep and clear."

Then said my lady: "Thou art Passion of Love,
   And this Love's Worship: both he plights to me.10
   Thy mastering music walks the sunlit sea:

But where wan water trembles in the grove
And the wan moon is all the light thereof,
   This harp still makes my name its voluntary."
(1870)

Sonnet X. The Portrait

O Lord of all compassionate control,
   O Love! let this my lady's picture glow
   Under my hand to praise her name, and show
Even of her inner self the perfect whole:
That he who seeks her beauty's furthest goal,   5
   Beyond the light that the sweet glances throw
   And refluent wave of the sweet smile, may know
The very sky and sea-line of her soul.

Lo! it is done. Above the enthroning throat
   The mouth's mould testifies of voice and kiss,   10
      The shadowed eyes remember and foresee.
Her face is made her shrine. Let all men note
   That in all years (O Love, thy gift is this!)
      They that would look on her must come to me.
(1870)

Sonnet XI. The Love-Letter

Warmed by her hand and shadowed by her hair
   As close she leaned and poured her heart through thee,
   Whereof the articulate throbs accompany
The smooth black stream that makes thy whiteness fair, —
Sweet fluttering sheet, even of her breath aware, —   5
   Oh let thy silent song disclose to me
   That soul wherewith her lips and eyes agree
Like married music in Love's answering air.

Fain had I watched her when, at some fond thought,
   Her bosom to the writing closelier press'd,   10
   And her breast's secrets peered into her breast;
When, through eyes raised an instant, her soul sought
My soul, and from the sudden confluence caught
   The words that made her love the loveliest.
(1870)

Sonnet XII. The Lovers' Walk

Sweet twining hedgeflowers wind-stirred in no wise
   On this June day; and hand that clings in hand: —
   Still glades; and meeting faces scarcely fann'd: —
An osier-odoured stream that draws the skies
Deep to its heart; and mirrored eyes in eyes: —   5
   Fresh hourly wonder o'er the Summer land
   Of light and cloud; and two souls softly spann'd
With one o'erarching heaven of smiles and sighs: —

Even such their path, whose bodies lean unto
   Each other's visible sweetness amorously, —   10
   Whose passionate hearts lean by Love's high decree
Together on his heart for ever true,
As the cloud-foaming firmamental blue
   Rest on the blue line of a foamless sea.

Sonnet XIII. Youth's Antiphony

"I love you, sweet: how can you ever learn
   How much I love you?" "You I love even so,
   And so I learn it." "Sweet, you cannot know
How fair you are." "If fair enough to earn
Your love, so much is all my love's concern."   5
   "My love grows hourly, sweet." "Mine too doth grow,
   Yet love seemed full so many hours ago!"
Thus lovers speak, till kisses claim their turn.

Ah! happy they to whom such words as these
   In youth have served for speech the whole day long,   10
   Hour after hour, remote from the world's throng,
Work, contest, fame, all life's confederate pleas, —
What while Love breathed in sighs and silences
   Through two blent souls one rapturous undersong.

Sonnet XIV. Youth's Spring-Tribute

On this sweet bank your head thrice sweet and dear
   I lay, and spread your hair on either side,
   And see the newborn woodflowers bashful-eyed

Look through the golden tresses here and there.
On these debateable borders of the year   5
   Spring's foot half falters; scarce she yet may know
   The leafless blackthorn-blossom from the snow;
And through her bowers the wind's way still is clear.

But April's sun strikes down the glades to-day;
   So shut your eyes upturned, and feel my kiss   10
Creep, as the Spring now thrills through every spray,
   Up your warm throat to your warm lips: for this
   Is even the hour of Love's sworn suitservice,
With whom cold hearts are counted castaway.

Sonnet XV. The Birth-Bond

Have you not noted, in some family
   Where two were born of a first marriage-bed,
   How still they own their gracious bond, though fed
And nursed on the forgotten breast and knee? —
How to their father's children they shall be   5
   In act and thought of one goodwill; but each
   Shall for the other have, in silence speech,
And in a word complete community?

Even so, when first I saw you, seemed it, love,
   That among souls allied to mine was yet   10
One nearer kindred than life hinted of.
   O born with me somewhere that men forget,
   And though in years of sight and sound unmet,
Known for my soul's birth-partner well enough!
(1870)

Sonnet XVI. A Day of Love

Those envied places which do know her well,
   And are so scornful of this lonely place,
   Even now for once are emptied of her grace:
Nowhere but here she is: and while Love's spell
From his predominant presence doth compel   5
   All alien hours, an outworn populace,
   The hours of Love fill full the echoing space
With sweet confederate music favourable.

Now many memories make solicitous
   The delicate love-lines of her mouth, till, lit   10
   With quivering fire, the words take wing from it;
As here between our kisses we sit thus
   Speaking of things remembered, and so sit
Speechless while things forgotten call to us.
(1870)

Sonnet XVII. Beauty's Pageant

What dawn-pulse at the heart of heaven, or last
   Incarnate flower of culminating day, —
   What marshalled marvels on the skirts of May,
Or song full-quired, sweet June's encomiast;
What glory of change by nature's hand amass'd   5
   Can vie with all those moods of varying grace
   Which o'er one loveliest woman's form and face
Within this hour, within this room, have pass'd?

Love's very vesture and elect disguise
   Was each fine movement, — wonder new-begot   10
   Of lily or swan or swan-stemmed galiot;
Joy to his sight who now the sadlier sighs,
Parted again; and sorrow yet for eyes
   Unborn, that read these words and saw her not.

Sonnet XVIII. Genius in Beauty

Beauty like hers is genius. Not the call
   Of Homer's or of Dante's heart sublime, —
   Not Michael's hand furrowing the zones of time, —
Is more with compassed mysteries musical;
Nay, not in Spring's or Summer's sweet footfall   5
   More gathered gifts exuberant Life bequeathes
   Than doth this sovereign face, whose love-spell breathes
Even from its shadowed contour on the wall.

As many men are poets in their youth,
   But for one sweet-strung soul the wires prolong   10
   Even through all change the indomitable song;
So in likewise the envenomed years, whose tooth
Rends shallower grace with ruin void of ruth,
   Upon this beauty's power shall wreak no wrong.

Sonnet XIX. Silent Noon

Your hands lie open in the long fresh grass, —
   The finger-points look through like rosy blooms:
   Your eyes smile peace. The pasture gleams and glooms
'Neath billowing skies that scatter and amass.
All round our nest, far as the eye can pass,   5
   Are golden kingcup-fields with silver edge
   Where the cow-parsley skirts the hawthorn-hedge.
'Tis visible silence, still as the hour-glass.

Deep in the sun-searched growths the dragon-fly
Hangs like a blue thread loosened from the sky: —   10
   So this wing'd hour is dropt to us from above.
Oh! clasp we to our hearts, for deathless dower,
This close-companioned inarticulate hour
   When twofold silence was the song of love.

Sonnet XX. Gracious Moonlight

Even as the moon grows queenlier in mid-space
   When the sky darkens, and her cloud-rapt car
   Thrills with intenser radiance from afar, —
So lambent, lady, beams thy sovereign grace
When the drear soul desires thee. Of that face   5
   What shall be said, — which, like a governing star,
   Gathers and garners from all things that are
Their silent penetrative loveliness?

O'er water-daisies and wild waifs of Spring,
   There where the iris rears its gold-crowned sheaf   10
   With flowering rush and sceptred arrow-leaf,
So have I marked Queen Dian, in bright ring
Of cloud above and wave below, take wing
   And chase night's gloom, as thou the spirit's grief.

Sonnet XXI. Love-Sweetness

Sweet dimness of her loosened hair's downfall
   About thy face; her sweet hands round thy head
   In gracious fostering union garlanded;
Her tremulous smiles; her glances' sweet recall

Of love; her murmuring sighs memorial;   5
    Her mouth's culled sweetness by thy kisses shed
    On cheeks and neck and eyelids, and so led
Back to her mouth which answers there for all: —

What sweeter than these things, except the thing
    In lacking which all these would lose their sweet: —   10
    The confident heart's still fervour: the swift beat
And soft subsidence of the spirit's wing,
Then when it feels, in cloud-girt wayfaring,
    The breath of kindred plumes against its feet?
(1870)

Sonnet XXII. Heart's Haven

Sometimes she is a child within mine arms,
    Cowering beneath dark wings that love must chase, —
    With still tears showering and averted face,
Inexplicably filled with faint alarms:
And oft from mine own spirit's hurtling harms   5
    I crave the refuge of her deep embrace, —
    Against all ills the fortified strong place
And sweet reserve of sovereign counter-charms

And Love, our light at night and shade at noon,
    Lulls us to rest with songs, and turns away   10
    All shafts of shelterless tumultuous day
Like the moon's growth, his face gleams through his tune;
And as soft waters warble to the moon,
    Our answering spirits chime one roundelay.

Sonnet XXIII. Love's Baubles

I stood where Love in brimming armfuls bore
    Slight wanton flowers and foolish toys of fruit:
    And round him ladies thronged in warm pursuit,
Fingered and lipped and proffered the strange store.
And from one hand the petal and the core   5
    Savoured of sleep; and cluster and curled shoot
    Seemed from another hand like shame's salute, —
Gifts that I felt my cheek was blushing for.

At last Love bade my Lady give the same:
   And as I looked, the dew was light thereon;
   And as I took them, at her touch they shone
With inmost heaven-hue of the heart of flame.
   And then Love said: "Lo! when the hand is hers,
   Follies of love are love's true ministers."
(1870)

Sonnet XXIV. Pride of Youth

Even as a child, of sorrow that we give
   The dead, but little in his heart can find,
   Since without need of thought to his clear mind
Their turn it is to die and his to live: —
Even so the winged New Love smiles to receive
   Along his eddying plumes the auroral wind,
   Nor, forward glorying, casts one look behind
Where night-rack shrouds the Old Love fugitive.

There is a change in every hour's recall,
   And the last cowslip in the fields we see
   On the same day with the first corn-poppy.
Alas for hourly change! Alas for all
The loves that from his hand proud Youth lets fall,
   Even as the beads of a told rosary!

Sonnet XXV. Winged Hours

Each hour until we meet is as a bird
   That wings from far his gradual way along
   The rustling covert of my soul, — his song
Still loudlier trilled through leaves more deeply stirr'd:
But at the hour of meeting, a clear word
   Is every note he sings, in Love's own tongue;
   Yet, Love, thou know'st the sweet strain suffers wrong,
Full oft through our contending joys unheard.

What of that hour at last, when for her sake
   No wing may fly to me nor song may flow;
   When, wandering round my life unleaved, I know

The bloodied feathers scattered in the brake,
    And think how she, far from me, with like eyes
Sees through the untuneful bough the wingless skies?
(1870)

Sonnet XXVI. Mid-Rapture

Thou lovely and beloved, thou my love;
    Whose kiss seems still the first; whose summoning eyes,
    Even now, as for our love-world's new sunrise,
Shed very dawn; whose voice, attuned above
All modulation of the deep-bowered dove,   5
    Is like a hand laid softly on the soul;
    Whose hand is like a sweet voice to control
Those worn tired brows it hath the keeping of: —

What word can answer to thy word, — what gaze
    To thine, which now absorbs within its sphere   10
    My worshipping face, till I am mirrored there
Light-circled in a heaven of deep-drawn rays?
    What clasp, what kiss mine inmost heart can prove,
    O lovely and beloved, O my love?

Sonnet XXVII. Heart's Compass

Sometimes thou seem'st not as thyself alone,
    But as the meaning of all things that are;
    A breathless wonder, shadowing forth afar
Some heavenly solstice hushed and halcyon;
Whose unstirred lips are music's visible tone;   5
    Whose eyes the sun-gate of the soul unbar,
    Being of its furthest fires oracular; —
The evident heart of all life sown and mown.

Even such Love is; and is not thy name Love?
    Yea, by thy hand the Love-god rends apart   10
    All gathering clouds of Night's ambiguous art;
Flings them far down, and sets thine eyes above;
And simply, as some gage of flower or glove,
    Stakes with a smile the world against thy heart.

Sonnet XXVIII. Soul-Light

What other woman could be loved like you,
   Or how of you should love possess his fill?
   After the fulness of all rapture, still, —
As at the end of some deep avenue
A tender glamour of day, — there comes to view   5
   Far in your eyes a yet more hungering thrill, —
   Such fire as Love's soul-winnowing hands distil
Even from his inmost ark of light and dew.

And as the traveller triumphs with the sun,
   Glorying in heat's mid-height, yet startide brings   10
   Wonder new-born, and still fresh transport springs
From limpid lambent hours of day begun; —
   Even so, through eyes and voice, your soul doth move
   My soul with changeful light of infinite love.

Sonnet XXIX. The Moonstar

Lady, I thank thee for thy loveliness,
   Because my lady is more lovely still.
   Glorying I gaze, and yield with glad goodwill
To thee thy tribute; by whose sweet-spun dress
Of delicate life Love labours to assess   5
   My lady's absolute queendom; saying, "Lo!
   How high this beauty is, which yet doth show
But as that beauty's sovereign votaress."

Lady, I saw thee with her, side by side;
   And as, when night's fair fires their queen surround,   10
An emulous star too near the moon will ride, —
   Even so thy rays within her luminous bound
   Were traced no more; and by the light so drown'd,
Lady, not thou but she was glorified.

Sonnet XXX. Last Fire

Love, through your spirit and mine what summer eve
   Now glows with glory of all things possess'd,
   Since this day's sun of rapture filled the west

And the light sweetened as the fire took leave?
Awhile now softlier let your bosom heave,   5
   As in Love's harbour, even that loving breast,
   All care takes refuge while we sink to rest,
And mutual dreams the bygone bliss retrieve.

Many the days that Winter keeps in store,
   Sunless throughout, or whose brief sun-glimpses   10
   Scarce shed the heaped snow through the naked trees.
This day at least was Summer's paramour,
Sun-coloured to the imperishable core
   With sweet well-being of love and full heart's ease.

Sonnet XXXI. Her Gifts

High grace, the dower of queens; and therewithal
   Some wood-born wonder's sweet simplicity;
   A glance like water brimming with the sky
Or hyacinth-light where forest-shadows fall;
Such thrilling pallor of cheek as doth enthral   5
   The heart; a mouth whose passionate forms imply
   All music and all silence held thereby;
Deep golden locks, her sovereign coronal;
A round reared neck, meet column of Love's shrine
   To cling to when the heart takes sanctuary;   10
   Hands which for ever at Love's bidding be,
And soft-stirred feet still answering to his sign: —
   These are her gifts, as tongue may tell them o'er.
   Breathe low her name, my soul; for that means more.

Sonnet XXXII. Equal Troth

Not by one measure mayst thou mete our love;
   For how should I be loved as I love thee? —
   I, graceless, joyless, lacking absolutely
All gifts that with thy queenship best behove; —
Thou, throned in every heart's elect alcove,   5
   And crowned with garlands culled from every tree,
   Which for no head but thine, by Love's decree,
All beauties and all mysteries interwove.

But here thine eyes and lips yield soft rebuke: —
  "Then only," (say'st thou) "could I love thee less,   10
    When thou couldst doubt my love's equality."
Peace, sweet! If not to sum but worth we look, —
  Thy heart's transcendence, not my heart's excess, —
  Then more a thousandfold thou lov'st than I.

Sonnet XXXIII. Venus Victrix

Could Juno's self more sovereign presence wear
  Than thou, 'mid other ladies throned in grace? —
  Or Pallas, when thou bend'st with soul-stilled face
O'er poet's page gold-shadowed in thy hair?
Dost thou than Venus seem less heavenly fair   5
  When o'er the sea of love's tumultuous trance
  Hovers thy smile, and mingles with thy glance
That sweet voice like the last wave murmuring there?

Before such triune loveliness divine
  Awestruck I ask, which goddess here most claims   10
The prize that, howsoe'er adjudged, is thine?
  Then Love breathes low the sweetest of thy names;
And Venus Victrix to my heart doth bring
Herself, the Helen of her guerdoning.

Sonnet XXXIV. The Dark Glass

Not I myself know all my love for thee:
  How should I reach so far, who cannot weigh
  To-morrow's dower by gage of yesterday?
Shall birth and death, and all dark names that be
As doors and windows bared to some loud sea,   5
  Lash deaf mine ears and blind my face with spray;
  And shall my sense pierce love, — the last relay
And ultimate outpost of eternity?

Lo! what am I to Love, the lord of all?
  One murmuring shell he gathers from the sand, —   10
  One little heart-flame sheltered in his hand.
Yet through thine eyes he grants me clearest call
And veriest touch of powers primordial
  That any hour-girt life may understand.

Sonnet XXXV. The Lamp's Shrine

Sometimes I fain would find in thee some fault,
    That I might love thee still in spite of it:
    Yet how should our Lord Love curtail one whit
Thy perfect praise whom most he would exalt?
Alas! he can but make my heart's low vault   5
    Even in men's sight unworthier, being lit
    By thee, who thereby show'st more exquisite
Like fiery chrysoprase in deep basalt.

Yet will I nowise shrink; but at Love's shrine
    Myself within the beams his brow doth dart   10
    Will set the flashing jewel of thy heart
In that dull chamber where it deigns to shine:
    For lo! in honour of thine excellencies
    My heart takes pride to show how poor it is.

Sonnet XXXVI. Life-in-Love

Not in thy body is thy life at all
    But in this lady's lips and hands and eyes;
    Through these she yields thee life that vivifies
What else were sorrow's servant and death's thrall.
Look on thyself without her, and recall   5
    The waste remembrance and forlorn surmise
    That lived but in a dead-drawn breath of sighs
O'er vanished hours and hours eventual.

Even so much life hath the poor tress of hair
    Which, stored apart, is all love hath to show   10
    For heart-beats and for fire-heats long ago;
Even so much life endures unknown, even where,
    'Mid change the changeless night environeth,
    Lies all that golden hair undimmed in death.
(1870)

Sonnet XXXVII. The Love-Moon

"When that dead face, bowered in the furthest years,
    Which once was all the life years held for thee,
    Can now scarce bid the tides of memory

Cast on thy soul a little spray of tears, —
How canst thou gaze into these eyes of hers   5
    Whom now thy heart delights in, and not see
    Within each orb Love's philtred euphrasy
Make them of buried troth remembrancers?"

"Nay, pitiful Love, nay, loving Pity! Well
    Thou knowest that in these twain I have confess'd   10
Two very voices of thy summoning bell.
    Nay, Master, shall not Death make manifest
In these the culminant changes which approve
The love-moon that must light my soul to Love?"
(1870)

Sonnet XXXVIII. The Morrow's Message

"Thou Ghost," I said, "and is thy name To-day? —
    Yesterday's son, with such an abject brow! —
    And can To-morrow be more pale than thou?"
While yet I spoke, the silence answered: "Yea,
Henceforth our issue is all grieved and grey,   5
    And each beforehand makes such poor avow
    As of old leaves beneath the budding bough
Or night-drift that the sundawn shreds away."

Then cried I: "Mother of many malisons,
    O Earth, receive me to thy dusty bed!"   10
    But therewithal the tremulous silence said:
"Lo! Love yet bids thy lady greet thee once: —
Yea, twice, — whereby thy life is still the sun's;
    And thrice, — whereby the shadow of death is dead."
(1870)

Sonnet XXXIX. Sleepless Dreams

Girt in dark growths, yet glimmering with one star,
    O night desirous as the nights of youth!
    Why should my heart within thy spell, forsooth,
Now beat, as the bride's finger-pulses are
Quickened within the girdling golden bar?   5
    What wings are these that fan my pillow smooth?
    And why does Sleep, waved back by Joy and Ruth,
Tread softly round and gaze at me from far?

Nay, night deep-leaved! And would Love feign in thee
   Some shadowy palpitating grove that bears
   Rest for man's eyes and music for his ears?
O lonely night! art thou not known to me,
A thicket hung with masks of mockery
   And watered with the wasteful warmth of tears?
(1870)

Sonnet XL. Severed Selves

Two separate divided silences,
   Which, brought together, would find loving voice;
   Two glances which together would rejoice
In love, now lost like stars beyond dark trees;
Two hands apart whose touch alone gives ease;   5
   Two bosoms which, heart-shrined with mutual flame,
   Would, meeting in one clasp, be made the same;
Two souls, the shores wave-mocked of sundering seas: —

Such are we now. Ah! may our hope forecast
   Indeed one hour again, when on this stream   10
   Of darkened love once more the light shall gleam? —
An hour how slow to come, how quickly past, —
Which blooms and fades, and only leaves at last,
   Faint as shed flowers, the attenuated dream.

Sonnet XLI. Through Death to Love

Like labour-laden moonclouds faint to flee
   From winds that sweep the winter-bitten wold, —
   Like multiform circumfluence manifold
Of night's flood-tide, — like terrors that agree
Of hoarse-tongued fire and inarticulate sea, —   5
   Even such, within some glass dimmed by our breath,
   Our hearts discern wild images of Death,
Shadows and shoals that edge eternity.

Howbeit athwart Death's imminent shade doth soar
   One Power, than flow of stream or flight of dove   10
   Sweeter to glide around, to brood above.
Tell me, my heart, — what angel-greeted door
Or threshold of wing-winnowed threshing-floor
   Hath guest fire-fledged as thine, whose lord is Love?

Sonnet XLII. Hope Overtaken

I deemed thy garments, O my Hope, were grey,
    So far I viewed thee. Now the space between
    Is passed at length; and garmented in green
Even as in days of yore thou stand'st to-day.
Ah God! and but for lingering dull dismay,   5
    On all that road our footsteps erst had been
    Even thus commingled, and our shadows seen
Blent on the hedgerows and the water-way.

O Hope of mine whose eyes are living love,
    No eyes but hers, — O Love and Hope the same! —   10
    Lean close to me, for now the sinking sun
That warmed our feet scarce gilds our hair above.
    O hers thy voice and very hers thy name!
    Alas, cling round me, for the day is done!

Sonnet XLIII. Love and Hope

Bless love and hope. Full many a withered year
    Whirled past us, eddying to its chill doomsday;
    And clasped together where the blown leaves lay,
We long have knelt and wept full many a tear.
Yet lo! one hour at last, the Spring's compeer,   5
    Flutes softly to us from some green byeway:
    Those years, those tears are dead, but only they: —
Bless love and hope, true soul; for we are here.

Cling heart to heart; nor of this hour demand
    Whether in very truth, when we are dead,   10
    Our hearts shall wake to know Love's golden head
Sole sunshine of the imperishable land;
    Or but discern, through night's unfeatured scope,
    Scorn-fired at length the illusive eyes of Hope.

Sonnet XLIV. Cloud and Wind

Love, should I fear death most for you or me?
    Yet if you die, can I not follow you,
    Forcing the straits of change? Alas! but who
Shall wrest a bond from night's inveteracy,

Ere yet my hazardous soul put forth, to be   5
   Her warrant against all her haste might rue? —
   Ah! in your eyes so reached what dumb adieu,
What unsunned gyres of waste eternity?

And if I die the first, shall death be then
   A lampless watchtower whence I see you weep? —   10
   Or (woe is me!) a bed wherein my sleep
Ne'er notes (as death's dear cup at last you drain),
The hour when you too learn that all is vain
   And that Hope sows what Love shall never reap?

Sonnet XLV. Secret Parting

Because our talk was of the cloud-control
   And moon-track of the journeying face of Fate,
   Her tremulous kisses faltered at love's gate
And her eyes dreamed against a distant goal:
But soon, remembering her how brief the whole   5
   Of joy, which its own hours annihilate,
   Her set gaze gathered, thirstier than of late,
And as she kissed, her mouth became her soul.

Thence in what ways we wandered, and how strove
   To build with fire-tried vows the piteous home   10
   Which memory haunts and whither sleep may roam, —
They only know for whom the roof of Love
Is the still-seated secret of the grove,
   Nor spire may rise nor bell be heard therefrom.
(1870)

Sonnet XLVI. Parted Love

What shall be said of this embattled day
   And armed occupation of this night
   By all thy foes beleaguered, — now when sight
Nor sound denotes the loved one far away?
Of these thy vanquished hours what shalt thou say, —   5
   As every sense to which she dealt delight
   Now labours lonely o'er the stark noon-height
To reach the sunset's desolate disarray?

Stand still, fond fettered wretch! while Memory's art
   Parades the Past before thy face, and lures   10
   Thy spirit to her passionate portraitures:
Till the tempestuous tide-gates flung apart
Flood with wild will the hollows of thy heart,
   And thy heart rends thee, and thy body endures.
(1870)

Sonnet XLVII. Broken Music

The mother will not turn, who thinks she hears
   Her nursling's speech first grow articulate;
   But breathless with averted eyes elate
She sits, with open lips and open ears,
That it may call her twice. 'Mid doubts and fears   5
   Thus oft my soul has hearkened; till the song,
   A central moan for days, at length found tongue,
And the sweet music welled and the sweet tears.

But now, whatever while the soul is fain
   To list that wonted murmur, as it were   10
The speech-bound sea-shell's low importunate strain, —
   No breath of song, thy voice alone is there,
O bitterly beloved! and all her gain
   Is but the pang of unpermitted prayer.
(1870)

Sonnet XLVIII. Death-in-Love

There came an image in Life's retinue
   That had Love's wings and bore his gonfalon:
   Fair was the web, and nobly wrought thereon,
O soul-sequestered face, thy form and hue!
Bewildering sounds, such as Spring wakens to,   5
   Shook in its folds; and through my heart its power
   Sped trackless as the immemorable hour
When birth's dark portal groaned and all was new.

But a veiled woman followed, and she caught
   The banner round its staff, to furl and cling, —   10
   Then plucked a feather from the bearer's wing,

And held it to his lips that stirred it not,
   And said to me, "Behold, there is no breath:
   I and this Love are one, and I am Death."
(1870)

Sonnets XLIX, L, LI, LII. Willowwood

I.

I sat with Love upon a woodside well,
   Leaning across the water, I and he;
   Nor ever did he speak nor looked at me,
But touched his lute wherein was audible
The certain secret thing he had to tell: 5
   Only our mirrored eyes met silently
   In the low wave; and that sound came to be
The passionate voice I knew; and my tears fell.

And at their fall, his eyes beneath grew hers;
And with his foot and with his wing-feathers   10
   He swept the spring that watered my heart's drouth.
Then the dark ripples spread to waving hair,
And as I stooped, her own lips rising there
   Bubbled with brimming kisses at my mouth.
(1870)

II.

And now Love sang: but his was such a song,
   So meshed with half-remembrance hard to free,
   As souls disused in death's sterility
May sing when the new birthday tarries long.
And I was made aware of a dumb throng   5
   That stood aloof, one form by every tree,
   All mournful forms, for each was I or she,
The shades of those our days that had no tongue.

They looked on us, and knew us and were known;
   While fast together, alive from the abyss,   10
   Clung the soul-wrung implacable close kiss;
And pity of self through all made broken moan
Which said, "For once, for once, for once alone!"
   And still Love sang, and what he sang was this: —
(1870)

III.

"O ye, all ye that walk in Willowwood,
   That walk with hollow faces burning white;
What fathom-depth of soul-struck widowhood,
   What long, what longer hours, one lifelong night,
Ere ye again, who so in vain have wooed   5
   Your last hope lost, who so in vain invite
Your lips to that their unforgotten food,
   Ere ye, ere ye again shall see the light!

Alas! the bitter banks in Willowwood,
   With tear-spurge wan, with blood-wort burning red: 10
Alas! if ever such a pillow could
   Steep deep the soul in sleep till she were dead, —
Better all life forget her than this thing,
That Willowwood should hold her wandering!"
(1870)

IV.

So sang he: and as meeting rose and rose
   Together cling through the wind's wellaway
   Nor change at once, yet near the end of day
The leaves drop loosened where the heart-stain glows, —
So when the song died did the kiss unclose;   5
   And her face fell back drowned, and was as grey
   As its grey eyes; and if it ever may
Meet mine again I know not if Love knows.

Only I know that I leaned low and drank
A long draught from the water where she sank,   10
   Her breath and all her tears and all her soul:
And as I leaned, I know I felt Love's face
Pressed on my neck with moan of pity and grace,
   Till both our heads were in his aureole.
(1870)

Sonnet LIII. Without Her

What of her glass without her? The blank grey
   There where the pool is blind of the moon's face.
   Her dress without her? The tossed empty space
Of cloud-rack whence the moon has passed away.
Her paths without her? Day's appointed sway   5

Usurped by desolate night. Her pillowed place
   Without her? Tears, ah me! for love's good grace,
And cold forgetfulness of night or day.

What of the heart without her? Nay, poor heart,
   Of thee what word remains ere speech be still?   10
   A wayfarer by barren ways and chill,
Steep ways and weary, without her thou art,
Where the long cloud, the long wood's counterpart,
   Sheds doubled darkness up the labouring hill.

Sonnet LIV. Love's Fatality

Sweet Love, — but oh! most dread Desire of Love
   Life-thwarted. Linked in gyves I saw them stand,
   Love shackled with Vain-longing, hand to hand:
And one was eyed as the blue vault above:
But hope tempestuous like a fire-cloud hove   5
   I' the other's gaze, even as in his whose wand
   Vainly all night with spell-wrought power has spann'd
The unyielding caves of some deep treasure-trove.

Also his lips, two writhen flakes of flame,
   Made moan: "Alas O Love, thus leashed with me!   10
   Wing-footed thou, wing-shouldered, once born free:
And I, thy cowering self, in chains grown tame, —
Bound to thy body and soul, named with thy name, —
   Life's iron heart, even Love's Fatality."

Sonnet LV. Stillborn Love

The hour which might have been yet might not be,
   Which man's and woman's heart conceived and bore
   Yet whereof life was barren, — on what shore
Bides it the breaking of Time's weary sea?
Bondchild of all consummate joys set free,   5
   It somewhere sighs and serves, and mute before
   The house of Love, hears through the echoing door
His hours elect in choral consonancy.

But lo! what wedded souls now hand in hand
Together tread at last the immortal strand   10

With eyes where burning memory lights love home?
Lo! how the little outcast hour has turned
And leaped to them and in their faces yearned: —
   "I am your child: O parents, ye have come!"
(1870)

Sonnets LVI, LVII, LVIII. True Woman

I. Herself
To be a sweetness more desired than Spring;
  A bodily beauty more acceptable
  Than the wild rose-tree's arch that crowns the fell;
To be an essence more environing
Than wine's drained juice; a music ravishing   5
  More than the passionate pulse of Philomel; —
  To be all this 'neath one soft bosom's swell
That is the flower of life: — how strange a thing!

How strange a thing to be what Man can know
  But as a sacred secret! Heaven's own screen   10
Hides her soul's purest depth and loveliest glow;
  Closely withheld, as all things most unseen, —
  The wave-bowered pearl, — the heart-shaped seal of green
That flecks the snowdrop underneath the snow.

II. Her Love
She loves him; for her infinite soul is Love,
  And he her lodestar. Passion in her is
  A glass facing his fire, where the bright bliss
Is mirrored, and the heat returned. Yet move
That glass, a stranger's amorous flame to prove,   5
  And it shall turn, by instant contraries,
  Ice to the moon; while her pure fire to his
For whom it burns, clings close i' the heart's alcove.

Lo! they are one. With wifely breast to breast
  And circling arms, she welcomes all command
  Of love, — her soul to answering ardours fann'd: 10
Yet as morn springs or twilight sinks to rest,
Ah! who shall say she deems not loveliest
  The hour of sisterly sweet hand-in-hand?

III. Her Heaven
If to grow old in Heaven is to grow young,
  (As the Seer saw and said,) then blest were he

With youth for evermore, whose heaven should be
True Woman, she whom these weak notes have sung.
Here and hereafter, — choir-strains of her tongue, —
    Sky-spaces of her eyes, — sweet signs that flee
    About her soul's immediate sanctuary, —
Were Paradise all uttermost worlds among.

The sunrise blooms and withers on the hill
    Like any hillflower; and the noblest troth
    Dies here to dust. Yet shall Heaven's promise clothe
Even yet those lovers who have cherished still
    This test for love: — in every kiss sealed fast
    To feel the first kiss and forbode the last.

Sonnet LIX. Love's Last Gift

Love to his singer held a glistening leaf,
    And said: "The rose-tree and the apple-tree
    Have fruits to vaunt or flowers to lure the bee;
And golden shafts are in the feathered sheaf
Of the great harvest-marshal, the year's chief,
    Victorious Summer; aye, and 'neath warm sea
    Strange secret grasses lurk inviolably
Between the filtering channels of sunk reef.

All are my blooms; and all sweet blooms of love
    To thee I gave while Spring and Summer sang;
    But Autumn stops to listen, with some pang
From those worse things the wind is moaning of.
    Only this laurel dreads no winter days:
    Take my last gift; thy heart hath sung my praise."

PART II. CHANGE AND FATE

Sonnet LX. Transfigured Life

As growth of form or momentary glance
    In a child's features will recall to mind
    The father's with the mother's face combin'd, —
Sweet interchange that memories still enhance:
And yet, as childhood's years and youth's advance,
    The gradual mouldings leave one stamp behind,

Till in the blended likeness now we find
A separate man's or woman's countenance: —

So in the Song, the singer's Joy and Pain,
   Its very parents, evermore expand   10
To bid the passion's fullgrown birth remain,
     By Art's transfiguring essence subtly spann'd;
     And from that song-cloud shaped as a man's hand
There comes the sound as of abundant rain.

Sonnet LXI. The Song-Throe

By thine own tears thy song must tears beget,
   O Singer! Magic mirror thou hast none
   Except thy manifest heart; and save thine own
Anguish or ardour, else no amulet.
Cisterned in Pride, verse is the feathery jet   5
   Of soulless air-flung fountains; nay, more dry
   Than the Dead Sea for throats that thirst and sigh,
That song o'er which no singer's lids grew wet.

The Song-god — He the Sun-god — is no slave
   Of thine; thy Hunter he, who for thy soul   10
   Fledges his shaft: to no august control
Of thy skilled hand his quivered store he gave:
   But if thy lips' loud cry leap to his smart,
   The inspir'd recoil shall pierce thy brother's heart.

Sonnet LXII. The Soul's Sphere

Some prisoned moon in steep cloud-fastnesses, —
   Throned queen and thralled; some dying sun whose pyre
   Blazed with momentous memorable fire; —
Who hath not yearned and fed his heart with these?
Who, sleepless, hath not anguished to appease   5
   Tragical shadow's realm of sound and sight
   Conjectured in the lamentable night? . . .
Lo! the soul's sphere of infinite images!

What sense shall count them? Whether it forecast
   The rose-winged hours that flutter in the van   10

Of Love's unquestioning unrevealéd span, —
Visions of golden futures: or that last
Wild pageant of the accumulated past
    That clangs and flashes for a drowning man.

Sonnet LXIII. Inclusiveness

The changing guests, each in a different mood,
    Sit at the roadside table and arise:
    And every life among them in likewise
Is a soul's board set daily with new food.
What man has bent o'er his son's sleep, to brood   5
    How that face shall watch his when cold it lies? —
    Or thought, as his own mother kissed his eyes,
Of what her kiss was when his father wooed?

May not this ancient room thou sit'st in dwell
    In separate living souls for joy or pain?   10
    Nay, all its corners may be painted plain
Where Heaven shows pictures of some life spent well;
    And may be stamped, a memory all in vain,
Upon the sight of lidless eyes in Hell.
(1870)

Sonnet LXIV. Ardour and Memory

The cuckoo-throb, the heartbeat of the Spring;
    The rosebud's blush that leaves it as it grows
    Into the full-eyed fair unblushing rose;
The summer clouds that visit every wing
With fires of sunrise and of sunsetting;   5
    The furtive flickering streams to light re-born
    'Mid airs new-fledged and valorous lusts of morn,
While all the daughters of the daybreak sing: —

These ardour loves, and memory: and when flown
    All joys, and through dark forest-boughs in flight   10
    The wind swoops onward brandishing the light,
Even yet the rose-tree's verdure left alone
Will flush all ruddy though the rose be gone;
    With ditties and with dirges infinite.

Sonnet LXV. Known in Vain

As two whose love, first foolish, widening scope,
   Knows suddenly, to music high and soft,
   The Holy of holies; who because they scoff'd
Are now amazed with shame, nor dare to cope
With the whole truth aloud, lest heaven should ope;   5
   Yet, at their meetings, laugh not as they laugh'd
   In speech; nor speak, at length; but sitting oft
Together, within hopeless sight of hope
For hours are silent: — So it happeneth
   When Work and Will awake too late, to gaze   10
After their life sailed by, and hold their breath.
   Ah! who shall dare to search through what sad maze
   Thenceforth their incommunicable ways
Follow the desultory feet of Death?

Sonnet LXVI. The Heart of the Night

From child to youth; from youth to arduous man;
   From lethargy to fever of the heart;
   From faithful life to dream-dowered days apart;
From trust to doubt; from doubt to brink of ban; —
Thus much of change in one swift cycle ran   5
   Till now. Alas, the soul! — how soon must she
   Accept her primal immortality, —
The flesh resume its dust whence it began?

O Lord of work and peace! O Lord of life!
   O Lord, the awful Lord of will! though late,   10
   Even yet renew this soul with duteous breath:
That when the peace is garnered in from strife,
   The work retrieved, the will regenerate,
   This soul may see thy face, O Lord of death!

Sonnet LXVII. The Landmark

Was that the landmark? What, — the foolish well
   Whose wave, low down, I did not stoop to drink,
   But sat and flung the pebbles from its brink
In sport to send its imaged skies pell-mell,

(And mine own image, had I noted well!) —   5
   Was that my point of turning? — I had thought
   The stations of my course should rise unsought,
As altar-stone or ensigned citadel.

But lo! the path is missed, I must go back,
   And thirst to drink when next I reach the spring   10
Which once I stained, which since may have grown black.
   Yet though no light be left nor bird now sing
   As here I turn, I'll thank God, hastening,
That the same goal is still on the same track.
(1870)

Sonnet LXVIII. A Dark Day

The gloom that breathes upon me with these airs
   Is like the drops which strike the traveller's brow
   Who knows not, darkling, if they bring him now
Fresh storm, or be old rain the covert bears.
Ah! bodes this hour some harvest of new tares,   5
   Or hath but memory of the day whose plough
   Sowed hunger once, — the night at length when thou,
O prayer found vain, didst fall from out my prayers?

How prickly were the growths which yet how smooth,
   Along the hedgerows of this journey shed,   10
Lie by Time's grace till night and sleep may soothe!
   Even as the thistledown from pathsides dead
Gleaned by a girl in autumns of her youth,
   Which one new year makes soft her marriage-bed.
(1870)

Sonnet LXIX. Autumn Idleness

This sunlight shames November where he grieves
   In dead red leaves, and will not let him shun
   The day, though bough with bough be over-run.
But with a blessing every glade receives
High salutation; while from hillock-eaves   5
   The deer gaze calling, dappled white and dun,

As if, being foresters of old, the sun
Had marked them with the shade of forest-leaves.

Here dawn to-day unveiled her magic glass;
   Here noon now gives the thirst and takes the dew;   10
Till eve bring rest when other good things pass.
   And here the lost hours the lost hours renew
While I still lead my shadow o'er the grass,
   Nor know, for longing, that which I should do.
(1870)

Sonnet LXX. The Hill Summit

This feast-day of the sun, his altar there
   In the broad west has blazed for vesper-song;
   And I have loitered in the vale too long
And gaze now a belated worshipper.
Yet may I not forget that I was 'ware,   5
   So journeying, of his face at intervals
   Transfigured where the fringed horizon falls, —
A fiery bush with coruscating hair.

And now that I have climbed and won this height,
   I must tread downward through the sloping shade   10
And travel the bewildered tracks till night.
   Yet for this hour I still may here be stayed
   And see the gold air and the silver fade
And the last bird fly into the last light.
(1870)

Sonnets LXXI, LXXII, LXXIII. The Choice

I.
Eat thou and drink; to-morrow thou shalt die.
   Surely the earth, that's wise being very old,
   Needs not our help. Then loose me, love, and hold
Thy sultry hair up from my face; that I
May pour for thee this golden wine, brim-high,   5
   Till round the glass thy fingers glow like gold.
   We'll drown all hours: thy song, while hours are toll'd,
Shall leap, as fountains veil the changing sky.

Now kiss, and think that there are really those,
  My own high-bosomed beauty, who increase
    Vain gold, vain lore, and yet might choose our way!
    Through many years they toil; then on a day
  They die not, — for their life was death, — but cease;
And round their narrow lips the mould falls close.
(1870)

II.
Watch thou and fear; to-morrow thou shalt die.
  Or art thou sure thou shalt have time for death?
  Is not the day which God's word promiseth
To come man knows not when? In yonder sky,
Now while we speak, the sun speeds forth: can I
  Or thou assure him of his goal? God's breath
  Even at this moment haply quickeneth
The air to a flame; till spirits, always nigh
Though screened and hid, shall walk the daylight here.
  And dost thou prate of all that man shall do?
    Canst thou, who hast but plagues, presume to be
    Glad in his gladness that comes after thee?
  Will his strength slay thy worm in Hell? Go to:
Cover thy countenance, and watch, and fear.
(1870)

III.
Think thou and act; to-morrow thou shalt die.
  Outstretched in the sun's warmth upon the shore,
  Thou say'st: "Man's measured path is all gone o'er:
Up all his years, steeply, with strain and sigh,
Man clomb until he touched the truth; and I,
  Even I, am he whom it was destined for."
  How should this be? Art thou then so much more
Than they who sowed, that thou shouldst reap thereby?

Nay, come up hither. From this wave-washed mound
  Unto the furthest flood-brim look with me;
Then reach on with thy thought till it be drown'd.
  Miles and miles distant though the last line be,
And though thy soul sail leagues and leagues beyond, —
  Still, leagues beyond those leagues, there is more sea.
(1870)

Sonnets LXXIV, LXXV, LXXVI. Old and New Art

I. St. Luke the Painter
Give honour unto Luke Evangelist;
   For he it was (the aged legends say)
   Who first taught Art to fold her hands and pray.
Scarcely at once she dared to rend the mist
Of devious symbols: but soon having wist   5
   How sky-breadth and field-silence and this day
   Are symbols also in some deeper way,
She looked through these to God and was God's priest.

And if, past noon, her toil began to irk,
   And she sought talismans, and turned in vain   10
      To soulless self-reflections of man's skill, —
      Yet now, in this the twilight, she might still
   Kneel in the latter grass to pray again,
Ere the night cometh and she may not work.
(1870)

II. Not as These
"I am not as these are," the poet saith
   In youth's pride, and the painter, among men
   At bay, where never pencil comes nor pen,
And shut about with his own frozen breath.
To others, for whom only rhyme wins faith   5
   As poets, — only paint as painters, — then
   He turns in the cold silence; and again
Shrinking, "I am not as these are," he saith.

And say that this is so, what follows it?
   For were thine eyes set backwards in thine head,   10
      Such words were well; but they see on, and far.
Unto the lights of the great Past, new-lit
   Fair for the Future's track, look thou instead, —
      Say thou instead, "I am not as these are."

III. The Husbandman
Though God, as one that is an householder,
   Called these to labour in his vineyard first,
   Before the husk of darkness was well burst
Bidding them grope their way out and bestir,
(Who, questioned of their wages, answered, "Sir,   5
   Unto each man a penny":) though the worst
   Burthen of heat was theirs and the dry thirst:

Though God hath since found none such as these were
To do their work like them: — Because of this
   Stand not ye idle in the market-place. 10
      Which of ye knoweth he is not that last
Who may be first by faith and will? — yea, his
   The hand which after the appointed days
      And hours shall give a Future to their Past?

Sonnet LXXVII. Soul's Beauty

Under the arch of Life, where love and death,
   Terror and mystery, guard her shrine, I saw
   Beauty enthroned; and though her gaze struck awe,
I drew it in as simply as my breath.
Hers are the eyes which, over and beneath, 5
   The sky and sea bend on thee, — which can draw,
   By sea or sky or woman, to one law,
The allotted bondman of her palm and wreath.

This is that Lady Beauty, in whose praise
   Thy voice and hand shake still, — long known to thee 10
      By flying hair and fluttering hem, — the beat
      Following her daily of thy heart and feet,
   How passionately and irretrievably,
In what fond flight, how many ways and days!
(1870)

Sonnet LXXVIII. Body's Beauty

Of Adam's first wife, Lilith, it is told
   (The witch he loved before the gift of Eve,)
   That, ere the snake's, her sweet tongue could deceive,
And her enchanted hair was the first gold.
And still she sits, young while the earth is old, 5
   And, subtly of herself contemplative,
   Draws men to watch the bright web she can weave,
Till heart and body and life are in its hold.

The rose and poppy are her flowers; for where
   Is he not found, O Lilith, whom shed scent 10
And soft-shed kisses and soft sleep shall snare?

Lo! as that youth's eyes burned at thine, so went
Thy spell through him, and left his straight neck bent
And round his heart one strangling golden hair.
(1870)

Sonnet LXXIX. The Monochord

Is it this sky's vast vault or ocean's sound
  That is Life's self and draws my life from me,
  And by instinct ineffable decree
Holds my breath quailing on the bitter bound?
Nay, is it Life or Death, thus thunder-crown'd,   5
  That 'mid the tide of all emergency
  Now notes my separate wave, and to what sea
Its difficult eddies labour in the ground?

Oh! what is this that knows the road I came,
The flame turned cloud, the cloud returned to flame,   10
  The lifted shifted steeps and all the way? —
That draws round me at last this wind-warm space,
And in regenerate rapture turns my face
  Upon the devious coverts of dismay?
(1870)

Sonnet LXXX. From Dawn to Noon

As the child knows not if his mother's face
  Be fair; nor of his elders yet can deem
  What each most is; but as of hill or stream
At dawn, all glimmering life surrounds his place:
Who yet, tow'rd noon of his half-weary race,   5
  Pausing awhile beneath the high sun-beam
  And gazing steadily back, — as through a dream,
In things long past new features now can trace: —

Even so the thought that is at length fullgrown
  Turns back to note the sun-smit paths, all grey   10
And marvellous once, where first it walked alone;
  And haply doubts, amid the unblenching day,
  Which most or least impelled its onward way, —
Those unknown things or these things overknown.

Sonnet LXXXI. Memorial Thresholds

What place so strange, — though unrevealèd snow
  With unimaginable fires arise
  At the earth's end, — what passion of surprise
Like frost-bound fire-girt scenes of long ago?
Lo! this is none but I this hour; and lo!   5
  This is the very place which to mine eyes
  Those mortal hours in vain immortalize,
'Mid hurrying crowds, with what alone I know.

City, of thine a single simple door,
  By some new Power reduplicate, must be   10
  Even yet my life-porch in eternity,
Even with one presence filled, as once of yore:
Or mocking winds whirl round a chaff-strown floor
  Thee and thy years and these my words and me.

Sonnet LXXXII. Hoarded Joy

I said: "Nay, pluck not, — let the first fruit be:
  Even as thou sayest, it is sweet and red,
  But let it ripen still. The tree's bent head
Sees in the stream its own fecundity
And bides the day of fulness. Shall not we   5
  At the sun's hour that day possess the shade,
  And claim our fruit before its ripeness fade,
And eat it from the branch and praise the tree?"

I say: "Alas! our fruit hath wooed the sun
  Too long, — 'tis fallen and floats adown the stream.   10
Lo, the last clusters! Pluck them every one,
  And let us sup with summer; ere the gleam
Of autumn set the year's pent sorrow free,
And the woods wail like echoes from the sea."
(1870)

Sonnet LXXXIII. Barren Spring

Once more the changed year's turning wheel returns:
  And as a girl sails balanced in the wind,
  And now before and now again behind

Stoops as it swoops, with cheek that laughs and burns, —
So Spring comes merry towards me here, but earns   5
    No answering smile from me, whose life is twin'd
    With the dead boughs that winter still must bind,
And whom to-day the Spring no more concerns.

Behold, this crocus is a withering flame;
    This snowdrop, snow; this apple-blossom's part   10
    To breed the fruit that breeds the serpent's art.
Nay, for these Spring-flowers, turn thy face from them,
Nor stay till on the year's last lily-stem
    The white cup shrivels round the golden heart.
(1870)

Sonnet LXXXIV. Farewell to the Glen

Sweet stream-fed glen, why say "farewell" to thee
    Who far'st so well and find'st for ever smooth
    The brow of Time where man may read no ruth?
Nay, do thou rather say "farewell" to me,
Who now fare forth in bitterer fantasy   5
    Than erst was mine where other shade might soothe
    By other streams, what while in fragrant youth
The bliss of being sad made melancholy.

And yet, farewell! For better shalt thou fare
    When children bathe sweet faces in thy flow   10
And happy lovers blend sweet shadows there
    In hours to come, than when an hour ago
Thine echoes had but one man's sighs to bear
    And thy trees whispered what he feared to know.
(1870)

Sonnet LXXXV. Vain Virtues

What is the sorriest thing that enters Hell?
    None of the sins, — but this and that fair deed
    Which a soul's sin at length could supersede.
These yet are virgins, whom death's timely knell
Might once have sainted; whom the fiends compel   5
    Together now, in snake-bound shuddering sheaves

Of anguish, while the pit's pollution leaves
Their refuse maidenhood abominable.

Night sucks them down, the tribute of the pit,
    Whose names, half entered in the book of Life,   10
        Were God's desire at noon. And as their hair
And eyes sink last, the Torturer deigns no whit
    To gaze, but, yearning, waits his destined wife,
        The Sin still blithe on earth that sent them there.
(1870)

Sonnet LXXXVI. Lost Days

The lost days of my life until to-day,
    What were they, could I see them on the street
    Lie as they fell? Would they be ears of wheat
Sown once for food but trodden into clay?
Or golden coins squandered and still to pay?   5
    Or drops of blood dabbling the guilty feet?
    Or such spilt water as in dreams must cheat
The undying throats of Hell, athirst alway?

I do not see them here; but after death
    God knows I know the faces I shall see,   10
Each one a murdered self, with low last breath.
    "I am thyself, — what hast thou done to me?"
"And I — and I — thyself," (lo! each one saith,)
    "And thou thyself to all eternity!"
(1870)

Sonnet LXXXVII. Death's Songsters

When first that horse, within whose populous womb
    The birth was death, o'ershadowed Troy with fate,
    Her elders, dubious of its Grecian freight,
Brought Helen there to sing the songs of home;
She whispered, "Friends, I am alone; come, come!"   5
    Then, crouched within, Ulysses waxed afraid,
    And on his comrades' quivering mouths he laid
His hands, and held them till the voice was dumb.

The same was he who, lashed to his own mast,
    There where the sea-flowers screen the charnel-caves,   10

Beside the sirens' singing island pass'd,
    Till sweetness failed along the inveterate waves. . . .
Say, soul, — are songs of Death no heaven to thee,
Nor shames her lip the cheek of Victory?
(1870)

Sonnet LXXXVIII. Hero's Lamp*

That lamp thou fill'st in Eros' name to-night,
    O Hero, shall the Sestian augurs take
    To-morrow, and for drowned Leander's sake
To Anteros its fireless lip shall plight.
Aye, waft the unspoken vow: yet dawn's first light   5
    On ebbing storm and life twice ebb'd must break;
    While 'neath no sunrise, by the Avernian Lake,
Lo where Love walks, Death's pallid neophyte.

That lamp within Anteros' shadowy shrine
    Shall stand unlit (for so the gods decree)   10
    Till some one man the happy issue see
Of a life's love, and bid its flame to shine:
Which still may rest unfir'd; for, theirs or thine,
    O brother, what brought love to them or thee?

Sonnet LXXXIX. The Trees of the Garden

Ye who have passed Death's haggard hills; and ye
    Whom trees that knew your sires shall cease to know
    And still stand silent: — is it all a show, —
A wisp that laughs upon the wall? — decree
Of some inexorable supremacy   5
    Which ever, as man strains his blind surmise
    From depth to ominous depth, looks past his eyes,
Sphinx-faced with unabashèd augury?

Nay, rather question the Earth's self. Invoke
    The storm-felled forest-trees moss-grown to-day   10
    Whose roots are hillocks where the children play;

*After the deaths of Leander and of Hero, the signal-lamp was dedicated to Anteros, with the edict that no man should light it unless his love had proved fortunate.

Or ask the silver sapling 'neath what yoke
    Those stars, his spray-crown's clustering gems, shall wage
    Their journey still when his boughs shrink with age.

Sonnet XC. "Retro Me, Sathana!"

Get thee behind me. Even as, heavy-curled,
    Stooping against the wind, a charioteer
    Is snatched from out his chariot by the hair,
So shall Time be; and as the void car, hurled
Abroad by reinless steeds, even so the world: 5
    Yea, even as chariot-dust upon the air,
    It shall be sought and not found anywhere.
Get thee behind me, Satan. Oft unfurled,
Thy perilous wings can beat and break like lath
    Much mightiness of men to win thee praise.   10
    Leave these weak feet to tread in narrow ways.
Thou still, upon the broad vine-sheltered path,
Mayst wait the turning of the phials of wrath
    For certain years, for certain months and days.
(1870)

Sonnet XCI. Lost on Both Sides

As when two men have loved a woman well,
    Each hating each, through Love's and Death's deceit;
    Since not for either this stark marriage-sheet
And the long pauses of this wedding-bell;
Yet o'er her grave the night and day dispel   5
    At last their feud forlorn, with cold and heat;
    Nor other than dear friends to death may fleet
The two lives left that most of her can tell: —

So separate hopes, which in a soul had wooed
    The one same Peace, strove with each other long,   10
      And Peace before their faces perished since:
So through that soul, in restless brotherhood,
    They roam together now, and wind among
      Its bye-streets, knocking at the dusty inns.
(1870)

Sonnets XCII, XCIII. The Sun's Shame

I.

Beholding youth and hope in mockery caught
   From life; and mocking pulses that remain
   When the soul's death of bodily death is fain;
Honour unknown, and honour known unsought;
And penury's sedulous self-torturing thought   5
   On gold, whose master therewith buys his bane;
   And longed-for woman longing all in vain
For lonely man with love's desire distraught;
And wealth, and strength, and power, and pleasantness,
   Given unto bodies of whose souls men say,   10
   None poor and weak, slavish and foul, as they: —
Beholding these things, I behold no less
The blushing morn and blushing eve confess
   The shame that loads the intolerable day.
(1870)

II.

As some true chief of men, bowed down with stress
   Of life's disastrous eld, on blossoming youth
   May gaze, and murmur with self-pity and ruth, —
"Might I thy fruitless treasure but possess,
Such blessing of mine all coming years should bless"; —   5
   Then sends one sigh forth to the unknown goal,
   And bitterly feels breathe against his soul
The hour swift-winged of nearer nothingness: —

Even so the World's grey Soul to the green World
   Perchance one hour must cry: "Woe's me, for whom   10
   Inveteracy of ill portends the doom, —
Whose heart's old fire in shadow of shame is furl'd:
   While thou even as of yore art journeying,
   All soulless now, yet merry with the Spring!"

Sonnet XCIV. Michelangelo's Kiss

Great Michelangelo, with age grown bleak
   And uttermost labours, having once o'ersaid
   All grievous memories on his long life shed,
This worst regret to one true heart could speak: —
That when, with sorrowing love and reverence meek,   5

He stooped o'er sweet Colonna's dying bed,
  His Muse and dominant Lady, spirit-wed, —
Her hand he kissed, but not her brow or cheek.

O Buonarruoti, — good at Art's fire-wheels
  To urge her chariot! — even thus the Soul,   10
  Touching at length some sorely-chastened goal,
Earns oftenest but a little: her appeals
  Were deep and mute, — lowly her claim. Let be:
  What holds for her Death's garner? And for thee?

Sonnet XCV. The Vase of Life

Around the vase of Life at your slow pace
  He has not crept, but turned it with his hands,
  And all its sides already understands.
There, girt, one breathes alert for some great race;
Whose road runs far by sands and fruitful space;   5
  Who laughs, yet through the jolly throng has pass'd;
  Who weeps, nor stays for weeping; who at last,
A youth, stands somewhere crowned, with silent face.

And he has filled this vase with wine for blood,
  With blood for tears, with spice for burning vow,   10
    With watered flowers for buried love most fit;
And would have cast it shattered to the flood,
  Yet in Fate's name has kept it whole; which now
    Stands empty till his ashes fall in it.
(1870)

Sonnet XCVI. Life the Beloved

As thy friend's face, with shadow of soul o'erspread,
  Somewhile unto thy sight perchance hath been
  Ghastly and strange, yet never so is seen
In thought, but to all fortunate favour wed;
As thy love's death-bound features never dead   5
  To memory's glass return, but contravene
  Frail fugitive days, and alway keep, I ween,
Than all new life a livelier lovelihead: —

So Life herself, thy spirit's friend and love,
  Even still as Spring's authentic harbinger   10

Glows with fresh hours for hope to glorify;
Though pale she lay when in the winter grove
   Her funeral flowers were snow-flakes shed on her
   And the red wings of frost-fire rent the sky.

Sonnet XCVII. A Superscription

Look in my face; my name is Might-have-been;
   I am also called No-more, Too-late, Farewell;
   Unto thine ear I hold the dead-sea shell
Cast up thy Life's foam-fretted feet between;
Unto thine eyes the glass where that is seen   5
   Which had Life's form and Love's, but by my spell
   Is now a shaken shadow intolerable,
Of ultimate things unuttered the frail screen.

Mark me, how still I am! But should there dart
   One moment through thy soul the soft surprise   10
   Of that winged Peace which lulls the breath of sighs, —
Then shalt thou see me smile, and turn apart
Thy visage to mine ambush at thy heart
   Sleepless with cold commemorative eyes.
(1870)

Sonnet XCVIII. He and I

Whence came his feet into my field, and why?
   How is it that he sees it all so drear?
   How do I see his seeing, and how hear
The name his bitter silence knows it by?
This was the little fold of separate sky   5
   Whose pasturing clouds in the soul's atmosphere
   Drew living light from one continual year:
How should he find it lifeless? He, or I?

Lo! this new Self now wanders round my field,
   With plaints for every flower, and for each tree   10
   A moan, the sighing wind's auxiliary:
And o'er sweet waters of my life, that yield
Unto his lips no draught but tears unseal'd,
   Even in my place he weeps. Even I, not he.
(1870)

Sonnets XCIX, C. Newborn Death

I.

To-day Death seems to me an infant child
   Which her worn mother Life upon my knee
   Has set to grow my friend and play with me;
If haply so my heart might be beguil'd
To find no terrors in a face so mild, —   5
   If haply so my weary heart might be
   Unto the newborn milky eyes of thee,
O Death, before resentment reconcil'd.

How long, O Death? And shall thy feet depart
   Still a young child's with mine, or wilt thou stand   10
Fullgrown the helpful daughter of my heart,
   What time with thee indeed I reach the strand
Of the pale wave which knows thee what thou art,
   And drink it in the hollow of thy hand?
(1870)

II.

And thou, O Life, the lady of all bliss,
   With whom, when our first heart beat full and fast,
   I wandered till the haunts of men were pass'd,
And in fair places found all bowers amiss
Till only woods and waves might hear our kiss,   5
   While to the winds all thought of Death we cast: —
   Ah, Life! and must I have from thee at last
No smile to greet me and no babe but this?

Lo! Love, the child once ours; and Song, whose hair
   Blew like a flame and blossomed like a wreath;   10
And Art, whose eyes were worlds by God found fair;
   These o'er the book of Nature mixed their breath
With neck-twined arms, as oft we watched them there:
   And did these die that thou mightst bear me Death?
(1870)

Sonnet CI. The One Hope

When vain desire at last and vain regret
   Go hand in hand to death, and all is vain,
   What shall assuage the unforgotten pain
And teach the unforgetful to forget?

Shall Peace be still a sunk stream long unmet, —   5
    Or may the soul at once in a green plain
    Stoop through the spray of some sweet life-fountain
And cull the dew-drenched flowering amulet?

Ah! when the wan soul in that golden air
    Between the scriptured petals softly blown   10
    Peers breathless for the gift of grace unknown, —
Ah! let none other alien spell soe'er
But only the one Hope's one name be there, —
    Not less nor more, but even that word alone.
(1870)

THE SONGS (1870)

Song I. Love-Lily

Between the hands, between the brows,
    Between the lips of Love-Lily,
A spirit is born whose birth endows
    My blood with fire to burn through me;
Who breathes upon my gazing eyes,   5
    Who laughs and murmurs in mine ear,
At whose least touch my colour flies,
    And whom my life grows faint to hear.

Within the voice, within the heart,
    Within the mind of Love-Lily,   10
A spirit is born who lifts apart
    His tremulous wings and looks at me;
Who on my mouth his finger lays,
    And shows, while whispering lutes confer,
That Eden of Love's watered ways   15
    Whose winds and spirits worship her.

Brows, hands, and lips, heart, mind, and voice,
    Kisses and words of Love-Lily, —
Oh! bid me with your joy rejoice
    Till riotous longing rest in me!   20
Ah! let not hope be still distraught,
    But find in her its gracious goal,
Whose speech Truth knows not from her thought
    Nor Love her body from her soul.

Song II. First Love Remembered

Peace in her chamber, wheresoe'er
   It be, a holy place:
The thought still brings my soul such grace
   As morning meadows wear.

Whether it still be small and light, 5
   A maid's who dreams alone,
As from her orchard-gate the moon
   Its ceiling showed at night:

Or whether, in a shadow dense
   As nuptial hymns invoke, 10
Innocent maidenhood awoke
   To married innocence:

There still the thanks unheard await
   The unconscious gift bequeathed;
For there my soul this hour has breathed 15
   An air inviolate.

Song III. Plighted Promise

In a soft-complexioned sky,
   Fleeting rose and kindling grey,
Have you seen Aurora fly
   At the break of day?
So my maiden, so my plighted may 5
   Blushing cheek and gleaming eye
     Lifts to look my way.

Where the inmost leaf is stirred
   With the heart-beat of the grove,
Have you heard a hidden bird 10
   Cast her note above?
So my lady, so my lovely love,
   Echoing Cupid's prompted word,
     Makes a tune thereof.

Have you seen, at heaven's mid-height, 15
   In the moon-rack's ebb and tide,
Venus leap forth burning white,
   Dian pale and hide?

So my bright breast-jewel, so my bride,
   One sweet night, when fear takes flight,   20
      Shall leap against my side.

Song IV. Sudden Light

  I have been here before,
    But when or how I cannot tell:
  I know the grass beyond the door,
    The sweet keen smell,
The sighing sound, the lights around the shore.   5

  You have been mine before, —
    How long ago I may not know:
  But just when at that swallow's soar
    Your neck turned so,
Some veil did fall, — I knew it all of yore.   10

  Then, now, — perchance again! . . .
    O round mine eyes your tresses shake!
  Shall we not lie as we have lain
    Thus for Love's sake,
And sleep, and wake, yet never break the chain?   15

Song V. A Little While

A little while a little love
  The hour yet bears for thee and me
  Who have not drawn the veil to see
If still our heaven be lit above.
Thou merely, at the day's last sigh,   5
  Hast felt thy soul prolong the tone;
And I have heard the night-wind cry
    And deemed its speech mine own.

A little while a little love
  The scattering autumn hoards for us   10
  Whose bower is not yet ruinous
Nor quite unleaved our songless grove.
Only across the shaken boughs
  We hear the flood-tides seek the sea,
And deep in both our hearts they rouse   15
    One wail for thee and me.

A little while a little love
  May yet be ours who have not said
  The word it makes our eyes afraid
To know that each is thinking of.   20
Not yet the end: be our lips dumb
  In smiles a little season yet:
I'll tell thee, when the end is come,
    How we may best forget.

Song VI. The Song of the Bower

Say, is it day, is it dusk in thy bower,
  Thou whom I long for, who longest for me?
Oh! Be it light, be it night, 'tis Love's hour,
  Love's that is fettered as Love's that is free.
Free Love has leaped to that innermost chamber,   5
  Oh! the last time, and the hundred before:
Fettered Love, motionless, can but remember,
  Yet something that sighs from him passes the door.

Nay, but my heart when it flies to thy bower,
  What does it find there that knows it again?   10
There it must droop like a shower-beaten flower,
  Red at the rent core and dark with the rain.
Ah! yet what shelter is still shed above it, —
  What waters still image its leaves torn apart?
Thy soul is the shade that clings round it to love it,   15
  And tears are its mirror deep down in thy heart.

What were my prize, could I enter thy bower,
  This day, to-morrow, at eve or at morn?
Large lovely arms and a neck like a tower,
  Bosom then heaving that now lies forlorn.   20
Kindled with love-breath, (the sun's kiss is colder!)
  Thy sweetness all near me, so distant to-day;
My hand round thy neck and thy hand on my shoulder,
  My mouth to thy mouth as the world melts away.

What is it keeps me afar from thy bower, —   25
  My spirit, my body, so fain to be there?
Waters engulfing or fires that devour? —
  Earth heaped against me or death in the air?
Nay, but in day-dreams, for terror, for pity,
  The trees wave their heads with an omen to tell;   30

Nay, but in night-dreams, throughout the dark city,
    The hours, clashed together, lose count in the bell.

Shall I not one day remember thy bower,
    One day when all days are one day to me? —
Thinking, "I stirred not, and yet had the power," —
    Yearning, "Ah God, if again it might be!"
Peace, peace! such a small lamp illumes, on this highway,
    So dimly so few steps in front of my feet, —
Yet shows me that her way is parted from my way. . . .
    Out of sight, beyond light, at what goal may we meet?

35

40

Song VII. Penumbra

I did not look upon her eyes,
(Though scarcely seen, with no surprise,
'Mid many eyes a single look,)
Because they should not gaze rebuke,
Thenceforth, from stars in sky and brook.

5

I did not take her by the hand,
(Though little was to understand
From touch of hand all friends might take,)
Because it should not prove a flake
Burnt in my palm to boil and ache.

10

I did not listen to her voice,
(Though none had noted, where at choice
All might rejoice in listening,)
Because no such a thing should cling
In the wood's moan at evening.

15

I did not cross her shadow once,
(Though from the hollow west the sun's
Last shadow runs along so far,)
Because in June it should not bar
My ways, at noon when fevers are.

20

They told me she was sad that day,
(Though wherefore tell what love's soothsay,
Sooner than they, did register?)
And my heart leapt and wept to her,
And yet I did not speak nor stir.

25

So shall the tongues of the sea's foam
(Though many voices therewith come
From drowned hope's home to cry to me,)
Bewail one hour the more, when sea
And wind are one with memory. 30

Song VIII. The Woodspurge

The wind flapped loose, the wind was still,
Shaken out dead from tree and hill:
I had walked on at the wind's will, —
I sat now, for the wind was still.

Between my knees my forehead was, — 5
My lips, drawn in, said not Alas!
My hair was over in the grass,
My naked ears heard the day pass.

My eyes, wide open, had the run
Of some ten weeds to fix upon; 10
Among those few, out of the sun,
The woodspurge flowered, three cups in one.

From perfect grief there need not be
Wisdom or even memory:
One thing then learnt remains to me, — 15
The woodspurge has a cup of three.

Song IX. The Honeysuckle

I plucked a honeysuckle where
    The hedge on high is quick with thorn,
    And climbing for the prize, was torn,
And fouled my feet in quag-water;
    And by the thorns and by the wind 5
    The blossom that I took was thinn'd,
And yet I found it sweet and fair.

Thence to a richer growth I came,
    Where, nursed in mellow intercourse,
    The honeysuckles sprang by scores, 10

Not harried like my single stem,
   All virgin lamps of scent and dew.
   So from my hand that first I threw,
Yet plucked not any more of them.

Song X. A Young Fir-Wood

These little firs to-day are things
   To clasp into a giant's cap,
   Or fans to suit his lady's lap.
From many winters many springs
   Shall cherish them in strength and sap,   5
   Till they be marked upon the map,
A wood for the wind's wanderings.

All seed is in the sower's hands:
   And what at first was trained to spread
   Its shelter for some single head, —   10
Yea, even such fellowship of wands, —
   May hide the sunset, and the shade
   Of its great multitude be laid
Upon the earth and elder sands.

Song XI. The Sea-Limits

Consider the sea's listless chime:
   Time's self it is, made audible, —
   The murmur of the earth's own shell.
Secret continuance sublime
   Is the sea's end: our sight may pass   5
   No furlong further. Since time was,
This sound hath told the lapse of time.

No quiet, which is death's, — it hath
   The mournfulness of ancient life,
   Enduring always at dull strife.   10
As the world's heart of rest and wrath,
   Its painful pulse is in the sands.
   Last utterly, the whole sky stands,
Grey and not known, along its path.

Listen alone beside the sea,
   Listen alone among the woods;
   Those voices of twin solitudes
Shall have one sound alike to thee:
   Hark where the murmurs of thronged men
   Surge and sink back and surge again, —
Still the one voice of wave and tree.

Gather a shell from the strown beach
   And listen at its lips: they sigh
   The same desire and mystery,
The echo of the whole sea's speech.
   And all mankind is thus at heart
   Not anything but what thou art:
And Earth, Sea, Man, are all in each.

PART THREE

Sonnets for Pictures and Other Sonnets
(1850, 1870, 1881)

For "Our Lady of the Rocks" by Leonardo da Vinci

Mother, is this the darkness of the end,
  The Shadow of Death? and is that outer sea
  Infinite imminent Eternity?
And does the death-pang by man's seed sustain'd
In Time's each instant cause thy face to bend   5
  Its silent prayer upon the Son, while he
  Blesses the dead with his hand silently
To his long day which hours no more offend?

Mother of grace, the pass is difficult,
  Keen as these rocks, and the bewildered souls   10
    Throng it like echoes, blindly shuddering through.
  Thy name, O Lord, each spirit's voice extols,
    Whose peace abides in the dark avenue
Amid the bitterness of things occult.

For a Venetian Pastoral by Giorgione
(In the Louvre)

Water, for anguish of the solstice: — nay,
  But dip the vessel slowly, — nay, but lean
  And hark how at its verge the wave sighs in
Reluctant. Hush! Beyond all depth away
The heat lies silent at the brink of day: 5
  Now the hand trails upon the viol-string
  That sobs, and the brown faces cease to sing,
Sad with the whole of pleasure. Whither stray
Her eyes now, from whose mouth the slim pipes creep
  And leave it pouting, while the shadowed grass   10
    Is cool against her naked side? Let be: —
Say nothing now unto her lest she weep,
  Nor name this ever. Be it as it was, —
    Life touching lips with Immortality.

For an Allegorical Dance of Women by Andrea Mantegna
(In the Louvre)

Scarcely, I think; yet it indeed may be
   The meaning reached him, when this music rang
   Clear through his frame, a sweet possessive pang,
And he beheld these rocks and that ridged sea.
But I believe that, leaning tow'rds them, he   5
   Just felt their hair carried across his face
   As each girl passed him; nor gave ear to trace
How many feet; nor bent assuredly
His eyes from the blind fixedness of thought
   To know the dancers. It is bitter glad   10
     Even unto tears. Its meaning filleth it,
     A secret of the wells of Life: to wit: —
   The heart's each pulse shall keep the sense it had
With all, though the mind's labour run to nought.

For "Ruggiero and Angelica" by Ingres

I.
A remote sky, prolonged to the sea's brim:
   One rock-point standing buffeted alone,
   Vexed at its base with a foul beast unknown,
Hell-birth of geomaunt and teraphim:
A knight, and a winged creature bearing him,   5
   Reared at the rock: a woman fettered there,
   Leaning into the hollow with loose hair
And throat let back and heartsick trail of limb.

The sky is harsh, and the sea shrewd and salt:
   Under his lord the griffin-horse ramps blind   10
     With rigid wings and tail. The spear's lithe stem
   Thrills in the roaring of those jaws: behind,
That evil length of body chafes at fault.
     She doth not hear nor see — she knows of them.

II.
Clench thine eyes now, — 'tis the last instant, girl:
   Draw in thy senses, set thy knees, and take
   One breath for all: thy life is keen awake, —
Thou mayst not swoon. Was that the scattered whirl
Of its foam drenched thee? — or the waves that curl   5

And split, bleak spray wherein thy temples ache?
  Or was it his the champion's blood to flake
Thy flesh? — or thine own blood's anointing, girl?

Now, silence: for the sea's is such a sound
  As irks not silence; and except the sea,
    All now is still. Now the dead thing doth cease
To writhe, and drifts. He turns to her: and she,
Cast from the jaws of Death, remains there, bound,
  Again a woman in her nakedness.

For "The Wine of Circe" by Edward Burne-Jones

Dusk-haired and gold-robed o'er the golden wine
  She stoops, wherein, distilled of death and shame,
  Sink the black drops; while, lit with fragrant flame,
Round her spread board the golden sunflowers shine.
Doth Helios here with Hecaté combine
  (O Circe, thou their votaress?) to proclaim
  For these thy guests all rapture in Love's name,
Till pitiless Night give Day the countersign?

Lords of their hour, they come. And by her knee
  Those cowering beasts, their equals heretofore,
Wait; who with them in new equality
  To-night shall echo back the sea's dull roar
  With a vain wail from passion's tide-strown shore
Where the dishevelled seaweed hates the sea.

Mary's Girlhood
(For a Picture)

I.
This is that blessed Mary, pre-elect
  God's Virgin. Gone is a great while, and she
  Dwelt young in Nazareth of Galilee.
Unto God's will she brought devout respect,
Profound simplicity of intellect,
  And supreme patience. From her mother's knee
  Faithful and hopeful; wise in charity;
Strong in grave peace; in pity circumspect.

So held she through her girlhood; as it were
   An angel-watered lily, that near God   10
      Grows and is quiet. Till, one dawn at home,
She woke in her white bed, and had no fear
   At all, — yet wept till sunshine, and felt awed:
      Because the fulness of the time was come.

II.

These are the symbols. On that cloth of red
   I' the centre is the Tripoint: perfect each,
   Except the second of its points, to teach
That Christ is not yet born. The books — whose head
Is golden Charity, as Paul hath said —   5
   Those virtues are wherein the soul is rich:
   Therefore on them the lily standeth, which

Is Innocence, being interpreted.
The seven-thorn'd briar and the palm seven-leaved
   Are her great sorrow and her great reward.   10
      Until the end be full, the Holy One
Abides without. She soon shall have achieved
   Her perfect purity: yea, God the Lord
      Shall soon vouchsafe His Son to be her Son.

The Passover in the Holy Family
(For a Drawing*)

Here meet together the prefiguring day
   And day prefigured. "Eating, thou shalt stand,
   Feet shod, loins girt, thy road-staff in thine hand,
With blood-stained door and lintel," — did God say
By Moses' mouth in ages passed away.   5
   And now, where this poor household doth comprise
   At Paschal-Feast two kindred families, —
Lo! the slain lamb confronts the Lamb to slay.

The pyre is piled. What agony's crown attained,
   What shadow of Death the Boy's fair brow subdues   10
Who holds that blood wherewith the porch is stained

*The scene is in the house-porch, where Christ holds a bowl of blood from which
Zacharias is sprinkling the posts and lintel. Joseph has brought the lamb and Elizabeth
lights the pyre. The shoes which John fastens and the bitter herbs which Mary is gather-
ing form part of the ritual.

By Zachary the priest? John binds the shoes
He deemed himself not worthy to unloose;
And Mary culls the bitter herbs ordained.

Mary Magdalene at the Door of Simon the Pharisee
(For a Drawing*)

"Why wilt thou cast the roses from thine hair?
  Nay, be thou all a rose, — wreath, lips, and cheek.
  Nay, not this house, — that banquet-house we seek;
See how they kiss and enter; come thou there.
This delicate day of love we two will share   5
  Till at our ear love's whispering night shall speak.
  What, sweet one, — hold'st thou still the foolish freak?
Nay, when I kiss thy feet they'll leave the stair."

"Oh loose me! See'st thou not my Bridegroom's face
  That draws me to Him? For His feet my kiss,   10
    My hair, my tears He craves to-day: — and oh!
What words can tell what other day and place
  Shall see me clasp those blood-stained feet of His?
    He needs me, calls me, loves me: let me go!"

Cassandra
(For a Drawing†)

I.
Rend, rend thine hair, Cassandra: he will go.
  Yea, rend thy garments, wring thine hands, and cry
  From Troy still towered to the unreddened sky.
See, all but she that bore thee mock thy woe: —
He most whom that fair woman arms, with show   5
  Of wrath on her bent brows; for in this place

---

*In the drawing Mary has left a procession of revellers, and is ascending by a sudden impulse the steps of the house where she sees Christ. Her lover has followed her and is trying to turn her back.

† The subject shows Cassandra prophesying among her kindred, as Hector leaves them for his last battle. They are on the platform of a fortress, from which the Trojan troops are marching out. Helen is arming Paris; Priam soothes Hecuba; and Andromache holds the child to her bosom.

This hour thou bad'st all men in Helen's face
The ravished ravishing prize of Death to know.

What eyes, what ears hath sweet Andromache,
  Save for her Hector's form and step; as tear   10
    On tear make salt the warm last kiss he gave?
He goes. Cassandra's words beat heavily
  Like crows above his crest, and at his ear
    Ring hollow in the shield that shall not save.

II.
"O Hector, gone, gone, gone! O Hector, thee
  Two chariots wait, in Troy long bless'd and curs'd;
  And Grecian spear and Phrygian sand athirst
Crave from thy veins the blood of victory.
Lo! long upon our hearth the brand had we,   5
  Lit for the roof-tree's ruin: and to-day
    The ground-stone quits the wall, — the wind hath way, —
And higher and higher the wings of fire are free.

"O Paris, Paris! O thou burning brand,
  Thou beacon of the sea whence Venus rose,   10
Lighting thy race to shipwreck! Even that hand
  Wherewith she took thine apple let her close
  Within thy curls at last, and while Troy glows
Lift thee her trophy to the sea and land."

Venus Verticordia
(For a Picture)

She hath the apple in her hand for thee,
  Yet almost in her heart would hold it back;
  She muses, with her eyes upon the track
Of that which in thy spirit they can see.
Haply, "Behold, he is at peace," saith she;   5
  "Alas! the apple for his lips, — the dart
  That follows its brief sweetness to his heart, —
The wandering of his feet perpetually!"

A little space her glance is still and coy;
  But if she give the fruit that works her spell,   10
Those eyes shall flame as for her Phrygian boy.
  Then shall her bird's strained throat the woe foretell,
  And her far seas moan as a single shell,
And through her dark grove strike the light of Troy.

Pandora
(For a Picture)

What of the end, Pandora? Was it thine,
  The deed that set these fiery pinions free?
  Ah! wherefore did the Olympian consistory
In its own likeness make thee half divine?
Was it that Juno's brow might stand a sign   5
  For ever? and the mien of Pallas be
  A deadly thing? and that all men might see
In Venus' eyes the gaze of Proserpine?

What of the end? These beat their wings at will,
The ill-born things, the good things turned to ill, —   10
  Powers of the impassioned hours prohibited.
Aye, clench the casket now! Whither they go
Thou mayst not dare to think: nor canst thou know
  If Hope still pent there be alive or dead.

On Refusal of Aid between Nations

Not that the earth is changing, O my God!
  Nor that the seasons totter in their walk, —
  Not that the virulent ill of act and talk
Seethes ever as a winepress ever trod, —
Not therefore are we certain that the rod   5
  Weighs in thine hand to smite thy world; though now
  Beneath thine hand so many nations bow,
So many kings: — not therefore, O my God! —

But because Man is parcelled out in men
  To-day; because, for any wrongful blow,   10
    No man not stricken asks, "I would be told
Why thou dost thus"; but his heart whispers then,
  "He is he, I am I." By this we know
    That our earth falls asunder, being old.

On the "Vita Nuova" of Dante

As he that loves oft looks on the dear form
  And guesses how it grew to womanhood,
  And gladly would have watched the beauties bud
And the mild fire of precious life wax warm: —

So I, long bound within the threefold charm
   Of Dante's love sublimed to heavenly mood,
   Had marvelled, touching his Beatitude,
How grew such presence from man's shameful swarm.

At length within this book I found pourtrayed
   Newborn that Paradisal Love of his,
And simple like a child; with whose clear aid
   I understood. To such a child as this,
Christ, charging well his chosen ones, forbade
   Offence: "for lo! of such my kingdom is."

Dantis Tenebrae
(In Memory of My Father)

And did'st thou know indeed, when at the font
   Together with thy name thou gav'st me his,
   That also on thy son must Beatrice
Decline her eyes according to her wont,
Accepting me to be of those that haunt
   The vale of magical dark mysteries
   Where to the hills her poet's foot-track lies
And wisdom's living fountain to his chaunt
Trembles in music? This is that steep land
   Where he that holds his journey stands at gaze
     Tow'rd sunset, when the clouds like a new height
Seem piled to climb. These things I understand:
   For here, where day still soothes my lifted face,
     On thy bowed head, my father, fell the night.

A Match with the Moon

Weary already, weary miles to-night
   I walked for bed: and so, to get some ease,
   I dogged the flying moon with similes.
And like a wisp she doubled on my sight
In ponds; and caught in tree-tops like a kite;
   And in a globe of film all liquorish
   Swam full-faced like a silly silver fish; —
Last like a bubble shot the welkin's height

Where my road turned, and got behind me, and sent
   My wizened shadow craning round at me,
   And jeered, "So, step the measure, — one two three!" —
And if I faced on her, looked innocent.
   But just at parting, halfway down a dell,
   She kissed me for good-night. So you'll not tell.

10

The Holy Family, by Michelangelo
(In the National Gallery*)

Turn not the prophet's page, O Son! He knew
   All that thou hast to suffer, and hath writ.
   Not yet thine hour of knowledge. Infinite
The sorrows that thy manhood's lot must rue
And dire acquaintance of thy grief. That clue
   The spirits of thy mournful ministerings
   Seek through yon scroll in silence. For these things
The angels have desired to look into.

Still before Eden waves the fiery sword, —
   Her Tree of Life unransomed: whose sad Tree
   Of Knowledge yet to growth of Calvary
     Must yield its Tempter, — Hell the earliest dead
Of Earth resign, — and yet, O Son and Lord,
     The Seed o' the woman bruise the serpent's head.

5
10

For Spring, by Sandro Botticelli
(In the Accademia of Florence)

What masque of what old wind-withered New-Year
   Honours this Lady?† Flora, wanton-eyed
   For birth, and with all flowrets prankt and pied:
Aurora, Zephyrus, with mutual cheer
Of clasp and kiss: the Graces circling near,

5

  *In this picture the Virgin Mother is seen withholding from the Child Saviour the prophetic writings in which his sufferings are foretold. Angelic figures beside them examine a scroll.

  †The same lady, here surrounded by the masque of Spring, is evidently the subject of a portrait by Botticelli formerly in the Pourtalès collection in Paris. This portrait is inscribed "Smeralda Bandinelli."

'Neath bower-linked arch of white arms glorified:
And with those feathered feet which hovering glide
O'er Spring's brief bloom, Hermes the harbinger.

Birth-bare, not death-bare yet, the young stems stand,
   This Lady's temple-columns: o'er her head   10
   Love wings his shaft. What mystery here is read
Of homage or of hope? But how command
   Dead Springs to answer? And how question here
   These mummers of that wind-withered New-year?

"Found"
(For a Picture)

"There is a budding morrow in midnight": —
   So sang our Keats, our English nightingale.
   And here, as lamps across the bridge turn pale
In London's smokeless resurrection-light,
Dark breaks to dawn. But o'er the deadly blight   5
   Of love deflowered and sorrow of none avail
   Which makes this man gasp and this woman quail,
Can day from darkness ever again take flight?

Ah! gave not these two hearts their mutual pledge,
Under one mantle sheltered 'neath the hedge   10
   In gloaming courtship? And O God! to-day
He only knows he holds her; — but what part
Can life now take? She cries in her locked heart, —
   "Leave me — I do not know you — go away!"

A Sea-Spell
(For a Picture)

Her lute hangs shadowed in the apple-tree,
   While flashing fingers weave the sweet-strung spell
   Between its chords; and as the wild notes swell,
The sea-bird for those branches leaves the sea.
But to what sound her listening ear stoops she?   5
   What netherworld gulf-whispers doth she hear,

In answering echoes from what planisphere,
Along the wind, along the estuary?

She sinks into her spell: and when full soon
 Her lips move and she soars into her song,   10
 What creatures of the midmost main shall throng
In furrowed surf-clouds to the summoning rune:
 Till he, the fated mariner, hears her cry,
 And up her rock, bare-breasted, comes to die?

Fiammetta
(For a Picture)

Behold Fiammetta, shown in Vision here.
 Gloom-girt 'mid Spring-flushed apple-growth she stands;
 And as she sways the branches with her hands,
Along her arm the sundered bloom falls sheer,
In separate petals shed, each like a tear;   5
 While from the quivering bough the bird expands
 His wings. And lo! thy spirit understands
Life shaken and shower'd and flown, and Death drawn near.

All stirs with change. Her garments beat the air:
 The angel circling round her aureole   10
 Shimmers in flight against the tree's grey bole:
While she, with reassuring eyes most fair,
A presage and a promise stands; as 'twere
 On Death's dark storm the rainbow of the Soul.

The Day-Dream
(For a Picture)

The thronged boughs of the shadowy sycamore
 Still bear young leaflets half the summer through;
 From when the robin 'gainst the unhidden blue
Perched dark, till now, deep in the leafy core,
The embowered throstle's urgent wood-notes soar   5
 Through summer silence. Still the leaves come new;
 Yet never rosy-sheathed as those which drew
Their spiral tongues from spring-buds heretofore.

Within the branching shade of Reverie
Dreams even may spring till autumn; yet none be 10
    Like woman's budding day-dream spirit-fann'd.
Lo! tow'rd deep skies, not deeper than her look,
She dreams; till now on her forgotten book
    Drops the forgotten blossom from her hand.

Astarte Syriaca
(For a Picture)

Mystery: lo! betwixt the sun and moon
    Astarte of the Syrians: Venus Queen
    Ere Aphrodite was. In silver sheen
Her twofold girdle clasps the infinite boon
Of bliss whereof the heaven and earth commune: 5
    And from her neck's inclining flower-stem lean
    Love-freighted lips and absolute eyes that wean
The pulse of hearts to the spheres' dominant tune.

Torch-bearing her sweet ministers compel
    All thrones of light beyond the sky and sea 10
    The witnesses of Beauty's face to be:
That face, of Love's all-penetrative spell
Amulet, talisman, and oracle, —
    Betwixt the sun and moon a mystery.

Proserpina
(Per un Quadro)

Lunghi à la luce che in sù questo muro
    Rifrange appena, un breve istante scorta
    Del rio palazzo alla soprana porta.
Lungi quei fiori d'Enna, O lido oscuro,
Dal frutto tuo fatal che omai m'è duro. 5
    Lungi quel cielo dal tartareo manto
    Che quì mi cuopre: e lungi ahi lungi ahi quanto
Le notti che sarán dai dì che furo.

Lungi da me mi sento; e ognor sognando
    Cerco e ricerco, e resto ascoltatrice; 10
    E qualche cuore a qualche anima dice,

(Di cui mi giunge il suon da quando in quando,
Continuamente insieme sospirando,) —
   "Oimè per te, Proserpina infelice!"

Proserpina
(For a Picture)

Afar away the light that brings cold cheer
   Unto this wall, — one instant and no more
   Admitted at my distant palace-door.
Afar the flowers of Enna from this drear
Dire fruit, which, tasted once, must thrall me here.   5
   Afar those skies from this Tartarean grey
   That chills me: and afar, how far away,
The nights that shall be from the days that were.

Afar from mine own self I seem, and wing
   Strange ways in thought, and listen for a sign: 10
   And still some heart unto some soul doth pine,
(Whose sounds mine inner sense is fain to bring,
Continually together murmuring,) —
   "Woe's me for thee, unhappy Proserpine!"

La Bella Mano
(Per un Quadro)

O bella Mano, che ti lavi e piaci
   In quel medesmo tuo puro elemento
   Donde la Dea dell' amoroso avvento
Nacque, (e dall' onda s'infuocar le faci
Di mille inispegnibili fornaci): —   5
   Come a Venere a te l'oro e l'argento
   Offron gli Amori; e ognun riguarda attento
La bocca che sorride e te che taci.

In dolce modo dove onor t'invii
   Vattene adorna, e porta insiem fra tante   10
   Di Venere e di vergine sembiante;
Umilemente in luoghi onesti e pii
Bianca e soave ognora; infin che sii,
   O Mano, mansueta in man d'amante.

La Bella Mano
(For a Picture)

O lovely hand, that thy sweet self dost lave
  In that thy pure and proper element,
  Whence erst the Lady of Love's high advènt
Was born, and endless fires sprang from the wave: —
Even as her Loves to her their offerings gave,   5
  For thee the jewelled gifts they bear; while each
  Looks to those lips, of music-measured speech
The fount, and of more bliss than man may crave.

In royal wise ring-girt and bracelet-spann'd,
  A flower of Venus' own virginity,   10
Go shine among thy sisterly sweet band;
  In maiden-minded converse delicately
  Evermore white and soft; until thou be,
O hand! heart-handsel'd in a lover's hand.

PART FOUR

Ballads and Lyrics (1881)

Rose Mary

Of her two fights with the Beryl-stone:
Lost the first, but the second won.

Part I.
"Mary mine that art Mary's Rose
Come in to me from the garden-close.
The sun sinks fast with the rising dew,
And we marked not how the faint moon grew;
But the hidden stars are calling you.   5

"Tall Rose Mary, come to my side,
And read the stars if you'd be a bride.
In hours whose need was not your own,
While you were a young maid yet ungrown,
You've read the stars in the Beryl-stone.   10

"Daughter, once more I bid you read;
But now let it be for your own need:
Because to-morrow, at break of day,
To Holy Cross he rides on his way,
Your knight Sir James of Heronhaye.   15

"Ere he wed you, flower of mine,
For a heavy shrift he seeks the shrine.
Now hark to my words and do not fear;
Ill news next I have for your ear;
But be you strong, and our help is here.   20

"On his road, as the rumour's rife,
An ambush waits to take his life.
He needs will go, and will go alone;
Where the peril lurks may not be known;
But in this glass all things are shown."   25

Pale Rose Mary sank to the floor: —
"The night will come if the day is o'er!"

"Nay, heaven takes counsel, star with star,
And help shall reach your heart from afar:
A bride you'll be, as a maid you are."   30

The lady unbound her jewelled zone
And drew from her robe the Beryl-stone.
Shaped it was to a shadowy sphere, —
World of our world, the sun's compeer,
That bears and buries the toiling year.   35

With shuddering light 'twas stirred and strewn
Like the cloud-nest of the wading moon:
Freaked it was as the bubble's ball,
Rainbow-hued through a misty pall
Like the middle light of the waterfall.   40

Shadows dwelt in its teeming girth
Of the known and unknown things of earth;
The cloud above and the wave around, —
The central fire at the sphere's heart bound,
Like doomsday prisoned underground.   45

A thousand years it lay in the sea
With a treasure wrecked from Thessaly;
Deep it lay 'mid the coiled sea-wrack,
But the ocean-spirits found the track:
A soul was lost to win it back.   50

The lady upheld the wondrous thing: —
"Ill fare"(she said) "with a fiend's-fairing:
But Moslem blood poured forth like wine
Can hallow Hell, 'neath the Sacred Sign;
And my lord brought this from Palestine.   55

"Spirits who fear the Blessed Rood
Drove forth the accursed multitude
That heathen worship housed herein, —
Never again such home to win,
Save only by a Christian's sin.   60

"All last night at an altar fair
I burnt strange fires and strove with prayer;
Till the flame paled to the red sunrise,
All rites I then did solemnize;
And the spell lacks nothing but your eyes."   65

Low spake maiden Rose Mary: —
"O mother mine, if I should not see!"

"Nay, daughter, cover your face no more,
But bend love's heart to the hidden lore,
And you shall see now as heretofore."

Paler yet were the pale cheeks grown
As the grey eyes sought the Beryl-stone:
Then over her mother's lap leaned she,
And stretched her thrilled throat passionately,
And sighed from her soul, and said, "I see."

Even as she spoke, they two were 'ware
Of music-notes that fell through the air;
A chiming shower of strange device,
Drop echoing drop, once twice and thrice,
As rain may fall in Paradise.

An instant come, in an instant gone,
No time there was to think thereon.
The mother held the sphere on her knee: —
"Lean this way and speak low to me,
And take no note but of what you see."

"I see a man with a besom grey
That sweeps the flying dust away."
"Ay, that comes first in the mystic sphere;
But now that the way is swept and clear,
Heed well what next you look on there."

"Stretched aloft and adown I see
Two roads that part in waste-country:
The glen lies deep and the ridge stands tall;
What's great below is above seen small,
And the hill-side is the valley-wall."

"Stream-bank, daughter, or moor and moss,
Both roads will take to Holy Cross.
The hills are a weary waste to wage;
But what of the valley-road's presage?
That way must tend his pilgrimage."

"As 'twere the turning leaves of a book,
The road runs past me as I look;
Or it is even as though mine eye
Should watch calm waters filled with sky
While lights and clouds and wings went by."

"In every covert seek a spear;
They'll scarce lie close till he draws near."

"The stream has spread to a river now;
The stiff blue sedge is deep in the slough,
But the banks are bare of shrub or bough."   110

"Is there any roof that near at hand
Might shelter yield to a hidden band?"
"On the further bank I see but one,
And a herdsman now in the sinking sun
Unyokes his team at the threshold-stone."   115

"Keep heedful watch by the water's edge, —
Some boat might lurk 'neath the shadowed sedge."
"One slid but now 'twixt the winding shores,
But a peasant woman bent to the oars
And only a young child steered its course.   120

"Mother, something flashed to my sight! —
Nay, it is but the lapwing's flight. —
What glints there like a lance that flees? —
Nay, the flags are stirred in the breeze,
And the water's bright through the dart-rushes.   125

"Ah! vainly I search from side to side: —
Woe's me! and where do the foemen hide?
Woe's me! and perchance I pass them by,
And under the new dawn's blood-red sky
Even where I gaze the dead shall lie."   130

Said the mother: "For dear love's sake,
Speak more low, lest the spell should break."
Said the daughter: "By love's control,
My eyes, my words, are strained to the goal;
But oh! the voice that cries in my soul!"   135

"Hush, sweet, hush! be calm and behold."
"I see two floodgates broken and old:
The grasses wave o'er the ruined weir,
But the bridge still leads to the breakwater;
And — mother, mother, O mother dear!"   140

The damsel clung to her mother's knee,
And dared not let the shriek go free;
Low she crouched by the lady's chair,
And shrank blindfold in her fallen hair,
And whispering said, "The spears are there!"   145

The lady stooped aghast from her place,
And cleared the locks from her daughter's face.

"More's to see, and she swoons, alas!
Look, look again, 'ere the moment pass!
One shadow comes but once to the glass.   150

"See you there what you saw but now?"
"I see eight men 'neath the willow bough.
All over the weir a wild growth's spread:
Ah me! it will hide a living head
As well as the water hides the dead.   155

"They lie by the broken water-gate
As men who have a while to wait.
The chief's high lance has a blazoned scroll, —
He seems some lord of tithe and toll
With seven squires to his bannerole.   160

"The little pennon quakes in the air,
I cannot trace the blazon there: —
Ah! now I can see the field of blue,
The spurs and the merlins two and two; —
It is the Warden of Holycleugh!"   165

"God be thanked for the thing we know!
You have named your good knight's mortal foe.
Last Shrovetide in the tourney-game
He sought his life by treasonous shame;
And this way now doth he seek the same.   170

"So, fair lord, such a thing you are!
But we too watch till the morning star.
Well, June is kind and the moon is clear:
Saint Judas send you a merry cheer
For the night you lie in Warisweir!   175

"Now, sweet daughter, but one more sight,
And you may lie soft and sleep to-night.
We know in the vale what perils be:
Now look once more in the glass, and see
If over the hills the road lies free."   180

Rose Mary pressed to her mother's cheek,
And almost smiled but did not speak;
Then turned again to the saving spell,
With eyes to search and with lips to tell
The heart of things invisible.   185

"Again the shape with the besom grey
Comes back to sweep the clouds away.

Again I stand where the roads divide;
But now all's near on the steep hillside,
And a thread far down is the rivertide." 190

"Ay, child, your road is o'er moor and moss,
Past Holycleugh to Holy Cross.
Our hunters lurk in the valley's wake,
As they knew which way the chase would take:
Yet search the hills for your true love's sake." 195

"Swift and swifter the waste runs by,
And nought I see but the heath and the sky;
No brake is there that could hide a spear,
And the gaps to a horseman's sight lie clear;
Still past it goes, and there's nought to fear." 200

"Fear no trap that you cannot see, —
They'd not lurk yet too warily.
Below by the weir they lie in sight,
And take no heed how they pass the night
Till close they crouch with the morning light." 205

"The road shifts ever and brings in view
Now first the heights of Holycleugh:
Dark they stand o'er the vale below,
And hide that heaven which yet shall show
The thing their master's heart doth know. 210

"Where the road looks to the castle steep,
There are seven hill-clefts wide and deep:
Six mine eyes can search as they list,
But the seventh hollow is brimmed with mist:
If aught were there, it might not be wist." 215

"Small hope, my girl, for a helm to hide
In mists that cling to a wild moorside:
Soon they melt with the wind and sun,
And scarce would wait such deeds to be done:
God send their snares be the worst to shun." 220

"Still the road winds ever anew
As it hastens on towards Holycleugh;
And ever the great walls loom more near,
Till the castle-shadow, steep and sheer,
Drifts like a cloud, and the sky is clear." 225

"Enough, my daughter," the mother said,
And took to her breast the bending head;

"Rest, poor head, with my heart below,
While love still lulls you as long ago:
For all is learnt that we need to know.   230

"Long the miles and many the hours
From the castle-height to the abbey-towers;
But here the journey has no more dread;
Too thick with life is the whole road spread
For murder's trembling foot to tread."   235

She gazed on the Beryl-stone full fain
Ere she wrapped it close in her robe again:
The flickering shades were dusk and dun,
And the lights throbbed faint in unison,
Like a high heart when a race is run.   240

As the globe slid to its silken gloom,
Once more a music rained through the room;
Low it splashed like a sweet star-spray,
And sobbed like tears at the heart of May,
And died as laughter dies away.   245

The lady held her breath for a space,
And then she looked in her daughter's face:
But wan Rose Mary had never heard;
Deep asleep like a sheltered bird
She lay with the long spell minister'd.   250

"Ah! and yet I must leave you, dear,
For what you have seen your knight must hear.
Within four days, by the help of God,
He comes back safe to his heart's abode:
Be sure he shall shun the valley-road."   255

Rose Mary sank with a broken moan,
And lay in the chair and slept alone,
Weary, lifeless, heavy as lead:
Long it was ere she raised her head
And rose up all discomforted.   260

She searched her brain for a vanished thing,
And clasped her brows, remembering;
Then knelt and lifted her eyes in awe,
And sighed with a long sigh sweet to draw: —
"Thank God, thank God, thank God I saw!"   265

The lady had left her as she lay,
To seek the Knight of Heronhaye.

But first she clomb by a secret stair,
And knelt at a carven altar fair,
And laid the precious Beryl there. 270

Its girth was graved with a mystic rune
In a tongue long dead 'neath sun and moon:
A priest of the Holy Sepulchre
Read that writing and did not err;
And her lord had told its sense to her. 275

She breathed the words in an undertone: —
"None sees here but the pure alone."
"And oh!" she said, "what rose may be
In Mary's bower more pure to see
Than my own sweet maiden Rose Mary?" 280

Beryl-Song

> *We whose home is the Beryl,*
>> *Fire-spirits of dread desire,*
>>> *Who entered in*
>>> *By a secret sin,*
> *Gainst whom all powers that strive with ours are sterile, —* 5
>> *We cry, Woe to thee, mother!*
>> *What hast thou taught her, the girl thy daughter,*
>>> *That she and none other*
> *Should this dark morrow to her deadly sorrow imperil?*
>>> *What were her eyes* 10
>>> *But the fiend's own spies,*
>>>> *O mother,*
> *And shall We not fee her, our proper prophet and seër?*
>>> *Go to her, mother,*
>> *Even thou, yea thou and none other,* 15
>>> *Thou, from the Beryl:*
>> *Her fee must thou take her,*
>> *Her fee that We send, and make her,*
> *Even in this hour, her sin's unsheltered avower.*
>>> *Whose steed did neigh,* 20
>>>> *Riderless, bridle-less,*
>>> *At her gate before it was day?*
>>> *Lo! where doth hover*
>>> *The soul of her lover?*
> *She sealed his doom, she, she was the sworn approver, —* 25
>>> *Whose eyes were so wondrous wise,*
>>> *Yet blind, ah! blind to his peril!*

For stole not We in
Through a love-linked sin,
'Gainst whom all powers at war with ours are sterile, —   30
Fire-spirits of dread desire,
We whose home is the Beryl?

Part II.
"Pale Rose Mary, what shall be done
With a rose that Mary weeps upon?"
"Mother, let it fall from the tree,
And never walk where the strewn leaves be
Till winds have passed and the path is free."   5

"Sad Rose Mary, what shall be done
With a cankered flower beneath the sun?"
"Mother, let it wait for the night;
Be sure its shame shall be out of sight
Ere the moon pale or the east grow light."   10

"Lost Rose Mary, what shall be done
With a heart that is but a broken one?"
"Mother, let it lie where it must;
The blood was drained with the bitter thrust,
And dust is all that sinks in the dust."   15

"Poor Rose Mary, what shall I do, —
I, your mother, that lovèd you?"
"O my mother, and is love gone?
Then seek you another love anon:
Who cares what shame shall lean upon?"   20

Low drooped trembling Rose Mary,
Then up as though in a dream stood she.
"Come, my heart, it is time to go;
This is the hour that has whispered low
When thy pulse quailed in the nights we know.   25

"Yet O my heart, thy shame has a mate
Who will not leave thee desolate.
Shame for shame, yea and sin for sin:
Yet peace at length may our poor souls win
If love for love be found therein.   30

"O thou who seek'st our shrift to-day,"
She cried, "O James of Heronhaye —
Thy sin and mine was for love alone;

And oh! in the sight of God 'tis known
How the heart has since made heavy moan. 35

"Three days yet!" she said to her heart;
"But then he comes, and we will not part.
God, God be thanked that I still could see!
Oh! he shall come back assuredly,
But where, alas! must he seek for me? 40

"O my heart, what road shall we roam
Till my wedding-music fetch me home?
For love's shut from us and bides afar,
And scorn leans over the bitter bar
And knows us now for the thing we are." 45

Tall she stood with a cheek flushed high
And a gaze to burn the heart-strings by.
'Twas the lightning-flash o'er sky and plain
Ere labouring thunders heave the chain
From the floodgates of the drowning rain. 50

The mother looked on the daughter still
As on a hurt thing that's yet to kill.
Then wildly at length the pent tears came;
The love swelled high with the swollen shame,
And their hearts' tempest burst on them. 55

Closely locked, they clung without speech,
And the mirrored souls shook each to each,
As the cloud-moon and the water-moon
Shake face to face when the dim stars swoon
In stormy bowers of the night's mid-noon. 60

They swayed together, shuddering sore,
Till the mother's heart could bear no more.
'Twas death to feel her own breast shake
Even to the very throb and ache
Of the burdened heart she still must break. 65

All her sobs ceased suddenly,
And she sat straight up but scarce could see.
"O daughter, where should my speech begin?
Your heart held fast its secret sin:
How think you, child, that I read therein?" 70

"Ah me! but I thought not how it came
When your words showed that you knew my shame:
And now that you call me still your own,

I half forget you have ever known.
Did you read my heart in the Beryl-stone?"

The lady answered her mournfully: —
"The Beryl-stone has no voice for me:
But when you charged its power to show
The truth which none but the pure may know,
Did naught speak once of a coming woe?"

Her hand was close to her daughter's heart,
And it felt the life-blood's sudden start:
A quick deep breath did the damsel draw,
Like the struck fawn in the oakenshaw:
"O mother," she cried, "but still I saw!"

"O child, my child, why held you apart
From my great love your hidden heart?
Said I not that all sin must chase
From the spell's sphere the spirits of grace,
And yield their rule to the evil race?

"Ah! would to God I had clearly told
How strong those powers, accurst of old:
Their heart is the ruined house of lies;
O girl, they can seal the sinful eyes,
Or show the truth by contraries!"

The daughter sat as cold as a stone,
And spoke no word but gazed alone,
Nor moved, though her mother strove a space
To clasp her round in a close embrace,
Because she dared not see her face.

"Oh!" at last did the mother cry,
"Be sure, as he loved you, so will I!
Ah! still and dumb is the bride, I trow;
But cold and stark as the winter snow
Is the bridegroom's heart, laid dead below!

"Daughter, daughter, remember you
That cloud in the hills by Holycleugh?
'Twas a Hell-screen hiding truth away:
There, not i' the vale, the ambush lay,
And thence was the dead borne home to-day."

Deep the flood and heavy the shock
When sea meets sea in the riven rock:
But calm is the pulse that shakes the sea

To the prisoned tide of doom set free
In the breaking heart of Rose Mary. 115

Once she sprang as the heifer springs
With the wolf's teeth at its red heart-strings:
First 'twas fire in her breast and brain,
And then scarce hers but the whole world's pain,
As she gave one shriek and sank again. 120

In the hair dark-waved the face lay white
As the moon lies in the lap of night;
And as night through which no moon may dart
Lies on a pool in the woods apart,
So lay the swoon on the weary heart. 125

The lady felt for the bosom's stir,
And wildly kissed and called on her;
Then turned away with a quick footfall,
And slid the secret door in the wall,
And clomb the strait stair's interval. 130

There above in the altar-cell
A little fountain rose and fell:
She set a flask to the water's flow,
And, backward hurrying, sprinkled now
The still cold breast and the pallid brow. 135

Scarce cheek that warmed or breath on the air,
Yet something told that life was there.
"Ah! not with the heart the body dies!"
The lady moaned in a bitter wise;
Then wrung her hands and hid her eyes. 140

"Alas! and how may I meet again
In the same poor eyes the self-same pain?
What help can I seek, such grief to guide?
Ah! one alone might avail," she cried, —
"The priest who prays at the dead man's side." 145

The lady arose, and sped down all
The winding stairs to the castle-hall.
Long-known valley and wood and stream,
As the loopholes passed, naught else did seem
Than the torn threads of a broken dream. 150

The hall was full of the castle-folk;
The women wept, but the men scarce spoke.
As the lady crossed the rush-strewn floor,

The throng fell backward, murmuring sore,
And pressed outside round the open door.   155

A stranger shadow hung on the hall
Than the dark pomp of a funeral.
'Mid common sights that were there alway,
As 'twere a chance of the passing day,
On the ingle-bench the dead man lay.   160

A priest who passed by Holycleugh
The tidings brought when the day was new.
He guided them who had fetched the dead;
And since that hour, unwearièd,
He knelt in prayer at the low bier's head.   165

Word had gone to his own domain
That in evil wise the knight was slain:
Soon the spears must gather apace
And the hunt be hard on the hunters' trace;
But all things yet lay still for a space.   170

As the lady's hurried step drew near,
The kneeling priest looked up to her.
"Father, death is a grievous thing;
But oh! the woe has a sharper sting
That craves by me your ministering.   175

"Alas for the child that should have wed
This noble knight here lying dead!
Dead in hope, with all blessed boon
Of love thus rent from her heart ere noon,
I left her laid in a heavy swoon.   180

"O haste to the open bower-chamber
That's topmost as you mount the stair:
Seek her, father, ere yet she wake;
Your words, not mine, be the first to slake
This poor heart's fire, for Christ's sweet sake!   185

"God speed!" she said as the priest passed through,
"And I ere long will be with you."
Then low on the hearth her knees sank prone;
She signed all folk from the threshold-stone,
And gazed in the dead man's face alone.   190

The fight for life found record yet
In the clenched lips and the teeth hard-set;
The wrath from the bent brow was not gone,

And stark in the eyes the hate still shone
Of that they last had looked upon.   195

The blazoned coat was rent on his breast
Where the golden field was goodliest;
But the shivered sword, close-gripped, could tell
That the blood shed round him where he fell
Was not all his in the distant dell.   200

The lady recked of the corpse no whit,
But saw the soul and spoke to it:
A light there was in her steadfast eyes, —
The fire of mortal tears and sighs
That pity and love immortalize.   205

"By thy death have I learnt to-day
Thy deed, O James of Heronhaye!
Great wrong thou hast done to me and mine;
And haply God hath wrought for a sign
By our blind deed this doom of thine.   210

"Thy shrift, alas! thou wast not to win;
But may death shrive thy soul herein!
Full well do I know thy love should be
Even yet — had life but stayed with thee —
Our honour's strong security."   215

She stooped, and said with a sob's low stir, —
"Peace be thine, — but what peace for her?"
But ere to the brow her lips were press'd,
She marked, half-hid in the riven vest,
A packet close to the dead man's breast.   220

'Neath surcoat pierced and broken mail
It lay on the blood-stained bosom pale.
The clot clung round it, dull and dense,
And a faintness seized her mortal sense
As she reached her hand and drew it thence.   225

'Twas steeped in the heart's flood welling high
From the heart it there had rested by:
'Twas glued to a broidered fragment gay, —
A shred by spear-thrust rent away
From the heron-wings of Heronhaye.   230

She gazed on the thing with piteous eyne: —
"Alas, poor child, some pledge of thine!
Ah me! in this troth the hearts were twain,

And one hath ebbed to this crimson stain,
And when shall the other throb again?"   235

She opened the packet heedfully;
The blood was stiff, and it scarce might be.
She found but a folded paper there,
And round it, twined with tenderest care,
A long bright tress of golden hair.   240

Even as she looked, she saw again
That dark-haired face in its swoon of pain:
It seemed a snake with a golden sheath
Crept near, as a slow flame flickereth,
And stung her daughter's heart to death.   245

She loosed the tress, but her hand did shake
As though indeed she had touched a snake;
And next she undid the paper's fold,
But that too trembled in her hold,
And the sense scarce grasped the tale it told.   250

"My heart's sweet lord," ('twas thus she read,)
"At length our love is garlanded.
At Holy Cross, within eight days' space,
I seek my shrift; and the time and place
Shall fit thee too for thy soul's good grace.   255

"From Holycleugh on the seventh day
My brother rides, and bides away:
And long or e'er he is back, mine own,
Afar where the face of fear's unknown
We shall be safe with our love alone.   260

"Ere yet at the shrine my knees I bow,
I shear one tress for our holy vow.
As round these words these threads I wind,
So, eight days hence, shall our loves be twined,
Says my lord's poor lady, JOCELIND."   265

She read it twice, with a brain in thrall,
And then its echo told her all.
O'er brows low-fall'n her hands she drew: —
"O God!" she said, as her hands fell too, —
"The Warden's sister of Holycleugh!"   270

She rose upright with a long low moan,
And stared in the dead man's face new-known.
Had it lived indeed? She scarce could tell:

'Twas a cloud where fiends had come to dwell, —
A mask that hung on the gate of Hell.

She lifted the lock of gleaming hair
And smote the lips and left it there.
"Here's gold that Hell shall take for thy toll!
Full well hath thy treason found its goal,
O thou dead body and damnèd soul!"

She turned, sore dazed, for a voice was near,
And she knew that some one called to her.
On many a column fair and tall
A high court ran round the castle-hall;
And thence it was that the priest did call.

"I sought your child where you bade me go,
And in rooms around and rooms below;
But where, alas! may the maiden be?
Fear nought, — we shall find her speedily, —
But come, come hither, and seek with me."

She reached the stair like a lifelorn thing,
But hastened upward murmuring: —
"Yea, Death's is a face that's fell to see;
But bitterer pang Life hoards for thee,
Thou broken heart of Rose Mary!"

Beryl-Song
   We whose throne is the Beryl,
   Dire-gifted spirits of fire,
      Who for a twin
     Leash Sorrow to Sin,
Who on no flower refrain to lour with peril, —
   We cry, — O desolate daughter!
Thou and thy mother share newer shame with each other
     Than last night's slaughter.
   Awake and tremble, for our curses assemble!
   What more, that thou know'st not yet, —
     That life nor death shall forget?
No help from Heaven, — thy woes heart-riven are sterile!
     O, once a maiden,
With yet worse sorrow can any morrow be laden?
     It waits for thee,
    It looms, it must be,
   O lost among women, —
  It comes and thou canst not flee.

> Amen to the omen,
>   Says the voice of the Beryl.   20
>   Thou sleep'st? Awake, —
>   What dar'st thou yet for his sake,
> Who each for other did God's own Future imperil?
>   Dost dare to live
>   'Mid the pangs each hour must give?   25
>   Nay, rather die, —
> With him thy lover 'neath Hell's cloud-cover to fly, —
>   Hopeless, yet not apart,
>   Cling heart to heart,
> And beat through the nether storm-eddying winds together?   30

>   Shall this be so?
> There thou shalt meet him, but may'st thou greet him? ah no!
> He loves, but thee he hoped never more to see, —
>   He sighed as he died,
>   But with never a thought for thee.   35
>   Alone!
>   Alone, for ever alone, —
> Whose eyes were such wondrous spies for the fate foreshown!
>   Lo! have not We leashed the twin
>   Of endless Sorrow to Sin, —   40
> Who on no flower refrain to lour with peril, —
>   Dire-gifted spirits of fire,
>   We whose throne is the Beryl?

Part III.
A swoon that breaks is the whelming wave
When help comes late but still can save.
With all blind throes is the instant rife, —
Hurtling clangour and clouds at strife, —
The breath of death, but the kiss of life.   5

The night lay deep on Rose Mary's heart,
For her swoon was death's kind counterpart:
The dawn broke dim on Rose Mary's soul, —
No hill-crown's heavenly aureole,
But a wild gleam on a shaken shoal.   10

Her senses gasped in the sudden air,
And she looked around, but none was there.
She felt the slackening frost distil
Through her blood the last ooze dull and chill:
Her lids were dry and her lips were still.   15

Her tears had flooded her heart again;
As after a long day's bitter rain,
At dusk when the wet flower-cups shrink,
The drops run in from the beaded brink,
And all the close-shut petals drink.   20

Again her sighs on her heart were rolled;
As the wind that long has swept the wold, —
Whose moan was made with the moaning sea, —
Beats out its breath in the last torn tree,
And sinks at length in lethargy.   25

She knew she had waded bosom-deep
Along death's bank in the sedge of sleep:
All else was lost to her clouded mind;
Nor, looking back, could she see defin'd
O'er the dim dumb waste what lay behind.   30

Slowly fades the sun from the wall
Till day lies dead on the sun-dial:
And now in Rose Mary's lifted eye
'Twas shadow alone that made reply
To the set face of the soul's dark sky.   35

Yet still through her soul there wandered past
Dread phantoms borne on a wailing blast, —
Death and sorrow and sin and shame;
And, murmured still, to her lips there came
Her mother's and her lover's name.   40

How to ask, and what thing to know?
She might not stay and she dared not go.
From fires unseen these smoke-clouds curled;
But where did the hidden curse lie furled?
And how to seek through the weary world?   45

With toiling breath she rose from the floor
And dragged her steps to an open door:
'Twas the secret panel standing wide,
As the lady's hand had let it bide
In hastening back to her daughter's side.   50

She passed, but reeled with a dizzy brain
And smote the door which closed again.
She stood within by the darkling stair,
But her feet might mount more freely there, —
'Twas the open light most blinded her.   55

Within her mind no wonder grew
At the secret path she never knew:
All ways alike were strange to her now, —
One field bare-ridged from the spirit's plough,
One thicket black with the cypress-bough.   60

Once she thought that she heard her name;
And she paused, but knew not whence it came.
Down the shadowed stair a faint ray fell
That guided the weary footsteps well
Till it led her up to the altar-cell.   65

No change there was on Rose Mary's face
As she leaned in the portal's narrow space:
Still she stood by the pillar's stem,
Hand and bosom and garment's hem,
As the soul stands by at the requiem.   70

The altar-cell was a dome low-lit,
And a veil hung in the midst of it:
At the pole-points of its circling girth
Four symbols stood of the world's first birth, —
Air and water and fire and earth.   75

To the north, a fountain glittered free;
To the south, there glowed a red fruit-tree;
To the east, a lamp flamed high and fair;
To the west, a crystal casket rare
Held fast a cloud of the fields of air.   80

The painted walls were a mystic show
Of time's ebb-tide and overflow;
His hoards long-locked and conquering key,
His service-fires that in heaven be,
And earth-wheels whirled perpetually.   85

Rose Mary gazed from the open door
As on idle things she cared not for, —
The fleeting shapes of an empty tale;
Then stepped with a heedless visage pale,
And lifted aside the altar-veil.   90

The altar stood from its curved recess
In a coiling serpent's life-likeness:
Even such a serpent evermore
Lies deep asleep at the world's dark core
Till the last Voice shake the sea and shore.   95

From the altar-cloth a book rose spread
And tapers burned at the altar-head;
And there in the altar-midst alone,
'Twixt wings of a sculptured beast unknown,
Rose Mary saw the Beryl-stone.   100

Firm it sat 'twixt the hollowed wings,
As an orb sits in the hand of kings:
And lo! for that Foe whose curse far-flown
Had bound her life with a burning zone,
Rose Mary knew the Beryl-stone.   105

Dread is the meteor's blazing sphere
When the poles throb to its blind career;
But not with a light more grim and ghast
Thereby is the future doom forecast,
Than now this sight brought back the past.   110

The hours and minutes seemed to whirr
In a clanging swarm that deafened her;
They stung her heart to a writhing flame,
And marshalled past in its glare they came, —
Death and sorrow and sin and shame.   115

Round the Beryl's sphere she saw them pass
And mock her eyes from the fated glass:
One by one in a fiery train
The dead hours seemed to wax and wane,
And burned till all was known again.   120

From the drained heart's fount there rose no cry,
There sprang no tears, for the source was dry.
Held in the hand of some heavy law,
Her eyes she might not once withdraw
Nor shrink away from the thing she saw.   125

Even as she gazed, through all her blood
The flame was quenched in a coming flood:
Out of the depth of the hollow gloom
On her soul's bare sands she felt it boom, —
The measured tide of a sea of doom.   130

Three steps she took through the altar-gate,
And her neck reared and her arms grew straight:
The sinews clenched like a serpent's throe,
And the face was white in the dark hair's flow,
As her hate beheld what lay below.   135

Dumb she stood in her malisons, —
A silver statue tressed with bronze:
As the fabled head by Perseus mown,
It seemed in sooth that her gaze alone
Had turned the carven shapes to stone.   140

O'er the altar-sides on either hand
There hung a dinted helm and brand:
By strength thereof, 'neath the Sacred Sign,
That bitter gift o'er the salt sea-brine
Her father brought from Palestine.   145

Rose Mary moved with a stern accord
And reached her hand to her father's sword;
Nor did she stir her gaze one whit
From the thing whereon her brows were knit;
But gazing still, she spoke to it.   150

"O ye, three times accurst," she said,
"By whom this stone is tenanted!
Lo! here ye came by a strong sin's might;
Yet a sinner's hand that's weak to smite
Shall send you hence ere the day be night.   155

"This hour a clear voice bade me know
My hand shall work your overthrow:
Another thing in mine ear it spake, —
With the broken spell my life shall break.
I thank Thee, God, for the dear death's sake!   160

"And he Thy heavenly minister
Who swayed erewhile this spell-bound sphere, —
My parting soul let him haste to greet,
And none but he be guide for my feet
To where Thy rest is made complete."   165

Then deep she breathed, with a tender moan: —
"My love, my lord, my only one!
Even as I held the cursed clue,
When thee, through me, these foul ones slew, —
By mine own deed shall they slay me too!   170

"Even while they speed to Hell, my love,
Two hearts shall meet in Heaven above.
Our shrift thou sought'st, but might'st not bring:
And oh! for me 'tis a blessed thing
To work hereby our ransoming.   175

"One were our hearts in joy and pain,
And our souls e'en now grow one again.
And O my love, if our souls are three,
O thine and mine shall the third soul be, —
One threefold love eternally."   180

Her eyes were soft as she spoke apart,
And the lips smiled to the broken heart:
But the glance was dark and the forehead scored
With the bitter frown of hate restored,
As her two hands swung the heavy sword.   185

Three steps back from her Foe she trod: —
"Love, for thy sake! In Thy Name, O God!"
In the fair white hands small strength was shown;
Yet the blade flashed high and the edge fell prone,
And she cleft the heart of the Beryl-stone.   190

What living flesh in the thunder-cloud
Hath sat and felt heaven cry aloud?
Or known how the levin's pulse may beat?
Or wrapped the hour when the whirlwinds meet
About its breast for a winding-sheet?   195

Who hath crouched at the world's deep heart
While the earthquake rends its loins apart?
Or walked far under the seething main
While overhead the heavens ordain
The tempest-towers of the hurricane?   200

Who hath seen or what ear hath heard
The secret things unregister'd
Of the place where all is past and done
And tears and laughter sound as one
In Hell's unhallowed unison?   205

Nay, is it writ how the fiends despair
In earth and water and fire and air?
Even so no mortal tongue may tell
How to the clang of the sword that fell
The echoes shook the altar-cell.   210

When all was still on the air again
The Beryl-stone lay cleft in twain;
The veil was rent from the riven dome;
And every wind that's winged to roam
Might have the ruined place for home.   215

The fountain no more glittered free;
The fruit hung dead on the leafless tree;
The flame of the lamp had ceased to flare;
And the crystal casket shattered there
Was emptied now of its cloud of air.   220

And lo! on the ground Rose Mary lay,
With a cold brow like the snows ere May,
With a cold breast like the earth till Spring,
With such a smile as the June days bring
When the year grows warm for harvesting.   225

The death she had won might leave no trace
On the soft sweet form and gentle face:
In a gracious sleep she seemed to lie;
And over her head her hand on high
Held fast the sword she triumphed by.   230

'Twas then a clear voice said in the room: —
"Behold the end of the heavy doom.
O come, — for thy bitter love's sake blest;
By a sweet path now thou journeyest,
And I will lead thee to thy rest.   235

"Me thy sin by Heaven's sore ban
Did chase erewhile from the talisman:
But to my heart, as a conquered home,
In glory of strength thy footsteps come
Who hast thus cast forth my foes therefrom.   240

"Already thy heart remembereth
No more his name thou sought'st in death:
For under all deeps, all heights above, —
So wide the gulf in the midst thereof, —
Are Hell of Treason and Heaven of Love.   245

"Thee, true soul, shall thy truth prefer
To blessed Mary's rose-bower:
Warmed and lit is thy place afar
With guerdon-fires of the sweet Love-star
Where hearts of steadfast lovers are: —   250

"Though naught for the poor corpse lying here
Remain to-day but the cold white bier,
But burial-chaunt and bended knee,
But sighs and tears that heaviest be,
But rent rose-flower and rosemary."   255

Beryl-Song

> *We, cast forth from the Beryl,*
> *Gyre-circling spirits of fire,*
>> *Whose pangs begin*
>> *With God's grace to sin,*
> *For whose spent powers the immortal hours are sterile, —* 5
>
> *Woe! must We behold this mother*
> *Find grace in her dead child's face, and doubt of none other*
> *But that perfect pardon, alas! hath assured her guerdon?*
> *Woe! must We behold this daughter,*
> *Made clean from the soil of sin wherewith We had fraught her,* 10
>
>> *Shake off a man's blood like water?*
>> *Write up her story*
>> *On the Gate of Heaven's glory,*
> *Whom there We behold so fair in shining apparel,*
>> *And beneath her the ruin* 15
>> *Of our own undoing!*
>> *Alas, the Beryl!*
>> *We had for a foeman*
>> *But one weak woman;*
>> *In one day's strife,* 20
> *Her hope fell dead from her life;*
>> *And yet no iron,*
>> *Her soul to environ,*
> *Could this manslayer, this false soothsayer imperil!*
>> *Lo, where she bows* 25
>> *In the Holy House!*
> *Who now shall dissever her soul from its joy for ever,*
>> *While every ditty*
>> *Of love and plentiful pity*
>> *Fills the White City,* 30
> *And the floor of Heaven to her feet for ever is given?*
>
>> *Hark, a voice cries "Flee!"*
> *Woe! woe! what shelter have We,*
>> *Whose pangs begin*
>> *With God's grace to sin,* 35
> *For whose spent powers the immortal hours are sterile,*
>
>> *Gyre-circling spirits of fire,*
>> *We, cast forth from the Beryl?*

The White Ship.
Henry I of England—25th Nov., 1120

By none but me can the tale be told,
The butcher of Rouen, poor Berold.
   (*Lands are swayed by a King on a throne.*)
'Twas a royal train put forth to sea,
Yet the tale can be told by none but me.   5
   (*The sea hath no King but God alone.*)

King Henry held it as life's whole gain
That after his death his son should reign.

'Twas so in my youth I heard men say,
And my old age calls it back to-day.   10

King Henry of England's realm was he,
And Henry Duke of Normandy.

The times had changed when on either coast
"Clerkly Harry" was all his boast.

Of ruthless strokes full many an one   15
He had struck to crown himself and his son;
And his elder brother's eyes were gone.

And when to the chase his court would crowd,
The poor flung ploughshares on his road,
And shrieked: "Our cry is from King to God!"   20

But all the chiefs of the English land
Had knelt and kissed the Prince's hand.

And next with his son he sailed to France
To claim the Norman allegiance:

And every baron in Normandy   25
Had taken the oath of fealty.

'Twas sworn and sealed, and the day had come
When the King and the Prince might journey home:

For Christmas cheer is to home hearts dear,
And Christmas now was drawing near.   30

Stout Fitz-Stephen came to the King, —
A pilot famous in seafaring;

And he held to the King, in all men's sight,
A mark of gold for his tribute's right.

"Liege Lord! my father guided the ship   35
From whose boat your father's foot did slip
When he caught the English soil in his grip,

"And cried: 'By this clasp I claim command
O'er every rood of English land!'

"He was borne to the realm you rule o'er now   40
In that ship with the archer carved at her prow:

"And thither I'll bear, an' it be my due,
Your father's son and his grandson too.

"The famed White Ship is mine in the bay;
From Harfleur's harbour she sails to-day,   45

"With masts fair-pennoned as Norman spears
And with fifty well-tried mariners."

Quoth the King: "My ships are chosen each one,
But I'll not say nay to Stephen's son.

"My son and daughter and fellowship   50
Shall cross the water in the White Ship."

The King set sail with the eve's south wind,
And soon he left that coast behind.

The Prince and all his, a princely show,
Remained in the good White Ship to go.   55

With noble knights and with ladies fair,
With courtiers and sailors gathered there,
Three hundred living souls we were:

And I Berold was the meanest hind
In all that train to the Prince assign'd.   60

The Prince was a lawless shameless youth;
From his father's loins he sprang without ruth:

Eighteen years till then he had seen,
And the devil's dues in him were eighteen.

And now he cried: "Bring wine from below;   65
Let the sailors revel ere yet they row:

"Our speed shall o'ertake my father's flight
Though we sail from the harbour at midnight."

The rowers made good cheer without check;
The lords and ladies obeyed his beck;   70
The night was light, and they danced on the deck.

But at midnight's stroke they cleared the bay,
And the White Ship furrowed the water-way.

The sails were set, and the oars kept tune
To the double flight of the ship and the moon: 75

Swifter and swifter the White Ship sped
Till she flew as the spirit flies from the dead:

As white as a lily glimmered she
Like a ship's fair ghost upon the sea.

And the Prince cried, "Friends, 'tis the hour to sing!   80
Is a songbird's course so swift on the wing?"

And under the winter stars' still throng,
From brown throats, white throats, merry and strong,
The knights and the ladies raised a song.

A song, — nay, a shriek that rent the sky,   85
That leaped o'er the deep! — the grievous cry
Of three hundred living that now must die.

An instant shriek that sprang to the shock
As the ship's keel felt the sunken rock.

'Tis said that afar — a shrill strange sigh —   90
The King's ships heard it and knew not why.

Pale Fitz-Stephen stood by the helm
'Mid all those folk that the waves must whelm.

A great King's heir for the waves to whelm,
And the helpless pilot pale at the helm!   95

The ship was eager and sucked athirst,
By the stealthy stab of the sharp reef pierc'd:

And like the moil round a sinking cup,
The waters against her crowded up.

A moment the pilot's senses spin, —   100
The next he snatched the Prince 'mid the din,
Cut the boat loose, and the youth leaped in.

A few friends leaped with him, standing near.
"Row! the sea's smooth and the night is clear!"

"What! none to be saved but these and I?"   105
"Row, row as you'd live! All here must die!"

Out of the churn of the choking ship,
Which the gulf grapples and the waves strip,
They struck with the strained oars' flash and dip.

'Twas then o'er the splitting bulwarks' brim   110
The Prince's sister screamed to him.

He gazed aloft, still rowing apace,
And through the whirled surf he knew her face.

To the toppling decks clave one and all
As a fly cleaves to a chamber-wall.   115

I Berold was clinging anear;
I prayed for myself and quaked with fear,
But I saw his eyes as he looked at her.

He knew her face and he heard her cry,
And he said, "Put back! she must not die!"   120

And back with the current's force they reel
Like a leaf that's drawn to a water-wheel.

'Neath the ship's travail they scarce might float,
But he rose and stood in the rocking boat.

Low the poor ship leaned on the tide: 125
O'er the naked keel as she best might slide,
The sister toiled to the brother's side.

He reached an oar to her from below,
And stiffened his arms to clutch her so.

But now from the ship some spied the boat,   130
And "Saved!" was the cry from many a throat.

And down to the boat they leaped and fell:
It turned as a bucket turns in a well,
And nothing was there but the surge and swell.

The Prince that was and the King to come,   135
There in an instant gone to his doom,

Despite of all England's bended knee
And maugre the Norman fealty!

He was a Prince of lust and pride;
He showed no grace till the hour he died.   140

When he should be King, he oft would vow,
He'd yoke the peasant to his own plough.
O'er him the ships score their furrows now.

God only knows where his soul did wake,
But I saw him die for his sister's sake.   145

By none but me can the tale be told,
The butcher of Rouen, poor Berold.
  (*Lands are swayed by a King on a throne.*)

'Twas a royal train put forth to sea,
Yet the tale can be told by none but me.   150
  (*The sea hath no King but God alone.*)

And now the end came o'er the waters' womb
Like the last great Day that's yet to come.

With prayers in vain and curses in vain,
The White Ship sundered on the mid-main: 155

And what were men and what was a ship
Were toys and splinters in the sea's grip.

I Berold was down in the sea;
And passing strange though the thing may be,
Of dreams then known I remember me.   160

Blithe is the shout on Harfleur's strand
When morning lights the sails to land:

And blithe is Honfleur's echoing gloam
When mothers call the children home:

And high do the bells of Rouen beat   165
When the Body of Christ goes down the street.

These things and the like were heard and shown
In a moment's trance 'neath the sea alone;

And when I rose, 'twas the sea did seem,
And not these things, to be all a dream.   170

The ship was gone and the crowd was gone,
And the deep shuddered and the moon shone:

And in a strait grasp my arms did span
The mainyard rent from the mast where it ran;
And on it with me was another man.   175

Where lands were none 'neath the dim sea-sky,
We told our names, that man and I.

"O I am Godefroy de l'Aigle hight,
And son I am to a belted knight."

"And I am Berold the butcher's son   180
Who slays the beasts in Rouen town."

Then cried we upon God's name, as we
Did drift on the bitter winter sea.

But lo! a third man rose o'er the wave,
And we said, "Thank God! us three may He save!"   185

He clutched to the yard with panting stare,
And we looked and knew Fitz-Stephen there.

He clung, and "What of the Prince?" quoth he.
"Lost, lost!" we cried. He cried, "Woe on me!"
And loosed his hold and sank through the sea.   190

And soul with soul again in that space
We two were together face to face:

And each knew each, as the moments sped,
Less for one living than for one dead:

And every still star overhead   195
Seemed an eye that knew we were but dead.

And the hours passed; till the noble's son
Sighed, "God be thy help! my strength's foredone!"

"O farewell, friend, for I can no more!"
"Christ take thee!" I moaned; and his life was o'er. 200

Three hundred souls were all lost but one,
And I drifted over the sea alone.

At last the morning rose on the sea
Like an angel's wing that beat tow'rds me.

Sore numbed I was in my sheepskin coat;   205
Half dead I hung, and might nothing note,
Till I woke sun-warmed in a fisher-boat.

The sun was high o'er the eastern brim
As I praised God and gave thanks to Him.

That day I told my tale to a priest, 210
Who charged me, till the shrift were releas'd,
That I should keep it in mine own breast.

And with the priest I thence did fare
To King Henry's court at Winchester.

We spoke with the King's high chamberlain, 215
And he wept and mourned again and again,
As if his own son had been slain:

And round us ever there crowded fast
Great men with faces all aghast:

And who so bold that might tell the thing 220
Which now they knew to their lord the King?
Much woe I learnt in their communing.

The King had watched with a heart sore stirred
For two whole days, and this was the third:

And still to all his court would he say, 225
"What keeps my son so long away?"

And they said: "The ports lie far and wide
That skirt the swell of the English tide;

"And England's cliffs are not more white
Than her women are, and scarce so light 230
Her skies as their eyes are blue and bright;

"And in some port that he reached from France
The Prince has lingered for his pleasaùnce."

But once the King asked: "What distant cry
Was that we heard 'twixt the sea and sky?" 235

And one said: "With suchlike shouts, pardie!
Do the fishers fling their nets at sea."

And one: "Who knows not the shrieking quest
When the sea-mew misses its young from the nest?"

'Twas thus till now they had soothed his dread, 240
Albeit they knew not what they said:

But who should speak to-day of the thing
That all knew there except the King?

Then pondering much they found a way,
And met round the King's high seat that day: 245

And the King sat with a heart sore stirred,
And seldom he spoke and seldom heard.

'Twas then through the hall the King was 'ware
Of a little boy with golden hair,

As bright as the golden poppy is   250
That the beach breeds for the surf to kiss:

Yet pale his cheek as the thorn in Spring,
And his garb black like the raven's wing.

Nothing heard but his foot through the hall,
For now the lords were silent all.   255

And the King wondered, and said, "Alack!
Who sends me a fair boy dressed in black?

"Why, sweet heart, do you pace through the hall
As though my court were a funeral?"

Then lowly knelt the child at the dais,   260
And looked up weeping in the King's face.

"O wherefore black, O King, ye may say,
For white is the hue of death to-day.

"Your son and all his fellowship
Lie low in the sea with the White Ship."   265

King Henry fell as a man struck dead;
And speechless still he stared from his bed
When to him next day my rede I read.

There's many an hour must needs beguile
A King's high heart that he should smile, —   270

Full many a lordly hour, full fain
Of his realm's rule and pride of his reign: —

But this King never smiled again.

By none but me can the tale be told,
The butcher of Rouen, poor Berold.   275
   (*Lands are swayed by a King on a throne.*)
'Twas a royal train put forth to sea,
Yet the tale can be told by none but me.
   (*The sea hath no King but God alone.*)

Soothsay

Let no man ask thee of anything
Not yearborn between Spring and Spring.
More of all worlds that he can know,
Each day the single sun doth show.
A trustier gloss than thou canst give   5
From all wise scrolls demonstrative,
The sea doth sigh and the wind sing.

Let no man awe thee on any height
Of earthly kingship's mouldering might.
The dust his heel holds meet for thy brow   10
Hath all of it been what both are now;
And thou and he may plague together
A beggar's eyes in some dusty weather
When none that is now knows sound or sight.

Crave thou no dower of earthly things   15
Unworthy Hope's imaginings.
To have brought true birth of Song to be
And to have won hearts of Poesy,
Or anywhere in the sun or rain
To have loved and been beloved again,   20
Is loftiest reach of Hope's bright wings.

The wild waifs cast up by the sea
Are diverse ever seasonably.
Even so the soul-tides still may land
A different drift upon the sand.   25
But one the sea is evermore:
And one be still, 'twixt shore and shore,
As the sea's life, thy soul in thee.

Say, hast thou pride? How then may fit
Thy mood with flatters' silk-spun wit?   30
Haply the sweet voice lifts thy crest,
A breeze of fame made manifest.
Nay, but then chaf'st at flattery? Pause:
Be sure thy wrath is not because
It makes thee feel thou lovest it.   35

Let thy soul strive that still the same
Be early friendship's sacred flame.
The affinities have strongest part

In youth, and draw men heart to heart:
As life wears on and finds no rest,
The individual in each breast
Is tyrannous to sunder them.

In the life-drama's stern cue-call,
A friend's a part well-prized by all:
And if thou meet an enemy,
What art thou that none such should be?
Even so: but if the two parts run
Into each other and grow one,
Then comes the curtain's cue to fall.

Whate'er by other's need is claimed
More than by thine, — to him unblamed
Resign it: and if he should hold
What more than he thou lack'st, bread, gold,
Or any good whereby we live, —
To thee such substance let him give
Freely: nor he nor thou be shamed.

Strive that thy works prove equal: lest
That work which thou hast done the best
Should come to be to thee at length
(Even as to envy seems the strength
Of others) hateful and abhorr'd, —
Thine own above thyself made lord, —
Of self-rebuke the bitterest.

Unto the man of yearning thought
And aspiration, to do nought
Is in itself almost an act, —
Being chasm-fire and cataract
Of the soul's utter depths unseal'd.
Yet woe to thee if once thou yield
Unto the act of doing nought!

How callous seems beyond revoke
The clock with its last listless stroke!
How much too late at length! — to trace
The hour on its forewarning face,
The thing thou hast not dared to do! . . .
Behold, this may be thus! Ere true
It prove, arise and bear thy yoke.

Let lore of all Theology
Be to thy soul what it can be:

But know, — the Power that fashions man   80
Measured not out thy little span
For thee to take the meting-rod
In turn, and so approve on God
Thy science of Theometry.

To God at best, to Chance at worst,   85
Give thanks for good things, last as first.
But windstrown blossom is that good
Whose apple is not gratitude.
Even if no prayer uplift thy face,
Let the sweet right to render grace   90
As thy soul's cherished child be nurs'd.

Didst ever say, "Lo, I forget"?
Such thought was to remember yet.
As in a gravegarth, count to see
The monuments of memory.   95

Spheral Change

In this new shade of Death, the show
    Passes me still of form and face;
Some bent, some gazing as they go,
    Some swiftly, some at a dull pace,
    Not one that speaks in any case.   5

If only one might speak! — the one
    Who never waits till I come near;
But always seated all alone
    As listening to the sunken air,
    Is gone before I come to her.   10

O dearest! while we lived and died
    A living death in every day,
Some hours we still were side by side,
    When where I was you too might stay
    And rest and need not go away.   15

O nearest, furthest! Can there be
    At length some hard-earned heart-won home,
Where, — exile changed for sanctuary, —
    Our lot may fill indeed its sum,
    And you may wait and I may come?   20

Sunset Wings

To-night this sunset spreads two golden wings
    Cleaving the western sky;
Winged too with wind it is, and winnowings
Of birds; as if the day's last hour in rings
    Of strenuous flight must die.   5

Sun-steeped in fire, the homeward pinions sway
    Above the dovecote-tops;
And clouds of starlings, ere they rest with day,
Sink, clamorous like mill-water, at wild play,
    By turns in every copse: 10

Each tree heart-deep the wrangling rout receives, —
    Save for the whirr within,
You could not tell the starlings from the leaves;
Then one great puff of wings, and the swarm heaves
    Away with all its din.   15

Even thus Hope's hours, in ever-eddying flight,
    To many a refuge tend;
With the first light she laughed, and the last light
Glows round her still; who natheless in the night
    At length must make an end.   20

And now the mustering rooks innumerable
    Together sail and soar,
While for the day's death, like a tolling knell,
Unto the heart they seem to cry, Farewell,
    No more, farewell, no more!   25

Is Hope not plumed, as 'twere a fiery dart?
    And oh! thou dying day,
Even as thou goest must she too depart,
And Sorrow fold such pinions on the heart,
    As will not fly away?   30

Insomnia

Thin are the night-skirts left behind
    By daybreak hours that onward creep,
    And thin, alas! the shred of sleep
That wavers with the spirit's wind:
But in half-dreams that shift and roll   5

And still remember and forget,
My soul this hour has drawn your soul
   A little nearer yet.

Our lives, most dear, are never near,
   Our thoughts are never far apart,   10
   Though all that draws us heart to heart
Seems fainter now and now more clear.
To-night Love claims his full control,
   And with desire and with regret
My soul this hour has drawn your soul   15
   A little nearer yet.

Is there a home where heavy earth
   Melts to bright air that breathes no pain,
   Where water leaves no thirst again
And springing fire is Love's new birth?   20
If faith long bound to one true goal
   May there at length its hope beget,
My soul that hour shall draw your soul
    For ever nearer yet.

The Cloud Confines

The day is dark and the night
   To him that would search their heart;
   No lips of cloud that will part
Nor morning song in the light:
   Only, gazing alone,   5
   To him wild shadows are shown,
   Deep under deep unknown
And height above unknown height.
    Still we say as we go, —
     "Strange to think by the way,   10
   Whatever there is to know,
    That shall we know one day."

The Past is over and fled;
   Named new, we name it the old;
   Thereof some tale hath been told,   15
But no word comes from the dead;
   Whether at all they be,
   Or whether as bond or free,
   Or whether they too were we,

Or by what spell they have sped.   20
    Still we say as we go, —
      "Strange to think by the way,
    Whatever there is to know,
      That shall we know one day."

What of the heart of hate   25
  That beats in thy breast, O Time? —
  Red strife from the furthest prime,
And anguish of fierce debate;
  War that shatters her slain,
  And peace that grinds them as grain,   30
  And eyes fixed ever in vain
On the pitiless eyes of Fate.
    Still we say as we go, —
      "Strange to think by the way,
    Whatever there is to know,   35
      That shall we know one day."

What of the heart of love
  That bleeds in thy breast, O Man? —
  Thy kisses snatched 'neath the ban
Of fangs that mock them above;   40
  Thy bells prolonged unto knells,
  Thy hope that a breath dispels,
  Thy bitter forlorn farewells
And the empty echoes thereof?
    Still we say as we go, —   45
      "Strange to think by the way,
    Whatever there is to know,
      That shall we know one day."

The sky leans dumb on the sea,
  Aweary with all its wings;   50
  And oh! the song the sea sings
Is dark everlastingly.
  Our past is clean forgot,
  Our present is and is not,
  Our future's a sealed seedplot,   55
And what betwixt them are we? —
    We who say as we go, —
      "Strange to think by the way,
    Whatever there is to know,
      That shall we know one day."   60

PART FIVE

The Early Italian Poets (1861, 1874)

PREFACE TO THE FIRST EDITION (1861)

I need not dilate here on the characteristics of the first epoch of Italian Poetry; since the extent of my translated selections is sufficient to afford a complete view of it. Its great beauties may often remain unapproached in the versions here attempted; but, at the same time, its imperfections are not all to be charged to the translator. Among these I may refer to its limited range of subject and continual obscurity, as well as to its monotony in the use of rhymes or frequent substitution of assonances. But to compensate for much that is incomplete and inexperienced, these poems possess, in their degree, beauties of a kind which can never again exist in art; and offer, besides, a treasure of grace and variety in the formation of their metres. Nothing but a strong impression, first of their poetic value, and next of the biographical interest of some of them (chiefly of those in my first division), would have inclined me to bestow the time and trouble which have resulted in this collection.

Much has been said, and in many respects justly, against the value of metrical translation. But I think it would be admitted that the tributary art might find a not illegitimate use in the case of poems which come down to us in such a form as do these early Italian ones. Struggling originally with corrupt dialect and imperfect expression, and hardly kept alive through centuries of neglect, they have reached that last and worst state in which the *coup-de-grâce* has almost been dealt them by clumsy transcription and pedantic superstructure. At this stage the task of talking much more about them in any language is hardly to be entered upon; and a translation (involving as it does the necessity of settling many points without discussion), remains perhaps the most direct form of commentary.

The life-blood of rhythmical translation is this commandment, — that a good poem shall not be turned into a bad one. The only true motive for putting poetry into a fresh language must be to endow a fresh nation, as far as possible, with one more possession of beauty. Poetry not being an exact science, literality of rendering is altogether secondary to this chief law. I say *literality*, — not fidelity, which is by no means the same thing. When literality can be combined with what is thus the primary condition of success, the translator is fortunate, and must strive his utmost to unite them; when such object can only be attained by paraphrase, that is his only path.

Any merit possessed by these translations is derived from an effort to follow this principle; and, in some degree, from the fact that such painstaking in arrangement and descriptive heading as is often indispensable to old and especially to "occasional" poetry, has here been bestowed on these poets for the first time.

That there are many defects in this collection, or that the above merit is its defect, or that it has no merits but only defects, are discoveries so sure to be made if necessary (or perhaps here and there in any case), that I may safely leave them in other hands. The series has probably a wider scope than some readers might look for, and includes now and then (though I believe in rare instances) matter which may not meet with universal approval; and whose introduction, needed as it is by the literary aim of my work, is I know inconsistent with the principles of pretty bookmaking. My wish has been to give a full and truthful view of early Italian poetry; not to make it appear to consist only of certain elements to the exclusion of others equally belonging to it.

Of the difficulties I have had to encounter, — the causes of imperfections for which I have no other excuse, — it is the reader's best privilege to remain ignorant; but I may perhaps be pardoned for briefly referring to such among these as concern the exigencies of translation. The task of the translator (and with all humility be it spoken) is one of some self-denial. Often would he avail himself of any special grace of his own idiom and epoch, if only his will belonged to him: often would some cadence serve him but for his author's structure — some structure but for his author's cadence: often the beautiful turn of a stanza must be weakened to adopt some rhyme which will tally, and he sees the poet revelling in abundance of language where himself is scantily supplied. Now he would slight the matter for the music, and now the music for the matter; but no, — he must deal to each alike. Sometimes too a flaw in the work galls him, and he would fain remove it, doing for the poet that which his age denied him; but no, — it is not in the bond. His path is like that of Aladdin through the enchanted vaults: many are the precious fruits and flowers which he must pass by unheeded in search for the lamp alone; happy if at last, when brought to light, it does not prove that his old lamp has been exchanged for a new one, — glittering indeed to the eye, but scarcely of the same virtue nor with the same genius at its summons.

In relinquishing this work (which, small as it is, is the only contribution I expect to make to our English knowledge of old Italy), I feel, as it were, divided from my youth. The first associations I have are connected with my father's devoted studies, which, from his own point of view, have done so much towards the general investigation of Dante's writings. Thus, in those early days, all around me partook of the influence of the great Florentine; till, from viewing it as a natural element, I also, growing older, was drawn within the circle. I trust that from this the reader may place more confidence in a work not carelessly undertaken, though produced in the spare-time of other pursuits more closely followed. He should perhaps be told that it has occupied the leisure moments of not a few years; thus affording, often at long intervals, every opportunity for consideration and revision; and that on the score of care, at least, he has no need to mistrust it. Nevertheless, I know there is no great stir to be made by launching afresh, on high-seas busy with new traffic, the ships which have been long outstripped and the ensigns which are grown strange.

Canzone. Of the Gentle Heart (Guido Guinicelli)

Within the gentle heart Love shelters him,
  As birds within the green shade of the grove.
Before the gentle heart, in Nature's scheme,
  Love was not, nor the gentle heart ere Love.
    For with the sun, at once,   5
So sprang the light immediately; nor was
    Its birth before the sun's.
  And Love hath his effect in gentleness
    Of very self; even as
Within the middle fire the heat's excess.   10

The fire of Love comes to the gentle heart
  Like as its virtue to a precious stone;
To which no star its influence can impart
  Till it is made a pure thing by the sun:
    For when the sun hath smit   15
From out its essence that which there was vile,
    The star endoweth it.
  And so the heart created by God's breath
    Pure, true, and clean from guile,
A woman, like a star, enamoureth.   20

In gentle heart Love for like reason is
  For which the lamp's high flame is fanned and bow'd:
Clear, piercing bright, it shines for its own bliss;
  Nor would it burn there else, it is so proud.
    For evil natures meet   25
With Love as it were water met with fire,
    As cold abhorring heat.
Through gentle heart Love doth a track divine, —
    Like knowing like; the same
As diamond runs through iron in the mine.   30

The sun strikes full upon the mud all day;
  It remains vile, nor the sun's worth is less.
"By race I am gentle," the proud man doth say:
  He is the mud, the sun is gentleness.
    Let no man predicate   35

That aught the name of gentleness should have,
    Even in a king's estate,
Except the heart there be a gentle man's.
    The star-beam lights the wave, —
Heaven holds the star and the star's radiance.   40

God, in the understanding of high Heaven,
    Burns more than in our sight the living sun:
There to behold His Face unveiled is given;
    And Heaven, whose will is homage paid to One,
    Fulfils the things which live   45
In God, from the beginning excellent.
    So should my lady give
That truth which in her eyes is glorified,
    On which her heart is bent,
To me whose service waiteth at her side.   50

My lady, God shall ask, "What daredst thou?"
    (When my soul stands with all her acts review'd);
"Thou passedst Heaven, into My sight, as now,
    To make Me of vain love similitude.
    To Me doth praise belong,   55
And to the Queen of all the realm of grace
    Who slayeth fraud and wrong."
Then may I plead: "As though from Thee he came,
    Love wore an angel's face:
Lord, if I loved her, count it not my shame."   60

Of His Lady in Heaven (Jacopo da Lentino)

I have it in my heart to serve God so
    That into Paradise I shall repair, —
    The holy place through the which everywhere
I have heard say that joy and solace flow.
Without my lady I were loth to go, —   5
    She who has the bright face and the bright hair;
    Because if she were absent, I being there,
My pleasure would be less than nought, I know.
Look you, I say not this to such intent
    As that I there would deal in any sin: 10
    I only would behold her gracious mien,
    And beautiful soft eyes, and lovely face,
That so it should be my complete content
    To see my lady joyful in her place.

Of His Lady, and of Her Portrait (Jacopo da Lentino)

Marvellously elate,
   Love makes my spirit warm
      With noble sympathies;
As one whose mind is set
   Upon some glorious form,   5
      To paint it as it is; —
I verily who bear
Thy face at heart, most fair,
      Am like to him in this.

Not outwardly declared,   10
   Within me dwells enclosed
      Thine image as thou art.
Ah! strangely hath it fared!
   I know not if thou know'st
      The love within my heart.   15
Exceedingly afraid,
My hope I have not said,
      But gazed on thee apart.

Because desire was strong,
   I made a portraiture   20
      In thine own likeness, love;
When absence has grown long,
   I gaze, till I am sure
      That I behold thee move;
As one who purposeth   25
To save himself by faith,
      Yet sees not, nor can prove.

Then comes the burning pain;
   As with the man that hath
      A fire within his breast, —
When most he struggles, then   30
   Most boils the flame in wrath,
      And will not let him rest.
So still I burned and shook,
To pass, and not to look   35
      In thy face, loveliest.

For where thou art I pass,
   And do not lift mine eyes,
      Lady, to look on thee:

But, as I go, alas!   40
   With bitterness of sighs
      I mourn exceedingly.
Alas! the constant woe!
Myself I do not know,
      So sore it troubles me.   45

And I have sung thy praise,
   Lady, and many times
      Have told thy beauties o'er.
Hast heard in anyways,
   Perchance, that these my rhymes   50
      Are song-craft and no more?
Nay, rather deem, when thou
Shalt see me pass and bow,
   These words I sicken for.

Delicate song of mine,   55
   Go sing thou a new strain:
Seek, with the first sunshine,
Our lady, mine and thine, —
   The rose of Love's domain,
Than red gold comelier.   60
   "Lady, in Love's name hark
   To Jacopo the clerk,
Born in Lentino here."

Canzone. Of His Dead Lady (Giacomo Pugliesi)

Death, why hast thou made life so hard to bear,
   Taking my lady hence? Hast thou no whit
Of shame? The youngest flower and the most fair
   Thou hast plucked away, and the world wanteth it.
O leaden Death, hast thou no pitying?   5
Our warm love's very spring
   Thou stopp'st, and endest what was holy and meet;
And of my gladdening
Mak'st a most woful thing,
And in my heart dost bid the bird not sing   10
   That sang so sweet.

Once the great joy and solace that I had
   Was more than is with other gentlemen: —
Now is my love gone hence, who made me glad.
   With her that hope I lived in she hath ta'en,   15

And left me nothing but these sighs and tears, —
Nothing of the old years
   That come not back again,
Wherein I was so happy, being hers.
Now to mine eyes her face no more appears,   20
Nor doth her voice make music in mine ears,
   As it did then.

O God, why hast thou made my grief so deep?
   Why set me in the dark to grope and pine?
Why parted me from her companionship,   25
   And crushed the hope which was a gift of thine?
To think, dear, that I never any more
Can see thee as before!
   Who is it shuts thee in?
Who hides that smile for which my heart is sore,   30
And drowns those words that I am longing for,
   Lady of mine?

Where is my lady, and the lovely face
   She had, and the sweet motion when she walk'd?
Her chaste, mild favour — her so delicate grace —   35
   Her eyes, her mouth, and the dear way she talk'd? —
Her courteous bending — her most noble air —
The soft fall of her hair? . . .
My lady — she who to my soul so rare
   A gladness brought!   40
Now I do never see her anywhere,
And may not, looking in her eyes, gain there
   The blessing which I sought.

So if I had the realm of Hungary,
   With Greece, and all the Almayn even to France,   45
Or Saint Sophia's treasure-hoard, you see
   All could not give me back her countenance.
For since the day when my dear lady died
From us, (with God being born and glorified),
   No more pleasaunce   50
Her image bringeth, seated at my side,
But only tears. Ay me! the strength and pride
   Which it brought once.

Had I my will, beloved, I would say
   To God, unto whose bidding all things bow,   55
That we were still together night and day:
   Yet be it done as His behests allow.
I do remember that while she remain'd

With me, she often called me her sweet friend;
   But does not now,   60
Because God drew her towards Him, in the end.
Lady, that peace which none but He can send
   Be thine. Even so.

How He Dreams of His Lady (Bonaggiunto Urbiciani, da Lucca)

Lady, my wedded thought,
When to thy shape 'tis wrought,
Can think of nothing else
   But only of thy grace,
   And of those gentle ways   5
Wherein thy life excels.
For ever, sweet one, dwells
Thine image on my sight,
   (Even as it were the gem
   Whose name is as thy name)*   10
And fills the sense with light.

Continual ponderings
That brood upon these things
Yield constant agony:
   Yea, the same thoughts have crept   15
   About me as I slept.
My spirit looks at me,
And asks, "Is sleep for thee?
Nay, mourner, do not sleep,
   But fix thine eyes, for lo!   20
   Love's fulness thou shalt know
By steadfast gaze and deep."

Then, burning, I awake,
Sore tempted to partake
Of dreams that seek thy sight: 25
   Until, being greatly stirr'd,
   I turn to where I heard
That whisper in the night;
And there a breath of light
Shines like a silver star.   30
   The same is mine own soul,

*The lady was probably called Diamante, Margherita, or some similar name. (Note to Flor. Ed. 1816.)

Which lures me to the goal
Of dreams that gaze afar.

But now my sleep is lost;
And through this uttermost   35
Sharp longing for thine eyes,
   At length it may be said
   That I indeed am mad
With love's extremities.
Yet when in such sweet wise   40
Thou passest and dost smile,
   My heart so fondly burns,
   That unto sweetness turns
Its bitter pang the while.

Even so Love rends apart   45
My spirit and my heart,
Lady, in loving thee;
   Till when I see thee now,
   Life beats within my brow
And would be gone from me.   50
So hear I ceaselessly
Love's whisper, well fulfill'd, —
   Even I am he, even so,
   Whose flame thy heart doth know:
And while I strive I yield.   55

His Portrait of His Lady, Angiola of Verona (Fazio degli Uberti)

I look at the crisp golden-threaded hair
   Whereof, to thrall my heart, Love twists a net;
   Using at times a string of pearls for bait,
     And sometimes with a single rose therein.
I look into her eyes which unaware   5
   Through mine own eyes to my heart penetrate;
   Their splendour, that is excellently great,
     To the sun's radiance seeming near akin,
     Yet from herself a sweeter light to win.
So that I, gazing on that lovely one,   10
   Discourse in this wise with my secret thought: —
   "Woe's me! why am I not,
Even as my wish, alone with her alone? —
   That hair of hers, so heavily uplaid,
   To shed down braid by braid,   15

And make myself two mirrors of her eyes
Within whose light all other glory dies."

I look at the amorous beautiful mouth,
   The spacious forehead which her locks enclose,
     The small white teeth, the straight and shapely nose,   20
      And the clear brows of a sweet pencilling.
And then the thought within me gains full growth,
   Saying, "Be careful that thy glance now goes
     Between her lips, red as an open rose,
      Quite full of every dear and precious thing;   25
      And listen to her gracious answering,
Born of the gentle mind that in her dwells,
   Which from all things can glean the nobler half.
   Look thou when she doth laugh
How much her laugh is sweeter than aught else."   30
   Thus evermore my spirit makes avow
   Touching her mouth; till now
I would give anything that I possess,
Only to hear her mouth say frankly, "Yes."

I look at her white easy neck, so well   35
   From shoulders and from bosom lifted out;
     And at her round cleft chin, which beyond doubt
      No fancy in the world could have design'd.
And then, with longing grown more voluble,
   "Were it not pleasant now," pursues my thought,   40
   "To have that neck within thy two arms caught
     And kiss it till the mark were left behind?"
     Then, urgently: "The eyelids of thy mind
Open thou: if such loveliness be given
   To sight here, — what of that which she doth hide?   45
   Only the wondrous ride
Of sun and planets through the visible heaven
   Tells us that there beyond is Paradise.
   Thus, if thou fix thine eyes,
Of a truth certainly thou must infer   50
That every earthly joy abides in her."

I look at the large arms, so lithe and round, —
   At the hands, which are white and rosy too, —
     At the long fingers, clasped and woven through,
      Bright with the ring which one of them doth wear.   55
Then my thought whispers: "Were thy body wound
   Within those arms, as loving women's do,
   In all thy veins were born a life made new

Which thou couldst find no language to declare.
  Behold if any picture can compare   60
With her just limbs, each fit in shape and size,
  Or match her angel's colour like a pearl.
    She is a gentle girl
To see; yet when it needs, her scorn can rise.
  Meek, bashful, and in all things temperate,   65
    Her virtue holds its state;
In whose least act there is that gift express'd
Which of all reverence makes her worthiest."

Soft as a peacock steps she, or as a stork
  Straight on herself, taller and statelier: 70
  'Tis a good sight how every limb doth stir
    For ever in a womanly sweet way.
"Open thy soul to see God's perfect work,"
  (My thought begins afresh), "and look at her
  When with some lady-friend exceeding fair   75
    She bends and mingles arms and locks in play.
    Even as all lesser lights vanish away,
When the sun moves, before his dazzling face,
  So is this lady brighter than all these.
  How should she fail to please, —   80
Love's self being no more than her loveliness?
  In all her ways some beauty springs to view;
    All that she loves to do
Tends alway to her honour's single scope;
And only from good deeds she draws her hope."   85

Song, thou canst surely say, without pretence,
  That since the first fair woman ever made,
    Not one can have display'd
      More power upon all hearts than this one doth
      Because in her are both   90
Loveliness and the soul's true excellence: —
And yet (woe's me!) is pity absent thence?

THE NEW LIFE (Dante Alighieri)

In that part of the book of my memory before the which is little that can be read, there is a rubric, saying, *Incipit Vita Nova.** Under such rubric I find written many things; and among them the words which I purpose to copy into this little book; if not all of them, at the least their substance.

*"Here beginneth the new life."

Nine times already since my birth had the heaven of light returned to the self-same point almost, as concerns its own revolution, when first the glorious Lady of my mind was made manifest to mine eyes; even she who was called Beatrice by many who knew not wherefore.* She had already been in this life for so long as that, within her time, the starry heaven had moved towards the Eastern quarter one of the twelve parts of a degree; so that she appeared to me at the beginning of her ninth year almost, and I saw her almost at the end of my ninth year. Her dress, on that day, was of a most noble colour, a subdued and goodly crimson, girdled and adorned in such sort as best suited with her very tender age. At that moment, I say most truly that the spirit of life, which hath its dwelling in the secretest chamber of the heart, began to tremble so violently that the least pulses of my body shook therewith; and in trembling it said these words: *Ecce deus fortior me, qui veniens dominabitur mihi.*† At that moment the animate spirit, which dwelleth in the lofty chamber whither all the senses carry their perceptions, was filled with wonder, and speaking more especially unto the spirits of the eyes, said these words: *Apparuit jam beatitudo vestra.*‡ At that moment the natural spirit, which dwelleth there where our nourishment is administered, began to weep, and in weeping said these words: *Heu miser! quia frequenter impeditus ero deinceps.*§

I say that, from that time forward, Love quite governed my soul; which was immediately espoused to him, and with so safe and undisputed a lordship, (by virtue of strong imagination) that I had nothing left for it but to do all his bidding continually. He oftentimes commanded me to seek if I might see this youngest of the Angels: wherefore I in my boyhood often went in search of her, and found her so noble and praiseworthy that certainly of her might have been said those words of the poet Homer, "She seemed not to be the daughter of a mortal man, but of God."§ And albeit her image, that was with me always, was an exultation of Love to subdue me, it was yet of so perfect a quality that it never allowed me to be overruled by Love without the faithful counsel of reason, whensoever such counsel was useful to be heard. But seeing that were I to dwell overmuch on the passions and doings of such early youth, my words might be counted something fabulous, I will therefore put them aside; and passing many things that may be conceived by the pattern of these, I will come to such as are writ in my memory with a better distinctness.

After the lapse of so many days that nine years exactly were completed since the above-written appearance of this most gracious being, on the last of those

---

*In reference to the meaning of the name, "She who confers blessing." We learn from Boccaccio that this first meeting took place at a May Feast, given in the year 1274 by Folco Portinari, father of Beatrice, who ranked among the principal citizens of Florence: to which feast Dante accompanied his father, Alighiero Alighieri.

†"Here is a deity stronger than I; who, coming, shall rule over me."

‡"Your beatitude hath now been made manifest unto you."

§"Woe is me! how often shall I be disturbed from this time forth!"

§(*Iliad*, XXIV. 258.)

days it happened that the same wonderful lady appeared to me dressed all in pure white, between two gentle ladies elder than she. And passing through a street, she turned her eyes thither where I stood sorely abashed: and by her unspeakable courtesy, which is now guerdoned in the Great Cycle, she saluted me with so virtuous a bearing that I seemed then and there to behold the very limits of blessedness. The hour of her most sweet salutation was certainly the ninth of that day; and because it was the first time that any words from her reached mine ears, I came into such sweetness that I parted thence as one intoxicated. And betaking me to the loneliness of mine own room, I fell to thinking of this most courteous lady, thinking of whom I was overtaken by a pleasant slumber, wherein a marvellous vision was presented to me: for there appeared to be in my room a mist of the colour of fire, within the which I discerned the figure of a lord of terrible aspect to such as should gaze upon him, but who seemed therewithal to rejoice inwardly that it was a marvel to see. Speaking he said many things, among the which I could understand but few; and of these, this: *Ego dominus tuus.** In his arms it seemed to me that a person was sleeping, covered only with a blood-coloured cloth; upon whom looking very attentively, I knew that it was the lady of the salutation who had deigned the day before to salute me. And he who held her held also in his hand a thing that was burning in flames; and he said to me, *Vide cor tuum.*† But when he had remained with me a little while, I thought that he set himself to awaken her that slept; after the which he made her to eat that thing which flamed in his hand; and she ate as one fearing. Then, having waited again a space, all his joy was turned into most bitter weeping; and as he wept he gathered the lady into his arms, and it seemed to me that he went with her up towards heaven: whereby such a great anguish came upon me that my light slumber could not endure through it, but was suddenly broken. And immediately having considered, I knew that the hour wherein this vision had been made manifest to me was the fourth hour (which is to say, the first of the nine last hours) of the night.

Then, musing on what I had seen, I proposed to relate the same to many poets who were famous in that day: and for that I had myself in some sort the art of discoursing with rhyme, I resolved on making a sonnet, in the which, having saluted all such as are subject unto Love, and entreated them to expound my vision, I should write unto them those things which I had seen in my sleep. And the sonnet I made was this: —

> To every heart which the sweet pain doth move,
>   And unto which these words may now be brought
>   For true interpretation and kind thought,
> Be greeting in our Lord's name, which is Love.
> Of those long hours wherein the stars, above,   5

* "I am thy master."
† "Behold thy heart."

Wake and keep watch, the third was almost nought
When Love was shown me with such terrors fraught
As may not carelessly be spoken of.

He seem'd like one who is full of joy, and had
  My heart within his hand, and on his arm
    My lady, with a mantle round her, slept;
Whom (having wakened her) anon he made
  To eat that heart; she ate, as fearing harm.
    Then he went out; and as he went, he wept.

10

*This sonnet is divided into two parts. In the first part I give greeting, and ask an an-
swer; in the second, I signify what thing has to be answered to. The second part com-
mences here: "Of those long hours."*

To this sonnet I received many answers, conveying many different opinions; of
the which, one was sent by him whom I now call the first among my friends, and
it began thus, "Unto my thinking thou beheld'st all worth."* And indeed, it was
when he learned that I was he who had sent those rhymes to him, that our friend-
ship commenced. But the true meaning of that vision was not then perceived by
any one, though it be now evident to the least skilful.

From that night forth, the natural functions of my body began to be vexed and
impeded, for I was given up wholly to thinking of this most gracious creature:
whereby in short space I became so weak and so reduced that it was irksome to
many of my friends to look upon me; while others, being moved by spite, went
about to discover what it was my wish should be concealed. Wherefore I, (per-
ceiving the drift of their unkindly questions), by Love's will, who directed me ac-
cording to the counsels of reason, told them how it was Love himself who had
thus dealt with me: and I said so, because the thing was so plainly to be discerned
in my countenance that there was no longer any means of concealing it. But
when they went on to ask, "And by whose help hath Love done this?" I looked
in their faces smiling, and spake no word in return.

Now it fell on a day, that this most gracious creature was sitting where words
were to be heard of the Queen of Glory; † and I was in a place whence mine eyes
could behold their beatitude: and betwixt her and me, in a direct line, there sat
another lady of a pleasant favour; who looked round at me many times, marvel-
ling at my continued gaze which seemed to have *her* for its object. And many per-
ceived that she thus looked; so that departing thence, I heard it whispered after
me, "Look you to what a pass *such a lady* hath brought him"; and in saying this
they named her who had been midway between the most gentle Beatrice, and
mine eyes. Therefore I was reassured, and knew that for that day my secret had
not become manifest. Then immediately it came into my mind that I might make

*The friend of whom Dante here speaks was Guido Cavalcanti.
†i.e. in a church.

use of this lady as a screen to the truth: and so well did I play my part that the most of those who had hitherto watched and wondered at me, now imagined they had found me out. By her means I kept my secret concealed till some years were gone over; and for my better security, I even made divers rhymes in her honour; whereof I shall here write only as much as concerneth the most gentle Beatrice, which is but a very little. Moreover, about the same time while this lady was a screen for so much love on my part, I took the resolution to set down the name of this most gracious creature accompanied with many other women's names, and especially with hers whom I spake of. And to this end I put together the names of sixty of the most beautiful ladies in that city where God had placed mine own lady; and these names I introduced in an epistle in the form of a *sirvent,* which it is not my intention to transcribe here. Neither should I have said anything of this matter, did I not wish to take note of a certain strange thing, to wit: that having written the list, I found my lady's name would not stand otherwise than ninth in order among the names of these ladies.

Now it so chanced with her by whose means I had thus long time concealed my desire, that it behoved her to leave the city I speak of, and to journey afar: wherefore I, being sorely perplexed at the loss of so excellent a defence, had more trouble than even I could before have supposed. And thinking that if I spoke not somewhat mournfully of her departure, my former counterfeiting would be the more quickly perceived, I determined that I would make a grievous sonnet* thereof; the which I will write here, because it hath certain words in it whereof my lady was the immediate cause, as will be plain to him that understands. And the sonnet was this: —

All ye that pass along Love's trodden way,
Pause ye awhile and say
  If there be any grief like unto mine:
I pray you that you hearken a short space
Patiently, if my case   5
  Be not a piteous marvel and a sign.

Love (never, certes, for my worthless part,
But of his own great heart),
  Vouchsafed to me a life so calm and sweet
That oft I heard folk question as I went   10
What such great gladness meant: —
  They spoke of it behind me in the street.

But now that fearless bearing is all gone
  Which with Love's hoarded wealth was given me;

---

*It will be observed that this poem is not what we now call a sonnet. Its structure, however, is analogous to that of the sonnet, being two sextets followed by two quatrains, instead of two quatrains followed by two triplets. Dante applies the term sonnet to both these forms of composition, and to no other.

Till I am grown to be   15
So poor that I have dread to think thereon.

And thus it is that I, being like as one
   Who is ashamed and hides his poverty,
   Without seem full of glee,
And let my heart within travail and moan.   20

This poem has two principal parts; for, in the first, I mean to call the Faithful of Love
in those words of Jeremias the Prophet, "O vos omnes qui transitis per viam, atten-
dite et videte si est dolor sicut dolor meus," and to pray them to stay and hear me.
In the second I tell where Love had placed me, with a meaning other than that which
the last part of the poem shows, and I say what I have lost. The second part begins here:
"Love, (never, certes)."

A certain while after the departure of that lady, it pleased the Master of the An-
gels to call into His glory a damsel, young and of a gentle presence, who had been
very lovely in the city I speak of: and I saw her body lying without its soul among
many ladies, who held a pitiful weeping. Whereupon, remembering that I had
seen her in the company of excellent Beatrice, I could not hinder myself from a
few tears; and weeping, I conceived to say somewhat of her death, in guerdon of
having seen her somewhile with my lady; which thing I spake of in the latter end
of the verses that I writ in this matter, as he will discern who understands. And I
wrote two sonnets, which are these: —

I.

Weep, Lovers, sith Love's very self doth weep,
   And sith the cause for weeping is so great;
   When now so many dames, of such estate
In worth, show with their eyes a grief so deep:
For Death the churl has laid his leaden sleep   5
   Upon a damsel who was fair of late,
   Defacing all our earth should celebrate, —
Yea all save virtue, which the soul doth keep.
Now hearken how much Love did honour her.
   I myself saw him in his proper form   10
      Bending above the motionless sweet dead,
And often gazing into Heaven; for there
   The soul now sits which when her life was warm
      Dwelt with the joyful beauty that is fled.

This first sonnet is divided into three parts. In the first, I call and beseech the Faith-
ful of Love to weep; and I say that their Lord weeps, and that they, hearing the reason
why he weeps, shall be more minded to listen to me. In the second, I relate this reason. In
the third, I speak of honour done by Love to this Lady. The second part begins here,
"When now so many dames"; the third here, "Now hearken."

II.

Death, alway cruel, Pity's foe in chief,
Mother who brought forth grief,
  Merciless judgment and without appeal!
  Since thou alone hast made my heart to feel
  This sadness and unweal,   5
My tongue upbraideth thee without relief.

And now (for I must rid thy name of ruth)
Behoves me speak the truth
  Touching thy cruelty and wickedness:
  Not that they be not known; but ne'ertheless   10
  I would give hate more stress
With them that feed on love in very sooth.

Out of this world thou hast driven courtesy,
  And virtue, dearly prized in womanhood;
  And out of youth's gay mood   15
The lovely lightness is quite gone through thee.

Whom now I mourn, no man shall learn from me
  Save by the measures of these praises given.
  Whoso deserves not Heaven
May never hope to have her company.*   20

This poem is divided into four parts. In the first I address Death by certain proper names of hers. In the second, speaking to her, I tell the reason why I am moved to denounce her. In the third, I rail against her. In the fourth, I turn to speak to a person undefined, although defined in my own conception. The second part commences here, "Since thou alone"; the third here, "And now (for I must)"; the fourth here, "Whoso deserves not."

Some days after the death of this lady, I had occasion to leave the city I speak of, and to go thitherwards where she abode who had formerly been my protection; albeit the end of my journey reached not altogether so far. And notwithstanding that I was visibly in the company of many, the journey was so irksome that I had scarcely sighing enough to ease my heart's heaviness; seeing that as I went, I left my beatitude behind me. Wherefore it came to pass that he who ruled me by virtue of my most gentle lady was made visible to my mind, in the light

---

* The commentators assert that the last two lines here do not allude to the dead lady, but to Beatrice. This would make the poem very clumsy in construction; yet there must be some covert allusion to Beatrice, as Dante himself intimates. The only form in which I can trace it consists in the implied assertion that such person as *had* enjoyed the dead lady's society was worthy of heaven, and that person was Beatrice. Or indeed the allusion to Beatrice might be in the first poem, where he says that Love "*in forma vera*" (that is, Beatrice), mourned over the corpse; as he afterwards says of Beatrice, "*Quella ha nome Amor.*" Most probably *both* allusions are intended.

habit of a traveller, coarsely fashioned. He appeared to me troubled, and looked always on the ground; saving only that sometimes his eyes were turned towards a river which was clear and rapid, and which flowed along the path I was taking. And then I thought that Love called me and said to me these words: "I come from that lady who was so long thy surety; for the matter of whose return, I know that it may not be. Wherefore I have taken that heart which I made thee leave with her, and do bear it unto another lady, who, as she was, shall be thy surety"; (and when he named her, I knew her well.) "And of these words I have spoken, if thou shouldst speak any again, let it be in such sort as that none shall perceive thereby that thy love was feigned for her, which thou must now feign for another." And when he had spoken thus, all my imagining was gone suddenly, for it seemed to me that Love became a part of myself: so that, changed as it were in mine aspect, I rode on full of thought the whole of that day, and with heavy sighing. And the day being over, I wrote this sonnet: —

> A day agone, as I rode sullenly
>   Upon a certain path that liked me not,
>   I met Love midway while the air was hot,
> Clothed lightly as a wayfarer might be.
> And for the cheer he showed, he seemed to me   5
>   As one who hath lost lordship he had got;
>   Advancing tow'rds me full of sorrowful thought,
> Bowing his forehead so that none should see.
> Then as I went, he called me by my name,
>   Saying: "I journey since the morn was dim   10
>   Thence where I made thy heart to be: which now
> I needs must bear unto another dame."
>   Wherewith so much passed into me of him
>   That he was gone, and I discerned not how.

This sonnet has three parts. In the first part, I tell how I met Love, and of his aspect. In the second, I tell what he said to me, although not in full, through the fear I had of discovering my secret. In the third, I say how he disappeared. The second part commences here, "Then as I went"; the third here, "Wherewith so much."

On my return, I set myself to seek out that lady whom my master had named to me while I journeyed sighing. And because I would be brief, I will now narrate that in a short while I made her my surety, in such sort that the matter was spoken of by many in terms scarcely courteous; through the which I had oftenwhiles many troublesome hours. And by this it happened (to wit: by this false and evil rumour which seemed to misfame me of vice) that she who was the destroyer of all evil and the queen of all good, coming where I was, denied me her most sweet salutation, in the which alone was my blessedness.

And here it is fitting for me to depart a little from this present matter, that it may be rightly understood of what surpassing virtue her salutation was to me. To the which end I say that when she appeared in any place, it seemed to me, by the hope of her excellent salutation, that there was no man mine enemy any longer; and such warmth of charity came upon me that most certainly in that moment I would have pardoned whosoever had done me an injury; and if one should then have questioned me concerning any matter, I could only have said unto him "Love," with a countenance clothed in humbleness. And what time she made ready to salute me, the spirit of Love, destroying all other perceptions, thrust forth the feeble spirits of my eyes, saying, "Do homage unto your mistress," and putting itself in their place to obey: so that he who would, might then have beheld Love, beholding the lids of mine eyes shake. And when this most gentle lady gave her salutation, Love, so far from being a medium beclouding mine intolerable beatitude, then bred in me such an overpowering sweetness that my body, being all subjected thereto, remained many times helpless and passive. Whereby it is made manifest that in her salutation alone was there any beatitude for me, which then very often went beyond my endurance.

And now, resuming my discourse, I will go on to relate that when, for the first time, this beatitude was denied me, I became possessed with such grief that parting myself from others, I went into a lonely place to bathe the ground with most bitter tears: and when, by this heat of weeping, I was somewhat relieved, I betook myself to my chamber, where I could lament unheard. And there, having prayed to the Lady of all Mercies, and having said also, "O Love, aid thou thy servant"; I went suddenly asleep like a beaten sobbing child. And in my sleep, towards the middle of it, I seemed to see in the room, seated at my side, a youth in very white raiment, who kept his eyes fixed on me in deep thought. And when he had gazed some time, I thought that he sighed and called to me in these words: *"Fili mi, tempus est ut praetermittantur simulata nostra."** And thereupon I seemed to know him; for the voice was the same wherewith he had spoken at other times in my sleep. Then looking at him, I perceived that he was weeping piteously, and that he seemed to be waiting for me to speak. Wherefore, taking heart, I began thus: "Why weepest thou, Master of all honour?" And he made answer to me: *"Ego tanquam centrum circuli, cui similimodo se habent circumferentiae partes: tu autem non sic."*† And thinking upon his words, they seemed to me obscure; so that again compelling myself unto speech, I asked of him: "What thing is this,

---

*"My son, it is time for us to lay aside our counterfeiting."
†"I am as the centre of a circle, to the which all parts of the circumference bear an equal relation: but with thee it is not thus." This phrase seems to have remained as obscure to commentators as Dante found it at the moment. No one, as far as I know, has even fairly tried to find a meaning for it. To me the following appears a not unlikely one. Love is weeping on Dante's account, and not on his own. He says, "I am the centre of a circle (*Amor che muove il sole e le altre stelle*): therefore all loveable objects, whether in heaven or earth, or any part of the circle's circumference, are equally near to me. Not so thou, who wilt one day lose Beatrice when she goes to heaven." The phrase would thus contain an intimation of the death of Beatrice, accounting for Dante being next told not to inquire the meaning of the speech, — "Demand no more than may be useful to thee."

Master, that thou hast spoken thus darkly?" To the which he made answer in the vulgar tongue: "Demand no more than may be useful to thee." Whereupon I began to discourse with him concerning her salutation which she had denied me; and when I had questioned him of the cause, he said these words: "Our Beatrice hath heard from certain persons, that the lady whom I named to thee while thou journeyedst full of sighs, is sorely disquieted by thy solicitations: and therefore this most gracious creature, who is the enemy of all disquiet, being fearful of such disquiet, refused to salute thee. For the which reason (albeit, in very sooth, thy secret must needs have become known to her by familiar observation) it is my will that thou compose certain things in rhyme, in the which thou shalt set forth how strong a mastership I have obtained over thee, through her; and how thou wast hers even from thy childhood. Also do thou call upon him that knoweth these things to bear witness to them, bidding him to speak with her thereof; the which I, who am he, will do willingly. And thus she shall be made to know thy desire; knowing which, she shall know likewise that they were deceived who spake of thee to her. And so write these things, that they shall seem rather to be spoken by a third person; and not directly by thee to her, which is scarce fitting. After the which, send them, not without me, where she may chance to hear them; but have fitted them with a pleasant music, into the which I will pass whensoever it needeth." With this speech he was away, and my sleep was broken up.

Whereupon, remembering me, I knew that I had beheld this vision during the ninth hour of the day; and I resolved that I would make a ditty, before I left my chamber, according to the words my master had spoken. And this is the ditty that I made: —

Song, 'tis my will that thou do seek out Love,
  And go with him where my dear lady is;
    That so my cause, the which thy harmonies
Do plead, his better speech may clearly prove.

Thou goest, my Song, in such a courteous kind,   5
  That even companionless
    Thou may'st rely on thyself anywhere.
And yet, an' thou wouldst get thee a safe mind,
  First unto Love address
    Thy steps; whose aid, mayhap, 'twere ill to spare: 10
    Seeing that she to whom thou mak'st thy prayer
Is, as I think, ill-minded unto me,
And that if Love do not companion thee,
  Thou'lt have perchance small cheer to tell me of.

With a sweet accent, when thou com'st to her,   15
  Begin thou in these words,
    First having craved a gracious audience:
"He who hath sent me as his messenger,
  Lady, thus much records,

An thou but suffer him, in his defence.   20
    Love, who comes with me, by thine influence
Can make this man do as it liketh him:
Wherefore, if this fault is or doth but seem
    Do thou conceive: for his heart cannot move."

Say to her also: "Lady, his poor heart   25
    Is so confirmed in faith
       That all its thoughts are but of serving thee:
'Twas early thine, and could not swerve apart."
    Then, if she wavereth,
       Bid her ask Love, who knows if these things be.   30
    And in the end, beg of her modestly
To pardon so much boldness: saying too: —
"If thou declare his death to be thy due,
    The thing shall come to pass, as doth behove."

Then pray thou of the Master of all ruth,   35
    Before thou leave her there,
       That he befriend my cause and plead it well.
"In guerdon of my sweet rhymes and my truth"
    (Entreat him) "stay with her;
       Let not the hope of thy poor servant fail;   40
    And if with her thy pleading should prevail,
Let her look on him and give peace to him."
    Gentle my Song, if good to thee it seem,
    Do this: so worship shall be thine and love.

*This ditty is divided into three parts. In the first, I tell it whither to go, and I encour-
age it, that it may go the more confidently, and I tell it whose company to join if it would
go with confidence and without any danger. In the second, I say that which it behoves the
ditty to set forth. In the third, I give it leave to start when it pleases, recommending its
course to the arms of Fortune. The second part begins here, "With a sweet accent"; the
third here, "Gentle my Song." Some might contradict me, and say that they understand
not whom I address in the second person, seeing that the ditty is merely the very words I
am speaking. And therefore I say that this doubt I intend to solve and clear up in this
little book itself, at a more difficult passage, and then let him understand who now
doubts, or would now contradict as aforesaid.*

After this vision I have recorded, and having written those words which Love
had dictated to me, I began to be harassed with many and divers thoughts, by
each of which I was sorely tempted; and in especial, there were four among them
that left me no rest. The first was this: "Certainly the lordship of Love is good;
seeing that it diverts the mind from all mean things." The second was this: "Cer-
tainly the lordship of Love is evil; seeing that the more homage his servants pay
to him, the more grievous and painful are the torments wherewith he torments
them." The third was this: "The name of Love is so sweet in the hearing that it

would not seem possible for its effects to be other than sweet; seeing that the name must needs be like unto the thing named: as it is written: *Nomina sunt consequentia rerum.*"* And the fourth was this: "The lady whom Love hath chosen out to govern thee is not as other ladies, whose hearts are easily moved."

And by each one of these thoughts I was so sorely assailed that I was like unto him who doubteth which path to take, and wishing to go, goeth not. And if I bethought myself to seek out some point at the which all these paths might be found to meet, I discerned but one way, and that irked me; to wit, to call upon Pity, and to commend myself unto her. And it was then that, feeling a desire to write somewhat thereof in rhyme, I wrote this sonnet: —

> All my thoughts always speak to me of Love,
>   Yet have between themselves such difference
>   That while one bids me bow with mind and sense,
> A second saith, "Go to: look thou above";
> The third one, hoping, yields me joy enough;   5
>   And with the last come tears, I scarce know whence:
>   All of them craving pity in sore suspense,
> Trembling with fears that the heart knoweth of.
> And thus, being all unsure which path to take,
>   Wishing to speak I know not what to say,   10
>   And lose myself in amorous wanderings:
> Until, (my peace with all of them to make),
>   Unto mine enemy I needs must pray,
>   My lady Pity, for the help she brings.

This sonnet may be divided into four parts. In the first, I say and propound that all my thoughts are concerning Love. In the second, I say that they are diverse, and I relate their diversity. In the third, I say wherein they all seem to agree. In the fourth, I say that, wishing to speak of Love, I know not from which of these thoughts to take my argument; and that if I would take it from all, I shall have to call upon mine enemy, my Lady Pity. "Lady" I say as in a scornful mode of speech. The second begins here, "Yet have between themselves"; the third, "All of them craving"; the fourth, "And thus."

After this battling with many thoughts, it chanced on a day that my most gracious lady was with a gathering of ladies in a certain place; to the which I was conducted by a friend of mine; he thinking to do me a great pleasure by showing me the beauty of so many women. Then I, hardly knowing whereunto he conducted me, but trusting in him (who yet was leading his friend to the last verge of life), made question: "To what end are we come among these ladies?" and he answered: "To the end that they may be worthily served." And they were assembled around a gentlewoman who was given in marriage on that day; the custom of the city being that these should bear her company when she sat down for the first

*"Names are the consequents of things."

time at table in the house of her husband. Therefore I, as was my friend's pleasure, resolved to stay with him and do honour to those ladies.

But as soon as I had thus resolved, I began to feel a faintness and a throbbing at my left side, which soon took possession of my whole body. Whereupon I remember that I covertly leaned my back unto a painting that ran round the walls of that house; and being fearful lest my trembling should be discerned of them, I lifted mine eyes to look on those ladies, and then first perceived among them the excellent Beatrice. And when I perceived her, all my senses were overpowered by the great lordship that Love obtained, finding himself so near unto that most gracious being, until nothing but the spirits of sight remained to me; and even these remained driven out of their own instruments because Love entered in that honoured place of theirs, that so he might the better behold her. And although I was other than at first, I grieved for the spirits so expelled which kept up a sore lament, saying: "If he had not in this wise thrust us forth, we also should behold the marvel of this lady." By this, many of her friends, having discerned my confusion, began to wonder; and together with herself, kept whispering of me and mocking me. Whereupon my friend, who knew not what to conceive, took me by the hands, and drawing me forth from among them, required to know what ailed me. Then, having first held me at quiet for a space until my perceptions were come back to me, I made answer to my friend: "Of a surety I have now set my feet on that point of life, beyond the which he must not pass who would return."*

Afterwards, leaving him, I went back to the room where I had wept before; and again weeping and ashamed, said: "If this lady but knew of my condition, I do not think that she would thus mock at me; nay, I am sure that she must needs feel some pity." And in my weeping I bethought me to write certain words, in the which, speaking to her, I should signify the occasion of my disfigurement, telling her also how I knew that she had no knowledge thereof: which, if it were known, I was certain must move others to pity. And then, because I hoped that peradventure it might come into her hearing, I wrote this sonnet.

> Even as the others mock, thou mockest me;
>   Not dreaming, noble lady, whence it is
>   That I am taken with strange semblances,
> Seeing thy face which is so fair to see:
> For else, compassion would not suffer thee   5
>   To grieve my heart with such harsh scoffs as these.
>   Lo! Love, when thou art present, sits at ease,

*It is difficult not to connect Dante's agony at this wedding-feast with our knowledge that in her twenty-first year Beatrice was wedded to Simone de' Bardi. That she herself was the bride on this occasion might seem out of the question, from the fact of its not being in any way so stated: but on the other hand, Dante's silence throughout the *Vita Nuova* as regards her marriage (which must have brought deep sorrow even to his ideal love) is so startling, that we might almost be led to conceive in this passage the only intimation of it which he thought fit to give.

And bears his mastership so mightily,
That all my troubled senses he thrusts out,
   Sorely tormenting some, and slaying some,   10
      Till none but he is left and has free range
      To gaze on thee. This makes my face to change
   Into another's; while I stand all dumb,
And hear my senses clamour in their rout.

*This sonnet I divide not into parts, because a division is only made to open the mean-
ing of the thing divided: and this, as it is sufficiently manifest through the reasons given,
has no need of division. True it is that, amid the words whereby is shown the occasion of
this sonnet, dubious words are to be found; namely, when I say that Love kills all my spir-
its, but that the visual remain in life, only outside of their own instruments. And this
difficulty it is impossible for any to solve who is not in equal guise liege unto Love; and,
to those who are so, that is manifest which would clear up the dubious words. And there-
fore it were not well for me to expound this difficulty, inasmuch as my speaking would be
either fruitless or else superfluous.*

A while after this strange disfigurement, I became possessed with a strong con-
ception which left me but very seldom, and then to return quickly. And it was
this: "Seeing that thou comest into such scorn by the companionship of this lady,
wherefore seekest thou to behold her? If she should ask thee this thing, what an-
swer couldst thou make unto her? yea, even though thou wert master of all thy
faculties, and in no way hindered from answering." Unto the which, another very
humble thought said in reply: "If I were master of all my faculties, and in no way
hindered from answering, I would tell her that no sooner do I image to myself
her marvellous beauty than I am possessed with the desire to behold her, the
which is of so great strength that it kills and destroys in my memory all those
things which might oppose it; and it is therefore that the great anguish I have en-
dured thereby is yet not enough to restrain me from seeking to behold her." And
then, because of these thoughts, I resolved to write somewhat, wherein, having
pleaded mine excuse, I should tell her of what I felt in her presence. Whereupon
I wrote this sonnet: —

The thoughts are broken in my memory,
   Thou lovely Joy, whene'er I see thy face;
   When thou art near me, Love fills up the space,
Often repeating, "If death irk thee, fly."
My face shows my heart's colour, verily,   5
   Which, fainting, seeks for any leaning-place;
   Till, in the drunken terror of disgrace,
The very stones seem to be shrieking, "Die!"
It were a grievous sin, if one should not
   Strive then to comfort my bewildered mind   10
      (Though merely with a simple pitying)

For the great anguish which thy scorn has wrought
  In the dead sight o' the eyes grown nearly blind,
    Which look for death as for a blessed thing.

This sonnet is divided into two parts. In the first, I tell the cause why I abstain not from coming to this lady. In the second, I tell what befalls me through coming to her; and this part begins here, "When thou art near." And also this second part divides into five distinct statements. For, in the first, I say what Love, counselled by Reason, tells me when I am near the lady. In the second, I set forth the state of my heart by the example of the face. In the third, I say how all ground of trust fails me. In the fourth, I say that he sins who shows not pity of me, which would give me some comfort. In the last, I say why people should take pity; namely, for the piteous look which comes into mine eyes; which piteous look is destroyed, that is, appeareth not unto others, through the jeering of this lady, who draws to the like action those who peradventure would see this piteousness. The second part begins here, "My face shows"; the third, "Till, in the drunken terror"; the fourth, "It were a grievous sin"; the fifth, "For the great anguish."

Thereafter, this sonnet bred in me desire to write down in verse four other things touching my condition, the which things it seemed to me that I had not yet made manifest. The first among these was the grief that possessed me very often, remembering the strangeness which Love wrought in me; the second was, how Love many times assailed me so suddenly and with such strength that I had no other life remaining except a thought which spake of my lady: the third was, how when Love did battle with me in this wise, I would rise up all colourless, if so I might see my lady, conceiving that the sight of her would defend me against the assault of Love, and altogether forgetting that which her presence brought unto me; and the fourth was, how, when I saw her, the sight not only defended me not, but took away the little life that remained to me. And I said these four things in a sonnet, which is this: —

At whiles (yea oftentimes) I muse over
  The quality of anguish that is mine
  Through Love: then pity makes my voice to pine,
Saying, "Is any else thus, anywhere?"
Love smiteth me, whose strength is ill to bear;   5
  So that of all my life is left no sign
  Except one thought; and that, because 'tis thine,
Leaves not the body but abideth there.
And then if I, whom other aid forsook,
  Would aid myself, and innocent of art   10
    Would fain have sight of thee as a last hope,
No sooner do I lift mine eyes to look
  Than the blood seems as shaken from my heart,
    And all my pulses beat at once and stop.

This sonnet is divided into four parts, four things being therein narrated; and as these are set forth above, I only proceed to distinguish the parts by their beginnings. Wherefore I say that the second part begins, "Love smiteth me"; the third, "And then if I"; the fourth, "No sooner do I lift."

After I had written these three last sonnets, wherein I spake unto my lady, telling her almost the whole of my condition, it seemed to me that I should be silent, having said enough concerning myself. But albeit I spake not to her again, yet it behoved me afterward to write of another matter, more noble than the foregoing. And for that the occasion of what I then wrote may be found pleasant in the hearing, I will relate it as briefly as I may.

Through the sore change in mine aspect, the secret of my heart was now understood of many. Which thing being thus, there came a day when certain ladies to whom it was well known (they having been with me at divers times in my trouble) were met together for the pleasure of gentle company. And as I was going that way by chance, (but I think rather by the will of fortune), I heard one of them call unto me, and she that called was a lady of very sweet speech. And when I had come close up with them, and perceived that they had not among them mine excellent lady, I was reassured; and saluted them, asking of their pleasure. The ladies were many; divers of whom were laughing one to another, while divers gazed at me as though I should speak anon. But when I still spake not, one of them, who before had been talking with another, addressed me by my name, saying, "To what end lovest thou this lady, seeing that thou canst not support her presence? Now tell us this thing, that we may know it: for certainly the end of such a love must be worthy of knowledge." And when she had spoken these words, not she only, but all they that were with her, began to observe me, waiting for my reply. Whereupon, I said thus unto them: — "Ladies, the end and aim of my Love was but the salutation of that lady of whom I conceive that ye are speaking; wherein alone I found that beatitude which is the goal of desire. And now that it hath pleased her to deny me this, Love, my Master, of his great goodness, hath placed all my beatitude there where my hope will not fail me." Then those ladies began to talk closely together; and as I have seen snow fall among the rain, so was their talk mingled with sighs. But after a little, that lady who had been the first to address me, addressed me again in these words: "We pray thee that thou wilt tell us wherein abideth this thy beatitude." And answering, I said but thus much: "In those words that do praise my lady." To the which she rejoined, "If thy speech were true, those words that thou didst write concerning thy condition would have been written with another intent."

Then I, being almost put to shame because of her answer, went out from among them; and as I walked, I said within myself: "Seeing that there is so much beatitude in those words which do praise my lady, wherefore hath my speech of her been different?" And then I resolved that thenceforward I would choose for the theme of my writings only the praise of this most gracious being. But when I had thought exceedingly, it seemed to me that I had taken to myself a theme which was much too lofty, so that I dared not begin; and I remained during several days in the desire of speaking, and the fear of beginning. After which it happened, as I passed one day along a path which lay beside a stream of very clear water, that there came upon me a great desire to say somewhat in rhyme; but when I began thinking how I should say it, methought that to speak of her were unseemly, unless I spoke to other ladies in the second person; which is to say, not to *any* other ladies; but only to such as are so called because they are gentle, let alone for mere womanhood. Whereupon I declare that my tongue spake as though by its own impulse, and said, "Ladies that have intelligence in love." These words I laid up in my mind with great gladness, conceiving to take them as my commencement. Wherefore, having returned to the city I spake of, and considered thereof during certain days, I began a poem with this beginning, constructed in the mode which will be seen below in its division. The poem begins here: —

Ladies that have intelligence in love,
    Of mine own lady I would speak with you;
    Not that I hope to count her praises through,
        But telling what I may, to ease my mind.
And I declare that when I speak thereof,   5
    Love sheds such perfect sweetness over me
    That if my courage failed not, certainly
        To him my listeners must be all resign'd.
        Wherefore I will not speak in such large kind
That mine own speech should foil me, which were base;   10
But only will discourse of her high grace
    In these poor words, the best that I can find,
With you alone, dear dames and damozels:
'Twere ill to speak thereof with any else.

An Angel, of his blessed knowledge, saith   15
    To God: "Lord, in the world that Thou hast made,
    A miracle in action is display'd
        By reason of a soul whose splendors fare
Even hither: and since Heaven requireth
    Nought saving her, for her it prayeth Thee,   20
    Thy Saints crying aloud continually."
        Yet Pity still defends our earthly share
        In that sweet soul; God answering thus the prayer:
"My well-belovèd, suffer that in peace
    Your hope remain, while so My pleasure is,   25
    There where one dwells who dreads the loss of her;
And who in Hell unto the doomed shall say,
"I have looked on that for which God's chosen pray.""

My lady is desired in the high Heaven:
    Wherefore, it now behoveth me to tell,   30

Saying: Let any maid that would be well
  Esteemed keep with her: for as she goes by,
Into foul hearts a deathly chill is driven
  By Love, that makes ill thought to perish there;
  While any who endures to gaze on her   35
    Must either be made noble, or else die.
    When one deserving to be raised so high
Is found, 'tis then her power attains its proof,
Making his heart strong for his soul's behoof
    With the full strength of meek humility.   40
Also this virtue owns she, by God's will:
Who speaks with her can never come to ill.

Love saith concerning her: "How chanceth it
  That flesh, which is of dust, should be thus pure?"
  Then, gazing always, he makes oath: "Forsure,   45
    This is a creature of God till now unknown."
She hath that paleness of the pearl that's fit
  In a fair woman, so much and not more;
  She is as high as Nature's skill can soar;
    Beauty is tried by her comparison.   50
    Whatever her sweet eyes are turned upon,
  Spirits of love do issue thence in flame,
  Which through their eyes who then may look on them
    Pierce to the heart's deep chamber every one.
And in her smile Love's image you may see;   55
Whence none can gaze upon her steadfastly.

Dear Song, I know thou wilt hold gentle speech
  With many ladies, when I send thee forth:
  Wherefore, (being mindful that thou hadst thy birth
    From Love, and art a modest, simple child),   60
Whomso thou meetest, say thou this to each:
  "Give me good speed! To her I wend along
  In whose much strength my weakness is made strong."
    And if, i' the end, thou wouldst not be beguiled
    Of all thy labour, seek not the defiled   65
And common sort; but rather choose to be
Where man and woman dwell in courtesy.
    So to the road thou shalt be reconciled,
And find the lady, and with the lady, Love.
Commend thou me to each, as doth behove.   70

*This poem, that it may be better understood, I will divide more subtly than the others
preceding; and therefore I will make three parts of it. The first part is a proem to the
words following. The second is the matter treated of. The third is, as it were, a handmaid*

to the preceding words. The second begins here, "An angel"; the third here, "Dear Song, I know." The first part is divided into four. In the first, I say to whom I mean to speak of my lady, and wherefore I will so speak. In the second, I say what she appears to myself to be when I reflect upon her excellence, and what I would utter if I lost not courage. In the third, I say what it is I purpose to speak, so as not to be impeded by faintheartedness. In the fourth, repeating to whom I purpose speaking, I tell the reason why I speak to them. The second begins here, "And I declare"; the third here, "Wherefore I will not speak"; the fourth here, "With you alone." Then, when I say "An Angel," I begin treating of this lady: and this part is divided into two. In the first, I tell what is understood of her in heaven. In the second, I tell what is understood of her on earth: here, "My lady is desired." This second part is divided into two; for, in the first, I speak of her as regards the nobleness of her soul, relating some of her virtues proceeding from her soul; in the second, I speak of her as regards the nobleness of her body, narrating some of her beauties: here, "Love saith concerning her." This second part is divided into two; for, in the first, I speak of certain beauties which belong to the whole person; in the second, I speak of certain beauties which belong to a distinct part of the person: here, "Whatever her sweet eyes." This second part is divided into two; for, in the one, I speak of the eyes, which are the beginning of love; in the second, I speak of the mouth, which is the end of love. And, that every vicious thought may be discarded herefrom, let the reader remember that it is above written that the greeting of this lady, which was an act of her mouth, was the goal of my desires, while I could receive it. Then, when I say, "Dear Song, I know," I add a stanza as it were hand-maid to the others, wherein I say what I desire from this my poem. And because this last part is easy to understand, I trouble not myself with more divisions. I say, indeed, that the further to open the meaning of this poem, more minute divisions ought to be used; but nevertheless he who is not of wit enough to understand it by these which have been already made is welcome to leave it alone; for certes I fear I have communicated its sense to too many by these present divisions, if it so happened that many should hear it.

When this song was a little gone abroad, a certain one of my friends, hearing the same, was pleased to question me, that I should tell him what thing love is; it may be, conceiving from the words thus heard a hope of me beyond my desert. Wherefore I, thinking that after such discourse it were well to say somewhat of the nature of Love, and also in accordance with my friend's desire, proposed to myself to write certain words in the which I should treat of this argument. And the sonnet that I then made is this: —

Love and the gentle heart are one same thing,
 Even as the wise man* in his ditty saith.
 Each, of itself, would be such life in death
As rational soul bereft of reasoning.
'Tis Nature makes them when she loves: a king   5
 Love is, whose palace where he sojourneth

*Guido Guinicelli, in the canzone which begins, "Within the gentle heart Love shelters him."

Is called the Heart; there draws he quiet breath
At first, with brief or longer slumbering.
Then beauty seen in virtuous womankind
   Will make the eyes desire, and through the heart   10
      Send the desiring of the eyes again;
Where often it abides so long enshrin'd
   That Love at length out of his sleep will start.
      And women feel the same for worthy men.

This sonnet is divided into two parts. In the first, I speak of him according to his power. In the second, I speak of him according as his power translates itself into act. The second part begins here, "Then beauty seen." The first is divided into two. In the first, I say in what subject this power exists. In the second, I say how this subject and this power are produced together, and how the one regards the other, as form does matter. The second begins here, "'Tis Nature." Afterwards when I say, "Then beauty seen in virtuous womankind," I say how this power translates itself into act; and, first, how it so translates itself in a man, then how it so translates itself in a woman: here, "And women feel."

Having treated of love in the foregoing, it appeared to me that I should also say something in praise of my lady, wherein it might be set forth how love manifested itself when produced by her; and how not only she could awaken it where it slept, but where it was not she could marvellously create it. To the which end I wrote another sonnet; and it is this: —

My lady carries love within her eyes;
   All that she looks on is made pleasanter;
   Upon her path men turn to gaze at her;
He whom she greeteth feels his heart to rise,
And droops his troubled visage, full of sighs,   5
   And of his evil heart is then aware:
   Hate loves, and pride becomes a worshipper.
O women, help to praise her in somewise.
Humbleness, and the hope that hopeth well,
   By speech of hers into the mind are brought,   10
      And who beholds is blessèd oftenwhiles.
      The look she hath when she a little smiles
      Cannot be said, nor holden in the thought;
'Tis such a new and gracious miracle.

This sonnet has three sections. In the first, I say how this lady brings this power into action by those most noble features, her eyes: and, in the third, I say this same as to that most noble feature, her mouth. And between these two sections is a little section, which asks, as it were, help for the previous section and the subsequent; and it begins here, "O women, help." The third begins here, "Humbleness." The first is divided into three; for, in the first, I say how she with power makes noble that which she looks upon; and this is as much as to say that she brings Love, in power, thither where he is not. In the second, I say how she brings Love, in act, into the hearts of all those whom she sees. In the third, I

*tell what she afterwards, with virtue, operates upon their hearts. The second begins,
"Upon her path"; the third, "He whom she greeteth." Then, when I say, "O women,
help," I intimate to whom it is my intention to speak, calling on women to help me to ho-
nour her. Then, when I say, "Humbleness," I say that same which is said in the first part,
regarding two acts of her mouth, one whereof is her most sweet speech, and the other her
marvellous smile. Only, I say not of this last how it operates upon the hearts of others, be-
cause memory cannot retain this smile, nor its operation.*

Not many days after this, (it being the will of the most High God, who also
from Himself put not away death), the father of wonderful Beatrice, going out
of this life, passed certainly into glory. Thereby it happened, as of very sooth it
might not be otherwise, that this lady was made full of the bitterness of grief: see-
ing that such a parting is very grievous unto those friends who are left, and that
no other friendship is like to that between a good parent and a good child; and
furthermore considering that this lady was good in the supreme degree, and her
father (as by many it hath been truly averred) of exceeding goodness. And be-
cause it is the usage of that city that men meet with men in such a grief, and
women with women, certain ladies of her companionship gathered themselves
unto Beatrice, where she kept alone in her weeping: and as they passed in and
out, I could hear them speak concerning her, how she wept. At length two of
them went by me, who said: "Certainly she grieveth in such sort that one might
die for pity, beholding her." Then, feeling the tears upon my face, I put up my
hands to hide them: and had it not been that I hoped to hear more concerning
her, (seeing that where I sat, her friends passed continually in and out), I should
assuredly have gone thence to be alone, when I felt the tears come. But as I still
sat in that place, certain ladies again passed near me, who were saying among
themselves: "Which of us shall be joyful any more, who have listened to this
lady in her piteous sorrow?" And there were others who said as they went by
me: "He that sitteth here could not weep more if he had beheld her as we have
beheld her"; and again: "He is so altered that he seemeth not as himself." And still
as the ladies passed to and fro, I could hear them speak after this fashion of her
and of me.

Wherefore afterwards, having considered and perceiving that there was herein
matter for poesy, I resolved that I would write certain rhymes in the which
should be contained all that those ladies had said. And because I would willingly
have spoken to them if it had not been for discreetness, I made in my rhymes as
though I had spoken and they had answered me. And thereof I wrote two son-
nets; in the first of which I addressed them as I would fain have done; and in the
second related their answer, using the speech that I had heard from them, as
though it had been spoken unto myself. And the sonnets are these: —

I.
You that thus wear a modest countenance
   With lids weigh'd down by the heart's heaviness,
   Whence come you, that among you every face

Appears the same, for its pale troubled glance?
Have you beheld my lady's face, perchance,   5
　　Bow'd with the grief that Love makes full of grace?
　　Say now, "This thing is thus"; as my heart says,
Marking your grave and sorrowful advance.
And if indeed you come from where she sighs
　　And mourns, may it please you (for his heart's relief)   10
　　　　To tell how it fares with her unto him
Who knows that you have wept, seeing your eyes,
　　And is so grieved with looking on your grief
　　　　That his heart trembles and his sight grows dim.

This sonnet is divided into two parts. In the first, I call and ask these ladies whether they come from her, telling them that I think they do, because they return the nobler. In the second, I pray them to tell me of her: and the second begins here, "And if indeed."

II.

Canst thou indeed be he that still would sing
　　Of our dear lady unto none but us?
　　For though thy voice confirms that it is thus,
Thy visage might another witness bring.
And wherefore is thy grief so sore a thing   5
　　That grieving thou mak'st others dolorous?
　　Hast thou too seen her weep, that thou from us
Canst not conceal thine inward sorrowing?
Nay, leave our woe to us: let us alone:
　　'Twere sin if one should strive to soothe our woe,   10
　　　　For in her weeping we have heard her speak:
Also her look's so full of her heart's moan
　　That they who should behold her, looking so,
　　　　Must fall aswoon, feeling all life grow weak.

This sonnet has four parts, as the ladies in whose person I reply had four forms of answer. And, because these are sufficiently shown above, I stay not to explain the purport of the parts, and therefore I only discriminate them. The second begins here, "And wherefore is thy grief"; the third here, "Nay, leave our woe"; the fourth, "Also her look."

A few days after this, my body became afflicted with a painful infirmity, whereby I suffered bitter anguish for many days, which at last brought me unto such weakness that I could no longer move. And I remember that on the ninth day, being overcome with intolerable pain, a thought came into my mind concerning my lady: but when it had a little nourished this thought, my mind returned to its brooding over mine enfeebled body. And then perceiving how frail a thing life is, even though health keep with it, the matter seemed to me so pitiful that I could not choose but weep; and weeping I said within myself: "Certainly it must some time come to pass that the very gentle Beatrice will die." Then, feeling bewildered, I closed mine eyes; and my brain began to be in travail as the brain of one frantic, and to have such imaginations as here follow.

And at the first, it seemed to me that I saw certain faces of women with their hair loosened, which called out to me, "Thou shalt surely die"; after the which, other terrible and unknown appearances said unto me, "Thou art dead." At length, as my phantasy held on in its wanderings, I came to be I knew not where, and to behold a throng of dishevelled ladies wonderfully sad, who kept going hither and thither weeping. Then the sun went out, so that the stars showed themselves, and they were of such a colour that I knew they must be weeping: and it seemed to me that the birds fell dead out of the sky, and that there were great earthquakes. With that, while I wondered in my trance, and was filled with a grievous fear, I conceived that a certain friend came unto me and said: "Hast thou not heard? She that was thine excellent lady hath been taken out of life." Then I began to weep very piteously; and not only in mine imagination, but with mine eyes, which were wet with tears. And I seemed to look towards Heaven, and to behold a multitude of angels who were returning upwards, having before them an exceedingly white cloud: and these angels were singing together gloriously, and the words of their song were these: "*Osanna in excelsis*": and there was no more that I heard. Then my heart that was so full of love said unto me: "It is true that our lady lieth dead": and it seemed to me that I went to look upon the body wherein that blessed and most noble spirit had had its abiding-place. And so strong was this idle imagining, that it made me to behold my lady in death; whose head certain ladies seemed to be covering with a white veil; and who was so humble of her aspect that it was as though she had said, "I have attained to look on the beginning of peace." And therewithal I came unto such humility by the sight of her, that I cried out upon Death, saying: "Now come unto me, and be not bitter against me any longer: surely, there where thou hast been, thou hast learned gentleness. Wherefore come now unto me who do greatly desire thee: seest thou not that I wear thy colour already?" And when I had seen all those offices performed that are fitting to be done unto the dead, it seemed to me that I went back unto mine own chamber, and looked up towards Heaven. And so strong was my phantasy, that I wept again in very truth, and said with my true voice: "O excellent soul! how blessed is he that now looketh upon thee!"

And as I said these words, with a painful anguish of sobbing and another prayer unto Death, a young and gentle lady, who had been standing beside me where I lay, conceiving that I wept and cried out because of the pain of mine infirmity, was taken with trembling and began to shed tears. Whereby other ladies, who were about the room, becoming aware of my discomfort by reason of the moan that she made, (who indeed was of my very near kindred), led her away from where I was, and then set themselves to awaken me, thinking that I dreamed, and saying: "Sleep no longer, and be not disquieted."

Then, by their words, this strong imagination was brought suddenly to an end, at the moment that I was about to say, "O Beatrice! peace be with thee." And already I had said, "O Beatrice!" when being aroused, I opened mine eyes, and knew that it had been a deception. But albeit I had indeed uttered her name, yet my voice was so broken with sobs, that it was not understood by these ladies; so that in spite of the sore shame that I felt, I turned towards them by Love's counselling. And when they beheld me, they began to say, "He seemeth as one dead," and to whisper among themselves, "Let us strive if we may not comfort him." Whereupon they spake to me many soothing words, and questioned me moreover touching the cause of my fear. Then I, being somewhat reassured, and having perceived that it was a mere phantasy, said unto them, "This thing it was that made me afeard"; and told them of all that I had seen, from the beginning even unto the end, but without once speaking the name of my lady. Also, after I had recovered from my sickness, I bethought me to write these things in rhyme; deeming it a lovely thing to be known. Whereof I wrote this poem: —

A very pitiful lady, very young,
   Exceeding rich in human sympathies,
      Stood by, what time I clamour'd upon Death;
And at the wild words wandering on my tongue
   And at the piteous look within mine eyes   5
      She was affrighted, that sobs choked her breath.
      So by her weeping where I lay beneath,
Some other gentle ladies came to know
My state, and made her go:
   Afterward, bending themselves over me,   10
   One said, "Awaken thee!"
      And one, "What thing thy sleep disquieteth?"
With that, my soul woke up from its eclipse,
The while my lady's name rose to my lips:

But utter'd in a voice so sob-broken,   15
   So feeble with the agony of tears,
      That I alone might hear it in my heart;
And though that look was on my visage then
   Which he who is ashamed so plainly wears,
      Love made that I through shame held not apart,   20
      But gazed upon them. And my hue was such
That they look'd at each other and thought of death;
Saying under their breath
   Most tenderly, "Oh, let us comfort him":
   Then unto me: "What dream   25
      Was thine, that it hath shaken thee so much?"
And when I was a little comforted,
"This, ladies, was the dream I dreamt," I said.

"I was a-thinking how life fails with us
   Suddenly after a little while;   30
      When Love sobb'd in my heart, which is his home.

Whereby my spirit wax'd so dolorous
    That in myself I said, with sick recoil:
        'Yea, to my lady too this Death must come.'
        And therewithal such a bewilderment   35
Possess'd me, that I shut mine eyes for peace;
And in my brain did cease
    Order of thought, and every healthful thing.
    Afterwards, wandering
        Amid a swarm of doubts that came and went,   40
Some certain women's faces hurried by,
And shriek'd to me, 'Thou too shalt die, shalt die!'

"Then saw I many broken hinted sights
    In the uncertain state I stepp'd into.
        Meseem'd to be I know not in what place,   45
Where ladies through the street, like mournful lights,
    Ran with loose hair, and eyes that frighten'd you
        By their own terror, and a pale amaze:
        The while, little by little, as I thought,
The sun ceased, and the stars began to gather,   50
And each wept at the other;
    And birds dropp'd in mid-flight out of the sky;
    And earth shook suddenly;
        And I was 'ware of one, hoarse and tired out,
Who ask'd of me: 'Hast thou not heard it said?   55
Thy lady, she that was so fair, is dead?'

"Then lifting up mine eyes, as the tears came,
    I saw the Angels, like a rain of manna,
        In a long flight flying back Heavenward;
Having a little cloud in front of them,   60
    After the which they went and said, 'Hosanna!'
        And if they had said more, you should have heard.
        Then Love spoke thus: 'Now all shall be made clear:
Come and behold our lady where she lies.'
These 'wildering phantasies   65
    Then carried me to see my lady dead:
    Even as I there was led,
        Her ladies with a veil were covering her;
And with her was such very humbleness
That she appeared to say, 'I am at peace.'   70

"And I became so humble in my grief,
    Seeing in her such deep humility,
        That I said: 'Death, I hold thee passing good
Henceforth, and a most gentle sweet relief,
    Since my dear love has chosen to dwell with thee: 75

Pity, not hate, is thine, well understood.
    Lo! I do so desire to see thy face
That I am like as one who nears the tomb;
My soul entreats thee, Come.'
    Then I departed, having made my moan;   80
    And when I was alone
      I said, and cast my eyes to the High Place:
'Blessed is he, fair soul, who meets thy glance!'
. . . . . . Just then you woke me, of your complaisaùnce."

This poem has two parts. In the first, speaking to a person undefined, I tell how I was aroused from a vain phantasy by certain ladies, and how I promised them to tell what it was. In the second, I say how I told them. The second part begins here, "I was a-thinking." The first part divides into two. In the first, I tell that which certain ladies, and which one singly, did and said because of my phantasy, before I had returned into my right senses. In the second, I tell what these ladies said to me after I had left off this wandering: and it begins here, "But utter'd in a voice." Then, when I say, "I was a-thinking," I say how I told them this my imagination; and concerning this I have two parts. In the first, I tell, in order, this imagination. In the second, saying at what time they called me, I covertly thank them: and this part begins here, "Just then you woke me."

After this empty imagining, it happened on a day, as I sat thoughtful, that I was taken with such a strong trembling at the heart, that it could not have been otherwise in the presence of my lady. Whereupon I perceived that there was an appearance of Love beside me, and I seemed to see him coming from my lady; and he said, not aloud but within my heart: "Now take heed that thou bless the day when I entered into thee; for it is fitting that thou shouldst do so." And with that my heart was so full of gladness, that I could hardly believe it to be of very truth mine own heart and not another.

A short while after these words which my heart spoke to me with the tongue of Love, I saw coming towards me a certain lady who was very famous for her beauty, and of whom that friend whom I have already called the first among my friends had long been enamoured. This lady's right name was Joan; but because of her comeliness (or at least it was so imagined) she was called of many *Primavera* (Spring), and went by that name among them. Then looking again, I perceived that the most noble Beatrice followed after her. And when both these ladies had passed by me, it seemed to me that Love spake again in my heart, saying: "She that came first was called Spring, only because of that which was to happen on this day. And it was I myself who caused that name to be given her; seeing that as the Spring cometh first in the year, so should she come first on this day,* when Beatrice was to show herself after the vision of her servant. And even if thou go about to consider her right name, it is also as one should say, 'She shall

---

*There is a play in the original upon the words *Primavera* (Spring) and *prima verrá* (she shall come first), to which I have given as near an equivalent as I could.

come first'; inasmuch as her name, Joan, is taken from that John who went before the True Light, saying: '*Ego vox clamantis in deserto: Parate viam Domini.*'"* And also it seemed to me that he added other words, to wit: "He who should inquire delicately touching this matter, could not but call Beatrice by mine own name, which is to say, Love; beholding her so like unto me."

Then I, having thought of this, imagined to write it with rhymes and send it unto my chief friend; but setting aside certain words† which seemed proper to be set aside, because I believed that his heart still regarded the beauty of her that was called Spring. And I wrote this sonnet: —

> I felt a spirit of love begin to stir
>   Within my heart, long time unfelt till then;
>   And saw Love coming towards me, fair and fain,
> (That I scarce knew him for his joyful cheer),
> Saying, "Be now indeed my worshipper!"   5
>   And in his speech he laugh'd and laugh'd again.
>   Then, while it was his pleasure to remain,
> I chanced to look the way he had drawn near,
> And saw the Ladies Joan and Beatrice
>   Approach me, this the other following,   10
>   One and a second marvel instantly.
> And even as now my memory speaketh this,
>   Love spake it then: "The first is christen'd Spring;
>   The second Love, she is so like to me."

This sonnet has many parts: whereof the first tells how I felt awakened within my heart the accustomed tremor, and how it seemed that Love appeared to me joyful from afar. The second says how it appeared to me that Love spake within my heart, and what was his aspect. The third tells how, after he had in such wise been with me a space, I saw and heard certain things. The second part begins here, "Saying, 'Be now'"; the third here, "Then, while it was his pleasure." The third part divides into two. In the first, I say what I saw. In the second, I say what I heard: and it begins here, "Love spake it then."

It might be here objected unto me, (and even by one worthy of controversy), that I have spoken of Love as though it were a thing outward and visible: not only a spiritual essence, but as a bodily substance also. The which thing, in absolute truth, is a fallacy; Love not being of itself a substance, but an accident of substance. Yet that I speak of Love as though it were a thing tangible and even human, appears by three things which I say thereof. And firstly, I say that I perceived Love coming towards me; whereby, seeing that to come bespeaks loco-

---

*"I am the voice of one crying in the wilderness: 'Prepare ye the way of the Lord.'"

†That is (as I understand it), suppressing, from delicacy towards his friend, the words in which Love describes Joan as merely the forerunner of Beatrice. And perhaps in the latter part of this sentence a reproach is gently conveyed to the fickle Guido Cavalcanti, who may already have transferred his homage (though Dante had not then learned it) from Joan to Mandetta. (See his Poems.)

motion, and seeing also how philosophy teacheth us that none but a corporeal substance hath locomotion, it seemeth that I speak of Love as of a corporeal substance. And secondly, I say that Love smiled; and thirdly, that Love spake; faculties (and especially the risible faculty) which appear proper unto man: whereby it further seemeth that I speak of Love as of a man. Now that this matter may be explained, (as is fitting), it must first be remembered that anciently they who wrote poems of Love wrote not in the vulgar tongue, but rather certain poets in the Latin tongue. I mean, among us, although perchance the same may have been among others, and although likewise, as among the Greeks, they were not writers of spoken language, but men of letters, treated of these things.* And indeed it is not a great number of years since poetry began to be made in the vulgar tongue; the writing of rhymes in spoken language corresponding to the writing in metre of Latin verse, by a certain analogy. And I say that it is but a little while, because if we examine the language of *oco* and the language of *sì* †we shall not find in those tongues any written thing of an earlier date than the last hundred and fifty years. Also the reason why certain of a very mean sort obtained at the first some fame as poets is, that before them no man had written verses in the language of *sì*: and of these, the first was moved to the writing of such verses by the wish to make himself understood of a certain lady, unto whom Latin poetry was difficult. This thing is against such as rhyme concerning other matters than love; that mode of speech having been first used for the expression of love alone.‡ Wherefore, seeing that poets have a license allowed them that is not allowed unto the writers of prose, and seeing also that they who write in rhyme are simply poets in the vulgar tongue, it becomes fitting and reasonable that a larger license should be given to these than to other modern writers; and that any metaphor or rhetorical similitude which is permitted unto poets, should also be counted not unseemly in the rhymers of the vulgar tongue. Thus, if we perceive that the former have caused inanimate things to speak as though they had sense and reason, and to discourse one with another; yea, and not only actual things, but such also as have no real existence, (seeing that they have made things which are not, to

---

*On reading Dante's treatise *De Vulgari Eloquio,* it will be found that the distinction which he intends here is not between one language, or dialect, and another; but between "vulgar speech" (that is, the language handed down from mother to son without any conscious use of grammar or syntax), and language as regulated by grammarians and the laws of literary composition, and which Dante calls simply "Grammar." A great deal might be said on the bearings of the present passage, but it is no part of my plan to enter on such questions.

†*i.e.* the languages of Provence and Tuscany.

‡It strikes me that this curious passage furnishes a reason, hitherto (I believe) overlooked, why Dante put such of his lyrical poems as relate to philosophy into the form of love-poems. He liked writing in Italian rhyme rather than Latin metre; he thought Italian rhyme ought to be confined to love-poems; therefore whatever he wrote (at this age) had to take the form of a love-poem. Thus any poem by Dante not concerning love is later than his twenty-seventh year (1291–92), when he wrote the prose of the *Vita Nuova;* the poetry having been written earlier, at the time of the events referred to.

speak; and often-times written of those which are merely accidents as though they were substances and things human); it should therefore be permitted to the latter to do the like; which is to say, not inconsiderately, but with such sufficient motive as may afterwards be set forth in prose.

That the Latin poets have done thus, appears through Virgil, where he saith that Juno (to wit, a goddess hostile to the Trojans) spake unto Aeolus, master of the Winds; as it is written in the first book of the Aeneid, *Aeole, namque tibi, etc.;* and that this master of the Winds made reply: *Tuus, o regina, quid optes — Explorare labor, mihi jussa capessere fas est.* And through the same poet, the inanimate thing speaketh unto the animate, in the third book of the Aeneid, where it is written: *Dardanidae duri, etc.* With Lucan, the animate thing speaketh to the inanimate; as thus: *Multum, Roma, tamen debes civilibus armis.* In Horace man is made to speak to his own intelligence as unto another person; (and not only hath Horace done this but herein he followeth the excellent Homer), as thus in his Poetics: *Dic mihi, Musa, virum, etc.* Through Ovid, Love speaketh as a human creature, in the beginning of his discourse *De Remediis Amoris:* as thus: *Bella mihi video, bella parantur, ait.* By which ensamples this thing shall be made manifest unto such as may be offended at any part of this my book. And lest some of the common sort should be moved to jeering hereat, I will here add, that neither did these ancient poets speak thus without consideration, nor should they who are makers of rhyme in our day write after the same fashion, having no reason in what they write; for it were a shameful thing if one should rhyme under the semblance of metaphor or rhetorical similitude, and afterwards, being questioned thereof, should be unable to rid his words of such semblance, unto their right understanding. Of whom, (to wit, of such as rhyme thus foolishly), myself and the first among my friends do know many.

But returning to the matter of my discourse. This excellent lady, of whom I spake in what hath gone before, came at last into such favour with all men, that when she passed anywhere folk ran to behold her; which thing was a deep joy to me: and when she drew near unto any, so much truth and simpleness entered into his heart, that he dared neither to lift his eyes nor to return her salutation: and unto this, many who have felt it can bear witness. She went along crowned and clothed with humility, showing no whit of pride in all that she heard and saw: and when she had gone by, it was said of many, "This is not a woman, but one of the beautiful angels of Heaven," and there were some that said: "This is surely a miracle; blessed be the Lord, who hath power to work thus marvellously." I say, of very sooth, that she showed herself so gentle and so full of all perfection, that she bred in those who looked upon her a soothing quiet beyond any speech; neither could any look upon her without sighing immediately. These things, and things yet more wonderful, were brought to pass through her miraculous virtue. Wherefore I, considering thereof and wishing to resume the endless tale of her praises, resolved to write somewhat wherein I might dwell on her surpassing influence; to the end that not only they who had beheld her, but others also, might know as much concerning her as words could give to the understanding. And it was then that I wrote this sonnet: —

My lady looks so gentle and so pure
  When yielding salutation by the way,
  That the tongue trembles and has nought to say,
And the eyes, which fain would see, may not endure.
And still, amid the praise she hears secure,   5
  She walks with humbleness for her array;
  Seeming a creature sent from Heaven to stay
On earth, and show a miracle made sure.
She is so pleasant in the eyes of men
That through the sight the inmost heart doth gain   10
  A sweetness which needs proof to know it by:
And from between her lips there seems to move
A soothing spirit that is full of love,
  Saying for ever to the spirit, "Sigh!"

This sonnet is so easy to understand, from what is afore narrated, that it needs no division: and therefore, leaving it, I say also that this excellent lady came into such favour with all men, that not only she herself was honoured and commended; but through her companionship, honour and commendation came unto others. Wherefore I, perceiving this and wishing that it should also be made manifest to those that beheld it not, wrote the sonnet here following; wherein is signified the power which her virtue had upon other ladies: —

For certain he hath seen all perfectness
  Who among other ladies hath seen mine:
  They that go with her humbly should combine
To thank their God for such peculiar grace.
So perfect is the beauty of her face   5
  That it begets in no wise any sign
  Of envy, but draws round her a clear line
Of love, and blessed faith, and gentleness.
Merely the sight of her makes all things bow:
  Not she herself alone is holier   10
    Than all; but hers, through her, are raised above.
From all her acts such lovely graces flow
  That truly one may never think of her
    Without a passion of exceeding love.

This sonnet has three parts. In the first, I say in what company this lady appeared most wondrous. In the second, I say how gracious was her society. In the third, I tell of the things which she, with power, worked upon others. The second begins here, "They that go with her"; the third here, "So perfect." This last part divides into three. In the first, I tell what she operated upon women, that is, by their own faculties. In the second, I tell what she operated in them through others. In the third, I say how she not only operated in women, but in all people; and not only while herself present, but, by memory of her, operated wondrously. The second begins here, "Merely the sight"; the third here, "From all her acts."

Thereafter on a day, I began to consider that which I had said of my lady: to wit, in these two sonnets aforegone: and becoming aware that I had not spoken of her immediate effect on me at that especial time, it seemed to me that I had spoken defectively. Whereupon I resolved to write somewhat of the manner wherein I was then subject to her influence, and of what her influence then was. And conceiving that I should not be able to say these things in the small compass of a sonnet, I began therefore a poem with this beginning: —

> Love hath so long possess'd me for his own
> $\quad$ And made his lordship so familiar
> That he, who at first irked me, is now grown
> $\quad$ Unto my heart as its best secrets are.
> $\quad$ And thus, when he in such sore wise doth mar $\hspace{2cm}$ 5
> My life that all its strength seems gone from it,
> Mine inmost being then feels throughly quit
> $\quad$ Of anguish, and all evil keeps afar.
> Love also gathers to such power in me
> $\quad$ That my sighs speak, each one a grievous thing, $\hspace{1.5cm}$ 10
> $\quad$ Always soliciting
> My lady's salutation piteously.
> Whenever she beholds me, it is so,
> Who is more sweet than any words can show.

$$* \quad * \quad * \quad * \quad * \quad *$$
$$* \quad * \quad * \quad * \quad * \quad *$$

Quomodo sedet sola civitas plena populo! facta est quasi vidua domina gentium.*

I was still occupied with this poem, (having composed thereof only the above-written stanza), when the Lord God of justice called my most gracious lady unto Himself, that she might be glorious under the banner of that blessed Queen Mary, whose name had always a deep reverence in the words of holy Beatrice. And because haply it might be found good that I should say somewhat concerning her departure, I will herein declare what are the reasons which make that I shall not do so.

And the reasons are three. The first is, that such matter belongeth not of right to the present argument, if one consider the opening of this little book. The second is, that even though the present argument required it, my pen doth not suffice to write in a fit manner of this thing. And the third is, that were it both

---

*"How doth the city sit solitary, that was full of people! how is she become as a widow, she that was great among the nations!" — *Lamentations of Jeremiah*, i, I.

possible and of absolute necessity, it would still be unseemly for me to speak thereof, seeing that thereby it must behove me to speak also mine own praises: a thing that in whosoever doeth it is worthy of blame. For the which reasons, I will leave this matter to be treated of by some other than myself.

Nevertheless, as the number nine, which number hath often had mention in what hath gone before, (and not, as it might appear, without reason), seems also to have borne a part in the manner of her death: it is therefore right that I should say somewhat thereof. And for this cause, having first said what was the part it bore herein, I will afterwards point out a reason which made that this number was so closely allied unto my lady.

I say, then, that according to the division of time in Italy, her most noble spirit departed from among us in the first hour of the ninth day of the month; and according to the division of time in Syria, in the ninth month of the year: seeing that Tismim, which with us is October, is there the first month. Also she was taken from among us in that year of our reckoning (to wit, of the years of our Lord) in which the perfect number was nine times multiplied within that century wherein she was born into the world: which is to say, the thirteenth century of Christians.*

And touching the reason why this number was so closely allied unto her, it may peradventure be this. According to Ptolemy, (and also to the Christian verity), the revolving heavens are nine; and according to the common opinion among astrologers, these nine heavens together have influence over the earth. Wherefore it would appear that this number was thus allied unto her for the purpose of signifying that, at her birth, all these nine heavens were at perfect unity with each other as to their influence. This is one reason that may be brought: but more narrowly considering, and according to the infallible truth, this number was her own self: that is to say by similitude. As thus. The number three is the root of the number nine; seeing that without the interposition of any other number, being multiplied merely by itself, it produceth nine, as we manifestly perceive that three times three are nine. Thus, three being of itself the efficient of nine, and the Great Efficient of Miracles being of Himself Three Persons (to wit: the Father, the Son, and the Holy Spirit), which, being Three, are also One: — this lady was accompanied by the number nine to the end that men might clearly perceive her to be a nine, that is, a miracle, whose only root is the Holy Trinity. It may be that a more subtile person would find for this thing a reason of greater subtilty: but such is the reason that I find, and that liketh me best.

After this most gracious creature had gone out from among us, the whole city came to be as it were widowed and despoiled of all dignity. Then I, left mourning in this desolate city, wrote unto the principal persons thereof, in an epistle, concerning its condition; taking for my commencement those words of Jere-

---

*Beatrice Portinari will thus be found to have died during the first hour of the 9th of June, 1290. And from what Dante says at the commencement of this work, (viz. that she was younger than himself by eight or nine months), it may also be gathered that her age, at the time of her death, was twenty-four years and three months. The "perfect number" mentioned in the present passage is the number ten.

mias: *Quomodo sedet sola civitas! etc.* And I make mention of this, that none may marvel wherefore I set down these words before, in beginning to treat of her death. Also if any should blame me, in that I do not transcribe that epistle whereof I have spoken, I will make it mine excuse that I began this little book with the intent that it should be written altogether in the vulgar tongue; wherefore, seeing that the epistle I speak of is in Latin, it belongeth not to mine undertaking: more especially as I know that my chief friend, for whom I write this book, wished also that the whole of it should be in the vulgar tongue.

When mine eyes had wept for some while, until they were so weary with weeping that I could no longer through them give ease to my sorrow, I bethought me that a few mournful words might stand me instead of tears. And therefore I proposed to make a poem, that weeping I might speak therein of her for whom so much sorrow had destroyed my spirit; and I then began "The eyes that weep."

That this poem may seem to remain the more widowed at its close, I will divide it before writing it; and this method I will observe henceforward. I say that this poor little poem has three parts. The first is a prelude. In the second, I speak of her. In the third I speak pitifully to the poem. The second begins here, "Beatrice is gone up"; the third here, "Weep, pitiful Song of mine." The first divides into three. In the first, I say what moves me to speak. In the second, I say to whom I mean to speak. In the third, I say of whom I mean to speak. The second begins here, "And because often, thinking"; the third here, "And I will say." Then, when I say, "Beatrice is gone up," I speak of her; and concerning this I have two parts. First, I tell the cause why she was taken away from us: afterwards, I say how one weeps her parting; and this part commences here, "Wonderfully." This part divides into three. In the first, I say who it is that weeps her not. In the second, I say who it is that doth weep her. In the third, I speak of my condition. The second begins here, "But sighing comes, and grief"; the third, "With sighs." Then, when I say, "Weep, pitiful Song of mine," I speak to this my song, telling it what ladies to go to, and stay with.

> The eyes that weep for pity of the heart
>   Have wept so long that their grief languisheth
>   And they have no more tears to weep withal:
> And now, if I would ease me of a part
>   Of what, little by little, leads to death,   5
>   It must be done by speech, or not at all.
>   And because often, thinking, I recall
> How it was pleasant, ere she went afar,
>   To talk of her with you, kind damozels,
>   I talk with no one else,   10
> But only with such hearts as women's are.
>   And I will say, — still sobbing as speech fails, —
> That she hath gone to Heaven suddenly,
> And hath left Love below, to mourn with me.
>
> Beatrice is gone up into high Heaven,   15
>   The kingdom where the angels are at peace;
>   And lives with them; and to her friends is dead.

Not by the frost of winter was she driven
  Away, like others; nor by summer-heats;
    But through a perfect gentleness, instead.
    For from the lamp of her meek lowlihead   20
Such an exceeding glory went up hence
  That it woke wonder in the Eternal Sire,
  Until a sweet desire
Entered Him for that lovely excellence,   25
  So that He bade her to Himself aspire:
Counting this weary and most evil place
Unworthy of a thing so full of grace.

Wonderfully out of the beautiful form
  Soared her clear spirit, waxing glad the while;
    And is in its first home, there where it is.   30
Who speaks thereof, and feels not the tears warm
  Upon his face, must have become so vile
    As to be dead to all sweet sympathies.
    Out upon him! an abject wretch like this   35
May not imagine anything of her, —
  He needs no bitter tears for his relief.
  But sighing comes, and grief,
And the desire to find no comforter,
  (Save only Death, who makes all sorrow brief),   40
To him who for a while turns in his thought
How she hath been among us, and is not.

With sighs my bosom always laboureth
  On thinking, as I do continually,
    Of her for whom my heart now breaks apace;   45
And very often when I think of death,
  Such a great inward longing comes to me
    That it will change the colour of my face;
    And, if the idea settles in its place,
All my limbs shake as with an ague-fit;   50
  Till, starting up in wild bewilderment,
  I do become so shent
That I go forth, lest folk misdoubt of it.
  Afterward, calling with a sore lament
On Beatrice, I ask, "Canst thou be dead?"   55
And calling on her, I am comforted.

Grief with its tears, and anguish with its sighs,
  Come to me now whene'er I am alone;
    So that I think the sight of me gives pain.
And what my life hath been, that living dies,   60

Since for my lady the New Birth's begun,
   I have not any language to explain.
   And so, dear ladies, though my heart were fain,
I scarce could tell indeed how I am thus.
   All joy is with my bitter life at war;   65
   Yea, I am fallen so far
That all men seem to say, "Go out from us,"
   Eyeing my cold white lips, how dead they are.
But she, though I be bowed unto the dust,
Watches me; and will guerdon me, I trust.   70

Weep, piteous Song of mine, upon thy way,
   To the dames going, and the damozels
   For whom and for none else
Thy sisters have made music many a day.
Thou, that art very sad and not as they,   75
   Go dwell thou with them as a mourner dwells.

After I had written this poem, I received the visit of a friend whom I counted as second unto me in the degrees of friendship, and who, moreover, had been united by the nearest kindred to that most gracious creature. And when we had a little spoken together, he began to solicit me that I would write somewhat in memory of a lady who had died; and he disguised his speech, so as to seem to be speaking of another who was but lately dead: wherefore I, perceiving that his speech was of none other than that blessed one herself, told him that it should be done as he required. Then afterwards, having thought thereof, I imagined to give vent in a sonnet to some part of my hidden lamentations; but in such sort that it might seem to be spoken by this friend of mine, to whom I was to give it. And the sonnet saith thus: "Stay now with me," &c.

This sonnet has two parts. In the first, I call the Faithful of Love to hear me. In the second, I relate my miserable condition. The second begins here, "Mark how they force."

Stay now with me, and listen to my sighs,
   Ye piteous hearts, as pity bids ye do.
   Mark how they force their way out and press through:
If they be once pent up, the whole life dies.
Seeing that now indeed my weary eyes   5
   Oftener refuse than I can tell to you,
   (Even though my endless grief is ever new),
To weep, and let the smothered anguish rise.
Also in sighing ye shall hear me call
   On her whose blessèd presence doth enrich   10
     The only home that well befitteth her:
And ye shall hear a bitter scorn of all
   Sent from the inmost of my spirit in speech
     That mourns its joy and its joy's minister.

But when I had written this sonnet, bethinking me who he was to whom I was to give it, that it might appear to be his speech, it seemed to me that this was but a poor and barren gift for one of her so near kindred. Wherefore, before giving him this sonnet, I wrote two stanzas of a poem: the first being written in very sooth as though it were spoken by him, but the other being mine own speech, albeit, unto one who should not look closely, they would both seem to be said by the same person. Nevertheless, looking closely, one must perceive that it is not so, inasmuch as one does not call this most gracious creature *his lady,* and the other does, as is manifestly apparent. And I gave the poem and the sonnet unto my friend, saying that I had made them only for him.

The poem begins, "Whatever while," and has two parts. In the first, that is, in the first stanza, this my dear friend, her kinsman, laments. In the second, I lament; that is, in the other stanza, which begins, "For ever." And thus it appears that in this poem two persons lament, of whom one laments as a brother, the other as a servant.

Whatever while the thought comes over me
  That I may not again
    Behold that lady whom I mourn for now,
About my heart my mind brings constantly
  So much of extreme pain   5
    That I say, Soul of mine, why stayest thou?
    Truly the anguish, soul, that we must bow
Beneath, until we win out of this life,
  Gives me full oft a fear that trembleth:
  So that I call on Death   10
Even as on Sleep one calleth after strife,
  Saying, Come unto me. Life showeth grim
  And bare; and if one dies, I envy him.

For ever, among all my sighs which burn,
  There is a piteous speech   15
    That clamours upon death continually:
Yea, unto him doth my whole spirit turn
  Since first his hand did reach
    My lady's life with most foul cruelty.
    But from the height of woman's fairness, she,   20
Going up from us with the joy we had,
  Grew perfectly and spiritually fair;
  That so she spreads even there
A light of Love which makes the Angels glad,
  And even unto their subtle minds can bring   25
  A certain awe of profound marvelling.

On that day which fulfilled the year since my lady had been made of the citizens of eternal life, remembering me of her as I sat alone, I betook myself to draw the resemblance of an angel upon certain tablets. And while I did thus, chancing to turn my head, I perceived that some were standing beside me to whom I should have given courteous welcome, and that they were observing what I did: also I learned afterwards that they had been there a while before I perceived them. Perceiving whom, I arose for salutation, and said: "Another was with me."*

Afterwards, when they had left me, I set myself again to mine occupation, to wit, to the drawing figures of angels: in doing which, I conceived to write of this matter in rhyme, as for her anniversary, and to address my rhymes unto those who had just left me. It was then that I wrote the sonnet which saith, "That lady": and as this sonnet hath two commencements, it behoveth me to divide it with both of them here.

I say that, according to the first, this sonnet has three parts. In the first, I say that this lady was then in my memory. In the second, I tell what Love therefore did with me. In the third, I speak of the effects of Love. The second begins here, "Love knowing"; the third here, "Forth went they." This part divides into two. In the one, I say that all my sighs issued speaking. In the other, I say how some spoke certain words different from the others. The second begins here, "And still." In this same manner is it divided with the other beginning, save that, in the first part, I tell when this lady had thus come into my mind, and this I say not in the other.

That lady of all gentle memories
   Had lighted on my soul; — whose new abode
   Lies now, as it was well ordained of God,
Among the poor in heart, where Mary is.
Love, knowing that dear image to be his,   5
   Woke up within the sick heart sorrow-bow'd,
   Unto the sighs which are its weary load,
Saying, "Go forth." And they went forth, I wis;
Forth went they from my breast that throbbed and ached;
   With such a pang as oftentimes will bathe   10
      Mine eyes with tears when I am left alone.
   And still those sighs which drew the heaviest breath
Came whispering thus: "O noble intellect!
      It is a year today that thou art gone."

Second Commencement
That lady of all gentle memories
   Had lighted on my soul; — for whose sake flow'd
   The tears of Love; in whom the power abode
Which led you to observe while I did this.
Love, knowing that dear image to be his, &c.

Then, having sat for some space sorely in thought because of the time that was now past, I was so filled with dolorous imaginings that it became outwardly man-

---

*Thus according to some texts. The majority, however, add the words, "And therefore was I in thought"; but the shorter speech is perhaps the more forcible and pathetic.

ifest in mine altered countenance. Whereupon, feeling this and being in dread lest any should have seen me, I lifted mine eyes to look; and then perceived a young and very beautiful lady, who was gazing upon me from a window with a gaze full of pity, so that the very sum of pity appeared gathered together in her. And seeing that unhappy persons, when they beget compassion in others, are then most moved unto weeping, as though they also felt pity for themselves, it came to pass that mine eyes began to be inclined unto tears. Wherefore, becoming fearful lest I should make manifest mine abject condition, I rose up, and went where I could not be seen of that lady; saying afterwards within myself: "Certainly with her also must abide most noble Love." And with that, I resolved upon writing a sonnet, wherein, speaking unto her, I should say all that I have just said. And as this sonnet is very evident, I will not divide it.

> Mine eyes beheld the blessed pity spring
>   Into thy countenance immediately
>   A while agone, when thou beheldst in me
> The sickness only hidden grief can bring;
> And then I knew thou wast considering   5
>   How abject and forlorn my life must be;
>   And I became afraid that thou shouldst see
> My weeping, and account it a base thing.
> Therefore I went out from thee; feeling how
>   The tears were straightway loosened at my heart   10
>   Beneath thine eyes' compassionate control.
>   And afterwards I said within my soul:
> 'Lo! with this lady dwells the counterpart
> Of the same Love who holds me weeping now."

It happened after this, that whensoever I was seen of this lady, she became pale and of a piteous countenance, as though it had been with love; whereby she remembered me many times of my own most noble lady, who was wont to be of a like paleness. And I know that often, when I could not weep nor in any way give ease unto mine anguish, I went to look upon this lady, who seemed to bring the tears into my eyes by the mere sight of her. Of the which thing I bethought me to speak unto her in rhyme, and then made this sonnet: which begins, "Love's pallor," and which is plain without being divided, by its exposition aforesaid: —

> Love's pallor and the semblance of deep ruth
>   Were never yet shown forth so perfectly
>   In any lady's face, chancing to see
> Grief's miserable countenance uncouth,
> As in thine, lady, they have sprung to soothe,   5
>   When in mine anguish thou hast looked on me;
>   Until sometimes it seems as if, through thee,
> My heart might almost wander from its truth.

Yet so it is, I cannot hold mine eyes
  From gazing very often upon thine   10
    In the sore hope to shed those tears they keep;
And at such time, thou mak'st the pent tears rise
  Even to the brim, till the eyes waste and pine;
    Yet cannot they, while thou art present, weep.

At length, by the constant sight of this lady, mine eyes began to be gladdened overmuch with her company; through which thing many times I had much unrest, and rebuked myself as a base person: also, many times I cursed the unsteadfastness of mine eyes, and said to them inwardly: "Was not your grievous condition of weeping wont one while to make others weep? And will ye now forget this thing because a lady looketh upon you? who so looketh merely in compassion of the grief ye then showed for your own blessed lady. But whatso ye can, that do ye, accursed eyes! many a time will I make you remember it! for never, till death dry you up, should ye make an end of your weeping." And when I had spoken thus unto mine eyes, I was taken again with extreme and grievous sighing. And to the end that this inward strife which I had undergone might not be hidden from all saving the miserable wretch who endured it, I proposed to write a sonnet, and to comprehend in it this horrible condition. And I wrote this which begins, "The very bitter weeping."

The sonnet has two parts. In the first, I speak to my eyes, as my heart spoke within myself. In the second, I remove a difficulty, showing who it is that speaks thus: and this part begins here, "'So far." It well might receive other divisions also; but this would be useless, since it is manifest by the preceding exposition.

"The very bitter weeping that ye made
  So long a time together, eyes of mine,
  Was wont to make the tears of pity shine
In other eyes full oft, as I have said.
But now this thing were scarce rememberèd   5
  If I, on my part, foully would combine
  With you, and not recall each ancient sign
Of grief, and her for whom your tears were shed.
It is your fickleness that doth betray
  My mind to fears, and makes me tremble thus   10
    What while a lady greets me with her eyes.
Except by death, we must not any way
  Forget our lady who is gone from us."
    So far doth my heart utter, and then sighs.

The sight of this lady brought me into so unwonted a condition that I often thought of her as of one too dear unto me; and I began to consider her thus: "This lady is young, beautiful, gentle, and wise: perchance it was Love himself who set her in my path, that so my life might find peace." And there were times when I thought yet more fondly, until my heart consented unto its reasoning. But when it had so consented, my thought would often turn round upon me, as moved by reason, and cause me to say within myself: "What hope is this which would console me after so base a fashion, and which hath taken the place of all other imagining?" Also there was another voice within me, that said: "And wilt thou, having suffered so much tribulation through Love, not escape while yet thou mayest from so much bitterness? Thou must surely know that this thought carries with it the desire of Love, and drew its life from the gentle eyes of that lady who vouchsafed thee so much pity." Wherefore I, having striven sorely and very often with myself, bethought me to say somewhat thereof in rhyme. And seeing that in the battle of doubts, the victory most often remained with such as inclined towards the lady of whom I speak, it seemed to me that I should address this sonnet unto her: in the first line whereof, I call that thought which spake of her a gentle thought, only because it spoke of one who was gentle; being of itself most vile.*

In this sonnet I make myself into two, according as my thoughts were divided one from the other. The one part I call Heart, that is, appetite; the other, Soul, that is, reason; and I tell what one saith to the other. And that it is fitting to call the appetite Heart, and the reason Soul, is manifest enough to them to whom I wish this to be open. True it is that, in the preceding sonnet, I take the part of the Heart against the Eyes; and that appears contrary to what I say in the present; and therefore I say that, there also, by the Heart I mean appetite, because yet greater was my desire to remember my most gentle lady than to see this other, although indeed I had some appetite towards her, but it appeared slight: wherefrom it appears that the one statement is not contrary to the other. This sonnet has three parts. In the first, I begin to say to this lady how my desires turn all towards her. In the second, I say how the Soul, that is, the reason, speaks to the Heart, that is, to the appetite. In the third, I say how the latter answers. The second begins here, "And what is this?" the third here, "And the heart answers."

A gentle thought there is will often start,
    Within my secret self, to speech of thee:
    Also of Love it speaks so tenderly
That much in me consents and takes its part.
"And what is this," the soul saith to the heart,   5
    "That cometh thus to comfort thee and me,
    And thence where it would dwell, thus potently
Can drive all other thoughts by its strange art?"
And the heart answers: "Be no more at strife

---

*Boccaccio tells us that Dante was married to Gemma Donati about a year after the death of Beatrice. Can Gemma then be "the lady of the window," his love for whom Dante so contemns? Such a passing conjecture (when considered together with the interpretation of this passage in Dante's later work, the *Convito*) would of course imply an admission of what I believe to lie at the heart of all true Dantesque commentary; that is, the existence always of the actual events even where the allegorical superstructure has been raised by Dante himself.

'Twixt doubt and doubt: this is Love's messenger
  And speaketh but his words, from him received;
And all the strength it owns and all the life
  It draweth from the gentle eyes of her
    Who, looking on our grief, hath often grieved."

But against this adversary of reason, there rose up in me on a certain day, about the ninth hour, a strong visible phantasy, wherein I seemed to behold the most gracious Beatrice, habited in that crimson raiment which she had worn when I had first beheld her; also she appeared to me of the same tender age as then. Whereupon I fell into a deep thought of her: and my memory ran back according to the order of time, unto all those matters in the which she had borne a part; and my heart began painfully to repent of the desire by which it had so basely let itself be possessed during so many days, contrary to the constancy of reason.

And then, this evil desire being quite gone from me, all my thoughts turned again unto their excellent Beatrice. And I say most truly that from that hour I thought constantly of her with the whole humbled and ashamed heart; the which became often manifest in sighs, that had among them the name of that most gracious creature, and how she departed from us. Also it would come to pass very often, through the bitter anguish of some one thought, that I forgot both it, and myself, and where I was. By this increase of sighs, my weeping, which before had been somewhat lessened, increased in like manner; so that mine eyes seemed to long only for tears and to cherish them, and came at last to be circled about with red as though they had suffered martyrdom: neither were they able to look again upon the beauty of any face that might again bring them to shame and evil: from which things it will appear that they were fitly guerdoned for their unsteadfastness. Wherefore I, (wishing that mine abandonment of all such evil desires and vain temptations should be certified and made manifest, beyond all doubts which might have been suggested by the rhymes aforewritten), proposed to write a sonnet, wherein I should express this purport. And I then wrote, "Woe's me!"

I said, "Woe's me!" because I was ashamed of the trifling of mine eyes. This sonnet I do not divide, since its purport is manifest enough.

Woe's me! by dint of all these sighs that come
  Forth of my heart, its endless grief to prove,
  Mine eyes are conquered, so that even to move
Their lids for greeting is grown troublesome.
They wept so long that now they are grief's home   5
  And count their tears all laughter far above:
  They wept till they are circled now by Love
With a red circle in sign of martyrdom.
These musings, and the sighs they bring from me,
  Are grown at last so constant and so sore   10
    That Love swoons in my spirit with faint breath;

Hearing in those sad sounds continually
   The most sweet name that my dead lady bore,
     With many grievous words touching her death.

About this time, it happened that a great number of persons undertook a pilgrimage, to the end that they might behold that blessed portraiture bequeathed unto us by our Lord Jesus Christ as the image of His beautiful countenance,* (upon which countenance my dear lady now looketh continually.) And certain among these pilgrims, who seemed very thoughtful, passed by a path which is well-nigh in the midst of the city where my most gracious lady was born, and abode, and at last died.

Then I, beholding them, said within myself: "These pilgrims seem to be come from very far; and I think they cannot have heard speak of this lady, or know anything concerning her. Their thoughts are not of her, but of other things; it may be, of their friends who are far distant, and whom we, in our turn, know not." And I went on to say: "I know that if they were of a country near unto us, they would in some wise seem disturbed, passing through this city which is so full of grief." And I said also: "If I could speak with them a space, I am certain that I should make them weep before they went forth of this city; for those things that they would hear from me must needs beget weeping in any."

And when the last of them had gone by me, I bethought me to write a sonnet, showing forth mine inward speech; and that it might seem the more pitiful, I made as though I had spoken it indeed unto them. And I wrote this sonnet, which beginneth: "Ye pilgrim-folk." I made use of the word *pilgrim* for its general signification; for "pilgrim" may be understood in two senses, one general, and one special. General, so far as any man may be called a pilgrim who leaveth the place of his birth; whereas, more narrowly speaking, he only is a pilgrim who goeth towards or frowards the House of St. James. For there are three separate denominations proper unto those who undertake journeys to the glory of God. They are called Palmers who go beyond the seas eastward, whence often they bring palm-branches. And Pilgrims, as I have said, are they who journey unto the holy House of Gallicia; seeing that no other apostle was buried so far from his birth-place as was the blessed Saint James. And there is a third sort who are called Romers; in that they go whither these whom I have called pilgrims went: which is to say, unto Rome.

This sonnet is not divided, because its own words sufficiently declare it.

Ye pilgrim-folk, advancing pensively
   As if in thought of distant things, I pray,
     Is your own land indeed so far away

---

*The Veronica (*Vera icon,* or true image); that is, the napkin with which a woman was said to have wiped our Saviour's face on His way to the cross, and which miraculously retained its likeness. Dante makes mention of it also in the *Commedia* (Parad. xxi. 103), where he says: "forth of this city; for those things that they would hear from me must needs beget weeping in any."

As by your aspect it would seem to be, —
That this our heavy sorrow leaves you free 5
   Though passing through the mournful town mid-way;
   Like unto men that understand to-day
Nothing at all of her great misery?
Yet if ye will but stay, whom I accost,
   And listen to my words a little space, 10
     At going ye shall mourn with a loud voice.
It is her Beatrice that she hath lost;
   Of whom the least word spoken holds such grace
   That men weep hearing it, and have no choice.

A while after these things, two gentle ladies sent unto me, praying that I would bestow upon them certain of these my rhymes. And I, (taking into account their worthiness and consideration), resolved that I would write also a new thing, and send it them together with those others, to the end that their wishes might be more honourably fulfilled. Therefore I made a sonnet, which narrates my condition, and which I caused to be conveyed to them, accompanied with the one preceding, and with that other which begins, "Stay now with me and listen to my sighs." And the new sonnet is, "Beyond the sphere."

This sonnet comprises five parts. In the first, I tell whither my thought goeth, naming the place by the name of one of its effects. In the second, I say wherefore it goeth up, and who makes it go thus. In the third, I tell what it saw, namely, a lady honoured. And I then call it a "Pilgrim Spirit," because it goes up spiritually, and like a pilgrim who is out of his known country. In the fourth, I say how the spirit sees her such (that is, in such quality) that I cannot understand her; that is to say, my thought rises into the quality of her in a degree that my intellect cannot comprehend, seeing that our intellect is, towards those blessed souls, like our eye weak against the sun; and this the Philosopher says in the Second of the Metaphysics. In the fifth, I say that, although I cannot see there whither my thought carries me — that is, to her admirable essence — I at least understand this, namely, that it is a thought of my lady, because I often hear her name therein. And, at the end of this fifth part, I say, "Ladies mine," to show that they are ladies to whom I speak. The second part begins, "A new perception"; the third, "When it hath reach'd"; the fourth, "It sees her such"; the fifth, "And yet I know." It might be divided yet more nicely, and made yet clearer; but this division may pass, and therefore I stay not to divide it further.

Beyond the sphere which spreads to widest space
   Now soars the sigh that my heart sends above:
   A new perception born of grieving Love
Guideth it upward the untrodden ways.
When it hath reach'd unto the end, and stays, 5
   It sees a lady round whom splendors move
   In homage; till, by the great light thereof

Abashed, the pilgrim spirit stands at gaze.
It sees her such, that when it tells me this
    Which it hath seen, I understand it not,   10
        It hath a speech so subtile and so fine.
And yet I know its voice within my thought
    Often remembereth me of Beatrice:
        So that I understand it, ladies mine.

After writing this sonnet, it was given unto me to behold a very wonderful vision;* wherein I saw things which determined me that I would say nothing further of this most blessed one, until such time as I could discourse more worthily concerning her. And to this end I labour all I can; as she well knoweth. Wherefore if it be His pleasure through whom is the life of all things, that my life continue with me a few years, it is my hope that I shall yet write concerning her what hath not before been written of any woman. After the which, may it seem good unto Him who is the Master of Grace, that my spirit should go hence to behold the glory of its lady: to wit, of that blessed Beatrice who now gazeth continually on His countenance *qui est per omnia saecula benedictus. Laus Deo.* †

The End of the New Life

Sestina‡. Of the Lady Pietra degli Scrovigni (Dante Alighieri)

To the dim light and the large circle of shade
I have clomb, and to the whitening of the hills,
There where we see no colour in the grass.
Natheless my longing loses not its green,
It has so taken root in the hard stone   5
Which talks and hears as though it were a lady.

Utterly frozen is this youthful lady
Even as the snow that lies within the shade;

---

*This we may believe to have been the Vision of Hell, Purgatory, and Paradise, which furnished the triple argument of the *Divina Commedia*. The Latin words ending the *Vita Nuova* are almost identical with those at the close of the letter in which Dante, on concluding the *Paradise*, and accomplishing the hope here expressed, dedicates his great work to Can Grande della Scala.

†"Who is blessed throughout all ages."

‡I have translated this piece both on account of its great and peculiar beauty, and also because it affords an example of a form of composition which I have met with in no Italian writer before Dante's time, though it is not uncommon among the Provençal poets (see Dante, de Vulg. Eloq.). I have headed it with the name of a Paduan lady, to whom it is surmised by some to have been addressed during Dante's exile; but this must be looked upon as a rather doubtful conjecture. I have adopted the name chiefly to mark it at once as not referring to Beatrice.

For she is no more moved than is a stone
By the sweet season which makes warm the hills   10
And alters them afresh from white to green,
Covering their sides again with flowers and grass.

When on her hair she sets a crown of grass
The thought has no more room for other lady;
Because she weaves the yellow with the green   15
So well that Love sits down there in the shade, —
Love who has shut me in among low hills
Faster than between walls of granite-stone.

She is more bright than is a precious stone;
The wound she gives may not be healed with grass: 20
I therefore have fled far o'er plains and hills
For refuge from so dangerous a lady;
But from her sunshine nothing can give shade, —
Not any hill, nor wall, nor summer-green.

A while ago, I saw her dressed in green, —   25
So fair, she might have wakened in a stone
This love which I do feel even for her shade;
And therefore, as one woos a graceful lady,
I wooed her in a field that was all grass
Girdled about with very lofty hills.   30

Yet shall the streams turn back and climb the hills
Before Love's flame in this damp wood and green
Burn, as it burns within a youthful lady,
For my sake, who would sleep away in stone
My life, or feed like beasts upon the grass,   35
Only to see her garments cast a shade.

How dark soe'er the hills throw out their shade,
Under her summer-green the beautiful lady
Covers it, like a stone cover'd in grass.

Sonnet. A Rapture Concerning His Lady (Guido Cavalcanti)

Who is she coming, whom all gaze upon,
   Who makes the air all tremulous with light,
And at whose side is Love himself? that none
   Dare speak, but each man's sighs are infinite.

Ah me! how she looks round from left to right,   5
　　Let Love discourse: I may not speak thereon.
　　Lady she seems of such high benison
As makes all others graceless in men's sight.
The honour which is hers cannot be said;
　　To whom are subject all things virtuous,   10
　　　　While all things beauteous own her deity.
Ne'er was the mind of man so nobly led
　　Nor yet was such redemption granted us
　　　　That we should ever know her perfectly.

Ballata. Of His Lady Among Other Ladies (Guido Cavalcanti)

With other women I beheld my love; —
　　Not that the rest were women to mine eyes,
Who only as her shadows seemed to move.

I do not praise her more than with the truth,
　　Nor blame I these if it be rightly read.   5

But while I speak, a thought I may not soothe
　　Says to my senses: "Soon shall ye be dead,
　　If for my sake your tears ye will not shed."

And then the eyes yield passage, at that thought,
To the heart's weeping, which forgets her not.   10

**To Guido Orlandi. Sonnet. Of a Consecrated Image
Resembling His Lady** (Guido Cavalcanti)

Guido, an image of my lady dwells
　　At San Michele in Orto, consecrate
　　And duly worshipped. Fair in holy state
She listens to the tale each sinner tells:
And among them that come to her, who ails   5
　　The most, on him the most doth blessing wait.
　　She bids the fiend men's bodies abdicate;
Over the curse of blindness she prevails,
And heals sick languors in the public squares.
　　A multitude adores her reverently: 10
　　　　Before her face two burning tapers are;

Her voice is uttered upon paths afar.
   Yet through the Lesser Brethren's* jealousy
She is named idol, not being one of theirs.

Ballata. Of a Continual Death in Love (Guido Cavalcanti)

Though thou, indeed, hast quite forgotten ruth,
Its steadfast truth my heart abandons not;
But still its thought yields service in good part
   To that hard heart in thee.

Alas! who hears believes not I am so.   5
Yet who can know? of very surety, none.
From Love is won a spirit, in some wise,
   Which dies perpetually:

And, when at length in that strange ecstasy
   The heavy sigh will start,   10
   There rains upon my heart
   A love so pure and fine,
That I say: "Lady, I am wholly thine."†

To Dante Alighieri. Sonnet. He Conceives of Some Compensation in Death‡ (Cino da Pistoia)

Dante, whenever this thing happeneth, —
   That Love's desire is quite bereft of Hope,
   (Seeking in vain at ladies' eyes some scope
Of joy, through what the heart for ever saith), —
I ask thee, can amends be made by Death?   5
   Is such sad pass the last extremity? —
   Or may the Soul that never fear'd to die
Then in another body draw new breath?
Lo! thus it is through her who governs all
   Below, — that I, who enter'd at her door,   10

---

* The Franciscans, in profession of deeper poverty and humility than belonged to other Orders, called themselves *Fratres minores*.

† I may take this opportunity of mentioning that, in every case where an abrupt change of metre occurs in one of my translations, it is so also in the original poem.

‡ Among Dante's Epistles, there is a Latin letter to Cino, which I should judge was written in reply to this Sonnet.

Now at her dreadful window must fare forth.
Yea, and I think through her it doth befall
  That even ere yet the road is travell'd o'er
    My bones are weary and life is nothing worth.

Canzone. His Lament for Selvaggia (Cino da Pistoia)

Ay me, alas! the beautiful bright hair
  That shed reflected gold
    O'er the green growths on either side the way;
Ay me! the lovely look, open and fair,
  Which my heart's core doth hold   5
    With all else of that best-remember'd day;
      Ay me! the face made gay
With joy that Love confers;
Ay me! that smile of hers
  Where whiteness as of snow was visible   10
Among the roses at all seasons red!
  Ay me! and was this well,
O Death, to let me live when she is dead?

Ay me! the calm, erect, dignified walk;
  Ay me! the sweet salute, —   15
    The thoughtful mind, — the wit discreetly worn;
Ay me! the clearness of her noble talk,
  Which made the good take root
    In me, and for the evil woke my scorn;
      Ay me! the longing born   20
Of so much loveliness, —
The hope, whose eager stress
  Made other hopes fall back to let it pass,
Even till my load of love grew light thereby!
  These thou hast broken, as glass,   25
O Death, who makest me, alive, to die!

Ay me! Lady, the lady of all worth; —
  Saint, for whose single shrine
All other shrines I left, even as Love will'd; —
Ay me! what precious stone in the whole earth,   30
  For that pure fame of thine
    Worthy the marble statue's base to yield?
      Ay me! fair vase fullfill'd

With more than this world's good, —
By cruel chance and rude   35
  Cast out upon the steep path of the mountains
Where Death has shut thee in between hard stones!
  Ay me! two languid fountains
Of weeping are these eyes, which joy disowns.

Ay me, sharp Death! till what I ask is done   40
  And my whole life is ended utterly, —
Answer — must I weep on
  Even thus, and never cease to moan Ay me?

Sonnet. Of All He Would Do (Cecco Angiolieri)

If I were fire, I'd burn the world away;
  If I were wind, I'd turn my storms thereon;
  If I were water, I'd soon let it drown;
If I were God, I'd sink it from the day;
If I were Pope, I'd never feel quite gay   5
  Until there was no peace beneath the sun;
  If I were Emperor, what would I have done? —
I'd lop men's heads all round in my own way.
If I were Death, I'd look my father up;
  If I were Life, I'd run away from him;   10
    And treat my mother to like calls and runs.
If I were Cecco, (and that's all my hope),
  I'd pick the nicest girls to suit my whim,
    And other folk should get the ugly ones.

Sonnet. On the Death of His Father (Cecco Angiolieri)

Let not the inhabitants of Hell despair,
  For one's got out who seem'd to be lock'd in;
  And Cecco's the poor devil that I mean,
Who thought for ever and ever to be there.
But the leaf's turn'd at last, and I declare   5
  That now my state of glory doth begin;
  For Messer Angiolieri's slipp'd his skin,
Who plagued me, Summer and Winter, many a year.

Make haste to Cecco, sonnet, with a will,
 To him who no more at the Abbey dwells;
  Tell him that Brother Henry's half dried up.*   10
He'll never more be down-at-mouth, but fill
 His beak at his own beck,† till his life swells
  To more than Enoch's or Elijah's scope.

Sonnet. Of the Star of His Love (Dino Frescobaldi)

That star the highest seen in heaven's expanse
 Not yet forsakes me with its lovely light:
  It gave me her who from her heaven's pure height
Gives all the grace mine intellect demands.
Thence a new arrow of strength is in my hands   5
 Which bears good will whereso it may alight;
  So barb'd, that no man's body or soul its flight
Has wounded yet, nor shall wound any man's.
Glad am I therefore that her grace should fall
 Not otherwise than thus; whose rich increase   10
  Is such a power as evil cannot dim.
My sins within an instant perish'd all
 When I inhaled the light of so much peace.
  And this Love knows; for I have told it him.

To Dante Alighieri. Sonnet. He Commends the Work of Dante's Life, Then Drawing to Its Close; and Deplores His Own Deficiencies (Giovanni Quirino)

Glory to God and to God's Mother chaste,
 Dear friend, is all the labour of thy days:
  Thou art as he who evermore uplays
That heavenly wealth which the worm cannot waste:
So shalt thou render back with interest   5
 The precious talent given thee by God's grace:
  While I, for my part, follow in their ways
Who by the cares of this world are possess'd.

---

*It would almost seem as if Cecco, in his poverty, had at last taken refuge in a religious house under the name of Brother Henry (*Frate Arrigo*), and as if he here meant that Brother Henry was now decayed, so to speak, through the resuscitation of Cecco.

†In the original words, "Ma dital cibo imbecchi lo suo becco," a play upon the name of Becchina seems intended, which I have conveyed as well as I could.

For as the shadow of the earth doth make
  The moon's globe dark, when so she is debarr'd   10
    From the bright rays which lit her in the sky, —
So now, since thou my sun didst me forsake,
  (Being distant from me), I grow dull and hard,
    Even as a beast of Epicurus' sty.

Of His Last Sight of Fiammetta (Giovanni Boccaccio)

Round her red garland and her golden hair
  I saw a fire about Fiammetta's head;
  Thence to a little cloud I watch'd it fade,
Than silver or than gold more brightly fair;
And like a pearl that a gold ring doth bear,   5
  Even so an angel sat therein, who sped
  Alone and glorious throughout heaven, array'd
In sapphires and in gold that lit the air.
Then I rejoiced as hoping happy things,
Who rather should have then discern'd how God   10
  Had haste to make my lady all his own,
Even as it came to pass. And with these stings
  Of sorrow, and with life's most weary load
    I dwell, who fain would be where she is gone.

PART SIX

Other Translations

In Absence of Becchina (Cecco Angiolieri)

I'm better skill'd to frolic on a bed
  Than any man that goes upon two feet;
  And so, when I and certain moneys meet,
You'll fancy with what joys I shall be fed.
Meanwhile (alas!) I can but long instead   5
  To be within her arms held close and sweet
  To whom without reserve and past retreat
My soul and body and heart are subjected.
For often, when my mind is all distraught
  With this whereof I make my boast, I pass   10
    The day in deaths which never seem enough;
And all my blood within is boiling hot,
  Yet I've less strength than running water has;
    And this shall last as long as I'm in love.

From the *Roman de la Rose*

Tender as dew her cheeks' warm life;
She was as simple as a wife,
She was as white as lilies are.
Her face was sweet and smooth and fair:
Slender and very straight she was,   5
And on her cheeks no paint might pass.

Her fair hair was so long that it
Shook, when she walked, about her feet:
Eyes, nose, and mouth, were perfect art,
Exceeding pain is at my heart   10
When I remember me of her.

Lilith. From Goethe

Hold thou thy heart against her shining hair,
  If, by thy fate, she spread it once for thee;
For, when she nets a young man in that snare,
  So twines she him he never may be free.

"I saw the sibyl at Cumae"

*[And the Sibyl, you know. I saw her with my own eyes at Cumae, hanging in
a jar; and, when the boys asked her, "What would you, Sibyl?" she answered,
"I would die."*
— Petronius.]

"I saw the Sibyl at Cumae"
  (One said) "with mine own eye.
She hung in a cage, and read her rune
  To all the passers-by.
Said the boys, 'What wouldst thou, Sibyl?'   5
  She answered, 'I would die.'"

Francesca da Rimini (Dante)

When I made answer, I began: "Alas!
  How many sweet thoughts and how much desire
Led these two onward to the dolorous pass!"
  Then turned to them, as who would fain inquire,
And said: "Francesca, these thine agonies   5
  Wring tears for pity and grief that they inspire:
But tell me, — in the season of sweet sighs,
  When and what way did Love instruct you so
That he in your vague longings made you wise?"
  Then she to me: "There is no greater woe   10
Than the remembrance brings of happy days
  In misery; and this thy guide doth know.
But if the first beginnings to retrace
  Of our sad love can yield thee solace here,
So will I be as one that weeps and says.   15
  One day we read, for pastime and sweet cheer,
Of Lancelot, how he found Love tyrannous:
  We were alone and without any fear.

Our eyes were drawn together, reading thus,
　　Full oft, and still our cheeks would pale and glow;　　　　20
But one sole point it was that conquered us.
　　For when we read of that great lover, how
He kissed the smile which he had longed to win, —
　　Then he whom nought can sever from me now
For ever, kissed my mouth, all quivering.　　　　25
　　A Galahalt was the book, and he that writ:
Upon that day we read no more therein."
　　At the tale told, while one soul uttered it,
The other wept: a pang so pitiable
　　That I was seized, like death, in swooning-fit,　　　　30
And even as a dead body falls, I fell.

PART SEVEN

Prose

HAND AND SOUL (1850, 1869)

'Rivolsimi in quel lato
Là onde venìa la voce,
E parvemi una luce
Che lucea quanto stella:
La mia mente era quella.'

Bonaggiunta Urbiciani, (1250).

Before any knowledge of painting was brought to Florence, there were already painters in Lucca, and Pisa, and Arezzo, who feared God and loved the art. The workmen from Greece, whose trade it was to sell their own works in Italy and teach Italians to imitate them, had already found in rivals of the soil a skill that could forestall their lessons and cheapen their labours, more years than is supposed before the art came at all into Florence. The pre-eminence to which Cimabue was raised at once by his contemporaries, and which he still retains to a wide extent even in the modern mind, is to be accounted for, partly by the circumstances under which he arose, and partly by that extraordinary *purpose of fortune* born with the lives of some few, and through which it is not a little thing for any who went before, if they are even remembered as the shadows of the coming of such an one, and the voices which prepared his way in the wilderness. It is thus, almost exclusively, that the painters of whom I speak are now known. They have left little, and but little heed is taken of that which men hold to have been surpassed; it is gone like time gone, — a track of dust and dead leaves that merely led to the fountain.

Nevertheless, of very late years and in very rare instances, some signs of a better understanding have become manifest. A case in point is that of the triptych and two cruciform pictures at Dresden, by Chiaro di Messer Bello dell' Erma, to which the eloquent pamphlet of Dr. Aemmster has at length succeeded in attracting the students. There is another still more solemn and beautiful work, now proved to be by the same hand, in the Pitti gallery at Florence. It is the one to which my narrative will relate.

This Chiaro dell' Erma was a young man of very honorable family in Arezzo; where, conceiving art almost for himself, and loving it deeply, he endeavoured from early boyhood towards the imitation of any objects offered in nature. The extreme longing after a visible embodiment of his thoughts strengthened as his years increased, more even than his sinews or the blood of his life; until he would feel faint in sunsets and at the sight of stately persons. When he had lived nineteen years, he heard of the famous Giunta Pisano; and, feeling much of admiration, with perhaps a little of that envy which youth always feels until it has learned to measure success by time and opportunity, he determined that he would seek out Giunta, and, if possible, become his pupil.

Having arrived in Pisa, he clothed himself in humble apparel, being unwilling that any other thing than the desire he had for knowledge should be his plea with the great painter; and then, leaving his baggage at a house of entertainment, he took his way along the street, asking whom he met for the lodging of Giunta. It soon chanced that one of that city, conceiving him to be a stranger and poor, took him into his house and refreshed him; afterwards directing him on his way.

When he was brought to speech of Giunta, he said merely that he was a student, and that nothing in the world was so much at his heart as to become that which he had heard told of him with whom he was speaking. He was received with courtesy and consideration, and soon stood among the works of the famous artist. But the forms he saw there were lifeless and incomplete; and a sudden exultation possessed him as he said within himself, "I am the master of this man." The blood came at first into his face, but the next moment he was quite pale and fell to trembling. He was able, however, to conceal his emotion; speaking very little to Giunta, but when he took his leave, thanking him respectfully.

After this, Chiaro's first resolve was, that he would work out thoroughly some one of his thoughts, and let the world know him. But the lesson which he had now learned, of how small a greatness might win fame, and how little there was to strive against, served to make him torpid, and rendered his exertions less continual. Also Pisa was a larger and more luxurious city than Arezzo; and when, in his walks, he saw the great gardens laid out for pleasure, and the beautiful women who passed to and fro, and heard the music that was in the groves of the city at evening, he was taken with wonder that he had never claimed his share of the inheritance of those years in which his youth was cast. And women loved Chiaro; for, in despite of the burthen of study, he was well-favoured and very manly in his walking; and, seeing his face in front, there was a glory upon it, as upon the face of one who feels a light round his hair.

So he put thought from him, and partook of his life. But, one night, being in a certain company of ladies, a gentleman that was there with him began to speak of the paintings of a youth named Bonaventura, which he had seen in Lucca; adding that Giunta Pisano might now look for a rival. When Chiaro heard this, the lamps shook before him and the music beat in his ears. He rose up, alleging a sudden sickness, and went out of that house with his teeth set. And, being again within his room, he wrote up over the door the name of Bonaventura, that it might stop him when he would go out.

He now took to work diligently, not returning to Arezzo, but remaining in Pisa, that no day more might be lost; only living entirely to himself. Sometimes, after nightfall, he would walk abroad in the most solitary places he could find; hardly feeling the ground under him, because of the thoughts of the day which held him in fever.

The lodging Chiaro had chosen was in a house that looked upon gardens fast by the Church of San Petronio. It was here, and at this time, that he painted the Dresden pictures; as also, in all likelihood, the one — inferior in merit, but certainly his — which is now at Munich. For the most part he was calm and regular in his manner of study; though often he would remain at work through the whole of a day, not resting once so long as the light lasted; flushed, and with the hair from his face. Or, at times, when he could not paint, he would sit for hours in thought of all the greatness the world had known from of old; until he was weak with yearning, like one who gazes upon a path of stars.

He continued in this patient endeavour for about three years, at the end of which his name was spoken throughout all Tuscany. As his fame waxed, he began to be employed, besides easel-pictures, upon wall-paintings; but I believe that no traces remain to us of any of these latter. He is said to have painted in the Duomo; and D'Agincourt mentions having seen some portions of a picture by him which originally had its place above the high altar in the Church of the Certosa; but which, at the time he saw it, being very dilapidated, had been hewn out of the wall, and was preserved in the stores of the convent. Before the period of Dr. Aemmster's researches, however, it had been entirely destroyed.

Chiaro was now famous. It was for the race of fame that he had girded up his loins; and he had not paused until fame was reached; yet now, in taking breath, he found that the weight was still at his heart. The years of his labour had fallen from him, and his life was still in its first painful desire.

With all that Chiaro had done during these three years, and even before with the studies of his early youth, there had always been a feeling of worship and service. It was the peace-offering that he made to God and to his own soul for the eager selfishness of his aim. There was earth, indeed, upon the hem of his raiment; but *this* was of the heaven, heavenly. He had seasons when he could endure to think of no other feature of his hope than this. Sometimes it had even seemed to him to behold that day when his mistress — his mystical lady (now hardly in her ninth year, but whose smile at meeting had already lighted on his soul), — even she, his own gracious Italian Art — should pass, through the sun that never sets, into the shadow of the tree of life, and be seen of God and found good: and then it had seemed to him that he, with many who, since his coming, had joined the band of whom he was one (for, in his dream, the body he had worn on earth had been dead an hundred years), were permitted to gather round the blessed maiden, and to worship with her through all ages and ages of ages, saying, Holy, holy, holy. This thing he had seen with the eyes of his spirit; and in this thing had trusted, believing that it would surely come to pass.

But now, (being at length led to inquire closely into himself), even as, in the pursuit of fame, the unrest abiding after attainment had proved to him that he had misinterpreted the craving of his own spirit — so also, now that he would willingly have fallen back on devotion, he became aware that much of that reverence which he had mistaken for faith had been no more than the worship of beauty. Therefore, after certain days passed in perplexity, Chiaro said within himself, "My life and my will are yet before me: I will take another aim to my life."

From that moment Chiaro set a watch on his soul, and put his hand to no other works but only to such as had for their end the presentment of some moral greatness that should influence the beholder: and to this end, he multiplied abstractions, and forgot the beauty and passion of the world. So the people ceased to throng about his pictures as heretofore; and, when they were carried through town and town to their destination, they were no longer delayed by the crowds eager to gaze and admire: and no prayers or offerings were brought to them on their path, as to his Madonnas, and his Saints, and his Holy Children, wrought for the sake of the life he saw in the faces that he loved. Only the critical audience remained to him; and these, in default of more worthy matter, would have turned their scrutiny on a puppet or a mantle. Meanwhile, he had no more of fever upon him; but was calm and pale each day in all that he did and in his goings in and out. The works he produced at this time have perished — in all likelihood, not unjustly. It is said (and we may easily believe it), that, though more laboured than his former pictures, they were cold and unemphatic; bearing marked out upon them the measure of that boundary to which they were made to conform.

And the weight was still close at Chiaro's heart: but he held in his breath, never resting (for he was afraid), and would not know it.

Now it happened, within these days, that there fell a great feast in Pisa, for holy matters: and each man left his occupation; and all the guilds and companies of the city were got together for games and rejoicings. And there were scarcely any that stayed in the houses, except ladies who lay or sat along their balconies between open windows which let the breeze beat through the rooms and over the spread tables from end to end. And the golden cloths that their arms lay upon drew all eyes upward to see their beauty; and the day was long; and every hour of the day was bright with the sun.

So Chiaro's model, when he awoke that morning on the hot pavement of the Piazza Nunziata, and saw the hurry of people that passed him, got up and went along with them; and Chiaro waited for him in vain.

For the whole of that morning, the music was in Chiaro's room from the Church close at hand; and he could hear the sounds that the crowd made in the streets; hushed only at long intervals while the processions for the feast-day chanted in going under his windows. Also, more than once, there was a high clamour from the meeting of factious persons: for the ladies of both leagues were looking down; and he who encountered his enemy could not choose but draw upon him. Chiaro waited a long time idle; and then knew that his model was gone elsewhere. When at his work, he was blind and deaf to all else; but he feared sloth: for then his stealthy thoughts would begin to beat round and round him, seeking a point for attack. He now rose, therefore, and went to the window. It was within a short space of noon; and underneath him a throng of people was coming out through the porch of San Petronio.

The two greatest houses of the feud in Pisa had filled the church for that mass. The first to leave had been the Gherghiotti; who, stopping on the threshold, had fallen back in ranks along each side of the archway: so that now, in passing outward, the Marotoli had to walk between two files of men whom they hated, and whose fathers had hated theirs. All the chiefs were there and their whole adherence; and each knew the name of each. Every man of the Marotoli, as he came forth and saw his foes, laid back his hood and gazed about him, to show the badge upon the close cap that held his hair. And of the Gherghiotti there were some who tightened their girdles; and some shrilled and threw up their wrists scornfully, as who flies a falcon; for that was the crest of their house.

On the walls within the entry were a number of tall narrow pictures, presenting a moral allegory of Peace, which Chiaro had painted that year for the Church. The Gherghiotti stood with their backs to these frescoes; and among them Golzo Ninuccio, the youngest noble of the faction, called by the people Golaghiotta, for his debased life. This youth had remained for some while talking listlessly to his fellows, though with his sleepy sunken eyes fixed on them who passed: but now, seeing that no man jostled another, he drew the long silver shoe off his foot and struck the dust out of it on the cloak of him who was going by, asking him how far the tides rose at Viderza. And he said so because it was three months since, at that place, the Gherghiotti had beaten the Marotoli to the sands, and held them there while the sea came in; whereby many had been drowned. And, when he had spoken, at once the whole archway was dazzling with the light of confused swords; and they who had left turned back; and they who were still behind made haste to come forth: and there was so much blood cast up the walls on a sudden, that it ran in long streams down Chiaro's paintings.

Chiaro turned himself from the window; for the light felt dry between his lids, and he could not look. He sat down, and heard the noise of contention driven out of the church-porch and a great way through the streets; and soon there was a deep murmur that heaved and waxed from the other side of the city, where those of both parties were gathering to join in the tumult.

Chiaro sat with his face in his open hands. Once again he had wished to set his foot on a place that looked green and fertile; and once again it seemed to him that the thin rank mask was about to spread away, and that this time the chill of the water must leave leprosy in his flesh. The light still swam in his head, and bewildered him at first; but when he knew his thoughts, they were these: —

"Fame failed me: faith failed me: and now this also, — the hope that I nourished in this my generation of men, — shall pass from me, and leave my feet and my hands groping. Yet because of this are my feet become slow and my hands thin. I am as one who, through the whole night, holding his way diligently, hath smitten the steel unto the flint, to lead some whom he knew darkling; who hath kept his eyes always on the sparks that himself made, lest they should fail; and who, towards dawn, turning to bid them that he had guided God speed, sees the wet grass untrodden except of his own feet. I am as the last hour of the day, whose chimes are a perfect number; whom the next followeth not, nor light ensueth from him; but in the same darkness is the old order begun afresh. Men say, 'This is not God nor man; he is not as we are, neither above us: let him sit beneath us, for we are many.' Where I write Peace, in that spot is the drawing of swords, and there men's footprints are red. When I would sow, another harvest is ripe. Nay, it is much worse with me than thus much. Am I not as a cloth drawn before the light, that the looker may not be blinded; but which sheweth thereby the grain of its own coarseness; so that the light seems defiled, and men say, 'We will not walk by it.' Wherefore through me they shall be doubly accursed, seeing that through me they reject the light. May one be a devil and not know it?"

As Chiaro was in these thoughts, the fever encroached slowly on his veins, till he could sit no longer and would have risen; but suddenly he found awe within him, and held his head bowed, without stirring. The warmth of the air was not shaken; but there seemed a pulse in the light, and a living freshness, like rain. The silence was a painful music, that made the blood ache in his temples; and he lifted his face and his deep eyes.

A woman was present in his room, clad to the hands and feet with a green and grey raiment, fashioned to that time. It seemed that the first thoughts he had ever known were given him as at first from her eyes, and he knew her hair to be the golden veil through which he beheld his dreams. Though her hands were joined, her face was not lifted, but set forward; and though the gaze was austere, yet her mouth was supreme in gentleness. And as he looked, Chiaro's spirit appeared abashed of its own intimate presence, and his lips shook with the thrill of tears; it seemed such a bitter while till the spirit might be indeed alone.

She did not move closer towards him, but he felt her to be as much with him as his breath. He was like one who, scaling a great steepness, hears his own voice echoed in some place much higher than he can see, and the name of which is not known to him. As the woman stood, her speech was with Chiaro: not, as it were, from her mouth or in his ears; but distinctly between them.

"I am an image, Chiaro, of thine own soul within thee. See me, and know me as I am. Thou sayest that fame has failed thee, and faith failed thee; but because at least thou hast not laid thy life unto riches, therefore, though thus late, I am suffered to come into thy knowledge. Fame sufficed not, for that thou didst seek fame: seek thine own conscience (not thy mind's conscience, but thine heart's), and all shall approve and suffice. For Fame, in noble soils, is a fruit of the Spring: but not therefore should it be said: 'Lo! my garden that I planted is barren: the crocus is here, but the lily is dead in the dry ground, and shall not lift the earth that covers it: therefore I will fling my garden together, and give it unto the builders.' Take heed rather that thou trouble not the wise secret earth; for in the mould that thou throwest up shall the first tender growth lie to waste; which else had been made strong in its season. Yea, and even if the year fall past in all its months, and the soil be indeed, to thee, peevish and incapable, and though thou indeed gather all thy harvest, and it suffice for others, and thou remain vexed with emptiness; and others drink of thy streams, and the drouth rasp thy throat; — let it be enough that these have found the feast good, and thanked the giver: remembering that, when the winter is striven through, there is another year, whose wind is meek, and whose sun fulfilleth all."

While he heard, Chiaro went slowly on his knees. It was not to her that spoke, for the speech seemed within him and his own. The air brooded in sunshine, and though the turmoil was great outside, the air within was at peace. But when he looked in her eyes, he wept. And she came to him, and cast her hair over him, and took her hands about his forehead, and spoke again: —

"Thou hast said," she continued, gently, "that faith failed thee. This cannot be. Either thou hadst it not, or thou hast it. But who bade thee strike the point betwixt love and faith? Wouldst thou sift the warm breeze from the sun that quickens it? Who bade thee turn upon God and say: 'Behold, my offering is of earth, and not worthy: thy fire comes not upon it: therefore, though I slay not my brother whom thou acceptest, I will depart before thou smite me.' Why shouldst thou rise up and tell God He is not content? Had He, of his warrant, certified so to thee? Be not nice to seek out division; but possess thy love in sufficiency: assuredly this is faith, for the heart must believe first. What He hath set in thine heart to do, that do thou; and even though thou do it without thought of Him, it shall be well done; it is this sacrifice that He asketh of thee, and his flame is upon it for a sign. Think not of Him; but of his love and thy love. For God is no morbid exactor: He hath no hand to bow beneath, nor a foot, that thou shouldst kiss it."

And Chiaro held silence, and wept into her hair which covered his face; and the salt tears that he shed ran through her hair upon his lips; and he tasted the bitterness of shame.

Then the fair woman, that was his soul, spoke again to him, saying: —

"And for this thy last purpose, and for those unprofitable truths of thy teaching, — thine heart hath already put them away, and it needs not that I lay my bidding upon thee. How is it that thou, a man, wouldst say coldly to the mind what God hath said to the heart warmly? Thy will was honest and wholesome; but look well lest this also be folly, — to say, 'I, in doing this, do strengthen God among men.' When at any time hath He cried unto thee, saying, 'My son, lend me thy shoulder, for I fall?' Deemest thou that the men who enter God's temple in malice, to the provoking of blood and neither for his love nor for his wrath will abate their purpose, — shall afterwards stand with thee in the porch, midway between Him and themselves, to give ear unto thy thin voice, which merely the fall of their visors can drown, and to see thy hands, stretched feebly, tremble among their swords? Give thou to God no more than He asketh of thee; but to man also, that which is man's. In all that thou doest, work from thine own heart, simply; for his heart is as thine, when thine is wise and humble; and he shall have understanding of thee. One drop of rain is as another, and the sun's prism in all: and shalt thou not be as he, whose lives are the breath of One? Only by making thyself his equal can he learn to hold communion with thee, and at last own thee above him. Not till thou lean over the water shalt thou see thine image therein: stand erect, and it shall slope from thy feet and be lost. Know that there is but this means whereby thou mayest serve God with man: — Set thine hand and thy soul to serve man with God."

And when she that spoke had said these words within Chiaro's spirit, she left his side quietly, and stood up as he had first seen her: with her fingers laid together, and her eyes steadfast, and with the breadth of her long dress covering her feet on the floor. And, speaking again, she said: —

"Chiaro, servant of God, take now thine Art unto thee, and paint me thus, as I am, to know me: weak, as I am, and in the weeds of this time; only with eyes which seek out labour, and with a faith, not learned, yet jealous of prayer. Do this; so shall thy soul stand before thee always, and perplex thee no more."

And Chiaro did as she bade him. While he worked, his face grew solemn with knowledge: and before the shadows had turned, his work was done. Having finished, he lay back where he sat, and was asleep immediately: for the growth of that strong sunset was heavy about him, and he felt weak and haggard; like one just come out of a dusk, hollow country, bewildered with echoes, where he had lost himself, and who has not slept for many days and nights. And when she saw him lie back, the beautiful woman came to him, and sat at his head, gazing, and quieted his sleep with her voice.

The tumult of the factions had endured all that day through all Pisa, though Chiaro had not heard it: and the last service of that feast was a mass sung at midnight from the windows of all the churches for the many dead who lay about the city, and who had to be buried before morning, because of the extreme heats.

In the spring of 1847, I was at Florence. Such as were there at the same time with myself — those, at least, to whom Art is something, — will certainly recollect how many rooms of the Pitti Gallery were closed through that season, in order that some of the pictures they contained might be examined and repaired without the necessity of removal. The hall, the staircases, and the vast central suite of apartments, were the only accessible portions; and in these such paintings as they could admit from the sealed *penetralia* were profanely huddled together, without respect of dates, schools, or persons.

I fear that, through this interdict, I may have missed seeing many of the best pictures. I do not mean *only* the most talked of: for these, as they were restored, generally found their way somehow into the open rooms, owing to the clamours raised by the students; and I remember how old Ercoli's, the curator's, spectacles used to be mirrored in the reclaimed surface, as he leaned mysteriously over these works with some of the visitors, to scrutinize and elucidate.

One picture that I saw that spring, I shall not easily forget. It was among those, I believe, brought from the other rooms, and had been hung, obviously out of all chronology, immediately beneath that head by Raphael so long known as the "Berrettino," and now said to be the portrait of Cecco Ciulli.

The picture I speak of is a small one, and represents merely the figure of a woman, clad to the hands and feet with a green and grey raiment, chaste and early in its fashion, but exceedingly simple. She is standing: her hands are held together lightly, and her eyes set earnestly open.

The face and hands in this picture, though wrought with great delicacy, have the appearance of being painted at once, in a single sitting: the drapery is unfinished. As soon as I saw the figure, it drew an awe upon me, like water in shadow. I shall not attempt to describe it more than I have already done; for the most absorbing wonder of it was its literality. You knew that figure, when painted, had been seen; yet it was not a thing to be seen of men. This language will appear ridiculous to such as have never looked on the work; and it may be even to some among those who have. On examining it closely, I perceived in one corner of the canvass the words *Manus Animam pinxit,* and the date 1239.

I turned to my Catalogue, but that was useless, for the pictures were all displaced. I then stepped up to the Cavaliere Ercoli, who was in the room at the moment, and asked him regarding the subject and authorship of the painting. He treated the matter, I thought, somewhat slightingly, and said that he could show me the reference in the Catalogue, which he had compiled. This, when found, was not of much value, as it merely said, "Schizzo d'autore incerto," adding the inscription.* I could willingly have prolonged my inquiry, in the hope that it might somehow lead to some result; but I had disturbed the curator from certain yards of Guido, and he was not communicative. I went back therefore, and stood before the picture till it grew dusk.

The next day I was there again; but this time a circle of students was round the spot, all copying the "Berrettino." I contrived, however, to find a place whence I could see *my* picture, and where I seemed to be in nobody's way. For some minutes I remained undisturbed; and then I heard, in an English voice: "Might I beg of you, sir, to stand a little more to this side, as you interrupt my view."

I felt vexed, for, standing where he asked me, a glare struck on the picture from the windows, and I could not see it. However, the request was reasonably made, and from a countryman; so I complied, and turning away, stood by his easel. I knew it was not worth while; yet I referred in some way to the work underneath

---

*I should here say, that in the latest catalogues, (owing, as in cases before mentioned, to the zeal and enthusiasm of Dr. Aemmster), this, and several other pictures, have been more competently entered. The work in question is now placed in the *Sala Sessagona,* a room I did not see — under the number 161. It is described as "Figura mistica di Chiaro dell'Erma," and there is a brief notice of the author appended.

the one he was copying. He did not laugh, but he smiled as we do in England: "*Very* odd, is it not?" said he.

The other students near us were all continental; and seeing an Englishman select an Englishman to speak with, conceived, I suppose, that he could understand no language but his own. They had evidently been noticing the interest which the little picture appeared to excite in me.

One of them, an Italian, said something to another who stood next to him. He spoke with a Genoese accent, and I lost the sense in the villanous dialect. "Che so?" replied the other, lifting his eyebrows towards the figure; "roba mistica: 'st' Inglesi son matti sul misticismo: somiglia alle nebbie di là. Li fa pensare alla patria,

'e intenerisce il core
Lo di ch' han detto ai dolci amici adio.'"

"La notte, vuoi dire," said a third.

There was a general laugh. My compatriot was evidently a novice in the language, and did not take in what was said. I remained silent, being amused.

"Et toi donc?" said he who had quoted Dante, turning to a student, whose birthplace was unmistakable, even had he been addressed in any other language: "que dis-tu de ce genre-là?"

"Moi?" returned the Frenchman, standing back from his easel, and looking at me and at the figure, quite politely, though with an evident reservation: "Je dis, mon cher, que c'est une spécialité dont je me fiche pas mal. Je tiens que quand on ne comprend pas une chose, c'est qu'elle ne signifie rien."

My reader thinks possibly that the French student was right.

SAINT AGNES OF INTERCESSION

"In all my life," said my uncle in his customary voice, made up of goodness and trusting simplicity, and a spice of piety withal, which, an't pleased your worship, made it sound the sweeter,—"In all my life," quoth my uncle Toby, "I have never heard a stranger story than one which was told me by a sergeant in Maclure's regiment, and which, with your permission, Doctor, I will relate."

"No stranger, brother Toby," said my father testily, "than a certain tale to be found in Slawkenbergius (being the eighth of his third Decad), and called by him the History of an Icelandish Nose."

"Nor than the golden legend of Saint Anschankus of Lithuania," added Dr. Slop, "who, being troubled digestively while delivering his discourse de sanctis sanctorum, was tempted by the Devil *in imagine vasis in contumeliam*,—which is to say,—in the form of a vessel unto dishonour."

Now Excentrio, as one mocking, sayeth, etc., etc.

—TRISTRAM SHANDY

Among my earliest recollections, none is stronger than that of my father standing before the fire when he came home in the London winter evenings, and singing to us in his sweet, generous tones: sometimes ancient English ditties, —

such songs as one might translate from the birds, and the brooks might set to music; sometimes those with which foreign travel had familiarized his youth, — among them the great tunes which have rung the world's changes since '89. I used to sit on the hearth-rug, listening to him, and look between his knees into the fire till it burned my face, while the sights swarming up in it seemed changed and changed with the music: till the music and the fire and my heart burned together, and I would take paper and pencil, and try in some childish way to fix the shapes that rose within me. For my hope, even then, was to be a painter.

The first book I remember to have read, of my own accord, was an old-fashioned work on Art, which my mother had, — Hamilton's "English Conoscente." It was a kind of continental tour, — sufficiently Della-Cruscan, from what I can recall of it, — and contained notices of pictures which the author had seen abroad, with engravings after some of them. These were in the English fashion of that day, executed in stipple and printed with red ink; tasteless enough, no doubt, but I yearned towards them and would toil over them for days. One especially possessed for me a strong and indefinable charm: it was a Saint Agnes in glory, by Bucciolo d'Orli Angiolieri. This plate I could copy from the first with much more success than I could any of the others; indeed, it was mainly my love of the figure, and a desire to obtain some knowledge regarding it, which impelled me, by one magnanimous effort upon the "Conoscente," to master in a few days more of the difficult art of reading than my mother's laborious inculcations had accomplished till then. However, what I managed to spell and puzzle out related chiefly to the executive qualities of the picture, which could be little understood by a mere child; of the artist himself, or the meaning of his work, the author of the book appeared to know scarcely anything.

As I became older, my boyish impulse towards art grew into a vital passion; till at last my father took me from school and permitted me my own bent of study. There is no need that I should dwell much upon the next few years of my life. The beginnings of Art, entered on at all seriously, present an alternation of extremes: — on the one hand, the most bewildering phases of mental endeavour, on the other, a toil rigidly exact and dealing often with trifles. What was then the precise shape of the cloud within my tabernacle, I could scarcely say now; or whether through so thick a veil I could be sure of its presence there at all. And as to which statue at the Museum I drew most or learned least from, — or which Professor at the Academy "set" the model in the worst taste, — these are things which no one need care to know. I may say, briefly, that I was wayward enough in the pursuit, if not in the purpose; that I cared even too little for what could be taught me by others; and that my original designs greatly outnumbered my school-drawings.

In most cases where study (such study, at least, as involves any practical elements) has benumbed that subtle transition which brings youth out of boyhood, there comes a point, after some time, when the mind loses its suppleness and is riveted merely by the continuance of the mechanical effort. It is then that the constrained senses gradually assume their utmost tension, and any urgent impression from without will suffice to scatter the charm. The student looks up: the film of their own fixedness drops at once from before his eyes, and for the first time he sees his life in the face.

In my nineteenth year, I might say that, between one path of Art and another, I worked hard. One afternoon I was returning, after an unprofitable morning, from a class which I attended. The day was one of those oppressive lulls in autumn, when application, unless under sustained excitement, is all but impossible, — when the perceptions seem curdled and the brain full of sand. On ascending the stairs to my room, I heard voices there, and when I entered, found my sister Catharine, with another young lady, busily turning over my sketches and papers, as if in search of something. Catharine laughed, and introduced her companion as Miss Mary Arden. There might have been a little malice in the laugh, for I remembered to have heard the lady's name before, and to have then made in fun some teasing inquiries about her, as one will of one's sisters' friends. I bowed for the introduction, and stood rebuked. She had her back to the window, and I could not well see her features at the moment; but I made sure she was very beautiful, from her tranquil body and the way that she held her hands. Catharine told me they had been looking together for a book of hers which I had had by me for some time, and which she had promised to Miss Arden. I joined in the search, the book was found, and soon after they left my room. I had come in utterly spiritless; but now I fell to and worked well for several hours. In the evening, Miss Arden remained with our family circle till rather late: till she left I did not return to my room, nor, when there, was my work resumed that night. I had thought her more beautiful than at first.

After that, every time I saw her, her beauty seemed to grow on my sight by gazing, as the stars do in water. It was some time before I ceased to think of her beauty alone; and even then it was still of her that I thought. For about a year my studies somewhat lost their hold upon me, and when that year was upon its close, she and I were promised in marriage.

Miss Arden's station in life, though not lofty, was one of more ease than my own, but the earnestness of her attachment to me had deterred her parents from placing any obstacles in the way of our union. All the more, therefore, did I now long to obtain at once such a position as should secure me from reproaching myself with any sacrifice made by her for my sake: and I now set to work with all the energy of which I was capable, upon a picture of some labour, involving various aspects of study. The subject was a modern one, and indeed it has often seemed to me that all work, to be truly worthy, should be wrought out of the age itself, as well as out of the soul of its producer, which must needs be a soul of the age. At this picture I laboured constantly and unweariedly, my days and my nights; and Mary sat to me for the principal female figure. The exhibition to which I sent it opened a few weeks before the completion of my twenty-first year.

Naturally enough, I was there on the opening day. My picture, I knew, had been accepted, but I was ignorant of a matter perhaps still more important, — its situation on the walls. On that now depended its success; on its success the fulfilment of my most cherished hopes might almost be said to depend. That is not the least curious feature of life as evolved in society — which, where the average strength and the average mind are equal, as in this world, becomes to each life another name for destiny, — when a man, having endured labour, gives its fruits into the hands of other men, that they may do their work between him and mankind: confiding it to them, unknown, without seeking knowledge of them; to them, who have probably done in likewise before him, without appeal to the sympathy of kindred experience: submitting to them his naked soul, himself, blind and unseen: and with no thought of retaliation, when, it may be, by their judgment, more than one year, from his dubious threescore and ten, drops alongside, unprofitable, leaving its baffled labour for its successors to recommence. There is perhaps no proof more complete how sluggish and little arrogant, in aggregate life, is the sense of individuality.

I dare say something like this may have been passing in my mind as I entered the lobby of the exhibition, though the principle, with me as with others, was subservient to its application; my thoughts, in fact, starting from and tending towards myself and my own picture. The kind of uncertainty in which I then was is rather a nervous affair; and when, as I shouldered my way through the press, I heard my name spoken close behind me, I believe that I could have wished the speaker further off without being particular as to distance. I could not well, however, do otherwise than look round, and on doing so, recognised in him who had addressed me a gentleman to whom I had been introduced overnight at the house of a friend, and to whose remarks on the Corn question and the National Debt I had listened with a wish for deliverance somewhat akin to that which I now felt; the more so, perhaps, that my distaste was coupled with surprise; his name having been for some time familiar to me as that of a writer of poetry.

As soon as we were rid of the crush, we spoke and shook hands; and I said, to conceal my chagrin, some platitudes as to Poetry being present to support her sister Art in the hour of trial.

"Oh just so, thank you," said he; "have you anything here?"

While he spoke, it suddenly struck me that my friend, the night before, had informed me this gentleman was a critic as well as a poet. And indeed, for the hippopotamus-fronted man, with his splay limbs and wading gait, it seemed the more congenial vocation of the two. In a moment, the instinctive antagonism wedged itself between the artist and the reviewer, and I avoided his question.

He had taken my arm, and we were now in the gallery together. My companion's scrutiny was limited almost entirely to the "line," but my own glance wandered furtively among the suburbs and outskirts of the ceiling, as a misgiving possessed me that I might have a personal interest in those unenviable "high places" of art. Works, which at another time would have absorbed my whole attention, could now obtain from me but a restless and hurried examination: still I dared not institute an open search for my own, lest thereby I should reveal to my companion its presence in some dismal condemned corner which might otherwise escape his notice. Had I procured my catalogue, I might at least have known in which room to look; but I had omitted to do so, thinking thereby to know my fate the sooner, and never anticipating so vexatious an obstacle to my search. Meanwhile I must answer his questions, listen to his criticism, observe and discuss. After nearly an hour of this work, we were not through the first room. My thoughts were already bewildered, and my face burning with excitement.

By the time we reached the second room, the crowd was more dense than ever, and the heat more and more oppressive. A glance round the walls could reveal but little of the consecrated "line," before all parts of which the backs were clustered more or less thickly; except, perhaps, where at intervals hung the work of some venerable member, whose glory was departed from him. The seats in the middle of the room were, for the most part, empty as yet: here and there only an unenthusiastic lady had been left by her party, and sat in stately unruffled toilet, her eye ranging apathetically over the upper portion of the walls, where the gilt frames were packed together in desolate parade. Over these my gaze also passed uneasily, but without encountering the object of its solicitude.

In this room my friend the critic came upon a picture, conspicuously hung, which interested him prodigiously, and on which he seemed determined to have my opinion. It was one of those tender and tearful works, those "labours of love," since familiar to all print-shop *flâneurs*, — in which the wax doll is made to occupy a position in Art which it can never have contemplated in the days of its humble origin. The silks heaved and swayed in front of this picture the whole day long. All that we could do was to stand behind, and catch a glimpse of it now and then, through the whispering bonnets, whose "curtains" brushed our faces continually. I hardly knew what to say, but my companion was lavish of his admiration, and began to give symptoms of the gushing of the poet-soul. It appeared that he had already seen the picture in the studio, and being but little satisfied with my monosyllables, was at great pains to convince me. While he chattered, I trembled with rage and impatience.

"You must be tired," said he at last; "so am I; let us rest a little." He led the way to a seat. I was his slave, bound hand and foot: I followed him.

The crisis now proceeded rapidly. When seated, he took from his pocket some papers, one of which he handed to me. Who does not know the dainty action of a poet fingering MS.? The knowledge forms a portion of those wondrous instincts implanted in us for self-preservation. I was past resistance, however, and took the paper submissively.

"They are some verses," he said, "suggested by the picture you have just seen. I mean to print them in our next number, as being the only species of criticism adequate to such a work."

I read the poem twice over, for after the first reading I found I had not attended to a word of it, and was ashamed to give it him back. The repetition was not, however, much more successful, as regarded comprehension, — a fact which I have since believed (having seen it again) may have been dependent upon other causes besides my distracted thoughts. The poem, now included among the works of its author, runs as follows: —

O thou who art not as I am,
    Yet knowest all that I must be, —
    O thou who livest certainly
Full of deep meekness like a lamb
Close laid for warmth under its dam,   5
    On pastures bare towards the sea: —

Look on me, for my soul is bleak,
    Nor owns its labour in the years,
    Because of the deep pain of tears:
It hath not found and will not seek,   10
Lest that indeed remain to speak
    Which, passing, it believes it hears.

Like ranks in calm unipotence
    Swayed past, compact and regular,
    Time's purposes and portents are: 15
Yet the soul sleeps, while in the sense
The graven brows of Consequence
    Lie sunk, as in blind wells the star.

O gaze along the wind-strewn path
    That curves distinct upon the road   20
    To the dim purple-hushed abode.
Lo! autumntide and aftermath!
Remember that the year has wrath
    If the ungarnered wheat corrode.

It is not that the fears are sore   25
    Or that the evil pride repels:
    But there where the heart's knowledge dwells
The heart is gnawed within the core,
Nor loves the perfume from that shore
    Faint with bloom-pulvered asphodels.   30

Having atoned for non-attention by a second perusal, whose only result was non-comprehension, I thought I had done my duty towards this performance, which I accordingly folded up and returned to its author. He asked, in so many words, my opinion of it.

"I think," replied I coolly, "that when a poet strikes out for himself a new path in style, he should first be quite convinced that it possesses sufficient advantages to counterbalance the contempt which the swarm of his imitators will bring upon poetry."

My ambiguity was successful. I could see him take the compliment to himself, and inhale it like a scent, while a slow broad smile covered his face. It was much as if, at some meeting, on a speech being made complimentary to the chairman, one of the waiters should elbow that personage aside, plant his knuckles on the table, and proceed to return thanks.

And indeed, I believe my gentleman was about to do so in due form, but my thoughts, which had been unable to resist some enjoyment of his conceit, now suddenly reverted to their one dominant theme; and rising at once, in an indignant spleen at being thus harassed and beset, I declared that I must leave him, and hurry through the rest of the gallery by myself, for that I had an impending appointment. He rose also. As we were shaking hands, a part of the "line" opposite to where we stood was left bare by a lapse in the crowd. "There seems to be an odd-looking picture," said my companion. I looked in the same direction: the press was closing again; I caught only a glimpse of the canvas, but that sufficed: it was my own picture, *on the line!* For a moment my head swam with me.

He walked towards the place, and I followed him. I did not at first hear well what he said of the picture; but when I did, I found he was abusing it. He called it quaint, crude, even grotesque; and certainly the uncompromising adherence to nature as then present before me, which I had attempted throughout, gave it, in the exhibition, a more curious and unique appearance than I could have anticipated. Of course only a very few minutes elapsed before my companion turned to the catalogue for the artist's name.

"They thought the thing good," he drawled as he ran his eye down the pages, "or it wouldn't be on the line. 605, 606 — or else the fellow has interest somewhere. 630, what the deuce am I thinking of? — 613, 613, 613 — Here it is — Why," he exclaimed, short of breath with astonishment, "the picture is yours!"

"Well, it seems so," said I, looking over his shoulder; "I suppose they're likely to know."

"And so you wanted to get away before we came to it. And so the picture is yours!"

"Likely to remain so too," I replied laughing, "if every one thinks as well of it as you do."

"Oh! mind you," he exclaimed, "you must not be offended: one always finds fault first: I am sure to congratulate you."

The surprise he was in made him speak rather loud, so that people were beginning to nudge each other, and whisper that I was the painter. I therefore repeated hurriedly that I really must go, or I should miss my appointment.

"Stay a minute," ejaculated my friend the critic; "I am trying to think what the style of your picture is like. It is like the works of a very early man that I saw in Italy. Angioloni, Angellini, *Angiolieri*, — that was the name, — Bucciuolo Angiolieri. He always turned the toes in. The head of your woman there" (and he pointed to the figure painted from Mary) "is exactly like a St. Agnes of his at Bologna."

A flash seemed to strike before my eyes as he spoke. The name mentioned was a part of my first recollections; and the picture he spoke of. . . . Yes, indeed, there in the face of my betrothed bride, I beheld the once familiar features of the St. Agnes, forgotten since childhood! I gazed fixedly on the work of my own hands; and thought turned in my brain like a wheel.

When I looked again toward my companion, I could see that he was wondering at my evident abstraction. I did not explain, but abruptly bidding him goodbye, hastened out of the exhibition.

As I walked homewards, the cloud was still about me, and the street seemed to pass me like a shadow. My life had been, as it were, drawn by, and the child and the man brought together. How had I not at once recognized, in her I loved, the dream of my childhood? Yet, doubtless, the sympathy of relation, though unconscious, must have had its influence. The fact of the likeness was a mere casualty, however singular; but that which had cast the shadow of a man's love in the path of the child, and left the seed at his heart to work its growth blindly in darkness, was surely much more than chance.

Immediately on reaching home, I made inquiries of my mother concerning my old friend the "English Conoscente"; but learned, to my disappointment, that she had long since missed the book, and had never recovered it. I felt vexed in the extreme.

The joy with which the news of my picture was hailed at home may readily be imagined. There was one, however, to whom it may have been more welcome even than to my own household: to her, as to myself, it was hope seen nearer. I could scarcely have assigned a reason why I refrained from mentioning to her, or to any one, the strange point of resemblance which I had been led to perceive; but from some unaccountable reluctance I kept it to myself at the time. The matter was detailed in the journal of the worthy poet-critic who had made the discovery; such scraps of research being much too scarce not to be worked to their utmost; it may be too that my precipitate retreat had left him in the belief of my being a convicted plagiarist. I do not think, however, that either Mary's family or my own saw the paper; and indeed it was much too aesthetic to permit itself many readers.

Meanwhile, my picture was obtaining that amount of notice, favourable with unfavourable, which constitutes success, and was not long in finding a purchaser. My way seemed clearing before me. Still, I could not prevent my mind from dwelling on the curious incident connected with the painting, and which, by constant brooding upon it, had begun to assume, in my idea, almost the character of a mystery. The coincidence was the more singular that my work, being in subject, costume, and accessories, English, and of the present period, could scarcely have been expected to suggest so striking an affinity in style to the productions of one of the earliest Italian painters.

The gentleman who purchased my picture had commissioned me at the same time for another. I had always entertained a great wish to visit Italy, but now a still stronger impulse than before drew me thither. All substantial record having been lost, I could hardly persuade myself that the idol of my childhood, and the worship I had rendered it, was not all an unreal dream; and every day the longing possessed me more strongly to look with my own eyes upon the veritable St. Agnes. Not holding myself free to marry as yet, I therefore determined (having it now within my power) that I would seek Italy at once, and remain there while I painted my next picture. Nor could even the thought of leaving Mary deter me from this resolution.

On the day I quitted England, Mary's father again placed her hand in mine, and renewed his promise; but our own hearts were a covenant between us.

From this point, my narrative will proceed more rapidly to its issue. Some lives of men are as the sea is, continually vexed and trampled with winds. Others are, as it were, left on the beach. There the wave is long in reaching its tide-mark, where it abides but a moment; afterwards, for the rest of that day, the water is shifted back more or less slowly; the sand it has filled hardens; and hourly the wind drives lower till nightfall.

To dwell here on my travels any further than in so much as they concern the thread of my story, would be superfluous. The first place where I established myself, on arriving in the Papal States, was Bologna, since it was there, as I well remembered, that the St. Agnes of Bucciuolo Angiolieri was said to be. I soon became convinced, however, after ransacking the galleries and private collections, that I had been misinformed. The great Clementine is for the most part a dismal wilderness of Bolognese Art, "where nothing is that hath life," being rendered only the more ghastly by the "life-in-death" of Guido and the Caracci; and the private collectors seem to emulate the Clementine.

From Bologna I removed to Rome, where I stayed only for a month, and proceeded thence into Tuscany. Here, in the painter's native province, after all, I thought the picture was most likely to be found; as is generally the case with artists who have produced comparatively few works, and whose fame is not of the highest order of all. Having visited Siena and Arezzo, I took up my abode in Florence. Here, however, seeing the necessity of getting to work at once, I commenced my next picture, devoting to it a certain number of hours each day; the rest of my time being chiefly spent among the galleries, where I continued my search. The St. Agnes still eluded me; but in the Pitti and elsewhere, I met with several works of Bucciuolo; in all of which I thought, in fact, that I could myself recognize, despite the wide difference both of subject and occasional treatment, a certain mental approximation, not easily defined, to the style of my own productions. The peculiarities of feeling and manner which had attracted my boyish admiration had evidently sunk deep, and maintained, though hitherto unperceived, their influence over me.

I had been at Florence for about three months, and my picture was progressing, though slowly enough; moreover, the other idea which engrossed me was losing its energy, by the recurrence of defeat, so that I now determined on leaving the thing mainly to chance, and went here and there, during the hours when I was not at work, seeing what was to see. One day, however, being in a bookseller's shop, I came upon some numbers of a new Dictionary of Works of Art, then in course of publication, where it was stated that a painting of St. Agnes, by Bucciuolo Angiolieri, was in the possession of the Academy of Perugia. This then, doubtless, was the work I wished to see; and when in the Roman States, I must already have passed upon my search through the town which contained it. In how many books had I rummaged for the information which chance had at length thrown in my way! I was almost inclined to be provoked with so inglorious a success. All my interest in the pursuit, however, revived at once, and I immediately commenced taking measures for retracing my steps to Perugia. Before doing so I despatched a long letter to Mary, with whom I kept up a correspondence, telling her where to direct her next missive, but without informing her as to the motive of my abrupt removal, although in my letter I dwelt at some length, among other topics, on those works of Bucciuolo which I had met with at Florence.

I arrived at Perugia late in the evening, and to see the gallery before the next morning was out of the question. I passed a most restless night. The same one thought had been more or less with me during the whole of my journey, and would not leave me now until my wish was satisfied. The next day proved to be one on which the pictures were not visible; so that on hastening to the Academy in the morning, I was again disappointed. Upon the second day, had they refused me admittance, I believe I should have resorted to desperate measures. The doors however were at last wide open. Having put the swarm of guides to rout, I set my feet on the threshold; and such is the power of one absorbing idea, long suffered to dwell on the mind, that as I entered I felt my heart choke me as if with some vague apprehension.

This portion of my story which the reader has already gone through is so unromantic and easy of belief, that I fear the startling circumstances which remain to be told will jar upon him all the more by contrast as a clumsy fabrication. My course, however, must be to speak on, relating to the best of my memory things in which the memory is not likely to have failed; and reserving at least my own inward knowledge that all the events of this narrative (however unequal the measure of credit they may obtain) have been equally, with myself, matters of personal experience.

The Academy of Perugia is, in its little sphere, one of the high places of privilege; and the first room, the Council Chamber, full of rickety arm chairs, is hung with the presentation pictures of the members, a collection of indigenous grandeurs of the school of David. I purchased a catalogue of an old woman who was knitting in one corner, and proceeded to turn the leaves with nervous anxiety. Having found that the Florentine pictures were in the last room, I commenced hurrying across the rest of the gallery as fast as the polish of the waxed boards would permit. There was no visitor besides myself in the rooms, which were full of Roman, Bolognese, and Perugian handiwork: one or two students only, who had set up their easels before some masterpiece of the "advanced" style, stared round in wonder at my irreverent haste. As I walked, I continued my search in the catalogue; so that, by the time I reached the Florentine room, I had found the number, and walked, with a beating heart, straight up to the picture.

The picture is about half the size of life: it represents a beautiful woman, seated, in the costume of the painter's time, richly adorned with jewels; she holds a palm branch, and a lamb nestles to her feet. The glory round her head is a device pricked without colour on the gold background, which is full of the faces of angels. The countenance was the one known to me, by a feeble reflex, in childhood; it was also the exact portrait of Mary, feature by feature. I had been absent from her for more than five months, and it was like seeing her again.

As I looked, my whole life seemed to crowd about me, and to stun me like a pulse in my head. For some time I stood lost in astonishment, admiration, perplexity, helpless of conjecture, and an almost painful sense of love.

I had seen that in the catalogue there was some account of the picture; and now, after a long while, I removed my eyes, dizzy with gazing and with thought, from the face, and read in Italian as follows:

"*No. 212. St. Agnes, with a glory of angels. By Bucciuolo Angiolieri.*

"Bertuccio, Buccio, or Bucciuolo d'Orli Angiolieri, a native of Cignana in the Florentine territory, was born in 1405 and died in 1460. He was the friend, and has been described as the pupil, of Benozzo Gozzoli; which latter statement is not likely to be correct, since their ages were nearly the same, as are also the dates of their earliest known pictures.

"He is said by some to have been the first to introduce a perfectly nude figure in a devotional subject (the St. Sebastian now at Florence); an opinion which Professor Ehrenhaupt has called in question, by fixing the date of the five anonymous frescoes in the Church of Sant' Andrea d'Oltr' arno, which contain several nude figures, at a period antecedent to that in which he flourished. His works are to be met with at Florence, at Lucca, and in one or two cities of Germany. The present picture, though ostensibly representing St. Agnes, is the portrait of Blanzifiore dal l'Ambra, a lady to whom the painter was deeply attached, and who died early. The circumstances connected by tradition with the painting of this picture are of a peculiarly melancholy nature.

"It appears that, in the vicissitudes of faction, the lady's family were exiled from Florence, and took refuge at Lucca; where some of them were delivered by treachery to their enemies and put to death. These accumulated misfortunes (not the least among which was the separation from her lover, who, on account of his own ties and connections, could not quit Florence), preyed fatally on the mind and health of Blanzifiore; and before many months had passed, she was declared to be beyond medicinal aid. No sooner did she learn this, than her first thought was of the misery which her death would occasion her lover; and she insisted on his being summoned immediately from Florence, that they might at least see each other once again upon earth. When, on his arrival, she witnessed his anguish at thus losing her for ever, Blanzifiore declared that she would rise at once from her bed, and that Bucciuolo should paint her portrait before she died; for so, she said, there should still remain something to him whereby to have her in memory. In this will she persisted against all remonstrance occasioned by the fears of her friends; and for two days, though in a dying state, she sat with wonderful energy to her lover: clad in her most sumptuous attire, and arrayed with all her jewels: her two sisters remaining constantly at her side, to sustain her and supply restoratives. On the third day, while Bucciuolo was still at work, she died without moving.

"After her death, Bucciuolo finished the portrait, and added to it the attributes of St. Agnes, in honour of her purity. He kept it always near him during his lifetime; and, in dying, bequeathed it to the Church of Santa Agnese dei Lavoranti, where he was buried at her side. During all the years of his life, after the death of Blanzifiore, he remained at Lucca: where some of his works are still to be found.

"The present picture has been copied many times, but never competently engraved; and was among those conveyed to Paris by Bonaparte, in the days of his omnipotence."

The feeling of wonder which attained bewilderment, as I proceeded with this notice, was yet less strong than an intense penetrating sympathy excited in me by the unhappy narrative, which I could not easily have accounted for, but which so overcame me that, as I finished, the tears stung my eyes. I remained for some time leaning upon the bar which separated me from the picture, till at last my mind settled to more definite thought. But thought here only served to confound. A woman had then lived four hundred years since, of whom that picture was the portrait; and my own eyes bore me witness that it was also the surpassingly perfect resemblance of a woman now living and breathing, — of my own affianced bride! While I stood, these things grew and grew upon my mind, till my thoughts seemed to hustle about me like pent-up air.

The catalogue was still open in my hand; and now, as my eyes wandered, in aimless distraction, over the page, they were arrested by these words: *"No. 231. Portrait of Bucciuolo Angiolieri painted by himself."* At first my bewildered perceptions scarcely attached a meaning to the words; yet, owing no doubt to the direction of my thoughts, my eye dwelt upon them, and continued to peruse them over and over, until at last their purport flashed upon me. At the same instant that it did so, I turned round and glanced rapidly over the walls for the number: it was at the other end of the room. A trembling suspense, with something almost of involuntary awe, was upon me as I ran towards the spot; the picture was hung low; I stooped over the rail to look closely at it, and was face to face with *myself!* I can recall my feeling at that moment, only as one of the most lively and exquisite fear.

It was myself, of nearly the same age as mine was then, but perhaps a little older. The hair and beard were of my colour, trimmed in an antique fashion; and the dress belonged to the early part of the fifteenth century. In the background was a portion of the city of Florence. One of the upper corners contained this inscription: —

ALBERTUS* ORLITIS ANGELERIUS
Ipsum ipse
AETAT. SUAE XXIV.

That it *was* my portrait, — that the St. Agnes was the portrait of Mary, — and that both had been painted by myself four hundred years ago, — this now rose up distinctly before me as the one and only solution of so startling a mystery, and as being, in fact, that result round which, or some portion of which, my soul had been blindly hovering, uncertain of itself. The tremendous experience of that moment, the like of which has never, perhaps, been known to any other man, must remain undescribed; since the description, read calmly at common leisure, could seem but fantastic raving. I was as one who, coming after a wilderness to some city dead since the first world, should find among the tombs a human body in his own exact image, embalmed; having the blackened coin still within its lips, and the jars still at its side, in honour of gods whose very names are abolished.

After the first incapable pause, during which I stood rooted to the spot, I could no longer endure to look on the picture, and turning away, fled back through the rooms and into the street. I reached it with the sweat springing on my forehead, and my face felt pale and cold in the sun.

As I hurried homewards, amid all the chaos of my ideas, I had clearly resolved on one thing, — namely, that I would leave Perugia that night on my return to England. I had passports which would carry me as far as the confines of Italy; and when there I counted on somehow getting them signed at once by the requisite authorities, so as to pursue my journey without delay.

On entering my room in the hotel where I had put up, I found a letter from Mary lying on the table. I was too much agitated with conflicting thoughts to open it at once; and therefore allowed it to remain till my perturbation should in some measure have subsided. I drew the blinds before my windows, and covered my face to think; my forehead was still damp between my hands. At least an hour must have elapsed in that tumult of the spirit which leaves no impression behind, before I opened the letter.

It was an answer to the one which I had posted before leaving Florence. After many questions and much news of home, there was a paragraph which ran thus: —

"The account you give me of the works of Bucciuolo Angiolieri interested me greatly. I am surprised never to have heard you mention him before, as he appears to find so much favour with you. But perhaps he was unknown to you till now. How I wish I could stand by your side before his pictures, to enjoy them with

---

Alberto, Albertuccio, Bertuccio, Buccio, *Bucciuolo.*

you and hear you interpret their beauties! I assure you that what you say about them is so vivid, and shows so much insight into all the meanings of the painter, that, while reading, I could scarcely divest myself of the impression that you were describing some of your own works."

As I finished the last sentence, the paper fell from my hands. A solemn passage of Scripture had been running in my mind; and as I again lay back and hid my now burning and fevered face, I repeated it aloud: — "How unsearchable are Thy judgments, and Thy ways past finding out!"

As I have said, my intention was to set out from Perugia that same night; but on making inquiry, I found that it would be impossible to do so before the morning, as there was no conveyance till then. Post-horses, indeed, I might have had, but of this my resources would not permit me to think. That was a troubled and gloomy evening for me. I wrote, as well as my disturbed state would allow me, a short letter to my mother, and one to Mary, to apprise them of my return; after which, I went early to bed, and, contrary to my expectations, was soon asleep.

That night I had a dream, which has remained as clear and whole in my memory as the events of the day: and so strange were those events — so apart from the rest of my life till then, — that I could sometimes almost persuade myself that my dream of that night also was not without a mystic reality.

I dreamt that I was in London, at the exhibition where my picture had been; but in the place of my picture, which I could not see, there hung the St. Agnes of Perugia. A crowd was before it; and I heard several say that it was against the rules to hang that picture, for that the painter (naming me) was dead. At this, a woman who was there began to weep: I looked at her and perceived it to be Mary. She had her arm in that of a man who appeared to wear a masquerade dress; his back was towards me, and he was busily writing on some tablets; but on peering over his shoulder, I saw that his pencil left no mark where it passed, which he did not seem to perceive, however, going on as before. I spoke to Mary, but she continued crying and did not look up. I then touched her companion on the shoulder; but finding that he paid no attention, I shook him and told him to resign that lady's arm to me, as she was my bride. He then turned round suddenly, and showed me my own face with the hair and beard quaintly cut, as in the portrait of Bucciuolo. After looking mournfully at me, he said, "Not mine, friend, but neither thine": and while he spoke, his face fell in like a dead face. Meantime, every one seemed pale and uneasy, and they began to whisper in knots; and all at once I found opposite me the critic I met at the gallery, who was saying something I could not understand, but so fast that he panted and kept wiping his forehead. Then my dream changed. I was going upstairs to my room at home, where I thought Mary was waiting to sit for her portrait. The staircase was quite dark; and as I went up, the voices of several persons I knew passed by me, as if they were descending; and sometimes my own among them. I had reached the top, and was feeling for the handle of the door, when it was opened suddenly by an angel; and looking in, I saw, not Mary, but a woman whose face was hidden with white light, and who had a lamb beside her that was bleating aloud. She knelt in the middle of the room, and I heard her say several times: "O Lord, it is more than he can bear. Spare him, O Lord, for her sake whom he consecrated to me." After this, music came out of heaven, and I thought to have heard speech; but instead, there was silence that woke me.

This dream must have occurred repeatedly in the course of the night, for I remember waking up in perfect darkness, overpowered with fear, and crying out in the words which I had heard spoken by the woman; and when I woke in the morning, it was from the same dream, and the same words were on my lips.

During the two days passed at Perugia, I had not had time to think of the picture I was engaged upon, which had therefore remained in its packing-case, as had also the rest of my baggage. I was thus in readiness to start without further preliminaries. My mind was so confused and disturbed that I have but a faint recollection of that morning; to the agitating events of the previous day, my dream had now added, in spite of myself, a vague foreboding of calamity.

No obstacle occurred throughout the course of my journey, which was, even at that recent date, a longer one than it is now. The whole time, with me, was occupied by one haunting and despotic idea: it accompanied me all day on the road; and if we paused at night it either held me awake or drove all rest from my sleep. It is owing to this, I suppose, that the wretched mode of conveyance, the evil roads, the evil weather, the evil inns, the harassings of petty authorities, and all those annoyances which are set as close as milestones all over the Continent, remain in my memory only with a general sense of discomfort. Moreover, on the day when I left Perugia I had felt the seeds of fever already in my veins; and during the journey this oppression kept constantly on the increase. I was obliged, however, carefully to conceal it, since the panic of the cholera was again in Europe, and any sign of illness would have caused me to be left at once on the road.

By the night of my arrival in London, I felt that I was truly and seriously ill; and, indeed during the last part of the journey, physical suffering had for the first time succeeded in partially distracting my thought from the thing which possessed it. The first inquiries I made of my family were regarding Mary. I learned that she at least was still in good health, and anxiously looking for my arrival; that she would have been there, indeed, but that I had not been expected till a day later. This was a weight taken from my heart. After scarcely more than an hour passed among my family, I repaired to my bed; both body and mind had at length a perfect craving for rest. My mother, immediately on my arrival, had noticed my flushed and haggard appearance; but when questioned by her I attributed this to the fatigues of travelling.

In spite of my extreme need of sleep, and the wish I felt for it, I believe that I slept but little that night. I am not certain, however, for I can only remember that as soon as I lay down my head began to whirl till I seemed to be lifted out of my bed; but whether this were in waking or a part of some distempered dream, I cannot determine. This, however, is the last thing I can recall. The next morning I was in a raging fever, which lasted for five weeks.

Health and consciousness came back to me by degrees, as light and air towards the outlet of a long vault. At length, one day, I sat up in bed for the first time. My head felt light in the pillows; and the sunshine that warmed the room made my blood creep refreshingly. My father and mother were both with me.

As sense had deserted my mind, so had it returned, in the form of one constant thought. But this was now grown peremptory, absolute, uncompromising, and seemed to cry within me for speech, till silence became a torment. To-day, therefore, feeling for the first time, since my gradual recovery, enough of strength for the effort, I resolved that I would at last tell the whole to my parents. Having first warned them of the extraordinary nature of the disclosure I was about to make, I accordingly began. Before I had gone far with my story, however, my mother fell back in her seat, sobbing violently; then rose, and running up to me, kissed me many times, still sobbing and calling me her poor boy. She then left the room. I looked towards my father, and saw that he had turned away his face. In a few moments he rose also without looking at me, and went out as my mother had done.

I could not quite account for this, but was so weary of doubt and conjecture, that I was content to attribute it to the feelings excited by my narration and the pity for all those troubles which the events I spoke of had brought upon me. It may appear strange, but I believe it to have been the fact, that the startling and portentous reality which those events had for me, while it left me fully prepared for wonder and perturbation on the part of my hearers, prevented the idea from even occurring to me that, as far as belief went, there could be more hesitation in another's than in my own.

It was not long before my father returned. On my questioning him as to the cause of my mother's excitement, he made no explicit answer, but begged to hear the remainder of what I had to disclose. I went on, therefore, and told my tale to the end. When I had finished, my father again appeared deeply affected; but soon recovering himself, endeavoured, by reasoning, to persuade me either that the circumstances I had described had no foundation save in my own diseased fancy, or else that at the time of their occurrence incipient illness had caused me to magnify very ordinary events into marvels and omens. Finding that I still persisted in my conviction of their actuality, he then informed me that the matters I had related were already known to himself and to my mother through the disjointed ravings of my long delirium, in which I had dwelt on the same theme incessantly; and that their grief, which I had remarked, was occasioned by hearing me discourse thus connectedly on the same wild and unreal subject, after they had hoped me to be on the road to recovery. To convince me that this could merely be the effect of prolonged illness, he led me to remark that I had never till then alluded to the topic, either by word or in any of my letters, although, by my account, the chain of coincidences had already begun before I left England. Lastly, he implored me most earnestly at once to resist and dispel this fantastic brain sickness, lest the same idea, allowed to retain possession of my mind, might end, — as he dreaded to think that it indeed might, — by endangering my reason.

My father's last words struck me like a stone in the mouth; there was no longer any answer that I could make. I was very weak at the time, and I believe I lay down in my bed and sobbed. I remember it was on that day that it seemed to me of no use to see Mary again, or, indeed, to strive again after any aim I had had, and that for the first time I wished to die; and then it was that there came distinctly, such as it may never have come to any other man, the unutterable suspicion of the vanity of death.

From that day until I was able to leave my bed, I never in any way alluded to the same terrible subject; but I feared my father's eye as though I had been indeed a madman. It is a wonder that I did not really lose my senses. I lived in a continual panic lest I should again speak of that matter unconsciously, and used to repeat inwardly, for hours together, words enjoining myself to silence. Several friends of the family, who had made constant inquiries during my illness, now wished to see me; but this I strictly refused, being in fear that my incubus might get the better of me, and that I might suddenly implore them to say if they had any recollection of a former existence. Even a voice or a whistle from the street would set me wondering whether that man also had lived before, and if so, why I alone should be cursed with this awful knowledge. It was useless even to seek relief in books; for the name of any historical character occurring at once disturbed my fevered mind with conjectures as to what name its possessor *now* bore, who he was, and in what country his lot was cast.

For another week after that day I was confined to my room, and then at last I might go forth. Latterly, I had scarcely spoken to any one, but I do not think that either my father or my mother imagined I had forgotten. It was on a Sunday that I left the house for the first time. Some person must have been buried at the neighbouring church very early that morning, for I recollect that the first thing I heard upon waking was the funeral bell. I had had, during the night, but a restless throbbing kind of sleep; and I suppose it was my excited nerves which made me wait with a feeling of ominous dread through the long pauses of the tolling, unbroken as they were by any sound from the silent Sunday streets, except the twitter of birds about the housetops. The last knell had long ceased, and I had been lying for some time in bitter reverie, when the bells began to ring for church. I cannot express the sudden refreshing joy which filled me at that moment. I rose from my bed, and kneeling down, prayed while the sound lasted.

On joining my parents at breakfast, I made my mother repeat to me once more how many times Mary had called during my illness, and all that she had said and done. They told me that she would probably be there that morning; but my impatience would not permit me to wait; I must go and seek her myself at once. Often already, said my parents, she had wished and begged to see me, but they had feared for my strength. This was in my thoughts as I left the house; and when, shutting the door behind me, I stood once again in the living sunshine, it seemed as if her love burst around me like music.

I set out hastily in the well-known direction of Mary's house. While I walked through the crowded streets, the sense of reality grew upon me at every step, and for the first time during some months I felt a man among men. Any artist or thoughtful man whatsoever, whose life has passed in a large city, can scarcely fail, in course of time, to have some association connecting each spot continually passed and repassed with the labours of his own mind. In the woods and fields every place has its proper spell and mystery, and needs no consecration from thought; but wherever in the daily walk through the thronged and jarring city, the soul has read some knowledge from life, or laboured towards some birth within its own silence, there abides the glory of that hour, and the cloud rests there before an unseen tabernacle. And thus now, with myself, old trains of thought and the conceptions of former years came back as I passed from one swarming resort to another, and seemed, by contrast, to wake my spirit from its wild and fantastic broodings to a consciousness of something like actual existence; as the mere reflections of objects, sunk in the vague pathless water, appear almost to strengthen it into substance.

THE STEALTHY SCHOOL OF CRITICISM

Your paragraph, a fortnight ago, relating to the pseudonymous authorship of an article, violently assailing myself and other writers of poetry, in the *Contemporary Review* for October last, reveals a species of critical masquerade which I have expressed in the heading given to this letter. Since then, Mr. Sidney Colvin's note, qualifying the report that he intends to "answer" that article, has appeared in your pages: and my own view as to the absolute forfeit, under such conditions, of all claim to honourable reply, is precisely the same as Mr. Colvin's. For here a critical organ, professedly adopting the principle of open signature, would seem, in reality, to assert (by silent practice, however, not by enunciation), that if the anonymous in criticism was — as itself originally inculcated — but an early caterpillar stage, the nominate too is found to be no better than a homely transitional chrysalis, and that the ultimate butterfly form for a critic who likes to sport in sunlight and yet to elude the grasp, is after all the pseudonymous. But, indeed, what I may call the "Siamese" aspect of the entertainment provided by the *Review* will elicit but one verdict. Yet I may, perhaps, as the individual chiefly attacked, be excused for asking your assistance now in giving a specific denial to specific charges which, if unrefuted, may still continue, in spite of their author's strategic *fiasco,* to serve his purpose against me to some extent.

The primary accusation, on which this writer grounds all the rest, seems to be that others and myself "extol fleshliness as the distinct and supreme end of poetic and pictorial art; aver that poetic expression is greater than poetic thought; and, by inference, that the body is greater than the soul, and sound superior to sense."

As my own writings are alone formally dealt with in the article, I shall confine my answer to myself; and this must first take unavoidably the form of a challenge to prove so broad a statement. It is true, some fragmentary pretence at proof is put in here and there throughout the attack, and thus far an opportunity is given of contesting the assertion.

A Sonnet, entitled "Nuptial Sleep" is quoted and abused at page 338 of the *Review*, and is there dwelt upon as a "whole poem," describing "merely animal sensations." It is no more a whole poem in reality, than is any single stanza of any poem throughout the book. The poem, written chiefly in sonnets, and of which this is one sonnet-stanza, is entitled "The House of Life"; and even in my first published instalment of the whole work (as contained in the volume under notice) ample evidence is included that no such passing phase of description as the one headed "Nuptial Sleep" could possibly be put forward by the author of "The House of Life" as his own representative view of the subject of love. In proof of this, I will direct attention (among the love-sonnets of this poem) to Nos. 2, 8, 11, 17, 28, and more especially 13, which, indeed, I had better print here.

[“Love Sweetness” quoted]

Any reader may bring any artistic charge he pleases against the above sonnet; but one charge it would be impossible to maintain against the writer of the series in which it occurs, and that is, the wish on his part to assert that the body is greater than the soul. For here all the passionate and just delights of the body are declared — somewhat figuratively, it is true, but unmistakably — to be as naught if not ennobled by the concurrence of the soul at all times. Moreover, nearly one half of this series of sonnets has nothing to do with love, but treats of quite other life-influences. I would defy any one to couple with fair quotation of Sonnets 29, 30, 31, 39, 40, 41, 43, or others, the slander that their author was not impressed, like all other thinking men, with the responsibilities and higher mysteries of life; while Sonnets 35, 36, and 37, entitled "The Choice," sum up the general view taken in a manner only to be evaded by conscious insincerity. Thus much for "The House of Life," of which the Sonnet "Nuptial Sleep" is one stanza, embodying, for its small constituent share, a beauty of natural universal function, only to be reprobated in art if dwelt on (as I have shown that it is not here) to the exclusion of those other highest things of which it is the harmonious concomitant.

At page 342, an attempt is made to stigmatize four short quotations as being specially "my own property," that is, (for the context shows the meaning), as being grossly sensual; though all guiding reference to any precise page or poem in my book is avoided here. The first of these unspecified quotations is from the "Last Confession," and is the description referring to the harlot's laugh, the hideous character of which, together with its real or imagined resemblance to the laugh heard soon afterwards from the lips of one long cherished as an ideal, is the immediate cause which makes the maddened hero of the poem a murderer. Assailants may say what they please; but no poet or poetic reader will blame me for making the incident recorded in these seven lines as repulsive to the reader as it was to the hearer and beholder. Without this, the chain of motive and result would remain obviously incomplete. Observe also that these are but seven lines in a poem of some five hundred, not one other of which could be classed with them.

A second quotation gives the last two lines *only* of the following sonnet, which is the first of four sonnets in "The House of Life" jointly entitled "Willow-wood": —

["Willowwood I" quoted]

The critic has quoted (as I said) only the last two lines, and he has italicized the second as something unbearable and ridiculous. Of course the inference would be that this was really my own absurd bubble-and-squeak notion of an actual kiss. The reader will perceive at once, from the whole sonnet transcribed above, how untrue such an inference would be. The sonnet describes a dream or trance of divided love momentarily re-united by the longing fancy; and in the imagery of the dream, the face of the beloved rises through deep dark waters to kiss the lover. Thus the phrase, "Bubbled with brimming kisses," &c., bears purely on the special symbolism employed, and from that point of view will be found, I believe, perfectly simple and just.

A third quotation is from "Eden Bower," and says

What more prize than love to impel thee?
Grip and lip my limbs as I tell thee!

Here again no reference is given, and naturally the reader would suppose that a human embrace is described. The embrace, on the contrary, is that of a fabled snake-woman and a snake. It would be possible still, no doubt, to object on other grounds to this conception; but the ground inferred and relied on for full effect by the critic is none the less an absolute misrepresentation. These three extracts, it will be admitted, are virtually, though not verbally, garbled with malicious intention; and the same is the case, as I have shown, with the sonnet called "Nuptial Sleep" when purposely treated as a "whole poem."

The last of the four quotations grouped by the critic as conclusive examples, consists of two lines from "Jenny." Neither some thirteen years ago, when I wrote this poem, nor last year when I published it, did I fail to foresee impending charges of recklessness and aggressiveness, or to perceive that even some among those who could really read the poem and acquit me on these grounds, might still hold that the thought in it had better have dispensed with the situation which serves it for framework. Nor did I omit to consider how far a treatment from without might here be possible. But the motive powers of art reverse the requirement of science, and demand first of all an *inner* standing-point. The heart of such a mystery as this must be plucked from the very world in which it beats or bleeds; and the beauty and pity, the self-questionings and all-questionings which it brings with it, can come with full force only from the mouth of one alive to its whole appeal, such as the speaker put forward in the poem, — that is, of a young and thoughtful man of the world. To such a speaker, many half-cynical revulsions of feeling and reverie, and a recurrent presence of the impressions of beauty (however artificial) which first brought him within such a circle of influence, would be inevitable features of the dramatic relation portrayed. Here again I can give the lie, in hearing of honest readers, to the base or trivial ideas which my critic labours to connect with the poem. There is another little charge, however, which this minstrel in mufti brings against "Jenny," namely, one of plagiarism from that very poetic self of his which the tutelary prose does but enshroud for the moment. This question can, fortunately, be settled with ease by others who have read my critic's poems; and thus I need the less regret that, not happening myself to be in that position, I must be content to rank with those who cannot pretend to an opinion on the subject.

It would be humiliating, need one come to serious detail, to have to refute such an accusation as that of "binding oneself by solemn league and covenant to extol fleshliness as the distinct and supreme end of poetic and pictorial art"; and one cannot but feel that here every one will think it allowable merely to pass by with a smile the foolish fellow who has brought a charge thus framed against any reasonable man. Indeed, what I have said already is substantially enough to refute it, even did I not feel sure that a fair balance of my poetry must, of itself, do so in the eyes of every candid reader. I say nothing of my pictures; but those who know them will laugh at the idea. That I may, nevertheless, take a wider view than some poets or critics, of how much, in the material conditions absolutely given to man to deal with as distinct from his spiritual aspirations, is admissible within the limits of Art, — this, I say, is possible enough; nor do I wish to shrink from such responsibility. But to state that I do so to the ignoring or overshadowing of spiritual beauty, is an absolute falsehood, impossible to be put forward except in the indulgence of prejudice or rancour.

I have selected, amid much railing on my critic's part, what seemed the most representative indictment against me, and have, so far, answered it. Its remaining clauses set forth how others and myself "aver that poetic expression is greater than poetic thought . . . and sound superior to sense" — an accusation elsewhere, I observe, expressed by saying that we "wish to create form for its own sake." If writers of verse are to be listened to in such arraignment of each other, it might be quite competent to me to prove, from the works of my friends in question, that no such thing is the case with them; but my present function is to confine myself to my own defence. This, again, it is difficult to do quite seriously. It is no part of my undertaking to dispute the verdict of any "contemporary," however contemptuous or contemptible, on my own measure of executive success; but the accusation cited above is not against the poetic value of certain work, but against its primary and (by assumption) its admitted aim. And to this I must reply that so far, assuredly, not even Shakespeare himself could desire more arduous human tragedy for development in Art than belongs to the themes I venture to embody, however incalculably higher might be his power of dealing with them. What more inspiring for poetic effort than the terrible Love turned to Hate, — perhaps the deadliest of all passion-woven complexities, — which is the theme of "Sister Helen," and, in a more fantastic form, of "Eden Bower," — the surroundings of both poems being the mere machinery of a central universal meaning? What, again, more so than the savage penalty exacted for a lost ideal, as expressed in the "Last Confession"; — than the outraged love for man and burning compensations in art and memory of "Dante at Verona"; — than the baffling problems which the face of Jenny conjures up; — or than the analysis of passion and feeling attempted in "The House of Life," and others among the more purely lyrical poems? I speak here, as does my critic in the clause adduced, of *aim* not of *achievement;* and so far, the mere summary is instantly subversive of the preposterous imputation. To assert that the poet whose matter is such as this aims chiefly at "creating form for its own sake," is, in fact, almost an ingenuous kind of dishonesty; for surely it delivers up the asserter at once, bound hand and foot, to the tender mercies of contradictory proof. Yet this may fairly be taken as an example of the spirit in which a constant effort is here made against me to appeal to those who either are ignorant of what I write, or else belong to the large class too easily influenced by an assumption of authority in addressing them. The false name appended to the article must, as is evident, aid this position vastly; for who, after all, would not be apt to laugh at seeing one poet confessedly come forward as aggressor against another in the field of criticism?

It would not be worth while to lose time and patience in noticing minutely how the system of misrepresentation is carried into points of artistic detail, — giving us, for example, such statements as that the burthen employed in the ballad of "Sister Helen" "is repeated with little or no alteration through thirty-four verses," whereas the fact is, that the alteration of it in every verse is the very scheme of the poem. But these are minor matters quite thrown into the shade by the critic's more daring sallies. In addition to the class of attack I have answered above, the article contains, of course, an immense amount of personal paltriness; as, for instance, attributions of my work to this, that, or the other absurd derivative source; or again, pure nonsense (which can have no real meaning even to the writer) about "one art getting hold of another, and imposing on it its conditions and limitations"; or, indeed, what not besides? However, to such antics as this, no more attention is possible than that which Virgil enjoined Dante to bestow on the meaner phenomena of his pilgrimage.

Thus far, then, let me thank you for the opportunity afforded me to join issue with the Stealthy School of Criticism. As for any literary justice to be done on this particular Mr. Robert-Thomas, I will merely ask the reader whether, once identified, he does not become manifestly his own best "sworn tormentor"? For who will then fail to discern all the palpitations which preceded his final resolve in the great question whether to be or not to be his acknowledged self when he became an assailant? And yet this is he who, from behind his mask, ventures to charge another with "bad blood," with "insincerity," and the rest of it (and that where poetic fancies are alone in question); while every word on his own tongue is covert rancour, and every stroke from his pen perversion of truth. Yet, after all, there is nothing wonderful in the lengths to which a fretful poet-critic will carry such grudges as he may bear, while publisher and editor can both be found who are willing to consider such means admissible, even to the clear subversion of first professed tenets in the *Review* which they conduct.

In many phases of outward nature, the principle of chaff and grain holds good, — the base enveloping the precious continually; but an untruth was never yet the husk of a truth. Thresh and riddle and winnow it as you may, — let it fly in shreds to the four winds, — falsehood only will be that which flies and that which stays. And thus the sheath of deceit which this pseudonymous undertaking presents at the outset insures in fact what will be found to be its real character to the core.

PART EIGHT

Posthumously Published and Uncollected Writings

Filii Filia

[I]
The lilies stand before her like a screen
  Through which, upon this warm & solemn day,
  God surely hears. For there she kneels to pray
Who bore our Bourne of prayer, — Mary the Queen —
She was Faith's Present, parting what had been   5
  From what began with her and is for aye.
  On either side God's twofold system lay, —
With meek bowed face a Virgin prayed between.

So prays she, and the Dove flies in to her,
  And she has turned. Within the porch is one   10
    Who looks as though deep awe made him to smile.
Heavy with heat, the plants yield shadow there;
  The loud flies cross each other in the sun;
    And the aisled pillars meet the poplar-aisle.

[II]
Upon a sun-scorched road when noon was deep
  I passed a little consecrated shrine
  Where among simple pictures ranged in line
The blessed Mary holds her son asleep.
To kneel here, shepherd-children leave their sheep   5
  When silence broods at heart of the sunshine,
  And again kneel here in the day's decline,
And here, when their life ails them, come to weep.

Night being full, I passed on the same road
  By the same shrine. Within, a lamp was lit   10
  Which through the depth of utter darkness glow'd.
    Then, after heat of life, when doubts arise
  Dim-hurtling, faith's pure lamp must beam on it, —
    How oft unlit, alas! how oft that dies.

Another Love

Of her I thought who now is gone so far:
   And, the thought passing over, to fall thence
   Was like a fall from spirit into sense
Or from the heaven of heavens to sun and star.
None other than Love's self ordained the bar   5
   'Twixt her and me; so that if, going hence,
   I met her, it could only seem a dense
Film of the brain, — just nought, as phantoms are.

Now when I passed your threshold and came in,
   And glanced where you were sitting, and did see   10
      Your tresses in these braids and your hands thus, —
I knew that other figure, grieved and thin,
   That seemed there, yea that was there, could not be,
      Though like God's wrath it stood dividing us.

Praise and Prayer

Doubt spake no word in me as there I kneeled.
   Loathing, I could not praise: I could not thank
   God for the cup of evil that I drank:
I dared not cry upon His strength to shield
My soul from weapons it was bent to wield   5
   Itself against itself. And so I sank
   Into the furnished phrases smooth and blank
Which we all learn in childhood, — and did yield
A barren prayer for life. My voice might mix
   With hers, but mingled not. Hers was a full   10
      Grand burst of music, which the crownèd Seven
Must have leaned sideways from their seats to fix
   In their calm minds. The seraph-songs fell dull
      Doubtless, when heard again, throughout all heaven.

For a Virgin and Child by Hans Memmelinck
(In the Academy of Bruges)

Mystery: God, man's life, born into man
   Of woman. There abideth on her brow
   The ended pang of knowledge, the which now

Is calm assured. Since first her task began
She hath known all. What more of anguish than   5
   Endurance oft hath lived through, the whole space
   Through night till day, passed weak upon her face
While the heard lapse of darkness slowly ran?

All hath been told her touching her dear Son,
   And all shall be accomplished. Where He sits   10
      Even now, a babe, He holds the symbol fruit
   Perfect and chosen. Until God permits,
      His soul's elect still have the absolute
Harsh nether darkness, and make painful moan.

For a Marriage of St. Catherine by the Same
(In the Hospital of St. John at Bruges)

Mystery: Catherine the bride of Christ.
   She kneels, and on her hand the holy Child
   Now sets the ring. Her life is hushed and mild,
Laid in God's knowledge — ever unenticed
From God, and in the end thus fitly priced.   5
   Awe, and the music that is near her, wrought
   Of angels, have possessed her eyes in thought:
Her utter joy is hers, and hath sufficed.

There is a pause while Mary Virgin turns
   The leaf, and reads. With eyes on the spread book,   10
      That damsel at her knees reads after her.
      John whom He loved, and John His harbinger,
   Listen and watch. Whereon soe'er thou look,
The light is starred in gems and the gold burns.

A TRIP TO PARIS AND BELGIUM

London to Folkstone
(Half-past one to half-past five)

A constant keeping-past of shaken trees,
And a bewildered glitter of loose road;
Banks of bright growth, with single blades atop
Against white sky; and wires — a constant chain —

That seem to draw the clouds along with them   5
(Things which one stoops against the light to see
Through the low window; shaking by at rest,
Or fierce like water as the swiftness grows);
And, seen through fences or a bridge far off,
Trees that in moving keep their intervals   10
Still one 'twixt bar and bar; and then at times
Long reaches of green level, where one cow,
Feeding among her fellows that feed on,
Lifts her slow neck, and gazes for the sound.

There are six of us: I that write away;   15
Hunt reads Dumas, hard-lipped, with heavy jowl
And brows hung low, and the long ends of hair
Standing out limp. A grazier at one end
(Thank luck not my end!) has blocked out the air,
And sits in heavy consciousness of guilt.   20
The poor young muff who's face to face with me
Is pitiful in loose collar and black tie,
His latchet-button shaking as we go.
There are flowers by me, half upon my knees,
Owned by a dame who's fair in soul, no doubt: 25
The wind that beats among us carries off
Their scent, but still I have them for my eye.

Fields mown in ridges; and close garden-crops
Of the earth's increase; and a constant sky
Still with clear trees that let you see the wind;   30
And snatches of the engine-smoke, by fits
Tossed to the wind against the landscape, where
Rooks stooping heave their wings upon the day.

Brick walls we pass between, passed so at once
That for the suddenness I cannot know   35
Or what, or where begun, or where at end.
Sometimes a Station in grey quiet; whence,
With a short gathered champing of pent sound,
We are let out upon the air again.
Now nearly darkness; knees and arms and sides   40
Feel the least touch, and close about the face
A wind of noise that is along like God.
Pauses of water soon, at intervals,
That has the sky in it; — the reflexes
O' the trees move towards the bank as we go by,   45
Leaving the water's surface plain. I now

Lie back and close my eyes a space; for they
Smart from the open forwardness of thought
Fronting the wind —

            —I did not scribble more,
Be certain, after this; but yawned, and read,   50
And nearly dozed a little, I believe;
Till, stretching up against the carriage-back,
I was roused altogether, and looked out
To where, upon the desolate verge of light,
Yearned, pale and vast, the iron-coloured sea.   55

Boulogne to Amiens and Paris
(3 to 11 p.m.; 3rd class)

Strong extreme speed, that the brain hurries with,
Further than trees, and hedges, and green grass
Whitened by distance, — further than small pools
Held among fields and gardens, — further than
Haystacks and windmill-sails and roofs and herds, —   5
The sea's last margin ceases at the sun.

The sea has left us, but the sun remains.
Sometimes the country spreads aloof in tracts
Smooth from the harvest; sometimes sky and land
Are shut from the square space the window leaves   10
By a dense crowd of trees, stem behind stem
Passing across each other as we pass:
Sometimes tall poplar-wands stand white, their heads
Outmeasuring the distant hills. Sometimes
The ground has a deep greenness; sometimes brown   15
In stubble; and sometimes no ground at all,
For the close strength of crops that stand unreaped.
The water-plots are sometimes all the sun's, —
Sometimes quite green through shadows filling them,
Or islanded with growths of reeds, — or else   20
Masked in grey dust like the wide face o' the fields.
And still the swiftness lasts; that to our speed
The trees seem shaken like a press of spears.

There is some count of us: — folks travelling-capped,
Priesthood, and lank hard-featured soldiery,   25
Females (no women), blouses, Hunt, and I.

We are relayed at Amiens. The steam
Snorts, chafes, and bridles, like three-hundred horse,
And flings its dusky mane upon the air.
Our company is thinned, and lamps alight: 30
But still there are the folks in travelling-caps —
No priesthood now, but always soldiery,
And babies to make up for show in noise,
Females (no women), blouses, Hunt, and I.

Our windows at one side are shut for warmth;   35
Upon the other side, a leaden sky,
Hung in blank glare, makes all the country dim,
Which too seems bald and meagre, — be it truth,
Or of the waxing darkness. Here and there
The shade takes light, where in thin patches stand   40
The unstirred dregs of water.

                                        Hunt can see
A moon, he says; but I am too far back.
Still the same speed and thunder. We are stopped
Again, and speech tells clearer than in day.

Hunt has just stretched to tell me that he fears   45
I and my note-book may be taken for
The stuff that goes to make an "émissaire
De la perfide." Let me abate my zeal:
There is a stout gendarme within the coach.

This cursed pitching is too bad. My teeth   50
Jingle together in it; and my legs
(Which I got wet at Boulogne this good day
Wading for star-fish) are so chilled that I
Would don my coat, were not these seats too hard
To spare it from beneath me, and were not   55
The love of ease less than the love of sloth.

Hunt has just told me it is nearly eight:
We do not reach till half-past ten. Drat verse,
And steam, and Paris, and the fins of Time!
Marry, for me, look you, I will go sleep.   60

Most of them slept; I could not — held awake
By jolting clamour, with shut eyes; my head
Willing to nod and fancy itself vague.
Only at Stations I looked round me, when
Short silence paused among us, and I felt   65

A creeping in my feet from abrupt calm.
At such times Hunt would jerk himself, and then
Tumble uncouthly forward in his sleep.
This lasted near three hours. The darkness now
Stayeth behind us on the sullen road,   70
And all this light is Paris. Dieu merci.

Paris. *Saturday Night,* 29.
Send me, dear William, by return of post,
As much as you can manage of that rhyme
Incurred at Ventnor. Bothers and delays
Have still prevented me from copying this   75
Till now; now that I do so, let it be
Anticipative compensation.
Numéro 4 Rue Geoffroy Marie,
Faubourg Montmartre, près des Boulevards.
Dear William, labelled thus the thing will reach.   80

The Staircase of Notre Dame, Paris

As one who, groping in a narrow stair,
   Hath a strong sound of bells upon his ears,
   Which, being at a distance off, appears
Quite close to him because of the pent air:
So with this France. She stumbles file and square   5
   Darkling and without space for breath: each one
   Who hears the thunder says: "It shall anon
Be in among her ranks to scatter her."

This may be; and it may be that the storm
   Is spent in rain upon the unscathed seas,   10
   Or wasteth other countries ere it die:
Till she, — having climbed always through the swarm
   Of darkness and of hurtling sound, — from these
   Shall step forth on the light in a still sky.

Place de la Bastille, Paris

How dear the sky has been above this place!
   Small treasures of this sky that we see here
   Seen weak through prison-bars from year to year;
Eyed with a painful prayer upon God's grace

To save, and tears which stayed along the face   5
  Lifted at sunset. Yea, how passing dear
  Those nights when through the bars a wind left clear
The heaven, and moonlight soothed the limpid space!

So was it, till one night the secret kept
  Safe in low vault and stealthy corridor   10
    Was blown abroad on gospel-tongues of flame.
  O ways of God, mysterious evermore!
How many on this spot have cursed and wept
  That all might stand here now and own Thy Name.

On a Handful of French Money

These coins that jostle on my hand do own
  No single image: each name here and date
  Denoting in man's consciousness and state
New change. In some, the face is clearly known, —
In others marred. The badge of that old throne   5
  Of Kings is on the obverse; or this sign
  Which says, "I France am all — lo, I am mine!"
Or else the Eagle that dared soar alone.
Even as these coins, so are these lives and years
  Mixed and bewildered; yet hath each of them   10
    No less its part in what is come to be
    For France. Empire, Republic, Monarchy, —
  Each clamours or keeps silence in her name,
And lives within the pulse that now is hers.

The Can-Can at Valentino's

The first, a mare; the second, 'twixt bow-wow
  And pussy-cat, a cross; the third, a beast
  To baffle Buffon; the fourth, not the least
In hideousness, nor last; the fifth, a cow;
The sixth, Chimera; the seventh, Sphinx; . . . Come now,   5
  One woman, France, ere this frog-hop have ceased,
  And it shall be enough. A toothsome feast
Of blackguardism and whoreflesh and bald row,
No doubt for such as love those same. For me,

I confess, William, and avow to thee,   10
     (Soft in thine ear!) that such sweet female whims
     As nasty backsides out and wriggled limbs
Are not a passion of mine naturally;
     Nor bitch-squeaks, nor the smell of heated quims.

To the P.R.B.

Woolner and Stephens, Collinson, Millais,
     And my first brother, each and every one,
     What portion is theirs now beneath the sun
Which, even as here, in England makes to-day?
For most of them life runs not the same way   5
     Always, but leaves the thought at loss: I know
     Merely that Woolner keeps not even the show
Of work, nor is enough awake for play.
Meanwhile Hunt and myself race at full speed
     Along the Louvre, and yawn from school to school,   10
          Wishing worn-out those masters known as old.
And no man asks of Browning; though indeed
     (As the book travels with me) any fool
          Who would might hear Sordello's story told.

At the Station of the Versailles Railway

I waited for the train unto Versailles.
     I hung with bonnes and gamins on the bridge
     Watching the gravelled road where, ridge with ridge,
Under black arches gleam the iron rails
Clear in the darkness, till the darkness fails
     And they press on to light again — again
     To reach the dark. I waited for the train
Unto Versailles; I leaned over the bridge,
And wondered, cold and drowsy, why the knave
     Claude is in worship; and why (sense apart)   10
          Rubens preferred a mustard vehicle.
          The wind veered short. I turned upon my heel
Saying, "Correggio was a toad"; then gave
          Three dizzy yawns, and knew not of the Art.

In the Train, and at Versailles

In a dull swiftness we are carried by
   With bodies left at sway and shaking knees.
   The wind has ceased, or is a feeble breeze
Warm in the sun. The leaves are not yet dry
From yesterday's dense rain. All, low and high,   5
   A strong green country; but, among its trees,
   Ruddy and thin with Autumn. After these
There is the city still before the sky.
Versailles is reached. Pass we the galleries
   And seek the gardens. A great silence here,   10
      Through the long planted alleys, to the long
      Distance of water. More than tune or song,
Silence shall grow to awe within thine eyes,
   Till thy thought swim with the blue turning sphere.

Last Visit to the Louvre. The Cry of the P.R.B. after a Careful Examination of the Canvases of Rubens, Correggio, et hoc genus omne

Non Noi Pittori! God of Nature's truth,
   If these, not we! Be it not said, when one
   Of us goes hence: "As these did, he hath done;
His feet sought out their footprints from his youth."
Because, dear God! the flesh Thou madest smooth   5
   These carked and fretted, that it seemed to run
   With ulcers; and the daylight of thy sun
They parcelled into blots and glares, uncouth
With stagnant grouts of paint. Men say that these
   Had further sight than man's, but that God saw   10
      Their works were good. God that didst know them foul!
      In such a blindness, blinder than the owl,
Leave us! Our sight can reach unto thy seas
   And hills: and 'tis enough for tears of awe.

Last Sonnets at Paris

I

Chins that might serve the new Jerusalem;
   Streets footsore; minute whisking milliners,

Dubbed graceful, but at whom one's eye demurs,
Knowing of England; ladies, much the same;
Bland smiling dogs with manes — a few of them   5
    At pains to look like sporting characters;
    Vast humming tabbies smothered in their furs;
Groseille, orgeat, meringues á la crême —
Good things to study; ditto bad — the maps
    Of sloshy colour in the Louvre; cinq-francs   10
    The largest coin; and at the restaurants
Large Ibrahim Pachas in Turkish caps
    To pocket them. Un million d'habitants:
Cast up, they'll make an Englishman — perhaps.

2

Tiled floors in bedrooms; trees (now run to seed —
    Such seed as the wind takes) of Liberty;
    Squares with new names that no one seems to see;
Scrambling Briarean passages, which lead
To the first place you came from; urgent need   5
    Of unperturbed nasal philosophy;
    Through Paris (what with church and gallery)
Some forty first-rate paintings, — or indeed
Fifty mayhap; fine churches; splendid inns;
    Fierce sentinels (toy-size without the stands)   10
        Who spit their oaths at you and grind their r's
    If at a fountain you would wash your hands;
        One Frenchman (this is fact) who thinks he spars: —
Can even good dinners cover all these sins?

3

Yet in the mighty French metropolis
    Our time has not gone from us utterly
    In waste. The wise man saith, "An ample fee
For toil, to work thine end." Aye that it is.
Should England ask, "Was narrow prejudice   5
    Stretched to its utmost point unflinchingly,
    Even unto lying, at all times, by ye?"
We can say firmly: "Lord, thou knowest this,
Our soil may own us." Having but small French,
    Hunt passed for a stern Spartan all the while,   10
        Uncompromising, of few words: for me —
    I think I was accounted generally
A fool, and just a little cracked. Thy smile
May light on us, Britannia, healthy wench.

From Paris to Brussels
(11 p.m. 15 October to half-past 1 p.m. 16).
Proem at the Paris Station

In France (to baffle thieves and murderers)
A journey takes two days of passport work
At least. The plan's sometimes a tedious one,
But bears its fruit. Because, the other day,
In passing by the Morgue, we saw a man   5
(The thing is common, and we never should
Have known of it, only we passed that way)
Who had been stabbed and tumbled in the Seine,
Where he had stayed some days. The face was black,
And, like a negro's, swollen; all the flesh   10
Had furred, and broken into a green mould.

Now, very likely, he who did the job
Was standing among those who stood with us,
To look upon the corpse. You fancy him —
Smoking an early pipe, and watching, as   15
An artist, the effect of his last work.
This always if it had not struck him that
'Twere best to leave while yet the body took
Its crust of rot beneath the Seine. It may:
But, if it did not, he can now remain   20
Without much fear. Only, if he should want
To travel, and have not his passport yet,
(Deep dogs these French police!) he may be caught.

Therefore you see (lest, being murderers,
We should not have the sense to go before   25
The thing were known, or to stay afterwards)
There is good reason why — having resolved
To start for Belgium — we were kept three days
To learn about the passports first, then do
As we had learned. This notwithstanding, in   30
The fullness of the time 'tis come to pass.

On the Road

October, and eleven after dark:
Both mist and night. Among us in the coach
Packed heat on which the windows have been shut:
Our backs unto the motion — Hunt's and mine.

The last lamps of the Paris Station move   5
Slow with wide haloes past the clouded pane;
The road in secret empty darkness. One
Who sits beside me, now I turn, has pulled
A nightcap to his eyes. A woman here,
Knees to my knees — a twenty-nine-year-old —   10
Smiles at the mouth I open, seeing him:
I look her gravely in the jaws, and write.
Already while I write heads have been leaned
Upon the wall, — the lamp that's overhead
Dropping its shadow to the waist and hands.   15

Some time 'twixt sleep and wake. A dead pause then,
With giddy humming silence in the ears.
It is a Station. Eyes are opening now,
And mouths collecting their propriety.
From one of our two windows, now drawn up,   20
A lady leans, hawks a clear throat, and spits.

Hunt lifts his head from my cramped shoulder where
It has been lying — long stray hairs from it
Crawling upon my face and teazing me.
Ten minutes' law. Our feet are in the road.   25
A weak thin dimness at the sky, whose chill
Lies vague and hard. The mist of crimson heat
Hangs, a spread glare, about our engine's bulk.
I shall get in again, and sleep this time.

A heavy clamour that fills up the brain   30
Like thought grown burdensome; and in the ears
Speed that seems striving to o'ertake itself;
And in the pulses torpid life, which shakes
As water to a stir of wind beneath.

Poor Hunt, who has the toothache and can't smoke,   35
Has asked me twice for brandy. I would sleep;
But man proposes, and no more. I sit
With open eyes, and a head quite awake,
But which keeps catching itself lolled aside
And looking sentimental. In the coach,   40
If any one tries talking, the voice jolts,
And stuns the ear that stoops for it.

    Amiens.
Half-an-hour's rest. Another shivering walk
Along the station, waiting for the bell.
Ding-dong. Now this time, by the Lord, I'll sleep.   45

I must have slept some while. Now that I wake,
Day is beginning in a kind of haze
White with grey trees. The hours have had their lapse.

A sky too dull for cloud. A country lain
In fields, where teams drag up the furrow yet;   50
Or else a level of trees, the furthest ones
Seen like faint clouds at the horizon's point.
Quite a clear distance, though in vapour. Mills
That turn with the dry wind. Large stacks of hay
Made to look bleak. Dead autumn, and no sun.   55

The smoke upon our course is borne so near
Along the earth, the earth appears to steam.
Blanc-Misseron, the last French station, passed.
We are in Belgium. It is just the same: —
Nothing to write of, and no good in verse.   60

Curse the big mounds of sand-weed! curse the miles
Of barren chill, — the twentyfold relays!
Curse every beastly Station on the road!

As well to write as swear. Hunt was just now
Making great eyes because outside the pane   65
One of the stokers passed whom he declared
A stunner. A vile mummy with a bag
Is squatted next me: a disgusting girl
Broad opposite. We have a poet, though,
Who is a gentleman, and looks like one;   70
Only he seems ashamed of writing verse,
And heads each new page with "Mon cher Ami."
Hunt's stunner has just come into the coach,
And set us hard agrin from ear to ear.

Another Station. There's a stupid horn   75
Set wheezing. Now I should just like to know
— Just merely for the whim — what good that is.
These Stations for the most part are a kind
Of London coal-merchant's back premises;
Whitewashed, but as by hands of coal-heavers;   80
Grimy themselves, and always circled in
With foul coke-loads that make the nose aroint.

Here is a Belgian village, — no, a town
Moated and buttressed. Next, a water-track
Lying with draggled reeds in a flat slime.   85

Next, the old country, always all the same.
Now by Hans Hemmling and by John Van Eyck,
You'll find, till something's new, I write no more.

(4 HOURS)
There is small change of country; but the sun
Is out, and it seems shame this were not said: 90
For upon all the grass the warmth has caught;
And betwixt distant whitened poplar-stems
Makes greener darkness; and in dells of trees
Shows spaces of a verdure that was hid;
And the sky has its blue floated with white,   95
And crossed with falls of the sun's glory aslant
To lay upon the waters of the world;
And from the road men stand with shaded eyes
To look; and flowers in gardens have grown strong,
And our own shadows here within the coach   100
Are brighter; and all colour has more bloom.

So, after the sore torments of the route: —
Toothache, and headache, and the ache of wind,
And huddled sleep, and smarting wakefulness,
And night, and day, and hunger sick at food,   105
And twentyfold relays, and packages
To be unlocked, and passports to be found,
And heavy well-kept landscape; — we were glad
Because we entered Brussels in the sun.

L'Envoi: Brussels, Hotel du Midi, 18 October

It's copied out at last: very poor stuff
Writ in the cold, with pauses of the cramp.
Direct, dear William, to the Poste Restante
At Ghent — here written Gand — Gong, Hunticè.
We go to Antwerp first, but shall not stay;   5
After, to Ghent and Bruges; and after that
To Ostend, and thence home. To Waterloo
Was yesterday. Thither, and there, and back,
I managed to scrawl something, — most of it
Bad, and the sonnet at the close mere slosh.   10
'Twas only made because I was knocked up,
And it helped yawning. Take it, and the rest.

On the Road to Waterloo: 17 October
(En Vigilante, 2 Hours)

It is grey tingling azure overhead
   With silver drift. Beneath, where from the green
   The trees are reared, the distance stands between
At peace: and on this side the whole is spread
For sowing and for harvest, subjected   5
   Clear to the sky and wind. The sun's slow height
   Holds it through noon, and at the furthest night
It lies to the moist starshine and is fed.
Sometimes there is no country seen (for miles
   You think) because of the near roadside path   10
   Dense with long forest. Where the waters run
   They have the sky sunk into them — a bath
Of still blue heat; and in their flow, at whiles,
   There is a blinding vortex of the sun.

A Half-Way Pause

The turn of noontide has begun.
   In the weak breeze the sunshine yields.
   There is a bell upon the fields.
On the long hedgerow's tangled run
   A low white cottage intervenes: 5
   Against the wall a blind man leans,
And sways his face to have the sun.

Our horses' hoofs stir in the road,
   Quiet and sharp. Light hath a song
   Whose silence, being heard, seems long.   10
The point of noon maketh abode,
   And will not be at once gone through.
   The sky's deep colour saddens you,
And the heat weighs a dreamy load.

On the Field of Waterloo

So then, the name which travels side by side
   With English life from childhood — Waterloo —
   Means this. The sun is setting. "Their strife grew
Till the sunset, and ended," says our guide.
It lacked the "chord" by stage-use sanctified,   5

Yet I believe one should have thrilled. For me,
 I grinned not, and 'twas something; — certainly
These held their point, and did not turn but died:

So much is very well. "Under each span
 Of these ploughed fields" ('tis the guide still) "there rot   10
  Three nations' slain, a thousand-thousandfold."
  Am I to weep? Good sirs, the earth is old:
 Of the whole earth there is no single spot
But hath among its dust the dust of man.

Returning to Brussels

Upon a Flemish road, when noon was deep,
 I passed a little consecrated shrine,
 Where, among simple pictures ranged in line,
The blessed Mary holds her child asleep.
To kneel here, shepherd-maidens leave their sheep   5
 When they feel grave because of the sunshine,
 And again kneel here in the day's decline;
And here, when their life ails them, come to weep.
Night being full, I passed on the same road
 By the same shrine; within, a lamp was lit   10
Which through the silence of clear darkness glowed.
 Thus, when life's heat is past and doubts arise
Darkling, the lamp of Faith must strengthen it,
 Which sometimes will not light and sometimes dies.

Sir Peter Paul Rubens (Antwerp)

"Messieurs, le Dieu des peintres": We felt odd:
 'Twas Rubens, sculptured. A mean florid church
 Was the next thing we saw, — from vane to porch
His drivel. The museum: as we trod
Its steps, his bust held us at bay. The clod   5
 Has slosh by miles along the wall within.
 ("I say, I somehow feel my gorge begin
To rise.") — His chair in a glass case, by God!
. . . To the Cathedral. Here too the vile snob
 Has fouled in every corner. ("Wherefore brave   10
  Our fate? Let's go.") There is a monument
We pass. "Messieurs, you tread upon the grave

Of the great Rubens." "Well, that's one good job!
　　　　What time this evening is the train for Ghent?"

Antwerp to Ghent

　We are upon the Scheldt. We know we move
Because there is a floating at our eyes
Whatso they seek; and because all the things
Which on our outset were distinct and large
Are smaller and much weaker and quite grey,　　　　　　　5
And at last gone from us. No motion else.

　We are upon the road. The thin swift moon
Runs with the running clouds that are the sky,
And with the running water runs — at whiles
Weak 'neath the film and heavy growth of reeds.　　　　　10
The country swims with motion. Time itself
Is consciously beside us, and perceived.
Our speed is such the sparks our engine leaves
Are burning after the whole train has passed.

The darkness is a tumult. We tear on,　　　　　　　　　　15
The roll behind us and the cry before,
Constantly, in a lull of intense speed
And thunder. Any other sound is known
Merely by sight. The shrubs, the trees your eye
Scans for their growth, are far along in haze.　　　　　　20
The sky has lost its clouds, and lies away
Oppressively at calm: the moon has failed:
Our speed has set the wind against us. Now
Our engine's heat is fiercer, and flings up
Great glares alongside. Wind and steam and speed　　　25
And clamour and the night. We are in Ghent.

Between Ghent and Bruges (Wednesday night, 24 October)

Ah yes, exactly so; but when a man
　　Has trundled out of England into France
　　And half through Belgium, always in this prance
Of steam, and still has stuck to his first plan —
Blank verse or sonnets; and as he began　　　　　　　　5
　　Would end; — why, even the blankest verse may chance
　　To falter in default of circumstance,

And even the sonnet miss its mystic span.
Trees will be trees, grass grass, pools merely pools,
   Unto the end of time and Belgium — points   10
Of fact which Poets (very abject fools)
   Get scent of — once their epithets grown tame
   And scarce. Even to these foreign rails — my joints
   Begin to find their jolting much the same.

Antwerp to Bruges

I climbed the stair in Antwerp church,
   What time the circling thews of sound
   At sunset seem to heave it round.
Far up, the carillon did search
The wind, and the birds came to perch   5
   Far under, where the gables wound.

In Antwerp harbour on the Scheldt
   I stood along, a certain space
   Of night. The mist was near my face;
Deep on, the flow was heard and felt.   10
The carillon kept pause, and dwelt
   In music through the silent place.

John Memmeling and John van Eyck
   Hold state at Bruges. In sore shame
   I scanned the works that keep their name.   15
The carillon, which then did strike
Mine ears, was heard of theirs alike:
   It set me closer unto them.

I climbed at Bruges all the flight
   The belfry has of ancient stone.
   For leagues I saw the east wind blown;   20
The earth was grey, the sky was white.
I stood so near upon the height
   That my flesh felt the carillon.

On Leaving Bruges

The city's steeple-towers remove away,
   Each singly; as each vain infatuate Faith
   Leaves God in heaven, and passes. A mere breath

Each soon appears, so far. Yet that which lay
The first is now scarce further or more grey   5
    Than the last is. Now all are wholly gone.
    The sunless sky has not once had the sun
Since the first weak beginning of the day.
The air falls back as the wind finishes,
    And the clouds stagnate. On the water's face   10
        The current breathes along, but is not stirred.
        There is no branch that thrills with any bird.
    Winter is to possess the earth a space,
And have its will upon the extreme seas.

Ashore at Dover

On landing, the first voice one hears is from
    An English police-constable; a man
    Respectful, conscious that at need he can
Enforce respect. Our custom-house at home
Strict too, but quiet. Not the foul-mouthed scum   5
    Of passport-mongers who in Paris still
    Preserve the Reign of Terror; not the till
Where the King haggles, all through Belgium.
The country somehow seems in earnest here,
    Grave and sufficient: — England, so to speak;   10
No other word will make the thing as clear.
    "Ah! habit," you exclaim, "and prejudice!"
    If so, so be it. One don't care to shriek,
"Sir, this shall be!" But one believes it is.

THE ORCHARD PIT

Men tell me that sleep has many dreams; but all my life I have dreamt one dream alone.

I see a glen whose sides slope upward from the deep bed of a dried-up stream, and either slope is covered with wild apple-trees. In the largest tree, within the fork whence the limbs divide, a fair, golden-haired woman stands and sings, with one white arm stretched along a branch of the tree, and with the other holding forth a bright red apple, as if to some one coming down the slope. Below her feet the trees grow more and more tangled, and stretch from both sides across the deep pit below: and the pit is full of the bodies of men.

They lie in heaps beneath the screen of boughs, with her apples bitten in their hands; and some are no more than ancient bones now, and some seem dead but yesterday. She stands over them in the glen, and sings for ever, and offers her apple still.

This dream shows me no strange place. I know the glen, and have known it from childhood, and heard many tales of those who have died there by the Siren's spell.

I pass there often now, and look at it as one might look at a place chosen for one's grave. I see nothing, but I know that it means death for me. The apple-trees are like others, and have childish memories connected with them, though I was taught to shun the place.

No man sees the woman but once, and then no other is near; and no man sees that man again.

One day, in hunting, my dogs tracked the deer to that dell, and he fled and crouched under that tree, but the dogs would not go near him. And when I approached, he looked in my eyes as if to say, "Here you shall die, and will you here give death?" And his eyes seemed the eyes of my soul, and I called off the dogs, who were glad to follow me, and we left the deer to fly.

I know that I must go there and hear the song and take the apple. I join with the young knights in their games; and have led our vassals and fought well. But all seems to me a dream, except what only I among them all shall see. Yet who knows? Is there one among them doomed like myself, and who is silent, like me? We shall not meet in the dell, for each man goes there alone: but in the pit we shall meet each other, and perhaps know.

Each man who is the Siren's choice dreams the same dream, and always of some familiar spot wherever he lives in the world, and it is there that he finds her when his time comes. But when he sinks in the pit, it is the whole pomp of her dead gathered through the world that awaits him there; for all attend her to grace her triumph. Have they any souls out of those bodies? Or are the bodies still the house of the soul, the Siren's prey till the day of judgment?

We were ten brothers. One is gone there already. One day we looked for his return from a border foray, and his men came home without him, saying that he had told them he went to seek his love who would come to meet him by another road. But anon his love met them, asking for him; and they sought him vainly all that day. But in the night his love rose from a dream; and she went to the edge of the Siren's dell, and there lay his helmet and his sword. And her they sought in the morning, and there she lay dead. None has ever told this thing to my love, my sweet love who is affianced to me.

One day at table my love offered me an apple. And as I took it she laughed, and said, "Do not eat, it is the fruit of the Siren's dell." And I laughed and ate: and at the heart of the apple was a red stain like a woman's mouth; and as I bit it I could feel a kiss upon my lips.

The same evening I walked with my love by that place, and she would needs have me sit with her under the apple-tree in which the Siren is said to stand. Then she stood in the hollow fork of the tree, and plucked an apple, and stretched it to me and would have sung: but at that moment she cried out, and leaped from the tree into my arms, and said that the leaves were whispering other words to her, and my name among them. She threw the apple to the bottom of the dell, and followed it with her eyes, to see how far it would fall, till it was hidden by the tangled boughs. And as we still looked, a little snake crept up through them.

She would needs go with me afterwards to pray in the church, where my ancestors and hers are buried; and she looked round on the effigies, and said, "How long will it be before we lie here carved together?" And I thought I heard the wind in the apple trees that seemed to whisper, "How long?"

And late that night, when all were asleep, I went back to the dell, and said in my turn, "How long?" And for a moment I seemed to see a hand and apple stretched from the middle of the tree where my love had stood. And then it was gone: and I plucked the apples and bit them, and cast them in the pit, and said, "Come."

I speak of my love, and she loves me well; but I love her only as the stone whirling down the rapids loves the dead leaf that travels with it and clings to it, and that the same eddy will swallow up.

Last night, at last, I dreamed how the end will come, and now I know it is near. I not only saw, in sleep, the lifelong pageant of the glen, but I took my part in it at last, and learned for certain why that dream was mine.

I seemed to be walking with my love among the hills that lead downward to the glen: and still she said, "It is late;" but the wind was glenwards, and said, "Hither." And still she said, "Home grows far;" but the rooks flew glenwards, and said, "Hither." And still she said, "Come back;" but the sun had set, and the moon laboured towards the glen, and said, "Hither." And my heart said in me, "Aye, thither at last." Then we stood on the margin of the slope, with the apple-trees beneath us; and the moon bade the clouds fall from her, and sat in her throne like the sun at noonday: and none of the apple-trees were bare now, though autumn was far worn, but fruit and blossom covered them together. And they were too thick to see through clearly; but looking far down I saw a white hand holding forth an apple, and heard the first notes of the Siren's song. Then my love clung to me and wept; but I began to struggle down the slope through the thick wall of bough and fruit and blossom, scattering them as the storm scatters the dead leaves; for that one apple only would my heart have. And my love snatched at me as I went; but the branches I thrust away sprang back on my path, and tore her hands and face: and the last I knew of her was the lifting of her hands to heaven as she cried aloud above me, while I still forced my way downwards. And now the Siren's song rose clearer as I went. At first she sang, "Come to Love;" and of the sweetness of Love she said many things. And next she sang, "Come to Life;" and Life was sweet in her song. But long before I reached her, she knew that all her will was mine: and then her voice rose softer than ever, and her words were, "Come to Death;" and Death's name in her mouth was the very swoon of all sweetest things that be. And then my path cleared; and she stood over against me in the fork of the tree I knew so well, blazing now like a lamp beneath the moon. And one kiss I had of her mouth, as I took the apple from her hand. But while I bit it, my brain whirled and my foot stumbled; and I felt my crashing fall through the tangled boughs beneath her feet, and saw the dead white faces that welcomed me in the pit. And so I woke cold in my bed: but it still seemed that I lay indeed at last among those who shall be my mates for ever, and could feel the apple still in my hand.

THE DOOM OF THE SIRENS.
A LYRICAL TRAGEDY

ACT I

Scene I

Hermitage near the Sirens' Rock. A Christianized Prince, flying from persecution in the latter days of the Roman Empire, is driven that way by stress of weather (having with him his wife and infant child), and succeeds in taking refuge in the Hermitage. The Hermit relates to him the legend of the Sirens, and how they are among the Pagan powers not yet subdued but still acting as demons against the human race. The spell upon them is that their power cannot be destroyed until one of them shall yield to human love and become enamoured of some one among her intended victims. The Hermit has, therefore, established himself hard by to pray for travellers in danger, and, if possible, to warn them off in time, and he implores the Prince to pursue his voyage by some other course. The Prince, however, says that he shall not be able to do so, and trusts in Heaven and in his love for his wife to guard him against danger. He dwells on his being a Christian, and therefore beyond the power of Pagan demons, who had as yet destroyed only those unprotected by true faith. The storm having subsided (this scene occurs the morning after he had taken refuge), the Prince and his family re-embark, leaving the Hermit praying for their safety.

Scene 2

The ship arrives at the Sirens' Rock, amid the songs of the three Sirens, Thelxiope, Thelxione, and Ligeia. The first offers wealth, the second greatness and triumph over his enemies, the third (Ligeia) offers her love. Here a chorus in which the three contend and the wife strives against them. The Prince gradually, in spite of his efforts, succumbs to Ligeia and climbs the rock, his wife following him. Here the choral contention is continued, the Prince clinging to Ligeia, rapt by her spells into the belief that it is the time of his first love and that he is surrounded by the scenes of that time. At last he dies in her arms, as she sings, under her poisonous breath, calling her as he dies by his wife's name, and shrinking from his wife without recognition. The Queen makes a prayer begging God to make him know her. During this he dies, and Ligeia then says,

"He knows us now; woman, take back your dead!"

The Queen pronounces a despairing curse against Ligeia, praying that she may yet love and be hated and so destroy herself and her sisters. The Queen then flings herself in madness from the rock into the sea.

Scene 3

The Hermit puts out in a boat to where the Prince's ship is still lying, and takes the infant to his Hermitage. He soliloquizes over him, saying how, if the faith prevails in his father's kingdom, he will take him in due time to occupy the throne, but how otherwise the youth shall stay with himself to serve him as an acolyte, and so escape the storms of human passion more baneful than those of the sea.

Twenty-one years elapse between Acts I. and II.

ACT 2

Scene 1

At the court of the Byzantine Prince. The courtiers are conversing about the approaching marriage of the young Prince, now come to the throne. One of them relates particulars respecting his being brought there as a boy by the Hermit, who revealed the secret of his father's and mother's death only to a trusted counsellor, the father of the girl he is now about to marry. They also refer to the troubles of the time when the former Prince had to fly from his kingdom on account of his faith, and recall to each other the progress of events since, and the establishment of Christianity in the country, after which the young Prince was brought back by the Hermit, and seated on his father's throne. Allusions are made to various omens and portents appearing to bear on the mysterious death of the Prince's father and mother, and on the vengeance still to be taken for it.

Scene 2

A grove, formerly sacred to an Oracle. The Prince and his betrothed meet here and speak of their love and approaching nuptials, which are to take place the next day. They are both, however, troubled by dreams they have had and which they relate to each other at length. These bear fantastically on the death of the Prince's parents, but without clearly revealing anything, though seeming to prognosticate misfortunes still unaccomplished, and a fatal issue to their love. The Prince connects these things with the events of his early boyhood, which he dimly remembers in the hermitage by the Sirens' Rock, before the Hermit brought him to his kingdom; and he confesses to his betrothed the gloomy uncertainty with which his mind is clouded. However, they try to forget all forebodings and dwell on the happiness in store for them. They sing to each other and together, but their songs seem to find an ominous burden in the echoes of the sacred grove, and they part at last, saddened in spite of themselves. The Prince goes, leaving the lady, who says that she will stay there till her maidens join her. Being left alone, she suddenly hears a voice calling her, and finds that it comes from the Oracle of the grove, whose shrine is forgotten and almost overgrown. She forces the tangled growth aside and enters the precincts.

Scene 3

The Shrine of the Oracle. Here the Oracle speaks to her; at first in dark sentences, but at length more explicitly, as to a great task awaiting her lover, without accomplishing which he must not hope for love or peace. It speaks of the evil powers which caused his parents' death, and are doomed themselves to annihilation by the just vengeance transmitted to him. It then tells her clearly how it is the heavenly will that the Prince shall only wed if he survives the vengeance due for his parents' death, but that he had been chosen now to fulfil the doom of the Sirens, and must at once accomplish his mission. Finally the Oracle announces that its function has been so far renewed for the last time that it may be compelled to denounce its fellow powers of Paganism; but that now its voice is silent for ever. At the end of this scene the Bride's maidens come to meet her, and find her bewildered and in tears, but cannot learn the cause from her.

Scene 4

The Bridal Chamber on the morning after the nuptials. The scene opens with a *réveillée* sung outside. The Prince and Princess are together, and he is speaking to her of his love and their future happiness; but after a time, in the midst of their endearments, he begins to perceive that she is disturbed and anxious, and presses her to tell him the cause. She at last informs him with tears of her conference with the Oracle on their last meeting in the grove. This (as she tells him) she had not the courage to reveal to him before their wedding, as, if obeyed, it must tear him from her arms, perhaps never to return; and she had then resolved to suppress the terrible secret at any risk to herself; but on the bridal night, while she lay in his arms, the Hermit, now a saint in heaven, had appeared to her in a dream, with a wrathful aspect. He had told her how by his means the Prince had been preserved in infancy; had reproached her with her silence as to the charge she had received; and had told her that if she did not now make known to her husband the will of Heaven, some fatal mischance would soon separate them for ever. All this she now tells him with many tears and with bitter upbraidings of the cruel fate which compelled her to avoid the certain wrath threatened to him by sending him on a mission of such terrible uncertainty. Before telling all this she had consented to speak only on his promising to grant the first favour she should afterwards ask for herself; and she now tells him that this favour is the permission to accompany him on his voyage. He endeavours in vain to dissuade her from this, and at last consents to it.

ACT 3

Scene 1

The hermitage near the Sirens' Rock, as in Act I. Arrival of the Prince, accompanied by his Bride, who is prevailed on by him to remain in prayer at the hermitage while he pursues his journey to the rock. Before they part, a paper is found written, by which they learn that the Hermit had died there a year and a day before, and that he named the day of their present arrival as the one on which his hermitage would again be tenanted, and yet on which its appointed use would cease.

Scene 2

The Sirens' Rock. The Sirens have been warned by the evil powers to whom they are tributary that this day is a signal one for them. They are uncertain whether for good or ill, but are possessed by a spirit of baneful exultation, and in their songs alternate from one to the other wild tales of their triumphs in past times and the renowned victims who have succumbed to them. As they reach the name of the Christian Prince and his wife who died by their means, a vessel comes in view, but almost before their songs have been directed towards it, they are surprised to see it make straight for the rock, and the occupant resolutely disembark and commence the ascent. As he nears them, they exchange scornful prophecies of his ruin between the pauses of their song; but gradually Ligeia, who has at first begged him of her sisters as her special prey, finds herself strangely overpowered by emotions she does not understand, and by the time he reaches the summit of the rock and stands before them, she is alternately beseeching him for his love and her sisters for his life. A long chorus here occurs: Ligeia yielding to the agony of her passion, while the Prince repulses and reviles her, and the other Sirens wail and curse, warning her of the impending doom. The Prince tells Ligeia of his parentage and mission, but she still madly craves for his love, and holds forth to him such promises of infernal sovereignty as her gods afford, if he will yield to her passion. He, meanwhile, though proof against her lures and loathing her in his heart, is physically absorbed into the death-agony of the expiring spell; and when, at his last word of reprobation, the curse seizes her and her sisters, and they dash themselves headlong from the rock, he also succumbs to the doom, calling with his last breath on his Bride to come to him. Throughout the scene the prayers of the Bride are fitfully wafted from the hermitage between the pauses of the Sirens' songs and the deadly chorus of love and hate.

Scene 3

Within the hermitage, the Bride still praying. The scene to commence with a few lines of prayer, after which the Spirit of the Prince appears, calling the Bride to come to him, in the same words with which the last scene ended. She then discourses to him, saying many things in gradually increasing ecstasy of love, he all the time speaking to her at intervals, only the same words as before. She ends by answering him in his own words, calling him to come to her, and so dies.

In case of representation — supposing the hermitage and rock to be visible on the stage at the same time — the conclusion might be that at the moment of the Prince's death, when he calls to his Bride, she breaks off her prayers; answering him in the same words, and dies. Scene 3 would thus be dispensed with.

Dennis Shand

The shadows fall along the wall,
    It's night at Haye-la-Serre;
The maidens weave since day grew eve,
    The lady's in her chair.

O passing slow the long hours go   5
    With time to think and sigh,
When weary maidens weave beneath
    A listless lady's eye.

It's two days that Earl Simon's gone
    And it's the second night;   10
At Haye-la-Serre the lady's fair,
    In June the moon is light.

O it's "Maids, ye'll wake till I come back,"
    And the hound's i' the lady's chair:
No shuttles fly, the work stands by,   15
    It's play at Haye-la-Serre.

The night is worn, the lamp's forlorn,
    The shadows waste and fail;
There's morning air at Haye-la-Serre,
    The watching maids look pale.   20

O all unmarked the birds at dawn
    Where drowsy maidens be;
But heard too soon the lark's first tune
    Beneath the trysting tree.

"Hold me thy hand, sweet Dennis Shand,"   25
    Says the Lady Joan de Haye,
"That thou to-morrow do forget
    To-day and yesterday.

"For many a weary month to come
    My lord keeps house with me,   30
And sighing summer must lie cold
    In winter's company.

"And many an hour I'll pass thee by
    And see thee and be seen;
Yet not a glance must tell by chance
    How sweet these hours have been.   35

"We've all to fear; there's Maud the spy,
    There's Ann whose face I scor'd,
There's Blanch tells Huot everything,
    And Huot loves my lord.   40

"But O and it's my Dennis 'll know,
    When my eyes look weary dim,
Who finds the gold for his girdle-fee
    And who keeps love for him."

The morrow's come and the morrow-night,   45
    It's feast at Haye-la-Serre,
And Dennis Shand the cup must hand
    Beside Earl Simon's chair.

And still when the high pouring's done
    And cup and flagon clink,   50
Till his lady's lips have touched the brim
    Earl Simon will not drink.

But it's, "Joan my wife," Earl Simon says,
    "Your maids are white and wan."
And it's, "O," she says, "they've watched the night   55
    With Maud's sick sister Ann."

But it's, "Lady Joan and Joan my bird,
    Yourself look white and wan."
And it's, "O, I've walked the night myself
    To pull the herbs for Ann: 60

"And some of your knaves were at the hutch
    And some in the cellarage,
But the only one that watched with us
    Was Dennis Shand your page.

"Look on the boy, sweet honey lord,   65
    How drooped his eyelids be:
The rosy colour's not yet back
    That paled in serving me."

O it's, "Wife, your maids are foolish jades,
    And you're a silly chuck,   70

And the lazy knaves shall get their staves
   About their ears for luck:

"But Dennis Shand may take the cup
   And pour the wine to his hand;
Wife, thou shalt touch it with thy lips,   75
   And drink thou, Dennis Shand!"

MacCracken
(Parody on Tennyson's "Kraken")

Getting his pictures, like his supper, cheap,
   Far, far away in Belfast by the sea,
His watchful one-eyed uninvaded sleep
   MacCracken sleepeth. While the P.R.B.
Must keep the shady side, he walks a swell   5
   Through spungings of perennial growth and height:
   And far away in Belfast out of sight,
By many an open do and secret sell,
Fresh daubers he makes shift to scarify,
   And fleece with pliant shears the slumbering "green."   10
There he has lied, though aged, and will lie,
     Fattening on ill-got pictures in his sleep,
     Till some Præraphael prove for him too deep.
    Then, once by Hunt and Ruskin to be seen,
Insolvent he will turn, and in the Queen's Bench die.   15

LIMERICKS

There is a big artist named Val,
The roughs' and the prize-fighters' pal:
   The mind of a groom
   And the head of a broom
Were Nature's endowments to Val.

There is a Creator named God
Whose creations are sometimes quite odd:
   I maintain — and I shall —
   The creation of Val
Reflects little credit on God.

There is a dull Painter named Wells
Who is duller than any one else:
   With the face of a horse
   He sits by you and snorts —
Which is very offensive in Wells.

There's an infantine Artist named Hughes —
Him and his the R.A.'s did refuse:
   At length, though, among
   The lot, one was hung —
But it was himself in a noose.

There's a babyish party named Burges
Who from infancy hardly emerges:
   If you had not been told
   He's disgracefully old,
You would offer a bull's-eye to Burges.

There is a young person named Georgie
Who indulges each night in an orgy:
   Soda-water and brandy
   Are always kept handy
To efface the effects of that orgy.

There is a young Artist named Jones
Whose conduct no genius atones:
   His behaviour in life
   Is a pang to the wife
And a plague to the neighbours of Jones.

There is a young Painter called Jones
(A cheer here, and hisses, and groans):
   The state of his mind
   Is a shame to mankind,
But a matter of triumph to Jones.

There's a Painter of Portraits named Chapman
Who in vain would catch woman or trap man
   To be painted life-size
   More preposterous guys
Than they care to be painted by Chapman.

There's a combative Artist named Whistler
Who is, like his own hog-hairs, a bristler:
   A tube of white lead
   And a punch on the head
Offer varied attractions to Whistler.

There's a publishing party named Ellis
Who's addicted to poets with bellies:
   He has at least two —
   One in fact, one in view —
And God knows what will happen to Ellis.

There's a Portuguese person named Howell
Who lays-on his lies with a trowel:
   Should he give-over lying,
   'Twill be when he's dying,
For living is lying with Howell.

There is a mad Artist named Inchbold
With whom you must be at a pinch bold:
   Or else you may score
   The brass plate on your door
With the name of J. W. Inchbold.

A Historical Painter named Brown
Was in manners and language a clown:
   At epochs of victual
   Both pudden and kittle
Were expressions familiar to Brown.

There was a young rascal called Nolly
Whose habits though dirty were jolly;
   And when this book comes
   To be marked with his thumbs
You may know that its owner is Nolly.

There are dealers in pictures named Agnew
Whose soft soap would make an old rag new:
   The Father of Lies
   With his tail to his eyes
Cries — "Go it, Tom Agnew, Bill Agnew!"

There's a solid fat German called Huffer
A hypochondriacal buffer:
   To declaim Schopenhauer
   From the top of a tower
Is the highest ambition of Huffer.

There's a Scotch correspondent named Scott
Thinks a penny for postage a lot:
   Books, verses, and letters,
   Too good for his betters,
Cannot screw out an answer from Scott.

There's a foolish old Scotchman called Scotus,
Most justly a Pictor Ignotus:
   For what he best knew
   He never would do,
This stubborn [old] donkey called Scotus.

There once was a painter named Scott
Who seemed to have hair, but had not.
   He seemed too to have sense:
   'Twas an equal pretence
On the part of the painter named Scott.

There's the Irishman Arthur O'Shaughnessy —
On the chessboard of poets a pawn is he:
   Though a bishop or king
   Would be rather the thing
To the fancy of Arthur O'Shaughnessy.

There is a young Artist named Knewstub,
Who for personal cleaning will use tub:
   But in matters of paint
   Not the holiest Saint
Was ever so dirty as Knewstub.

There is a poor sneak called Rossetti:
As a painter with many kicks met he —
   With more as a man —
   But sometimes he ran,
And that saved the rear of Rossetti.

As a critic, the Poet Buchanan
Thinks Pseudo much safer than Anon.
   Into Maitland he shrunk,
   But the smell of the skunk
Guides the shuddering nose to Buchanan.

Parted Love!

Oh how the family affections combat
Within this heart, and each hour flings a bomb at
My burning soul! Neither from owl nor from bat
Can peace be gained until I clasp my wombat.

At Last

Fate claimed hard toll from Love, and did not spare;
Are the dues paid, and is all Love's at last?
Cling round me, sacred sweetness — hold me fast, —

Oh! as I kneel, enfold mine eyes even there
Within thy breast; and to Love's deepest lair 5
Of memory bid thy soul with mine retreat
And let our past years and our future meet
In the warm darkness underneath thine hair.

Say once for all: "Me Love accepts, and thee:
Nor takes he other count of bygone years 10
Not his, than do the affranchised earth and sea
Of hours wherein the unyoked inordinate spheres
Hurtled tumultuous round Time's ringing ears
Ere yet one word gave light to victory."

First Fire

This hour be her sweet body all my song —
   Now the same heart-beat blends her gaze with mine, —
   One parted fire, Love's silent countersign:
Her arms lie open, throbbing with their throng
Of confluent pulses, bare and fair and strong: 5
   And her deep-freighted lips expect me now,
   Amid the clustering hair that throngs her brow
Five kisses broad, her neck ten kisses long.

Lo, Love! thy heaven of Beauty; where a sun
   Thou shin'st; and art a white-winged moon to press 10
   By hidden paths to every hushed recess;
Yea, and with sinuous lightnings here anon
Of passionate change, an instant seen & gone,
   Shalt light the tumult of this loveliness.

THE BLESSED DAMOZEL

Rossetti produced five distinct versions of this signature work. The first version (1846–47, never printed, manuscript now lost) consisted of stanzas 1–5, 12–13, 18–23. The four remaining versions are

1. the *Germ* text (1850), 25 stanzas (1, 2, 3, 4, 5, 6, 6.1 [stanza not subsequently included], 7, 8, 9, 12, 13, 14, 15, 16, 16.1, 16.2 [two stanzas not subsequently included], 18, 19, 20, 21, 22, 22.1 [stanza not subsequently included], 23, 24);

2. the Pierpont Morgan manuscript text (1855), 19 stanzas (1, 2, 3, 4, 5, 7, 8, 9, 12, 13, 14, 15, 16, 18, 19, 21, 22, 23, 24);

3. the *Oxford and Cambridge Magazine* text (1856), 23 stanzas (1, 2, 3, 4, 5, 6, 7, 8, 9, 10, 12, 13, 14, 15, 16, 11, 18, 19, 20, 21, 22, 23, 24);

4. the 1870 *Poems* text, 24 stanzas (1–24). Local revisions to the 1870 text appeared in Rossetti's new edition of *Poems* (1881). This text is printed in the present edition.

The poem draws its inspiration from Dante's *Vita Nuova,* especially the famous canzone "Donne ch'avete intelletto d'amore" (Ladies that have intelligence in love), which comes in section XIX. The canzone treats the position that Beatrice, the emparadised beloved, has in relation both to mortal creatures, including Dante, and to the beings of heaven, including God. Rossetti's approach is strongly eroticized in both the poetical and pictorial treatments of his subjects. The influence of Poe's "Raven" is significant because it provided Rossetti with a nineteenth-century point of reference for his own treatment. Ultimately the damozel, like Poe's Lenore, is the figural expression for a lost set of cultural values.

The poem operates at three levels, or from three points of vantage: the damozel's from heaven, the lover's from his dream-vision, and the lover's from his conscious reflection. The last of these is signalled in the text by parentheses, which enclose the lover's thoughts on the vision of his desire. As a double work (with Rossetti's paintings) the text's meanings are of course further complicated.

Title. *Damozel:* old French spelling, which signals the poem's conscious adoption of a medieval style.

6. Revelation 1:16 and 12:1. In the painting the damozel has a crown of six stars, not seven. The discrepancy defines the crown as the Pleiades, which traditional astrology saw as being composed of seven stars, though one—the "lost Pleiad"—was invisible. This lost Pleiad, a favorite subject in the romantic tradition since Byron, is Merope, who was cast from her starry place because she fell in love with a mortal man. In this context the Damozel is the lost Pleiad. Symbolically the Pleiades are a favorable sign, a forecast of good weather for navigation and agriculture. The number seven in this context also suggests the seven joys and seven sorrows of the Madonna. Compare "Mary's Girlhood I" lines 9–10.

54. Alluding to the ancient idea of the music of the spheres.

87. The dove is a traditional figure of the Holy Ghost.

107–8. St. Cecilia: an early virgin martyr. In the mythology of her life, she is closely associated with the Virgin Mary. In the middle ages she emerged as the patroness of sacred music.

Gertrude: patron saint of pilgrims and travellers. Margaret: either Margaret of Antioch, popu-larized in the Golden Legend, or perhaps the thirteenth-century Margaret of Cortona, a kind of Mary Magdalene surrogate. Rosalys: she summarizes Rossetti's procedure in handling these fe-male figures. Rosalys is a kind of pure signifier, a linguistic construct made from two of the Madonnna's most characteristic symbols (the rose and the lily). The extremity of Rossetti's sec-ular spirituality also appears in this signifier, for the rose = beauty/passion/love while the lily = chastity/purity/devotion.

SISTER HELEN

Composed in 1851–52, first printed in the *Düsseldorf Artists' Album* (1853), revised and augmented for both the 1870 and the 1881 editions of *Poems*. The 1881 text is printed in the present edition.

The poem is a sophisticated traditional ballad set in a generally medieval locus, though the scene is specifically Ireland. It employs a well-known folklore motif: killing someone by de-stroying an effigy fashioned by witchcraft. It is a remarkable work for both its psychological power and its technical virtuosity. The suggestively worked language of the refrains is particu-larly impressive.

STRATTON WATER

Composed in 1854, first printed in the 1870 *Poems,* collected thereafter. A pastiche medieval ballad.

105–6. These are spoken to the knave.
107–10. These lines are spoken to Janet.

THE STAFF AND THE SCRIP

Conceived in 1849, first drafted in 1851–52, revised substantially for its publication in 1856 (in the *Oxford and Cambridge Magazine*) and in 1870 for *Poems*. Further revisions came before its 1881 *Poems* printing, and that is the text in the present edition. The poem is based on one (and per-haps two) anecdotes from the *Gesta Romanorum:* no. 25 ("Of Ingratitude") and no. 66 ("Of Constancy").

AVE

Composed under the title "Mater Pulchrae Delectionis" (Mother of the fair delight) in 1847 as part of the project Rossetti called Songs of the Art Catholic. It was first published in the 1870 *Poems,* where it was heavily revised; collected thereafter. The 1870 printing provides the present text.

The poem represents itself as a kind of free translation or contemporary reconfiguration of an original Latin hymn to the Virgin Mary. The pastiche element in works like this reveals their es-sentially magical character: these are works aspiring to a kind of secular sacramentalism that might be imagined to reinstall (not simply reimagine) the ethos and spiritual agency of a lost set of spiritual agencies. The work should be compared with "The Girlhood of Mary Virgin," son-nets and associated pictorial works, as well as "The Blessed Damozel" and all of Rossetti's other medieval conjurings.

6. I.e., from Bethlehem to Golgotha.
32. The contemporary sign is important for establishing the poem's internal historicized ur-gency, i.e., its effort to produce a spiritual and aesthetic closure between the mid–nineteenth century and the medieval world evoked in the poem.
98–100. In the secular context of Rossetti's work, this question clearly suggests that the an-swer is not religious and hence that the faith, love, and hope have become secular, rather than theological, virtues.

107. See Revelation 12:1.

112. Echoes the opening of the "Magnificat."

DANTE AT VERONA

First draft written in 1848–50 under title "Dante in Exile," completed around 1852, revised in 1869 for its first publication in the 1870 *Poems*, collected thereafter, with some minor revisions between 1870 and 1881. The 1881 text is printed in the present edition.

Originally intended as an introduction to Rossetti 's translation of the *Vita Nuova*, the poem investigates Dante and the cultural condition of Italy in the thirteenth and early fourteenth centuries. The poem is a revisionary critique of the view that Dante had good relations with his Verona patron Can Grande della Scala. The poem exposes the conflict between Dante's artistic and spiritual interests and his alienated secular circumstances. Rossetti uses this view of Dante and his work as a vehicle for arguing that there exists a similar relation between the contemporary artist and the secular Victorian world.

The first epigraph defines the poem as a revelation of the prophetic words that Cacciaguida spoke to Dante but that, according to *Paradiso* canto XVII, Dante withheld from his poem (see lines 91–96 of canto XVII). Rossetti's poem represents itself as the revelation of that secret. Hence we see the importance of the studied archaic quality of the diction and poetical style. This feature of the poem aligns it closely with Rossetti 's translations and Art Catholic pastiche works of the same period. It suggests that the narrator of the poem is not to be seen transparently— that is, not simply as the voice of Rossetti in propria persona. The voice seems a contemporary (Victorian) one that has been invaded by the spirit of a much earlier culture.

TROY TOWN

Written in 1869–70 for publication in the 1870 *Poems*, collected thereafter.

A dark double of "The Blessed Damozel," the ballad is a disturbing and erotic meditation on cultural doom—a common Victorian preoccupation most famously treated in Tennyson's *Idyls*. In Rossetti's poem Paris dreams of his longed-for beloved Helen, whose prayer to Venus dominates the text and action. "The Blessed Damozel" operates under the horizon of paradise, "Troy Town" under the prophecy of the destruction of Troy, the symbol of flourishing civilization.

title. The phrase is a figurative expression designating a labyrinth or a scene of confusion (OED).

textual. In the first printings of the poem, Rossetti had included an introductory note citing Herodotus as the source of the story about the cup made from an impression of Helen's breast.

1. Helen was the daughter of Zeus and (depending on which tradition one followed) either Leda or Nemesis.

43–56. Referring to the heart of the myth, which tells of the fatal judgment of Paris made at the wedding of Thetis and King Peleus. The Fate Eris threw the apple of discord (inscribed "To the fairest") among the guests at the wedding, and Paris was asked to choose to whom to give it. In the end he had to choose between Minerva (glory), Venus (beauty), and Juno (power). His choice of Venus precipitated the events that led to the war of Troy.

59–60. These lines subtly glance at very different apples, the famous Dead Sea apples associated with Sodom and Gomorrah.

92–96. Paris is dreaming on the promise that Venus made to him after he awarded her the prize as the fairest: that he would marry the most beautiful woman in the world.

EDEN BOWER

Composed in August–September 1869 for publication in the 1870 *Poems*. Further revisions, particularly to the complex refrain, were made for the 1881 edition of the *Poems*, and it is that text that is printed in the present edition.

The poem cuts into the Eden story and the story of the Fall from Paradise via the myth of Lilith, Adam's first wife, which is not treated directly in the bible. The erotic intensity of the poem is deepened by the social and personal aspects of the subject that run through the text in dark undercurrents. An apocalyptic destruction (at once psychic and cultural/historical) is hinted throughout the ballad. Rossetti was fascinated by the Lilith story, which recurs in his paintings and writings. He called this poem "a central representative treatment of its splendid subject," and he later maintained his high valuation of the work. Along with "Jenny," "A Last Confession," and *The House of Life, (HL)* he placed it among the poems he "would wish to be known by."

The poem scatters echoes of Milton and especially the Book of Genesis (chapters 1–3).

THE CARD-DEALER

Originally written in 1848, first published in the *Athenæum* (1852) under the title "The Card-Dealer; or Vingt-et-un." It was much revised in 1869 for publication in the 1870 *Poems* and collected thereafter. The 1870 text is printed in this volume.

The poem illustrates very well Rossetti's involvement with the fantastic traditions of romanticism (both artistic and poetical). The poem is explicitly—as its original printed version showed—an interpretive meditation on Theodore Von Holst's painting *The Wish* (also called *The Fortune Teller* [1840]). Rossetti made some drawings of his own for a picture he planned to accompany the poem.

A letter to Holman Hunt (September 1848) explaining the original title is relevant: "'Vingt-et-un' is, as you of course know, the title of a game of cards, at which I have supposed the lady of the picture (personifying, according to me, intellectual enjoyment) to be playing, since twenty-one is the age at which the mind is most liable to be beguiled for a time from its proper purpose."

Rossetti invented two interesting epigraphs for the poem, which he removed when he came to print it in 1870. The first is in English: "'And the name of the first siren is Telxiope,—she it is who sings of high honour; the name of the second is Telsinoe, and riches is her song; and the third is named Aglaophemia, and her singing is all of pleasure and solace. And they three oftentimes sing together.' (*Travells of King Ulixes*—1550)." The second, in French, was printed with the 1852 text: "Ambition, Cupidité, / Et délicieuse Volupté, / Sont les soeurs de la Destinée / Après la vingt-première année. (Calendrier de la Vie, 1630.)"

LOVE'S NOCTURNE

Originally written in 1854, drastically revised in the summer of 1869 for publication in the 1870 *Poems;* collected thereafter.

Rossetti conceived the poem as a kind of dramatic monologue, as he wrote to his brother in September 1969: "The first conception of this poem was of a man not yet in love who dreams vaguely of a woman who he thinks must exist for him. This is not very plainly expressed, and not I think very valuable; and it might be better to refer the love to a known woman whom he wishes to approach." Rossetti revised the poem to encourage this latter interpretation, though it does not prevent the other.

Title. In music, a composition of a dreamy character (OED). In Catholic liturgy, the night office of Matins is divided into three nocturns; Rossetti is imagining a fourth where the prayers are addressed to "Love."

1. The Master is Love, here personified in the early Italian manner.

20. Interludes: a key word in the poem, here given an emphatic place. The word partly glances at the poem's dreams, which constitute "interludes" in the lover's waking life; and partly at the poem's principal technical exponent of those dreams, the musical elements—especially the rhymes—that fill up the spaces between the poem's semantic elements.

35. death's wicket: see *Paradise Lost* III, 484.

50–70. This central section connects the work directly with the doppelgänger theme that so fascinated Rossetti. The key pictorial work here is what Rossetti called his Bogie drawing, *How They Met Themselves*. Rossetti originally made this drawing in 1851 for G. P. Boyce.

94. sundial: a striking (off) rhyme. Rossetti liked this type of effect, where eye challenges the ear's customary authority over the rhyme. As a consequence, the word-as-such is powerfully foregrounded, as if it were a thing or object in its own right, with its own intrinsic (as opposed to its referential) significance.

143–44. Adam's dream of love is Eve, who is born when God's love puts Adam to sleep and creates Eve at and in that time-space: see Genesis 2:21.

THE STREAM'S SECRET

Composed between September 1869 and March 1870; first published in the 1870 *Poems,* collected thereafter.

Among the most recondite of Rossetti's poems, "The Stream's Secret" is also one of the most hauntingly beautiful. Much of its force follows from its complex metrical structure, where alternating line lengths play off a rhyme scheme suggestive of a sonnet quatrain. The highly alliterative stylistic treatment adds a further element of aesthetic subtlety. These surface features do not merely suggest the motion of a stream, as has been (aptly) said; they signify and even enact the poem's theme of secret messages—messages that their perceptible forms reveal and conceal simultaneously. One central secret is that the poem meditates on Rossetti's love for Jane Morris on one hand and recollects his love for his dead wife Elizabeth on the other. The poem is thus a close companion piece to *HL*.

Paull Baum has usefully noted that the poem falls into three broad sections: the address to the stream (1–72); the narrative of the love vision (73–138); the concluding address to the stream (139–234). The poem is littered with allusions to Rossetti's other works, and it has a particularly close relation with the sonnets of *HL* where Rossetti's secret life in love is also the main subject.

61–62. At the autobiographical level, the reference can be either to Jane Morris or to Rossetti's dead wife, Elizabeth. This ambiguity persists through all the poem's equivalent references.

167ff. The passage distinctly recalls the pictorial representation Rossetti created in his painting *Beata Beatrix.*

JENNY

First version composed in 1847–48; completely reworked in 1859–60 into a dramatic monologue; buried in 1862 with his other poems in his wife's coffin. Rossetti recovered it in 1869 and reworked it again for printing in the 1870 *Poems.* Collected thereafter.

The central critical text is Rossetti's brief explication in "The Stealthy School of Criticism," where he replied to Robert Buchanan's abusive attack on his 1870 *Poems.* In his explication Rossetti sketches his theory of art at "an *inner* standing-point," which this poem exhibits. The procedure subjects the speaker, Rossetti's "young and thoughtful man of the world," to the reader's judgment (both critical and sympathetic). It also allows the poet to include his own subjectivity in the poem under the mask of the speaker. (In this respect Rossetti's dramatic monologue is much closer to Tennyson's method than to Browning's.)

The key Rossettian theme of the dialectic of Sacred and Profane love—Soul's Beauty and Body's Beauty—is here powerfully treated in a contemporary context. One notes in particular lines 250–75, an addition made to the poem in October or November 1869: the passage seems a kind of oblique meditation on Rossetti's own book of poems and its many hidden (erotic) texts. These texts, by traditional moral measures, are "Puddled with shameful knowledge" (line 265) of various kinds. But it is as if Rossetti were imagining the figure of Jenny as an index of his own work and its effort to have its "erring heart unerringly" (line 251) exposed. The exposure would entail a reimagination of the relation of the dominions of the Sacred and the Profane.

More than anything else, "Jenny" is a dramatic representation of a broadly dispersed and shared set of social attitudes. It is a poem about a society dominated by well-meaning and bad faith. The equivalences between Jenny and the speaker's "cousin Nell" and between the speaker and the poet emblemize this subject, which embraces the reader as well—a reader assumed to be implicated in the same social nexus. Ruskin's 1860 critique of "Jenny"—that it would not be understood by most, and that it would offend those who could understand it—stands as an index of the poem's meaning, which is to say of the problems it poses and means to pose.

Epigraph. *Merry Wives of Windsor* IV.1.63–64.
18. Parodying the first lines of the Ave Maria.
20. See Mark 9:48.
88. serve: meaning here "push aside" (OED)
100. Matthew 6:28.
111–20. The passage, a late (Oct.–Nov. 1869) addition, uncannily recapitulates the figure of the poet's dead wife, and the figure of the "leaves" connects the passage to the poem's recurrent bibliographical imagery.
117. purfled: poetical for embroidered.
119–20. Christological allusions come in here, to the Sacred Heart of Jesus and to the Crucifixion.
142. The Haymarket theatre district was a known haunt of prostitutes.
166. middle street: the gutter ran through the middle of the street in the older parts of London.
180–84. Echoes Romans 9:20–21.
228–29. The text glances at the doctrine of Christ's redemption; in the context the allusion carries effective ironical overtones.
237. This line suggests the aesthetic vantage from which the figure of Jenny is being observed.
249. John 14:2.
282–97. According to the folklore on such fossils, the toad could survive in its earth cell without food or air.
304–9. The image recalls Rossetti's famous unfinished painting *Found,* begun in 1854.
316. Ironical reference to the parable of the wise and foolish virgins in Matthew 25.
322. Lovers would commonly scratch their names together on a mirror. The reference is of course ironic.

THE PORTRAIT

Rossetti wrote a version of this poem in 1847, "On Mary's Portrait Which I Painted Six Years Ago," which was to have been a part of the unfinished story "St. Agnes of Intercession." He completely reworked that text in 1869 and produced this poem for the 1870 *Poems.* Both versions illustrate Rossetti's programmatic treatment of art as a kind of sacramental action. Like "Hand and Soul" and the "Old and New Art" sonnets, this poem makes a key statement of Rossetti's ideas about art. In that regard it is closely related to the painting *Beata Beatrix,* Rossetti's portrait of his wife (begun before she died, completed afterwards). Like the sonnet titled "The Portrait," this poem recollects Fazio Degli Uberti's great "Canzone. His Portrait of His Lady, Angiola of Verona," a seminal work for Rossetti. And of course Dante's vision of Beatrice is a foundational presence in all these works.

1–2. Echoes the opening of Browning's "My Last Duchess."
91ff. Recalls the culminant vision in Dante's *Paradiso;* see especially canto XXXIII, 115–45.

MY SISTER'S SLEEP

Written mid-1848, first printed in the *New Monthly Belle Assemblée* (September 1848), then again in the *Germ,* no. 1 (1850), where it came under the general heading "Songs of One Household No. 1." Collected into the 1870 *Poems* and kept thereafter.

The hyperrealistic treatment of circumstantial detail makes this a paradigm example of a poem done in an early Pre-Raphaelite style on a contemporary subject. The mode—typical of William Michael's poetry—is uncharacteristic of Rossetti's. The poem is thus a kind of theoretical work, or poetical experiment. When Rossetti wrote it in 1847 he consciously strove to depart from the "hot" style that William Holman Hunt had reproached: "I quite agree with you in what you say of the 'hotness' of my verses, if you mean (as I suppose) a certain want of repose and straining after original modes of expression. Of these aspects I am endeavouring to rid myself, and hoped in some degree to have cast them off in 'My Sister's Sleep,' which is one of the last things I have written, and which, I confess, seems to me simpler and more like nature than I have shown you" (letter of September 1848). But of course the simplicity itself was a type of poetical self-consciousness and "original mode of expression," as Coventry Patmore noted when he commented on the poem in December 1849.

24. broken lights: i.e., the fire casts flickering shadows.

A LAST CONFESSION

Written 1848–49, much revised in the fall of 1869 for its first publication in the 1870 *Poems,* kept thereafter. Much influenced by Browning, the monologue is the confession of an Italian patriot mortally wounded during the 1848 uprising against Austrian rule of the kingdom of Lombardy-Venetia. The poem is a politically disillusioned commentary on the situation in Europe, and especially Italy, after 1848. It distinctly recalls the mordant critique apparent in poems like "On Refusal of Aid Between Nations," which dates from the period of this monologue. As in Browning's comparable texts, the Italy of this work is in a crucial sense a projection of English views, and hence as much a comment on English cultural politics as on current Italian events.

39. Iglio is an imaginary place.
183ff. The passage evokes the attitudes of Italian patriots to the rule and policies of the much-hated Prince Klemens Wenzel Furst Von Metternich (1773–1859), the Austrian chancellor who established the German Confederation which governed most of the Italian peninsula from 1820 until the revolution of 1848.
356. Rossetti has invented this statue of the Madonna.
376–80. The famous Iron Crown of the Lombard kings is housed in the Duomo of Monza. Being under Austrian occupation, Lombardy has at this point, the speaker observes, no proper authority.

THE BURDEN OF NINEVEH

Composed in 1850, much revised for its first printing in the 1856 *Oxford and Cambridge Magazine,* revised further for publication in the 1870 *Poems.* The 1170 text is printed in this volume. The work clearly relates to Rossetti's programmatic concerns about art and its relation to society, concerns that were most pressing for him in the years of his Pre-Raphaelite commitments in the late 40s and early 50s. The 1856 text treats these matters in a comic tone that tells much about his skeptical view of English art and society at large, including a "revolutionary" movement like the PRB, which was organized towards artistic and social reform. The contemporary setting focuses on the Near Eastern antiquities being acquired by the British Museum. Rossetti uses that setting to develop a broadly based critique of imperial cultures. The principal source for the poem is Sir Austin Layard, *Nineveh and Its Remains* and *A Popular Account of Discoveries at Nineveh,* the abridged edition (1851). Rossetti used the latter when he was recasting his poem but the former when he wrote the first version in 1850. Besides this reference work, Rossetti's poem clearly recalls Byron's earlier satiric treatment of British cultural imperialism in *Childe Harold's Pilgrimage* (1812; see especially canto II) and *The Curse of Minerva* (1812), as well as Shelley's sonnet "Ozymandias," which Rossetti specifically recalls in his final two stanzas.

2–3. The reference is to the Elgin Marbles, whose transportation to England at the beginning of the century Byron had fiercely condemned.
10. One of the monumental bulls brought to the museum from the excavations at Nineveh.

13. Strictly speaking, runes are Germanic glyphs.

23–24. Rossetti recalls passages from stanzas 1 and 4 of Keats's "Ode on a Grecian Urn."

53. See Jonah 4:6.

113. teraphim: small Jewish idols.

122. i.e., Sodom and Gomorrah (see Genesis 14:3).

126–27. Jonah 3:3.

131–42. Matthew 4:8–9.

AN OLD SONG ENDED

Composed mid-1869, first printed in the 1870 *Poems,* collected thereafter. The poem "completes" the fragmentary song sung by Ophelia when she enters in scene 5, act 4 of *Hamlet.* The poem has distinct biographical overtones, recollecting Rossetti's dead wife Elizabeth. It intimates a corresponding madness lying in store for the betraying man: the final two lines of the song sketch the figure of a man haunted by the presence of his dead love.

ASPECTA MEDUSA (FOR A PICTURE)

Composed in July 1867 "as an inscription" to the oil painting of the same name that was commissioned (and later rejected) by C. P. Mathews; first printed in the 1870 *Poems,* collected thereafter. It is an allegorical treatment of the subject of art's relation to the world. (Compare Shelley's sonnet "Lift not the painted veil.") The message seems ominous since Rossetti leaves only ominous alternatives: either a revelation that would bring destruction or a dangerous (because illusory) concealment. The version of the story used by Rossetti (see lines 4–5), in which Perseus overcame the monster by using the Medusa's head, is uncommon, but he probably found his authority for it in Lemprière's *Classical Dictionary.* Rossetti invented the idea that Andromeda "hankered" to see the Medusa.

Title. *Aspecta Medusa* means "Medusa beheld."

2. Hankered: a striking colloquialism.

THE BRIDE'S PRELUDE

Begun in the late 1840s, probably 1848, when it was titled "Bride Chamber Talk," but left incomplete. Rossetti revised and augmented it considerably in 1869 for printing in the 1870 *Poems* but decided against including it because its length would overbalance the other works in the book. He revised it again in 1880 and the completed Part I was first printed in the 1881 *Poems. A New Edition.* Part II was never written, though in 1878 Rossetti sketched out its contents: "Urscelyn has become celebrated as a soldier of fortune, selling his sword to the highest bidder, and in this character reports reach Aloyse and her family respecting him. Aloyse now becomes enamoured of a young knight who loves her deeply; this leads, after fears and hesitations, to her confessing to him the stain on her life; he still remains devoted to her. Urscelyn now reappears; his influence as a soldier renders a lasting bond with him desirable to the brothers of Aloyse, much as they hate him; and he, on his side, is bent on assuming an important position in the family to which he as yet only half belongs. He therefore offers marriage to Aloyse, supported by the will of her brothers, who moreover are well aware of the blot they have to efface, which would thus disappear. At a tournament Urscelyn succeeds in treacherously slaying the knight to whom Aloyse has betrothed herself; and this death is followed in due course by the bridal to which the poem relates. It winds up with the description of the last preparations preceding the bridal procession. Amelotte would draw attention to the passing of the time. Aloyse then says: 'There is much now that you remember; how we heard that Urscelyn had become a soldier of fortune, and how he returned here, etc. You must also remember well the death of that young knight at the tourney.' Amelotte should then describe the event, and say how well she remembers Urscelyn's bitter grief at the mischance. Aloyse would then tell her how she herself was betrothed secretly to the young knight, and how Urscelyn slew him intentionally. As the bridal procession appears, perhaps it might become apparent that the brothers mean to kill Urscelyn when he has married her." Swinburne apparently suggested the final incident to Rossetti.

A brilliant symbolist work, the poem never entirely pleased Rossetti. Paull Baum well described it as "a study of delayed narration, corresponding to the Bride's reluctance to reveal her story." He points out how Rossetti's inventive original stanza form contributes to this effect by dragging at the forward movement of the text—as do the poem's convoluted syntaxes, parentheses, and interruptions, all so typically Rossettian. The poem transforms the ballad from a narrative tale to a study of the text's own process of unfolding.

456–60. According to Rossetti's brother, these lines suggested to Rossetti the idea for his so-called bogie-picture, *How They Met Themselves*.

A NEW-YEAR'S BURDEN

Composed in 1858 or 1859, first printed in the 1870 *Poems* (as one of the Songs of the *HL* sequence), collected thereafter. As with the next poem, this is as much an experiment in verse technique as anything else.

EVEN SO

Composed in 1854 or 1859, first printed in the 1870 *Poems* (as one of the Songs of the *HL* sequence), collected thereafter. It arrests one with its abstract qualities—an arrest all the more effective because the subject (the dissolution of love) comes in at such an oblique angle. The poem's self-display of technical precision and deliberateness becomes an objective correlative for an immobilized emotional condition.

THREE TRANSLATIONS FROM FRANÇOIS VILLON, 1450

All three were composed in 1869 for inclusion in the 1870 *Poems,* where they were first printed. They emphasize the continuity of sacred and profane love. The interpenetration of the two, perhaps the most celebrated idea in all of Rossetti's work, grounds the (implicit but recurrent) mythic orientation of Rossetti's work. Rossetti and Swinburne planned to make a complete translation of Villon's poetry but the project never came to fruition.

A Ballad of Dead Ladies
2. Flora was a celebrated Roman courtesan.

3. Hipparchia is Rossetti's substitution for Archipiada, i.e., Alcibiades, who was taken for a woman in the Middle Ages. Hipparchia is the name of an obscure Greek woman of wealthy family in the fourth century B.C. who was devoted to the Cynic philosopher Crates. Thais: the famous Greek courtesan.

5. See Ovid, *Metamorphoses* III, 339ff.

9–12. The celebrated love of Heloise and Abelard is recounted by Jean de Meun in the *Roman de la Rose* V, 8729ff.

13–15. Villon recalls a legend regarding the medieval philosopher Jean Buridan (fl. 1300–1372) and the Queen of Navarre.

17–18. The identity of this queen is uncertain; perhaps Blanche of Castille; perhaps Blanche of Bourgogne, wife of Charles IV.

19. All heroines in the medieval chanson de geste *Hervis de Metz*.

20. Daughter of Count Helia, of Maine.

21–22. Joan of Arc.

His Mother's Service to Our Lady
13. Saint Mary of Egypt, a courtesan of Alexandria.

14–16. The Vidame of the Church of Adana, in Cilicia. The legend of his dealings with the devil appears throughout medieval literature.

JOHN OF TOURS. OLD FRENCH

Written in 1869 (probably), first printed in the 1870 *Poems*, collected thereafter. This and the next poem, "My Father's Close," are translations from Old French ballads that Rossetti found in the works of Gérard de Nerval, who made versions of them. The two poems underscore the connection between Rossetti's work and the symbolist movement in France. Among the Pre-Raphaelite poets only Swinburne is regularly connected with that important contemporary school of French writing, but it is clear that Rossetti's work connects with it as well.

MY FATHER'S CLOSE. OLD FRENCH

Written in 1869 (probably), first printed in the 1870 *Poems*, collected thereafter. See commentary for "John of Tours," above.

BEAUTY (A COMBINATION FROM SAPPHO)

Written in 1869 (probably), first printed in the 1870 *Poems* under the title "One Girl"; collected thereafter. Rossetti is translating Sappho fragments nos. 93 and 94. Rossetti's source text (Karl Otfried Müller's *History of the Literature of Ancient Greece* [1858] I, 237) shows that weighty themes are being lightly carried in this little poem, which closed Rossetti's 1870 volume. The poem delivers, in the language of flowers, a cryptic message out of the Eleusinian and Orphic mysteries, a message Nietzsche would make famous in his exposition of the myth of the Eternal Return. The poem's "One Girl" is Persephone/Euridice, although in Rossetti's imaginative lexicon she has as well many other particular names.

PART 2. THE HOUSE OF LIFE

This work occupied Rossetti for nearly the whole of his writing life. The earliest pieces were written in 1847–48, and he was revising it until its latest lifetime publication in the 1881 *Poems and Ballads*. He did not begin *HL* as an integral work until 1869, however, as he was preparing the work that would become the 1870 *Poems* volume, where he published a version of *HL* comprising 50 sonnets and 11 songs. Of these original sonnets, 16 were printed in March 1869 in the *Fortnightly Review*. The 1881 publication consisted of 101 sonnets. That version does not include the 1870 Songs and it removed as well one sonnet, the notorious "Nuptial Sleep," which was a special focus of the attack Robert Buchanan made on Rossetti's work in his celebrated review of the 1870 *Poems*, "The Fleshly School of Poetry." The so-called Kelmscott Love Poems—a collection of 28 sonnets and 2 love songs that Rossetti wrote for Jane Morris—is another, unpublished, version or state of this work. Most of the poems in that collection were composed in the summer of 1871 when the two were staying together at Kelmscott Manor. Rossetti wrote out these works in a notebook and gave them to her as a gift. The 1870 and the 1881 texts of *HL* are both organized in two parts that divide roughly into the two parts of an Italian sonnet.

Rossetti said the work was an effort "to put in action a complete 'dramatis personae' of the soul." The elaborate ornamental surface of the work creates a network of functional ambiguities which are the work's hallmark. Substantively considered, the ambiguities all pivot around Rossetti's complex love commitments: on one hand to the memory of his wife, Elizabeth, who died in early 1862; on the other to Jane Morris, with whom he fell in love in the late 1850s. Personal as the work is, Rossetti insisted on its impersonal and symbolic character, and it is in fact quite clear that *HL* models itself on Dante's half personal, half symbolical autobiography, the *Vita Nuova*, which of course Rossetti translated. Below the richly elaborated surface lies a relatively simple story: it narrates the onset of love in a young man (a poet and artist) followed by the loss of the beloved. A New Beloved enters the field of his love devotions, for the first time unmistakably in sonnet XXXVI (no. XVI in 1870), and the love loss recorded in the sequence may be taken to refer to the initial love or to the New Beloved, or to the Ideal Love that both clearly represent. In any case, the loss triggers a series of reflections that center on troubled memories about the possibility of the recovery of love and of an ultimate unity with the lost beloved. Mixed with these is Rossetti's recollection of the stillborn child his wife delivered on 1 May 1861. The figure of the child, which appears repeatedly through the sequence, apparently represents the consummation of the poet's love pursuits.

Readings of this work often misleadingly associate Rossetti's wife, Elizabeth, with "Soul's Beauty" and Jane Morris with "Body's Beauty." The work's love ideal is a fusion of spirit and flesh, however, and the two women rather represent—if they represent anything—two different conditions of lost love, one in life and one in death. One should note as well that the images of various women rise up in *HL*: for example, Alexa Wilding, Fanny Cornforth, and—the first of them all—Rossetti's mother, to whom the opening "Sonnet on the Sonnet" was dedicated.

SONNET XXXVII. THE LOVE-MOON

7. euphrasy: *euphrasis officinalis* (eyebright), a remedy for eye disease.

SONNET XLVIII. DEATH-IN-LOVE

In MSS the poem is headed "Dies atra 1st May 1869," referencing the anniversary of the birth of Rossetti and his wife's stillborn child.

SONNET LVIII. TRUE WOMAN. III. HER HEAVEN

2. the Seer: Emmanuel Swedenborg.

SONNET LX. TRANSFIGURED LIFE

13. See I Kings 18:44.

SONNETS LXXIV–LXXVI. OLD AND NEW ART

These sonnets, in particular the first, constitute a kind of aesthetic manifesto. All were written in the late 1840s.

SONNET LXXVII. SOUL'S BEAUTY

4, 6. drew, draw: this crucial wordplay recurs in the next two sonnets as well. The three together comprise a key moment in *HL*.

10. voice and hand shake still: recalling Dante's *Paradiso* XIII, 78, a central statement about artistic practice.

SONNET LXXIX. THE MONOCHORD

Title. The monochord is a single-stringed device for establishing the correct pitch for a musical instrument.

SONNET LXXXI. MEMORIAL THRESHOLDS

1ff. Rossetti's brother thought this comprised an allusion to the last part of Poe's "Narrative of Arthur Gordon Pym."

SONNET LXXXVII. DEATH'S SONGSTERS

13–14. See 1 Corinthians 15:55.

SONNET XCIV. MICHELANGELO'S KISS

4. true heart: i.e., Michelangelo's early biographer Condivi.

SONNET CI. THE ONE HOPE

In a letter to his friend Alice Boyd, Rossetti explicated "the one hope" as "the longing for accomplishment of individual desire after death."

SONG I. LOVE-LILY

Composed 1869, first printed among the *HL* "Songs" in the 1870 *Poems,* later collected separately. This is a hieratic, quasi-allegorical poem that works by recondite allusion: first to the biblical text "And a river went out of Eden to water the garden" (Genesis 2:10); then to Shelley's "Life of Life" lyric in *Prometheus Unbound* (act II, scene 5); to the Fire-Lily in E. T. A. Hoffmann's story "Der Goldene Topf"; and finally, in general, to the medieval troubador and *stil novisti* songs that recur throughout Rossetti's collection of *The Early Italian Poets.*

SONG II. FIRST LOVE REMEMBERED

Composed 1869, first printed among the *HL* "Songs" in the 1870 *Poems.* The extreme artifice of the poem throws a decorative and pictorial veil over the underlying romantic—indeed, Wordsworthian—thematic structure. The signal opening word ("Peace") transforms into the word "still" (line 13), a conceptual rhyme that realizes the poem's moral, psychic, and ultimately textual stillness. The poem is literally a prayer for peace that evolves into an image of that prayer, or perhaps an icon of it.

13–16. The stanza is signature Rossetti. The word "still" is carefully worked for its multiple meanings, and the verbal forms echo across to each other (There/there/air; unheard/unconscious/ inviolate), arresting the whole unit. Realizing "thanks" as the subject of the verb "await" further immobilizes the figuration, as it also doubles the possible references of "thanks" and "gift" (for either could be the speaker's or the maid's).

SONG III. PLIGHTED PROMISE

Composed 1869, first printed among the *HL* "Songs" in the 1870 *Poems,* later collected separately. Another poem of extreme textural artifice.

SONG IV. SUDDEN LIGHT

Written in 1854, first printed in *Poems: An Offering to Lancashire* (1863), then placed among the *HL* "Songs" in the 1870 *Poems;* later collected separately. This poem treats one of Rossetti's most deeply desired beliefs, the idea that true lovers occupy an eternal space that defines their relationship, and that this fact gets registered by déjà vu experiences. The belief structures the entire dynamic order of *HL,* and is explicitly present at various points, most notably perhaps in "The Birth-Bond."

SONG V. A LITTLE WHILE

Composed 1859, first printed among the *HL* "Songs" in the 1870 *Poems,* later collected separately. The poem's thought should be compared with various *HL* sonnets—e.g., "Autumn Idleness" and "The Hill Summit."

title. Echoes Jesus' words to the Pharisees (John 7:33) shortly before he goes to Jerusalem and his death.
9–16. Echoes Shakespeare, Sonnet 73.

SONG VI. THE SONG OF THE BOWER

Composed 1860 and titled at that point "Bocca Baciata"; first printed among the *HL* "Songs" in the 1870 *Poems,* later collected separately. The poem makes a reprise on the biblical "Song of Songs," a relation especially clear in stanza 3 (lines 19–23). The original title shows that the poem is a quasi double work with Rossetti's crucial picture of 1859, *Bocca Baciata.* And indeed, the beloved imagined in this poem resembles the more voluptuous women who populate Rossetti's paintings from the early 1860s—figures out of Venetian art rather than the more austere women inspired by Rossetti's interest in primitive and early Italian Renaissance painting.

SONG VII. PENUMBRA

Composed 1853, first printed among the *HL* "Songs" in the 1870 *Poems,* later collected separately. Though placed under a heading that calls this poem a song, its form owes much to Rossetti's study of Browning and the tradition of the dramatic monologue. Despite its oblique and imploding meter structure, which works against the essentially realistic inertia of the dramatic monologue, the poem has the same kind of objectivity as "My Sister's Sleep" and "The Woodspurge." The poem is a lover's critical self-assessment and it should be compared with *HL* sonnets like "Vain Virtues" and "Lost Days."

SONG VIII. THE WOODSPURGE

Composed 1856, first printed among the *HL* "Songs" in the 1870 *Poems,* later collected separately. Like "My Sister's Sleep," the poem is a paradigmatic instance of Rossetti's early Pre-Raphaelite handling of concrete details. Not exactly "realistic," the style functions primarily on two other thematic fronts. On one hand it conveys, obliquely, a picture of a traumatic moment, usually a moment following immediately upon some experience of intense psychic distress. On the other hand it carries an implicit argument for an aesthetic program in which phenomena are prized for their elemental, primary qualities. (The early Pre-Raphaelite ideal of "truth to nature" points in this direction.) The programmatic character of this kind of work is especially clear when the climactic stanzas introduce a potential for symbolic reading (via the trinitarian possibilities opened by a flower with "three cups in one"). The final stanza short-circuits the religious-symbolic reading, however, by insisting that, in crucial human moments, an ultimate Wisdom will be found in simple facticities. The Ruskinian connections to this kind of thought are clear.

SONG IX. THE HONEYSUCKLE

Composed 1853, first printed among the *HL* "Songs" in the 1870 *Poems,* later collected separately. The poem is an erotic parable, much in the manner of certain of Blake's *Songs*—for instance, "My Pretty Rose Tree" and "The Garden of Love." One might, as well, recall Wordsworth's "Nutting."

SONG X. A YOUNG FIR-WOOD

Composed 1850, first printed among the *HL* "Songs" in the 1870 *Poems,* later collected separately. Like "The Honeysuckle," this is a parable poem. The theme is in this case not love but mortality.

SONG XI. THE SEA-LIMITS

Composed 1849 as one of Rossetti's travel poems and then headed "At Boulogne. Upon the Cliffs: Noon," a distinctly Pre-Raphaelite title. First printed in the 1870 *Poems* as the concluding poem of the "Songs" in *HL,* and collected separately thereafter. Like the previous two poems this is a parable. Its subject is not love or mortality, however, but unity-of-being.

PART 3. SONNETS FOR PICTURES AND OTHER SONNETS

FOR "OUR LADY OF THE ROCKS" BY LEONARDO DA VINCI

Composed in 1848, first printed in the 1870 *Poems,* collected thereafter. Placed as it is, at the head of the final section of the 1870 volume (the "Sonnets for Pictures"), the poem inevitably recalls the first poem in the volume, "The Blessed Damozel." That bibliographical rhyme urges the reader to read this text, and its Madonna figure, in the context of the book as a whole, where the Beloved Woman—with all her symbolic meanings—is the organizing focus of attention. The picture referenced is not the one in the Louvre, but the one in the National Gallery in London.

Behind this sonnet stands the famous Pauline text (1 Corinthians 13:12): "For now we see through a glass, darkly, but then face to face." Rossetti uses this text to construct a statement about art as a glass through which to represent and view the occult order of things that are the ground of a religious experience. In Rossetti's reading, the picture is an occult construction, all of its representational forms dark and difficult. Rossetti's presentation follows Vasari more closely than one might expect: in his *Lives of the Painters* Vasari comments that Leonardo's success culminated in "paintings [that] were wholly devoid of light and the subjects looked as if they were being seen by night" (Penguin Classics edition [1965], p. 261).

13. "Whose" may refer to the Lord or to each spirit, and the subject of the verb "extols" is ambiguous.

FOR A VENETIAN PASTORAL BY GIORGIONE (IN THE LOUVRE)

Composed in Paris, 1849, first published in the *Germ*, no. 4 (30 April 1850), much revised for the 1870 *Poems,* collected thereafter. The picture, now regarded as Titian's, generally goes by the title *Fête Champêtre* (or *Pastorale*). The sonnet is very Keatsian in its appreciation of art, or aesthetic space, as emblematic of an "immortality" unavailable to flesh and blood humans. As in the "Ode on a Grecian Urn," here Rossetti suggests that the painting's figures, in particular the woman dipping the water pitcher, seem half-conscious of their aesthetic condition. To the degree that the woman is conscious, she recalls the Blessed Damozel, whose emparadised state is transacted by a melancholy that arises because her lover is not with her. In this sonnet the woman's purely imaginative status refines the textual melancholy to an exquisite degree.

1. I.e., the summer solstice, but also more figuratively a moment seen as both liminal and immobilized.

FOR AN ALLEGORICAL DANCE OF WOMEN BY ANDREA MANTEGNA (IN THE LOUVRE)

Composed in Paris, 1849, first published in the *Germ*, no. 4 (30 April 1850), much revised for the 1870 *Poems,* collected thereafter. The painting is Mantegna's *Mars et Vénus dit le Parnasse*. As Rossetti's note to the *Germ* text states, the "modern spectator may seek vainly to interpret" the painting, even though—paradoxically—"its meaning filleth it." As an interpretation of the picture, then, Rossetti's sonnet represents this interpretive failure, which culminates in the last two lines, which have the rhetorical form of a definite "meaning" (allegorical). But those lines are themselves only formally determinate (like the rest of the sonnet, like Mantegna's painting). They do not fix a specific "meaning," they define the difference between the knowledge opened through artistic acts and the knowledge prized by interpreters, whether positivist or hermeneutical. The play of language in lines 1–3 is crucial and pivots on the double meaning of "frame." Depending on how we take that word, we will read the lines as saying that (a) the unheard music governing the dance rang through Mantegna's body and resulted in this great picture, the execution of which involved him in an experience of profound conceptual awareness; (b) Mantegna embodied the unheard music that governs the dance in this picture, and when he himself saw what he had painted he experienced an understanding of ultimate meaning. Note that in either case Rossetti is emphasizing the cognitive power of pictorial forms of expression.

title. Rossetti's note in the *Germ* text reads: "It is necessary to mention, that this picture would appear to have been in the artist's mind an allegory, which the modern spectator may seek vainly to interpret."
2. The sonnet is equivocal about which "meaning" is meant here: whether it be the meaning of whatever vision or idea initially led Mantegna to make his painting, or the meaning of the painting itself; music: i.e., the (unapparent but implicit) music that orders the "Allegorical Dance of Women."

3. frame: a typical Rossettian wordplay; he imagines Mantegna being physically shaken by the music (and vision) and also by the act of looking at his own painting.

11. The pronoun has multiple references: to the dance, to the "thought," and to the painting itself.

FOR "RUGGIERO AND ANGELICA" BY INGRES

Composed 1849 in Paris, first published in the *Germ,* no. 4 (30 April 1850), included in the 1870 *Poems,* collected thereafter. The painting is the version now in the Louvre, though Rossetti saw it in the Luxembourg Palace. These sonnets—and in particular the first—exemplify Rossetti's peculiar gift for turning various types of words (especially nouns, verbs, and adjectives) into a "picturesque" state, so that different syntactic forms acquire the qualities of other forms. Terms like "harsh" and "shrewd" here operate with a certain nominal force, as does the verb "ramps"; and of course the noun "salt" is forced to operate in adjectival form. The startling words "geomaunt and teraphim" epitomize the sophistication of the treatment: these are nouns, but their substantive elements are so recondite that they become, as has often been noted, atmospheric and adjectival in their primary syntactic function. The sonnets derive from Ariosto's *Orlando Furioso,* canto X, as does the painting. The second sonnet is not a verbal rendering of the pictorial details but a report on the emotional and psychic content of the scene (a) as it is experienced by Angelica, and (b) as Angelica's experience is sympathetically recreated by the poet. Closer to Ariosto than to Ingres, it argues that interpretation is best undertaken as an act of imagination. That the scene represents a threat of rape scarcely needs to be said: Rossetti's gothic details in the octave are meant to stand as an objective correlative for the psychic catastrophe being undergone (by Angelica, but through her by the viewer/reader as well). Indeed, the textual injunctions in the octave appear to signal an observer's attitude to the painting. Seen in this way, the sestet then becomes a reflection on the aesthetic repose that (in Rossetti's argument of images here) one ought to realize as a function of even the most thrilling and energetic work of art. Seen in another (sexual) way, it represents a kind of postcoital lassitude; and it hardly needs mentioning that the poem is setting in the reader's way a series of disturbing and even outrageous complications. It is important to see, for example, that a certain equation is being drawn in Rossetti's re-presentation between Ruggiero and the orc.

I

4. geomaunt: one who practices divination by use of lines and figures; teraphim: idols or images (in particular household gods) used for purposes of divination in the Near East.

12. thrills: Rossetti plainly works this word for its primary (though now and in Rossetti's day unusual) meaning, "To bore, pierce, penetrate," and also for its more common meaning, "To feel . . . a thrill of emotion" (OED).

II

2. Draw: the most notable of Rossetti's worked words. The pun functions as an important device for connecting Angelica's (psychic) state with the reader/viewer's sympathetic response.

14. This image distinctly recalls the conclusion, and in particular the final line, of "Nuptial Sleep."

FOR "THE WINE OF CIRCE" BY EDWARD BURNE-JONES

Composed March 1870 and printed in the 1870 *Poems,* collected thereafter. Like Ruskin, Rossetti admired this picture greatly, but his sense of it is much more stern than the one Ruskin developed in *Munera Pulveris* (which came out in articles in *Fraser's* in 1862–63). Ruskin contrasts Circe ("pure Animal life . . . full vital pleasure") with the Sirens, who represent avarice. Rossetti's view is close to this, but his sense of the intimate relation between Soul's Beauty and Body's Beauty clearly leads him to a darker sense of Circe's enchanting powers (and hence to a darker view of the power of art than Ruskin had).

5. Helios and Hecate: sun and moon, hence intimating the period of twilight. Circe was the daughter of Helios and the nymph Perse.

MARY'S GIRLHOOD (FOR A PICTURE)

First sonnet composed 1848, the second in 1849. The first sonnet was published initially in the *Catalogue of the Association for Promoting the Free Exhibition of Modern Art. Gallery,* Hyde Park Corner (1849) as part of catalogue entry 368 for the picture Rossetti had exhibited (*The Girlhood of Mary Virgin,* 1848–49, his first important painting). The sonnet was revised and printed again in the 1870 *Poems* and collected thereafter. The second sonnet was first published by William Sharp in his 1882 study of Rossetti's works and collected thereafter. Rossetti apparently had both sonnets printed on a gold leaf that he attached to the frame of his picture in 1849, but this leaf seems no longer extant. These important sonnets, which involve Rossetti's first double work, are, like the painting to which they refer, consciously designed to suggest anachronism. The rhetorical impulse behind the work is pastiche, and the intellectual point of the pastiche is to dramatize the historical differential separating the contemporary Victorian world from the medieval ethos evoked through the pastiche. Like "Hand and Soul," the sonnets stand at the center of Rossetti's early programmatic ideas and plans for a renovation of poetical and artistic practise. The program is most succinctly defined in the first of the "Old and New Art" sonnets (also written in 1848–49 but not published until 1870). All such work emerges from an acute sense of the belated and excessively personal/commercial character of current art and poetry. Rossetti turns to medieval and primitive models as an artistic rather than a religious move. The example of such work means to promote an alternative to the "soulless self-reflections of man's skill" ("St. Luke the Painter," line 11) that characterize the traditions of Renaissance-inspired art descending to the present of Rossetti's period. Note that in the second sonnet iconography as such is the subject. The text is thus not an interpretation of the Christian iconography deployed in the painting but a pastiche of what such an interpretation might have looked like if the painting were a primitive work.

THE PASSOVER IN THE HOLY FAMILY (FOR A DRAWING)

Composed in 1867 for a drawing Rossetti worked at in 1849–56; first published in the 1870 *Poems,* collected thereafter. Like the picture it attends upon, the poem centers in the iconographical symbolism of Christian typology. In this symbolic structure, events from the Old Testament prefigure New Testament events, as type to antitype. The system is ultimately founded on the Christian belief—derived from the Jewish idea of the Messiah—that Jesus' life fulfilled the Old Testament promises associated with the Messiah. An important background text to the sonnet is the first chapter of Luke, and in particular the Benedictus of Zacharias, which is one of the most commonly cited prefigurative texts in the New Testament. The ritual of the Passover is set forth in Exodus 12:1–13. In its Victorian context, where the primitive Christian attitudes necessarily clash with their more attenuated contemporary residues, the sestet of the sonnet strongly suggests that more is "prefigured" in the scene and the poem than the original symbolic system would have been aware of. Rossetti's poem is acutely conscious of cultural belatedness. As such, the foreboding attitudes represented in all three figures come to suggest not only the future life of Jesus, especially his crucifixion, but the drained state of culture in nineteenth-century England and Europe. The figure of the young Jesus is especially interesting, for the poem suggests that he may be already aware of the death that lies in store for him. That typological situation in the Christian mythos turns the boy Jesus into a "type" of Rossetti, the contemporary artist who experiences the cultural death suggested in the poem.

title. Rossetti's note in the 1870 *Poems* (reprinted in this volume) explicates the picture's essential narrative features.

1–2. That is to say, the feast of the Passover prefigures the sacrificial death of Jesus, the event that brings about the new day of the Messiah also prefigured in the Passover.

2–4. Exodus 12:7, 11, 22.

12. Zacharias is the father of St. John the Baptist.

12–13. John 1:27.

MARY MAGDALENE AT THE DOOR OF SIMON THE PHARISEE
(FOR A DRAWING)

Composed in 1869 for a drawing Rossetti first executed in 1853 and reworked at various times be-tween 1853 and 1859; first published in the 1870 *Poems,* collected thereafter. The textual pivot for both the poem and the related drawing is the word "draws" (line 10), a key example of one of Rossetti's most characteristic wordplays. The word shows that this Magdalene is an artistic crea-ture who figures centrally in an argument Rossetti is making about an aesthetic ideal. The argu-ment is visibly instantiated in the drawing as a collision between two styles of representation: a realist style here associated with the street and its extreme pictorial recession; and an iconic style associated with the head of Jesus. The latter, aggressively "out of drawing," enters the picture as a recollection of primitivist pictorial methods. Rossetti and the other Pre-Raphaelites had been attacked, when they first appeared on the scene in the early 1850s, for their ignorance of the rules of perspective. The truth, of course, was that they wanted to call into question the authority of those rules and to argue the expressive power of more primitive styles. Rossetti in particular as-sociated the iconic style with the power of art to transcend normalized reality. The general liter-ary context for the sonnet is the gospel of Luke, chapter 7 (especially verses 36–47).

CASSANDRA (FOR A DRAWING)

Rossetti wrote the sonnet pair in 1869 for a drawing he made in 1860–61; first published in the 1870 *Poems,* collected thereafter. His inspiration for the drawing was George Meredith's poem "Cassandra" (and beyond that of course *The Iliad*). Like Tennyson, Rossetti read the myth of Troy as a prophetic allegory that bore ominous contemporary political meanings. The sonnets' placement in the 1870 *Poems* emphasizes a political significance: they form a group with "Venus Verticordia," "Pandora," and "On Refusal of Aid Between Nations."

VENUS VERTICORDIA (FOR A PICTURE)

Composed in 1868 for a drawing Rossetti made in 1863; first published in the 1870 *Poems,* col-lected thereafter. Rossetti's brother persuaded him to change the title of the poem to "Venus" in its 1870 printing. "Verticordia" referred, he said, to the Venus who turned hearts away from il-licit love to "cultivate chastity," but Rossetti's Venus clearly incorporated both Uranian and Pan-demian features. Rossetti returned to his more ambiguous title when he reprinted the poem in 1881. A key to negotiating its ambiguity lies in the double reference made by the apple held by Venus. It suggests both the apple of discord and the apple of the tree of knowledge: as if to say that whereas Paris gave it to Venus as a sign of her beauty, Eve offered it back as a sign of (for-bidden) knowledge. In each case a disaster followed. But in the Judeo-Christian mythos, the dis-aster occurs as a *felix culpa*. Rossetti's syncretic approach to myth here works to suggest, or even argue, a possible relation between beauty and knowledge—indeed, to suggest that a moral re-demption of physical love can be realized and understood when sensuous beauty comes to us in the forms of art. So while this work represents a prophetic insight into cultural disaster, it also intimates that a grace may operate through such legendary disasters. This grace comes about when an artistic practice reconsiders and represents the material. The grace of works like "Venus Verticordia," with their dark beauties and erotic challenges, emerges through the knowledge that they bring. In the most literal sense, such works, as works of art, "cultivate chastity" precisely by turning both their subjects and their audiences toward, and into, art. (In these respects the son-net clearly works in close relation with the two sonnets that surround it in the 1870 *Poems*—"Cas-sandra" and "Pandora.")

11. Phrygian boy: Adonis.

PANDORA (FOR A PICTURE)

Composed in 1869 for a drawing Rossetti made in 1868; first published in the 1870 *Poems*, collected thereafter. That the sonnet is an allegory for the situation of art as Rossetti saw it is suggested by the poet's source text, Lemprière's *Classical Dictionary* entry for Pandora ("the All-Gifted"): "She was made from clay by Vulcan, at the request of Jupiter, who wished to punish the impiety and artifice of Prometheus by giving him a wife. When this woman of clay had been made by the artist . . . all the gods vied in making her presents. . . . Jupiter, after this, gave her a beautiful box which she was ordered to present to the man who married her; and by the commission of the god, Mercury conducted her to Prometheus. The artful mortal was sensible of the deceit and . . . he sent away Pandora. . . . His brother Epimetheus . . . married Pandora, and when he opened the box which she presented to him, there issued from it a multitude of evils and distempers which dispersed themselves all over the world. . . . Hope was the only one who remained at the bottom of the box, and it is she alone who has the wonderful power of easing the labours of man, and of rendering his troubles and sorrows less painful in life."

5–8. The oblique allusion here is to the Judgment of Paris; Rossetti is suggesting that the all-gifted Pandora incarnates within herself the virtues and powers of Juno, Pallas Athene, and Venus. The sonnet's close connection to both "Cassandra" and "Venus Verticordia" is very clear at this point.

9–10. The *HL* sonnet "Vain Virtues" expands upon this thought.

14. This is both "The One Hope" of *HL*'s concluding sonnet, and the Hope left at the bottom of Pandora's box (according to the legend).

ON REFUSAL OF AID BETWEEN NATIONS

Written 1849, first printed in the 1870 *Poems*, collected thereafter. This sonnet refers to the apathy with which other countries witnessed the national struggles of Italy and Hungary against Austria in 1848–49. The sonnet's placement in the 1870 *Poems* extends its political significance: it closes the group that includes "Cassandra," "Venus Verticordia," and "Pandora." Although the literal content of those sonnets is mythic, Rossetti read the Matter of Troy as a prophetic allegory with ominous contemporary political meanings. The image of selfish behavior as a general cultural malaise is powerfully realized.

ON THE "VITA NUOVA" OF DANTE

Written in 1852 to accompany Rossetti's translation of Dante's autobiography, it was first printed in the 1870 *Poems*, collected thereafter. Along with its companion piece, "Dantis Tenebrae," the sonnet locates a key moment in the 1870 *Poems:* when the relation between Rossetti's original poetry and his translation work is sharply defined. The figure of the child is crucial, suggesting Rossetti's artistic ideal of simplicity which is realized in stylistic forms (like pastiche and translation) that emphasize the authority of the origin. So in Rossetti's Dantean frame of reference, the "child" is a figure that idealizes the spirit of submission and humility sought with such difficult deliberation by the proud and talented Dante. Dante's greatness as a poet arises from the devotional character of his work, and Rossetti here adopts a similar devotional posture towards his greatest master.

5. threefold charm: the *Divina Commedia*. But the phrase also suggests that the idea of a trinitarian God may be taken as a poetical figure for a beloved woman. The term "threefold" also suggests, in general, a magical condition (e.g., the third charm is always the most powerful). Rossetti is himself the "third" in a line of descent from ideal origin and a subsequent human model and guide.

10–11. The sonnet at this point makes close and even explicit contact with the important theme of the child in *HL:* see especially "Pride of Youth," "Stillborn Love," "Newborn Death," and "Transfigured Life." The Dantean connection is made through the oblique reference to the fact that Dante first saw Beatrice (he says) when she was eight and he was nine years old (in 1274).

14. Matthew 19:14.

DANTIS TENEBRAE (IN MEMORY OF MY FATHER)

Composed in 1861, first printed in the 1870 *Poems,* collected thereafter. The poem of course feeds upon Dante's works as well as on Rossetti's father's lifelong scholarly involvement with Dante. The octave refers directly to Gabriele Rossetti's study *La Beatrice di Dante* (1842). The sonnet forms a pair with "On the 'Vita Nuova' of Dante." This sonnet's conclusion—where Rossetti's father is seen under the dominion of the night—lifts the darkness explored in the poem to a position of great (and decidedly ambiguous) power. Rossetti's father died in 1854.

title. The memory refers partly to his father's decision about Rossetti's significant name, but also specifically to Gabriele Rossetti's important writings on Dante. Rossetti's critical remarks on these works are often quoted, as if they had no influence upon the poet; but in fact both father and son, each in their distinctive ways, approached Dante through Neoplatonic modes of thought.

3–4. The lines glance at the famous Salutation of Beatrice in the *Vita Nuova*—the event that comes nine years after Dante's first encounter with her. But reference is also being made to the meeting of Dante with Beatrice after her death in *Purgatorio* XXX.

6. magical dark mysteries: the phrase glances back to the Tenebrae of the title.

6–8. These three lines recall, respectively, the gloomy regions of Dante's hell, his mount of purgatory, and his paradisal regions of the Blessed where heavenly song is met by the divine music of Dante's poetical response. Line 6 also glances at Rossetti's father's famous scholarly investigations of Dante and medieval Neoplatonic thought.

9. steep: a Dantean word recalling the arduous climb through the regions of the *Commedia;* Dante rings the changes on the verb *scendere* and its past participial *sceso,* which signifies a steep and precipitous incline.

A MATCH WITH THE MOON

Composed in 1854, first printed in the 1870 *Poems,* collected thereafter. The playful tone is notable, especially in the poem's position in the 1870 printing following the Dante sonnets. The poem's central move is to play a poetical game of similes with the moon, which comes here *as* a figure of imagination and *in* the figure of a woman (see the closing lines). The poem's light eroticism distinctly recalls (and modifies) the Soul's Beauty/Body's Beauty dichotomy that dominates Rossetti's work.

THE HOLY FAMILY, BY MICHELANGELO (IN THE NATIONAL GALLERY)

Composed in 1880, first printed in *Ballads and Sonnets* (1881). The painting—*Madonna and Child with St. John and Angels*—is not by Michelangelo but by the so-called Master of Manchester. As usual, Rossetti reads the painting for its contemporary significance. Like the painter, Rossetti understands that a final redemption "Still" remains to be realized, and that it is somehow—mysteriously—bound up with "the woman" who is the center of the picture. Unlike Eve, the Virgin here withholds the temptation of ultimate knowledge.

9. See Genesis 3:24 and Milton, *Paradise Lost,* book XII.

10–12. The Tree of Knowledge in Eden transforms to the "Tree" of Calvary, the crucifix, on which Christ dies to undo the work of the "Tempter." This event brings about the harrowing of Hell, where Christ descends at his death to lead forth the souls of the just.

14. See *Paradise Lost,* book XII, 148–50, 161.

FOR SPRING BY SANDRO BOTTICELLI (IN THE ACCADEMIA OF FLORENCE)

Composed in 1880, first printed in *Ballads and Sonnets* (1881). Glossing the famous *Primavera,* the sonnet reflects Rossetti's strong admiration for Botticelli's work. In 1867 he bought a portrait ascribed to the master himself. As the first and last lines indicate, the poem is Rossetti's version of the theme famously rendered in Swinburne's "A Vision of Spring in Winter." Viewing this picture from his wintry present, Rossetti redoubles the ambiguities in the painting's masque, as the word "here" (line 13) indicates. The central "Lady" (line 10), Venus, epitomizes these ambiguities, as all of Rossetti's works indicate. The sonnet should be compared with the other late sonnets "Fiammetta," "A Sea-Spell," "Proserpina," and "Astarte Syriaca."

13. Dead Springs: an interesting example of Rossetti's "worked" language. The wordplay suggests that the picture is not just an allegory of spring, it is an embodiment of an artistic source or origin.

"FOUND" (FOR A PICTURE)

Composed in 1881, first printed in *Ballads and Sonnets* (1881). The sonnet is "for" Rossetti's famous (unfinished) oil painting of the same title, which he began in 1853–54. The picture represents the climactic moment of a countryman's search for his sweetheart, who has become a prostitute in London. The sentimental literature dealing with this double work's story-picture is very large. Goldsmith's *Deserted Village* (lines 325–36) is a classic point of reference, but Rossetti seems to have been most immediately inspired by William Bell Scott's "Rosabell." Coming so late to the picture, the sonnet acquires a singularly personal significance, as if it were a commentary on Rossetti's art in general, which he felt he had prostituted for the sake of worldly success.

1. Quoting the first line of Keats's sonnet "To Homer."

A SEA-SPELL (FOR A PICTURE)

Composed in 1869, first published in *Ballads and Sonnets* (1881) as the textual double of the painting he executed in 1877. Rossetti's brother described the picture thus: "The idea is that of a Siren, or Sea-Fairy, whose lute summons a sea-bird to listen, and whose song will soon prove fatal to some fascinated mariner." The work has much in common with "The Orchard Pit" and of course connects to Rossetti's many images of fatal ladies. The sonnet recalls as well Swinburne's "To a Seamew," which also identifies the poet/artist with a seabird.

7. planisphere: Rossetti typically works this word for its suggestiveness; it means, literally, a polar projection.

FIAMMETTA (FOR A PICTURE)

Composed in 1878 for Rossetti's just completed picture *A Vision of Fiammetta;* first printed in the *Athenæum,* 5 October 1878, collected in the 1881 *Ballads and Sonnets.* Although the relation between Boccaccio and Fiammetta is, like that between Petrarch and Laura, fundamentally a literary one, there has been a long-standing belief in the historicity of the lady, and while current scholarship discounts this tradition, Rossetti adhered to it, as he did to the historical reality of Beatrice. The Boccaccio/Fiammetta relation is most important for Rossetti's work because it sets a model for a secondary pursuit of Dante's primary idea and ideal of Beatrice. It is more important than the Petrarch/Laura relation exactly because, as all scholars agree, Laura was primarily a literary and aesthetic figure, not Petrarch's actual beloved. Rossetti's translations from Boccaccio's sonnets for Fiammetta are important related texts.

THE DAY-DREAM (FOR A PICTURE)

Composed in 1880 for Rossetti's just completed painting, printed in the 1881 *Ballads and Sonnets.* Jane Morris sat for the picture, and it is one of Rossetti's best portraits of her. Both picture and sonnet reflect, and reflect upon, the vicissitudes of beauty and of the artist's attachment to beauty. The poignant tone develops from a structure of present tenses borne down by a belated perspective, a spring attenuated by dream and haunted by its own departure. Phrases like "Still bear" and "Still the leaves come new" define the sonnet's ominous sadness. What flourishes in the poem are figures of speech rather than natural forms, an effect epitomized in the splendid opening two lines of the sestet.

ASTARTE SYRIACA (FOR A PICTURE)

Composed in 1877 for Rossetti's just completed painting (begun in 1875), printed in the 1881 *Ballads and Sonnets*. Once again, Jane Morris is the focus of both poem and picture. The sonnet opens with an allusion to the Book of Revelation 17:5. As Clarence Fry (who purchased the painting) observed in a letter to Rossetti, this reference could easily scandalize a traditional Christian, for it refers to "Babylon the Great, Mother of harlots and abominations of the earth" (letter to Rossetti of 10 March 1877). In Rossetti's syncretic, Blakean reading of Revelation, however, this figure is the double of the "woman clothed with the sun" of Revelation 12:1. So the first line announces Rossetti's revisionary revelation that identifies otherwise demonic and divine orders. The argument is the same as Rossetti's famous "Thy soul I know not from thy body, nor / Thee from myself, neither our love from God" (see "Heart's Hope").

The close of the octave touches on another key idea: that the Pythagorean music of the spheres becomes realized in one's encounter with Astarte. Notable here is Rossetti's startling use (or invention) of the expression "wean . . . to." That verb is regularly used with the preposition "from"; "to" here all but reverses the idea of deprivation that lies at the heart of the word's meaning. The suggestion is thus developed that desire (as a state of longing and deprivation) constitutes as well a condition for realizing an encounter with ideal orders.

Finally, the sestet develops a remarkable series of ideas and images that take a performative view of art and the visions it calls into being. The double meaning in the syntax of lines 9–11 argues that Astarte's "ministers," figured in the picture, are any act of artistic creation that operates with a performative or revelatory purpose. In this respect they carry out an action analogous to Astarte's primary agency. They are emblemized in line 13: "Amulet, talisman, and oracle" are not simply decorative terms for "symbol," they are three distinctive pieces of cultic—that is to say, magical—religious machinery.

1. Compare the similar openings for the poems on two pictures by Memmeling, "For a Virgin and Child, by Hans Memmeling (In the Academy of Bruges)" and "For a Marriage of St. Katherine, by the same (In the Hospital of St. John at Bruges)."

PROSERPINA (FOR A PICTURE)

Composed in 1872 for the first of a series of copies of the picture that Rossetti made during the 1870s, all portraits of Jane Morris; printed in the 1881 *Ballads and Sonnets*. This is in fact something more than a double work. Rossetti wrote an accompanying sonnet in Italian and then translated the sonnet into English. He also wrote a prose ekphrasis of the picture. The sonnet is remarkable in several ways. It is the only sonnet for a picture that gives the central subject's interior monologue: normally Rossetti's sonnets for pictures carry remarks upon the picture by an observer of some kind. Even more notable, the poem clearly involves a late reprise on the theme and situation famously taken up in "The Blessed Damozel." Carried off to Hades from the fields of Enna in Sicily by an enamoured Pluto, Proserpine was subsequently doomed to remain there for half the year because (see line 5) she had eaten food in hell—in fact, the pomegranate pictured in her hand in Rossetti's painting. In this poem the blessed damozel's separation from her lover and her happiness is raised to an explicitly mythical level. The sestet develops an uncanny sense that Proserpine is listening for the sounds and signs of the very poem she herself appears to be authoring, and hence that the final line is giving us, as it were, Rossetti's own words, here reported back to us from the underworld. The entire double work complex thus argues that the function of art is to restore the connection between the severed worlds of life and imagination.

LA BELLA MANO (FOR A PICTURE)

Composed in 1875 for a just-completed oil portrait done in Rossetti's high Venetian manner, elaborately decorative. As with "Proserpina," Rossetti wrote the Italian sonnet first. First published in the *Atheneum* (28 August 1875), collected in *Ballads and Sonnets* (1881). The title recalls the fifteenth-century book of Petrarchan lyrics of the same title by Giusto de' Conti (1389–1449), one of Sigismundo Malatesta's court poets.

14. heart-handsel'd: i.e., her act is made auspicious because it expresses a heartfelt love.

PART 4. BALLADS AND LYRICS

ROSE MARY

Rossetti made a prose sketch of the story—which is entirely his invention—early, perhaps in the late 1840s, but he did not write the poem until 1871 when he was at Kelmscott with Jane Morris. The Beryl-Songs were written later, 1878–79. First printed in *Ballads and Sonnets,* collected thereafter, though Rossetti said that he wanted to remove the songs in any later editions. The poem has various debts to the tradition of gothic fiction, in particular to the tales of E. T. A. Hoffman and to the *Arabian Nights* (the Lane translation). Christina Rossetti's "Goblin Market" tells an analogous story, but Coleridge's "Christabel" is probably the single most important work standing behind Rossetti's strange ballad, which seems an effort to complete Coleridge's famous fragment (in several senses). In conceptual terms, then, the poem is one of Rossetti's most important—an effort to work out a tale of redemption in a world where all the characters, including the redeemer, are sinners. The story also involves an investigation of the function of art, for the Beryl-stone is clearly a figural embodiment of art and poetry as conceived in terms of Romantic Imagination. The resolution offered in the poem is interesting precisely because it is so equivocal. When Rose Mary destroys the stone's magical powers, the spirits of evil are not eliminated—indeed, they flee abroad into the world. Rose Mary's act emblemizes a judgment on the illusions of Romantic Imagination. The poem's moral—an idea that preoccupies nearly all of Rossetti's work—centers in the need for truth telling and clarity of mind in a world riven by falsehood, secret fears, and hypocrisies.

Part I

51–65. A key passage. Rose Mary's mother explains how the powers of the stone function and prays that evil may not have its way. The stone's magic is founded in the Crusaders' spilling of "Moslem blood" and the subsequent Christian possession of the stone. If the magic is summoned by anyone but a sinless person, however, it will work against the user. In Rossetti's tale, of course, no such spotless person exists—nor, it is implied, *could* exist. The whole poem pivots around that situation.

98. wage: to travel through.

Part II

Beryl-Song 23. Referring to the sinful love of Rose Mary and Sir James.
Beryl-Song 27–30. The figure recalls Paolo and Francesca in hell.
Beryl-Song 36–37. Perhaps recalling Coleridge's "Rime of the Ancient Mariner," line 232.

Part III

138. Compare "Aspecta Medusa."

151. three times: Once by Muslim black magic, once by Christian hypocrisy, the third time by Rose Mary.

161. The stone's "Good Spirit," whose purposes are realized when the stone is destroyed.

171–85. The climax of the tale. Involved here is a benevolent recasting of the Paolo and Francesca story as well as Rossetti's own "Sister Helen."

193. levin: lightning.

THE WHITE SHIP

Composed early in 1881, printed in *Ballads and Sonnets,* collected thereafter. The ballad is quite successful, sophisticating the traditional ballad in ways that preserve the aura of the latter. Rossetti manages this by the spare and simple narrative, on one hand, and by the regulated irregularities in the meter and linear rhythms. Thus the poem's psychological impact depends greatly on Rossetti's management of the text's abstract forms. The figures that come before us—Berold, "the fair boy dressed in black," the king, his son, Fitz-Stephen, etc.—all are cast as in a tableau. This procedure torques the ballad into a symbolistic poem whose import—whose contemporary or even personal meaning—hovers about the ballad in elusive and suggestive ways. Rossetti took most of his materials from Ordericus Vitalis (1075–1143), *Ecclesiastical History* (book 12, chaps. 25–26), but some were drawn from Henry, Archdeacon of Huntingdon (1084–1155), *History of the English People,* and William of Malmesbury (d. 1143), *Chronicle of the Kings of England.* The ship actually sailed from Barfleur, not Harfleur.

8. his son: William.
14. Henry Beauclerc.
17. elder brother: Robert, captured by the barons in 1106.
50. daughter: Mathilda.
89. The ship struck the rocks near Raz de Gatteville, north of Barfleur.
215. Probably Theobald, Count of Blois.

SOOTHSAY

Composed initially in 1871, much augmented in 1880; first printed in *Ballads and Sonnets,* collected thereafter. Pater much admired this philosophical work. It is closely related to "The Cloud Confines," another reflective and philosophical poem written at the same time. Rossetti's resentment at Buchanan's attack on his work is a running subtext.

78–84. Recalls Dante's *Paradiso* XIX, 79–81.

SPHERAL CHANGE

Composed in 1881, first printed in *Ballads and Sonnets,* collected thereafter. The poem should be compared with "Insomnia," written at about the same time. Its biographical relevance—a poem shadowed by Rossetti's memory of his dead wife—seems clear.

SUNSET WINGS

Composed in 1871, first printed in the *Athenæum* (24 May 1873), then in *Ballads and Sonnets.* The poem focuses on a flight pattern of starlings that Rossetti noticed during his sojourns at Kelmscott. The birds seem invested with some mysterious dynamic form, as if under some significant and even signifying agency. Rossetti's explanatory similes are second-order figural forms that rhyme with the action of the birds.

INSOMNIA

Composed in 1881, first printed in *Ballads and Sonnets,* collected thereafter. Compare "Spheral Change."

THE CLOUD CONFINES

Composed in 1871, first printed in the *Fortnightly Review* (1 January 1872), printed again in *Ballads and Sonnets,* collected thereafter. Compare "Soothsay." The poem expresses Rossetti's theory of death not "of annihilation but of absorption": as he put it in a letter to William Bell Scott, "a real retributive future for the special atom of life to be re-embodied (if so it were) in a world which its own former identity had helped to fashion for pain or pleasure."

PART 5. THE EARLY ITALIAN POETS

Rossetti worked on these translations from 1845 to 1874, with the main effort coming early, between about 1845and 1850. The work was first published in late 1861 as *The Early Italian Poets* and reissued in 1874 in a revised and rearranged format as *Dante and His Circle*. They are the first attempt in English at a comprehensive representation of *stil novo* Italian poetry, especially Dante's, along with its Sicilian and other precursors. The influence of these translations was immense, not least of all on the Modernists. In developing English equivalences for his Italian texts, Rossetti turned hendecasyllables into iambic pentameters and septenarii into iambic trimeters. He flattened the accentual urgencies of English by the frequent use of simple, even monosyllabic, words; by working within a slightly antique lexicon; and by creating a syntactic structure that continually loops back upon itself, slowing the progress of the verse and producing a peculiar equivalent of Italian syllabic verse.

The poems have sometimes been faulted for their translational inaccuracies. In this connection two matters are relevant: first, Rossetti's source texts were often exceedingly corrupt; second, like the work of his imitator Ezra Pound, Rossetti's was an act of contemporary aesthetic (re)incarnation. These are late-nineteenth-century poems whose vitality rests in their ability to raise the dead—or more accurately, to create the poetic illusion that the dead can be raised. The contemporaneity of the poems is especially clear in a sonnet like "Of a consecrated Image resembling his Lady" ("Guido, an image of my lady dwells"), from Cavalcanti.

Not often noted is the significant presence of the work of Cecco Angiolieri in Rossetti's collections. In 1861 he included twenty-two poems he thought were by Cecco, and he added another in 1874 (and he kept back yet another he had translated—see below, "In Absence of Becchina"). Only Dante and Cavalcanti have more poems in the two collections, which tells a great deal about Rossetti's poetical interests. Cecco's raw wit, highly personal style, and colloquial manner were unpleasing to traditional Italian scholars, and it was not until the twentieth century that his notable poetic virtues were given proper attention. Indeed, Rossetti's admiration for Cecco is yet another instance of his unusually advanced aesthetic taste—a quality of his character we know very well from his work in English but that is less often remarked in relation to his work with Italian writers.

The order of the materials here is from the 1861 edition, but the texts are those of 1874.

PREFACE TO THE FIRST EDITION

239.12. in my first division: the "Poets before Dante," as Rossetti designated them in 1861.

CANZONE. OF THE GENTLE HEART (GUIDO GUINICELLI)

This and the next poem, "Of His Lady in Heaven," are excellent examples of Rossetti's translational effort to contrive English equivalents of thirteenth-century Italian poems. Notable here is Rossetti's rhyme scheme, which adheres to the *coblas capfinidas* of the famous original.

OF HIS LADY, AND OF HER PORTRAIT (JACOPO DA LENTINO)

The poem reflects Rossetti's commitment to the idea of the "double work of art," and it recalls several of Rossetti's key works: "Hand and Soul," "Saint Agnes of Intercession," and especially "On Mary's Portrait Which I Painted Six Years Ago."

CANZONE. OF HIS DEAD LADY (GIACOMO PUGLIESI)

Rossetti's source text for this poem was highly imperfect. In a prose note on Pugliesi and his work, Rossetti called this the only Italian poem on a lady's death written before Dante. But that idea is not at all correct.

HOW HE DREAMS OF HIS LADY (BONAGGIUNTO URBICIANI, DA LUCCA)

The translation intersects with ideas and even phrasings that come out in Rossetti's original poetry. Compare, e.g., "Love's Nocturne" or the sestet of "A Superscription." Modern scholars do not assign the original poem to Bonaggiunto, and it remains anonymous.

HIS PORTRAIT OF HIS LADY, ANGIOLA OF VERONA (FAZIO DEGLI UBERTI)

This translation is nearly as central a work in Rossetti's corpus as "The Blessed Damozel." The iconograph of "The Rossetti Woman" is fully articulated in this text, but even more important is the ambiguity—enforced in the title Rossetti supplied for his translation—about the reference of the word "Portrait." In one sense the portrait is the canzone; in another the canzone references a pictorial object: either a literal painting (like Rossetti's own related picture *Fazio's Mistress*, which "doubles" this poem) or the lady herself metaphorically imagined as an image. That way of thinking about his art, pictorial as well as textual, as well as his art's relation to the donne it represents, is foundational and provides the structure supporting all of Rossetti's double works.

THE NEW LIFE (DANTE ALIGHIERI)

The *Vita Nuova* is the organizing center for Rossetti's early Italian translations and is in many ways the inspirational source for all of Rossetti's work, literary and artistic both. From Dante's symbolistic autobiography springs Rossetti's new artistic life. Distinctly about Rossetti himself, this work constructs a myth of imaginative identification. Rossetti reads the original as if it were a key part of the book of his cultural memory that he has been called, in the nineteenth century, to rewrite and recopy. The translation is a rite of passage that sets Rossetti on the path of a new existence centered in a devotional pursuit of art and beauty. When he completed the work around 1850, he marked the event by changing his baptismal name from Gabriel Charles Dante to Dante Gabriel.

Dante's autobiography is a recollective reconstruction, written between 1292 and 1295, of events that occurred earlier—between 1274, when he first saw Beatrice, and 1290, when she died. The *Vita Nuova*'s account connects the writing of certain poems with specific events, but we know, as Rossetti knew, that the poems in the book were not all written, originally, as part of the narrative in which they are placed. Dante sometimes applies poems to events in his narrative that were written for different reasons and under other circumstances than those given in the story. That kind of appropriation is germane to Dante's project, which argues the presence of a prevenient spiritual order in Dante's life. His personal history is shadowed by divine purposes and a general economy of grace.

Rossetti is attracted to Dante's project exactly because it draws a relation between poetic practice and historical agency. The *Vita Nuova* argues that poetry, if properly executed, can cooperate with the divine economy that pervades historical events—indeed, can escape the quotidian order to participate directly in this transhistorical order. In that frame of reference, Rossetti's "New Life" texts are second-order acts of poetic "cooperation"—more akin to ritual acts of magic than to Romantic acts of self-expression. The magical purpose is to call back from the dead the power—Rossetti called it the "beauty"—of Dante's poetry. The focus of the summons is Dante and his poetic contemporaries, not God, just as the ultimate object is not religious, but cultural, redemption. "The New Life" is a secular *Imitatio Christi*. Indeed, for Rossetti it is the one far off sublime event to which the whole of Dante's creation moved.

Below are given a set of commentaries on a selection of Rossetti's "New Life" translations. They comprise a schematic reading of the autobiography as a whole in terms of certain key texts.

"To every heart which the sweet pain doth move"

Dante's opening sonnet is a reinterpretation of itself, for it is a poem written around 1283 under circumstances different from those under which it was placed in the *Vita Nuova* in 1292. It calls for yet other "true interpretations," and these came from a number of Dante's contemporaries, who wrote sonnets explaining Dante's. Rossetti's translation enters into that poetical scene as well. Notable are the translation's octave variances, which expand Dante's thought beyond the literal Italian. Rossetti is striving to replicate tonal qualities in the original—a certain decorous formality that pervades and indeed distinguishes Dante's style.

"A day agone, as I rode sullenly"

This is a riddle poem quite like the opening sonnet of the autobiography. Both examine the mysterious agency of Love, who is directing Dante's life in ways that he cannot always understand and that often bring pain and sorrow.

Most important is the way Rossetti "rhymes" the first and the final lines through the repetition of the word "gone." The word draws one's attention in line 1 because of the auditional play in the first three words (recalling certain similar effects in Keats, for instance, "Not to the sensual ear, but more endear'd"). With line 14 the word comes back to us in what Italian poets would call a *rima equivoca*. The move is important because of Dante's striking *rima equivoca* in lines 10 and 13 of his sonnet. Because this metrical device is so distinctively Italian rather than English, Rossetti's move "translates" it into an index or quasi-symbolic sign in his poem. It means to suggest that Dante's poem lives on, literally, in Rossetti's Victorian reprisal.

"All my thoughts always speak to me of Love"

The translation is as poetically successful as it is semantically free. Rossetti makes some fine turns on the Italian original—for instance in the opening six lines or even more spectacularly in line 11: "And lose myself in amorous wanderings." Special note should be made of the opening four words and that typical Rossettian move coming in the relation All/always (compare the opening of "A day agone, as I rode sullenly"). In this case the wit gains special force because of the thematic importance of the word "ways" so cunningly half-hidden from the eye.

The last two lines are recalling Beatrice's displeasure with Dante and her denial of her salutation: "Unto mine enemy I needs must pray, / My lady Pity, for the help she brings." But the paradoxical idea of Lady Pity as "mine enemy" is thematically important and suggests further meanings in Dante's text. Rossetti chooses the safest path here: a fairly literal translation.

"Even as the others mock, thou mockest me"

The central action of the poem, which comes in the sestet, carries an indirect allusion to "A day agone, as I rode sullenly," where Love disappears into some secret place within Dante himself. The "rout" of Dante's senses here thus leaves behind a remarkably ambiguous apparition of the poet—the "figura nova" ("strange semblances") of line 3 and again line 12 ("This makes my face to change / Into another's"). Dante's face is disfigured by his sorrow but this "disfigurement" conceals the secret presence of the god of Love in Dante. It scarcely needs remarking that, in the context, terms like "strange semblances" and "disfigurement" carry important, purely aesthetic, resonances.

The repetition of the word "face" in lines 4 and 12 is clearly deliberate. In both cases the translation deviates from the original text and the deviance signals Rossetti's effort to make his poem expose an important but inexplicit subject in the original sonnet: that Dante's facial "disfigurement" nonetheless, and paradoxically, mirrors the (Love) splendour reflected in Beatrice's "fair" face. That disfiguration then becomes an oblique index of the relation between Dante's poetry and its inspiring sources. And when this whole poetical dynamic falls into Rossetti's hands, it undergoes a further disfiguration, with Rossetti's sonnet.

Rossetti's source text for line 14 reads "de' discacciati" where the authorized reading is "de li scacciati." This misleads Rossetti away from Dante's striking final *figura* but does not spoil the English poem's special excellence.

"At whiles (yea oftentimes) I muse over"

The sonnet is stunning for its interpretive boldness and clarity. In the original everything hinges on the "spirto vivo solamente" (line 7), Dante's brilliant wordplay echoing "la mente" in line 1. The prose introduction underscores and prepares the reader for this key "pensero che parlava di questa donna"—specifically, in fact, Dante's own verse and the thought of writing of Beatrice in verse. As the canzone that follows makes clear, this sonnet's commitment to intellectual reflection signals what is involved in writing a love poetry that has transcended the subjectivity of its passion.

Rossetti's understanding of this poetical drama is very clear in lines 6 and 10, and particularly in the words "sign"and "art," which have no explicit equivalents in Dante. To translate this way is an act of "true interpretation," incarnating Dante's "spirto vivo"—what he will shortly reveal as "intelletto d'amore"—as the poetical act itself. For Dante, this act is bound up with a Christian scheme of redemption as it was reworked through the tradition of courtly love. For Rossetti, the act is modern and secular: an act of devotion to art *per se*.

The translation is also interesting for its metrical procedure. Line 1's final four syllables are not only startling, they make a signature for Rossetti's various efforts to flatten the effect of English stress-based verse. Line 6 marks another notable moment. Its ten single-syllable words take the breath from the English iambic line: "So that of all my life is left no sign." This device appears all over Rossetti's translations and is especially notable because of the variance from the Italian originals, where multisyllabic words abound.

"Ladies that have intelligence in love"
In this canzone Dante's poetry stands to Rossetti as Beatrice had stood to Dante. We see this when we reflect on the place of Dante's poem in the *Vita Nuova*. The elaborate *divisio* following the canzone reaches back to the prose passage introducing the canzone where Dante lays down his formula for a poetry of praise that lifts the Guinizzellian tradition to this new level. The key moment comes when Dante says, "dico che mia lingua parlò quasi come per se stessa mossa" ("I declare that my tongue spake as though by its own impulse"). The remark conceals a crucial play on the word "lingua," which signifies both Dante's own speech as well as his "mother tongue." We are introduced here to a sweet new style, Dante's poetry "in seconda persona"—the latter phrase in fact also involving a wordplay that signals the nonsubjective ground of Dante's "personal" poetry. The god of Love, according to this representation of the matter, authorizes Dante's verse.

Writing thus in his nineteenth-century post-Romantic context, Rossetti's translation involves an act of poetic ventriloquism very like Browning's in his dramatic monologues. But Browning had few resources for involving his subjectivity directly in the poetic action. Rossetti's translational model opens the possibility of an art of the "inner standing-point," as he called it, whereby the Romantic first person can be objectively introduced into the poetic field.

"Love and the gentle heart are one same thing"
This is an explication of the preceding canzone by way of Guinizzelli's famous canzone, also translated by Rossetti, "Within the gentle heart Love shelters him." The translation of line 3 ("Each, of itself, would be such life in death") stands out because it seems to have departed so far from Dante's Italian ("E così senza l'un l'altro esser osa"). But Rossetti is matching Dante's Italian allusion with his own English reference—in this case, to Coleridge and to the Romantic tradition of the organic poetical imagination. Dante's (and Rossetti's) argument for the intimate relation of form and matter (see Dante's *divisio* for this sonnet) has no force unless the "power [sustaining that relation] translates itself into act." That prose explanation from the *divisio* involves its own remarkable act of translation, for the Italian source of "translates itself" is "si riduce."

"Canst thou indeed be he that still would sing"
The fine wit of Dante's opening lines is difficult to render: "Se' tu colui, ch' hai trattato sovente / Di nostra donna" instantiates the style of writing "in seconda persona" by making the verb in the subordinate clause agree with "tu" rather than with "colui." The question is addressed to the preceding sonnet in the *Vita Nuova*, which is paired with this work. It asks the paired sonnet if it (or its voice?) is the same person (so to speak) as the one who addressed the ladies in the canzone "Ladies that have intelligence in love." Simply to ask that question in this way is to force attention to the poetry's stylistic and rhetorical program. Rossetti's awareness of the issues comes out most clearly when he departs from literal translation: in this case, for example, in line 4, "Thy visage might another witness bring." The elaborate construction, not in Dante, suggests that "another witness" might be this very sonnet, which is the sympathetic mirror of its paired sonnet spoken by the ambiguous "tu colui." The mistranslation—for it is that—in lines 5-6 ("And

wherefore is thy grief so sore a thing / That grieving thou mak'st others dolorous") underscores Rossetti's purpose here.

"I felt a spirit of love begin to stir"

Dante's prose introduction to this sonnet establishes its prefigurative character. He uses the discourse of prefiguration to forecast the coming of a life of love into his own life.

Rossetti's distinctively aesthetic reading of his source texts is never more apparent than it is here, for he turns Dante's poem into a sign-constellation prefiguring a second coming of the poetic imagination. In this reading the pronoun "I" simultaneously references Dante and Rossetti, forcing a correspondent mutation in the reference of the figure of Love, who now also signifies Dante. Rossetti's decision to translate "la mente" as "my memory" (line 12) flags his purpose, for the word recalls—in this strongly recollective moment—the "book of my memory" where the autobiography opened its narrative.

Dante's sonnet is one of the poems written before the *Vita Nuova* was conceived by Dante. That fact supplies yet another level of prefiguration to the original text, as it did for the opening sonnet of Dante's autobiography. In his major original work, *The House of Life,* Rossetti regularly takes poems written at one period and in one context and reworks them for new meanings by later putting them in different contexts. His model for doing this was almost certainly Dante and what he learned about Dante's poetic practices when he was translating the work of his Italian precursor.

"My lady looks so gentle and so pure"

This sonnet forms a pair with the next. Both are written—Dante's words are "con ragione" and "avendo . . . ragionamento"—to illustrate and *perform* the aesthetic program Dante sets forth in his prose. This is the program by which figurative and rhetorical language that is not strictly "realistic" is cultivated for transphenomenal ideas. So in this sonnet Beatrice seems "a creature sent from Heaven to stay / On earth, and show a miracle" (7–8). Even more dramatically, Beatrice's spiritual power is such that she inspires a poetry—this very poem, in fact—whose operations are essentially unexpressed and unapparent. This is a mute sonnet—"ogne lingua deven tremando muta" (it "has nought to say," line 3)—because its deep "ragione" functions beyond the order of physical expression. The argument gets sealed in the sonnet's last two lines, where Dante plays on the words "spirito" and "Sospira" to intimate an immaterial level of erotic response.

Rossetti's sonnet gives a distinctively aesthetic turn to that poetical economy, as we see in the final three lines where Rossetti consciously echoes Shelley's "Life of Life" lyric in *Prometheus Unbound* (II,5, 48–71, especially 48–49: "Life of Life! thy lips enkindle / With their love the breath between them"), which is itself a conscious recollection of this passage in Dante. Rossetti's "for ever" (line 14), which is not in his source, nonetheless captures perfectly, even performatively, the "spirit" of Dante's poetical argument.

"The eyes that weep for pity of the heart"

Although Rossetti's translation of the canzone reads "piteous" (line 71), he left the prose description that precedes the poem to read "pitiful" in all editions of this text. The slip would have been, originally, his brother's.

"Whatever while the thought comes over me"

The central event in this truncated canzone is purely textual—the angel reference in line 24. Immediately after Dante invokes that figural expression—according to the story being told here—the textual angels reappear in another medium, as if through an agency beyond Dante's conscious purposes. The import of the famous incident narrated here, of Dante caught drawing an angel by some unexpected Florentine visitors, lies concealed and anticipated in Dante's interrupted canzone.

The remarkable presentation of a secret spiritual ministry in Dante's life acquires a nineteenth-century Rossettian equivalence that seems to me scarcely less astonishing. The equation will remain unapparent, however, if one's attention is too narrowly focused—just as one won't see Beatrice's secret messaging if one stays within the text of Dante's incomplete canzone. The Rossettian "translation" becomes apparent as soon as Rossetti's "New Life" is viewed in terms of its three textual/historical states: the late 1840s (when it was written), 1860–61 (when it was first published), 1874 (when it was republished). The thirteenth-century action, as Rossetti came to see, would unfold itself in his own life (1) before he knew Elizabeth Siddal; (2) at the end of his life with her; (3) in the midst of his devotion to Jane Morris, Rossetti's "Donna della Finestra." In this sense Rossetti's "angel" is Dante, or (perhaps) the whole mythic constellation of Dante's life and works. Some such eventuality Rossetti clearly hoped to realize, though surely not in the dark form that it actually took.

"That lady of all gentle memories"

This sonnet completes the sequence of traumatized texts that began with "Stay with me now and listen to my sighs." It comes here in the narrative as the poem written to celebrate the first anniversary of the death of Beatrice, when Dante set himself to drawing angels. In terms of the action of the autobiography, the narrative shows Dante making a turn from his arrested state toward more deliberated action. This meaning, announced in Dante's two different acts of angel-drawing, is refigured in the sonnet's alternative commencements. Note that in the second commencement Dante, as if rethinking the first, says explicitly that Beatrice "led you to observe" the poet in his first, only half-conscious act of drawing. The acts of drawing and poem-making thus replicate each other as doubled events, the second in each case coming to repeat the first in a more self-conscious way. Because the second sonnet commencement refers back to the first act of drawing, the structural pattern reflects the order of the sonnet's quatrains, ABBA. It scarcely needs mentioning that Rossetti's own attachment to the "double work of art" gets a signal authorization in this Dantean event.

Rossetti's "lighted on my soul" (line 2) introduces a double meaning not in Dante, but one that seems especially apt for a poem so concerned with the idea of spiritual enlightenment. It is thus one of Rossetti's characteristically "interpretive" translational moments. The rendering of the sonnet's conclusion is more literal but equally effective in leaving open, as Dante does so carefully, the referent of the "noble intellect"; for of course Dante's own intellect has in a sense been "gone" since Beatrice left the poet. Dante's version of this double reference is altogether a more happy one, in several senses, than Rossetti's. In Dante the intellect is represented as having ascended to heaven ("oggi fa l'anno che nel ciel salisti"), whereas Rossetti's words inevitably carry a darker overtone.

"Mine eyes beheld the blessed pity spring"

This sonnet focuses the climactic sequence of the *Vita Nuova*, the episode of the Donna della Finestra when Dante turns back toward Beatrice with greater devotion than ever. Read in a Rossettian perspective, the Donna della Finestra episode makes its own uncanny forecast. Its four sonnets—besides this one, the sonnets "Love's pallor and the semblance of deep ruth," "The very bitter weeping that ye made," and "A gentle thought there is will often start"—all carry forward into the central texts of *HL*. The connection appears explicitly in line 11: "thine eyes' compassionate control" refers to the benignant look of the Donna della Finestra, but in *HL* that phrase comes to announce "The Portrait" and the countenance of that sequence's Beatrice figure, Elizabeth Siddal, not its Donna della Finestra, Jane Morris.

In the Donna della Finestra episode, Dante represents a final struggle between his Soul and his Heart. This struggle, for all the trouble it causes Dante, ultimately functions in a benevolent way in the economy of grace being celebrated in Dante's work. The benevolence appears subsequently as a condition of endless martyrdom for the soul whose commitments are ultimately toward divine realities; and the heart's Donna leads Dante to realize that martyrdom in the fullest possible way.

Rossetti understands this argument perfectly, as we see in his interpretive translation of the last two lines of this sonnet, which draw the expectable equations between the Donna, Beatrice, and Love: "'Lo! with this lady dwells the counterpart / Of the same Love who holds me weeping now.'" But the word "counterpart"—it has no Dantean equivalent—insinuates as well the set of distinctions and differences that Dante will also be working out through the whole of the Donna episode.

"A gentle thought there is will often start"

This sonnet captures the radical doubleness of Dante's original poem—indeed, it raises that doubleness to a more explicit level, as Rossetti regularly does in his reclamation of Dante. So various key locutions—for example, "secret self," "'twixt doubt and doubt," and "Love's messenger"—have no literal Dantean equivalents, though all perform equivalent functions. "Love's messenger" is perhaps most revealing in this regard since it picks up the angel theme that is so important in Dante's work.

An appreciation of the "strange art" of Rossetti's sonnet (that phrase also has no literal Dantean source) can be usefully sought in various poems and poem sequences in *HL*, where the strange art of the secret self is developed to such an extraordinary degree. Observing the nuances and ambiguities of a sonnet like "Life-in-Love," for example, not only illuminates this translation of Dante, it demonstrates how deeply Rossetti's reading of Dante's autobiography informs the English poet's work. Figural palimpsest is perhaps Rossetti's central poetic (and artistic) device, and in this sonnet we see that he has stolen this idea from Dante, or rather from his reading of Dante.

"Woe's me! by dint of all these sighs that come"

This sonnet shows Dante's restored integrity after his troubled passage through the Donna della Finestra texts. Rossetti replicates this by overtranslating the first two lines of the sestet. Besides introducing the wordplay "musings" (for Dante's "penseri"), Rossetti works Dante's text in several other important ways. Dante, for example, argues no causal relation between his "penseri" and his "sospir," as Rossetti does, nor is there any Dantean equivalent for Rossetti's "constant" (line 10). But Rossetti's poem insists on both of these points, so fundamental to Dante's general argument even if they aren't here specifically articulated.

The phrase "These musings" torques Rossetti's sonnet into a sharply reflexive condition, an effect heightened by rhyming "musings" with "Hearing" and thus building a clear structural parallel between the two final tercets. These formal relationships emphasize the agenting power of Dante's (and Rossetti's) verse and forecast the next chapter in the autobiography with its accompanying sonnet addressed to the pilgrim-folk passing through Florence. For while the sonnet says that Beatrice's "sweet name" (line 13) is heard continually in the poet's musings and sighs, we search the text in vain for visible or articulate signs of her. The name will come, unlooked for, in the next sonnet, generated from the desire expressed and brought to focus in this one.

"Ye pilgrim-folk, advancing pensively"

Dante's prose introduction to his sonnet explicitly calls for a symbolic reading of the pilgrims introduced into the narrative at this point and addressed in the sonnet. As a result, both the events of Dante's life and his textual passage through his narrative become identified as pilgrimages in what he calls a "general sense." Line 12 comes into the sonnet in a dramatic way because it fulfills the unheard melody announced in the previous sonnet, Beatrice's inexpressed sweet name. We want to see that she comes into presence here in words of grace, as Rossetti's free translation of lines 13–14 represents the matter. That *literal* beatific presence crowns Dante's argument about his double pilgrimage: for his *literal Vita Nuova* is a reflexive repetition of his life's experience. Rossetti translates this complex Dantean textual scene into contemporary terms. The move is established in the opening quatrain, whose uncanny effect comes from the suggestion that the pilgrim-folk include Rossetti and his Victorian readers. The illusion is raised of Dante speaking across the centuries through the exemplary mediumship of Rossetti's poetic traversal. Rossetti's readers pass through his verse "in thought of distant things"—like Dante, like Dante's pilgrims, like Rossetti.

"Beyond the sphere which spreads to widest space"

The Wordsworth allusion in line 4 is at once deft and shocking: deft because of the clear parallel between Wordsworth's Lucy figure and Dante's Beatrice; shocking because, as Byron would later say of Haidee and Aurora Raby, their beauties differ as between a flower and gem. Rossetti's implicit argument here forecasts his famous declaration: "Thy soul I know not from thy body" ("Heart's Hope," line 7).

In a Dantean perspective the sonnet looks forward to the *Commedia,* as Rossetti's prose note here indicates: Dante's "sospiro" (line 2) conceals his guiding "peregrino spirito" (line 8), an understanding hidden within a longing desire (lines 9–10, 14). The forecast *Paradiso* thus becomes here a kind of figure for this climactic moment in Dante's autobiography, where he seems poised in an exquisite vision of the relation of the text and journey he is just finishing and the text and journey he has yet to take. This sonnet incarnates that moment of poised awareness. In its Rossettian perspective, the entire dynamic is recuperated in the "lady round whom splendours move / In homage," i.e., the Ideal lady of every idealizing poet's imagination, Wordsworth's natural one as well as Dante's supernatural one. In Rossetti's later famous (and consciously Dantean) words: "This is that Lady Beauty, in whose praise / Thy voice and hand shake still"("Soul's Beauty," lines 9–10). Rossetti's final sonnet—not Dante's—is a poetic splendour risen to do homage to that figure.

SESTINA. OF THE LADY PIETRA DEGLI SCROVIGNI (DANTE ALIGHIERI)

This double work centers in the only one of Dante's *rime petrose* that Rossetti translated, the great sestina "Al poco giorno e al gran cerchio d'ombra." The nearly exact adherence to Dante's rhyme scheme makes the work a remarkable tour de force as well as a splendid poem in its own right. As Rossetti's note to the poem indicates, he is aware that the ascription to Pietra degli Scrovigni is uncertain—in fact, it is now known to be wrong (the lady's identity is not known). The picture that the poem doubles is the 1874 pastel *Madonna Pietra.*

SONNET. A RAPTURE CONCERNING HIS LADY (GUIDO CAVALCANTI)

Rossetti's poem is an unusually free translation, in technical respects, of Cavalcanti's famous sonnet. The poem brilliantly replicates the tone of the original.

BALLATA. OF HIS LADY AMONG OTHER LADIES (GUIDO CAVALCANTI)

Rossetti followed his source in ascribing this poem (incorrectly) to Cavalcanti.

TO GUIDO ORLANDI. SONNET. OF A CONSECRATED IMAGE RESEMBLING HIS LADY (GUIDO CAVALCANTI)

It is interesting that Rossetti would choose to translate this work, one of Cavalcanti's most irreverent and antireligious. The sonnet refers to a celebrated episode recorded in the chronicles of Florence for 3 July 1292: the report of great miracles effected through a painting of the Virgin in the church of San Michele d'Orto. Equally interesting is how well Rossetti replicates the spirit and import of Cavalcanti's wicked and witty sonnet, which works by reserve and implication. Especially admirable is the way Rossetti turns the topicality of Cavalcanti's sonnet to his own contemporary purposes. The effect is most striking in lines 13–14 (and the appended note), where Cavalcanti's reference to the Franciscans becomes Rossetti's to the "brethren" of the PRB.

BALLATA. OF A CONTINUAL DEATH IN LOVE (GUIDO CAVALCANTI)

Rossetti's source text is corrupt at some crucial places.

TO DANTE ALIGHIERI. SONNET. HE CONCEIVES OF SOME COMPENSATION IN DEATH (CINO DA PISTOIA)

Rossetti's source text was quite corrupt and his translational procedure moved freely in compensation. The result is an important original work with close connections to the *HL* sonnets (e.g., "The One Hope"). It clearly anticipates Rossetti's treatment of the relation of the Beloved of the sequence and the Innominata—a relation built upon the model fashioned by Dante in the *Vita Nuova* between Beatrice and the screen ladies. Finally, the last two lines of the octave force the translation into the kind of reflexive mode that characterizes so many of Rossetti's "New Life" poems. As a consequence the first-person pronouns in Rossetti's sonnet acquire a palimpsestic character, with Cino and Rossetti each playing a ghostly presence to the other.

CANZONE. HIS LAMENT FOR SELVAGGIA (CINO DA PISTOIA)

Rossetti's poem, like the original, enforces a relation between ritual and liturgical forms of prayer and a poetic "service" to a lady. It should be compared with Rossetti's translation of Fazio degli Uberti's "His Portrait of His Lady, Angiola of Verona."

SONNET. OF ALL HE WOULD DO (CECCO ANGIOLIERI)

Ironizing as it does the voice of the poet in the poem, Cecco's sonnet is finally a parodic transformation of the poetic tradition it is drawing upon. The sonnet triumphs in its bold skill and panache exactly because it skirts so close to travesty. In Rossetti's corpus, a close equivalent and analogue is the splendid burlesque "Parted Love!" which reflects upon and plays with Rossetti's serious love sonnet "Parted Love."

SONNET. ON THE DEATH OF HIS FATHER (CECCO ANGIOLIERI)

Cecco's sonnet represents a peak of the marvelously venomous poetry he directed at his father. Rossetti's source text was quite corrupt and led him to a free rendering of the original. A nice index of Rossetti's poetical success comes in line 3, which violates the literal sense but gains a far more important (and purely poetic) result that is completely true to the tone and colloquial spirit of the original. (A literal translation of line 3 would be something like "and that's Cecco, the one so called.")

SONNET. OF THE STAR OF HIS LOVE (DINO FRESCOBALDI)

The "new arrow" in line 5 is this poem, which has gained its power because the poet was struck with the light of the star of love.

OF HIS LAST SIGHT OF FIAMMETTA (GIOVANNI BOCCACCIO)

Most scholars do not accept this poem as Boccaccio's. In any case, it is important in the mythology of poetic influence that pervades Rossetti's work. Fiammetta—Boccaccio's Beatrice figure— is a second-order poetical construction, an imaginative response to and reprise on the Beatricean vision explicated in Dante's work. As such, Boccaccio becomes Rossetti's surrogate, an early inheritor of Dante's vision. The translation is closely connected to Rossetti's sonnet "Fiammetta" and its associated painting of 1878, *A Vision of Fiammetta*.

PART 6. OTHER TRANSLATIONS

IN ABSENCE OF BECCHINA (CECCO ANGIOLIERI)

Composed perhaps in 1849, which is Rossetti's brother's dating, but left unpublished by Rossetti in his lifetime; first printed posthumously (1911) by his brother. The poem (and translation) were probably judged too strong for Rossetti's Victorian audience.

FROM THE *ROMAN DE LA ROSE*

Composed in 1850; published posthumously (1911) by Rossetti's brother. Rossetti also executed a painting for this central text from the courtly love tradition.

LILITH. FROM GOETHE

Composed in 1866, published posthumously (1886). The text is most important for the relation it bears to Rossetti's various treatments of the figure and myth of Lilith. It translates a brief section of the famous Brocken scene in *Faust*.

"I SAW THE SIBYL AT CUMAE"

Written around 1870, first printed 1886. The translation is interesting partly because of the poem's famous reappearance in T. S. Eliot's *The Waste Land* (Eliot almost certainly came upon the poem through Rossetti's translation) and partly for the way it reflects on Rossetti's sense of the aptness of the fragment for his own place and time.

FRANCESCA DA RIMINI (DANTE)

Composed in 1862, the translation was first published in the *Athenaeum* (11 January 1879) then included in the 1881 *Poems* and collected thereafter. The text was to accompany the replica three-panel watercolor of *Paolo and Francesca* that Rossetti sold to James Leathart in 1862 (from a picture first done in 1855). Like many others before and since, Rossetti was fascinated by this famous story from Dante's *Inferno,* canto V.

PART 7. PROSE

HAND AND SOUL

Begun in September 1849, completed (after a hiatus) in December; first printed in the *Germ,* no. 1 (January 1850), reprinted in the *Fortnightly Review* (December 1869) and in a pamphlet, a few copies of which were printed privately at the same time. It is one of Rossetti's most important works—in fact, an aesthetic manifesto. It is set in the mid to late thirteenth century when Italian art is on the brink of the Renaissance. Giotto has not yet appeared, indeed (according to the story), even Cimabue is only just coming into public prominence. The point of all this is to develop a revisionist art history: that is, not only to try to imagine this primitive cultural scene, but to realize it in Vasarian terms. For Rossetti's tale, in the end, is an effort to rethink art history outside of the humanist paradigm that Vasari's *Lives* had laid down as the truth of the history of Italian art, and hence as the standard for measuring the truth and value of European art in general. The story of Chiaro is the story of an artist who refuses to take the Renaissance road. As such, it is a story with a profound contemporary (mid-Victorian) message. It is a message that in certain respects anticipates a similar refusal made by programmatic Modernist artists. The story's companion work is the set of sonnets, written about the same time, called "Old and New Art." Like its companion tale, "St. Agnes of Intercession," its greatest debt is to Poe's tales, especially hoaxing tales like "Von Kempelen and His Discovery." Most important is the imaginative form in which Rossetti casts his argument about art and art history. The procedure is exactly the same that he uses in his double works and his translations, where imaginative works are used to expound intellectual positions and ideas.

Epigraph. The passage is from the third stanza of Urbiciani's "How He Dreams of His Lady," which Rossetti translated.

309.13. Rossetti chooses Cimabue (1240?–1302) to establish the historical context for his imaginary tale of Chiaro, who is represented in the story as a kind of John the Baptist to Cimabue's Christ (see the reference in this paragraph to John 1:23: "I am the voice of one crying in the wilderness, 'Make straight the way of the Lord,' as said the prophet Esaias"). Chiaro, whose name means "clarity," is associated with Hermes, the gods' messenger.

310.5. Giunta Pisano was an obscure thirteenth-century painter.

311.32. of the heaven, heavenly: I Corinthians 15:47 ("of the earth, earthy"); hardly in her ninth year: Rossetti glances at the famous first meeting of Dante with Beatrice, recorded in the *Vita Nuova.*

314.23. The vision partly recalls the apparitions of the Virgin Mary recorded in the lore surrounding her and partly the figure of Diotima that Socrates speaks of in the *Symposium*.

316.1. "Give thou to God . . . ": recalls Christ's reply to the Pharisees in Matthew 22:15–22; "for his heart is as thine": this phrase is crucial for understanding the rest of the soul's remarks. One must note the lower case in the pronoun "his" as well as the sequence of similar lower case pronouns. These all reference the word "man," and they are to be sharply distinguished from the upper case pronouns that reference the word "God"; "Not till thou . . . be lost": this figure anticipates the scene Rossetti will stage much later in his "Willowwood" sonnets. It comprises an unusual interpretation of the Narcissus legend. The bent figure of Narcissus is imagined as a kneeling figure, and as such is invested with the virtues of devotion and humility.

317.5. The Raphael painting is a fiction.

317.19. *Manus Animam pinxit:* the hand painted the soul.

317.25. "Schizzo d'autore incerto": Sketch by an unknown author; yards of Guido: an ironic reference to the baroque painter Guido Reni (1575–1642), who epitomized an artistic practice Rossetti and the Pre-Raphaelites disapproved.

318.8ff. The Italian exchange runs, "How do I know?" . . . "mystic stuff. These English are mad about mysticism—it's like those fogs they have over there. It makes them think of their country: 'and melts their heart in sighs the day they have said farewell to their sweet friends.'" "The night, you mean."

318.16ff. The French reads, "And you . . . what do you think of this painting?" "Me? . . . I, my dear fellow, say that it's a specialty with which I cannot be bothered. I hold that when one can't understand a thing it's therefore of no importance."

SAINT AGNES OF INTERCESSION

Begun in March 1850, this work was left unfinished, though Rossetti augmented it in 1870 and again in 1881. First published posthumously in his brother's 1886 collected edition. The story is clearly a companion piece, set in the contemporary world, to "Hand and Soul." It is closely and explicitly associated with what Rossetti called his "bogey picture," *How They Met Themselves,* both being studies of the uncanny experience of meeting one's double. The title alludes to the thirteen-year-old Roman virgin who was martyred, according to tradition, in the early fourth century. Like Keats, Rossetti's interest focuses in the legend associated with St. Agnes: that a virgin who prayed to her on the eve of her feast day (21 January) would be granted a vision of her future spouse. Rossetti's tale shifts the Keatsian focus to encompass the issue of foreseeing, which is a recurrent Rossettian preoccupation. Special notice should be taken of the lyric embedded in the story. Written specifically for this tale, it stands in the work much as Stephen Daedalus's famous "Are thou not weary of ardent ways" stands in Joyce's *Portrait of the Artist as a Young Man*. Each poem is written partly as an index to the character of its fictive author—in this case, the character of the poet/critic being satirized by Rossetti in the story. Part of the wit of the poem in Rossetti's work lies in its parodic resemblance to certain features of Rossetti's own poetical style. Self-parody is a form of pastiche practiced by both Rossetti and Swinburne, and in this case it functions especially well. The story as a whole, for instance, is written under the parodic sign announced in the spurious epigraph from Sterne placed at the front of the tale.

319.10. Hamilton's "English Conoscente." . . . Della-Cruscan: the Hamilton reference is spurious. To call the engravings "Della-Cruscan" is to identify them with a sentimental engagement with Italian literature and culture; Bucciolo d'Orli Angiolieri: the Angiolieri named here is fictitious, though the name recalls the poet Cecco Angiolieri, translated by Rossetti.

321.24. Corn question and the National Debt: two political and economic problems that plagued England throughout the nineteenth century, particularly after the defeat of Napoleon and the end of the wars with France.

321.38. the "line": The critic is only focusing on the most readily seen pictures, those given a favorable position just above the molding (or line) that ran around the rooms at about eye level.

326.24. Guido Reni (1575–1642); Lodovico Carracci (1555–1619) founded a school with his nephews Agostino (1558–1601) and Annibale (1560–1609).

327.39. school of David: that is, neoclassical works from the late eighteenth and early nineteenth centuries.

328.23. Gozzoli: Benozzo Gozzoli (1420–1498), a Florentine master particularly important for Rossetti and the PRB because of his involvement with the Campo Santo frescoes reproduced in Lasinio's book of engravings.

331.7. Romans 11:33.

THE STEALTHY SCHOOL OF CRITICISM

Composed October–December 1871, this is the text of the essay published by Rossetti in the *Athenaeum* (December 1871). It is a reply to Robert Buchanan's abusive notice of Rossetti's 1870 *Poems*, "The Fleshly School of Poetry: Mr. D. G. Rossetti" (published in the *Contemporary Review*, Oct. 1871, under the pseudonym Thomas Maitland). Rossetti planned a pamphlet publication but was persuaded by his brother and his publisher to cut the opening half of his essay, which they considered possibly libelous. (The whole of the original text is available in the online *Rossetti Archive* (http://jefferson.village.virginia.edu/Rossetti). The two essays comprise one of the most notorious literary controversies in English literature. Originally written as an open letter to Buchanan, the published version is measured and restrained in tone—in sharp contrast to the original opening, which is riven by Rossetti's anger and anxiety. Apart from its biographical interest, the essay features a presentation of Rossetti's aesthetic "law" of the "inner standing-point"—a neglected but major contribution to the theory of art and poetry. Also notable is the fact that Buchanan's review led Rossetti to remove the sonnet "Nuptial Sleep" from the 1881 edition of *HL* and that Buchanan recanted his attack after Rossetti's death.

335.23. Sidney Colvin (1845–1927), art and literary historian.

PART 8. POSTHUMOUSLY PUBLISHED AND UNCOLLECTED WRITINGS

The texts of the writings in this section are taken from the most finished manuscript sources.

FILII FILIA

The first sonnet was composed in 1847, the second later, in 1849, on Rossetti's trip to the Continent; Rossetti's brother printed the first in his 1886 collected edition and collected it thereafter. The second sonnet was first published in The Rossetti Archive (online). The manuscript of these poems shows that they were arranged as a pair and that Rossetti thought in 1869 to publish them in the 1870 *Poems*. Their close relation to the sonnets "Mary's Girlhood" probably induced him to exclude them. Rossetti reworked the sonnet as a letter-poem to his brother (see "Returning to Brussels" in "A Trip to Paris and Belgium," below).

title. It means "Daughter of the Son," signifying that, while Jesus is her natural son, Mary, like all human beings, is the spiritual daughter of Christ. The most relevant text here is Dante's *Paradiso* XXXIII, 1ff. William Michael Rossetti said the sonnets refer to a painting—still unidentified—that Rossetti saw in an auction room.

ANOTHER LOVE

Composed about 1848, first published in 1898 by Rossetti's brother, collected thereafter. This and the next sonnet are from a group that Rossetti wrote to rhymes set for him by his brother. The two played this game several times in 1847–49, and the rule was that the sonnet had to be composed quickly, in five to ten minutes. Both poems were in the volume that Rossetti interred in his wife's grave in 1862. The early date of the poem is important because it reinforces the idea of fatality that grows increasingly important in Rossetti's work. Reading the sonnet with a self-conscious understanding of its history—which is what Rossetti would have done in 1862 (when he put it in the book he buried with his wife) and again in 1869 (when he exhumed the book for poems he wanted to publish in his 1870 *Poems*)—one is struck by its premonitory qualities. So the placement of the sonnet in the manuscript volume Rossetti interred with his wife's body amounts to a revisionary interpretation of the sonnet as a prophetic forecast of certain key events in his life.

PRAISE AND PRAYER

See commentary on "Another Love," above.

FOR A VIRGIN AND CHILD BY HANS MEMMELINCK (IN THE ACADEMY OF BRUGES)

Composed in 1849, first published with the "Sonnets for Pictures" in the *Germ*, no. 4 (30 April 1850); collected in 1886 and thereafter. Scholars associate this sonnet with the left panel of the Hospital of St. John's altarpiece, but it is almost certainly a response to another picture altogether: an outer wing of the *Altarpiece of the Baptism of Christ* by the Belgian master Gerard David. Rossetti saw the latter in the museum of the Academy of Bruges, which he visited in 1849. The painting was commonly attributed to Memling in the nineteenth century. The sonnet registers the importance of early Flemish art to Rossetti's experience and to his ideas about striking out on a new artistic course. See also "For a Marriage of St. Katherine, by the same."

FOR A MARRIAGE OF ST. KATHERINE BY THE SAME (IN THE HOSPITAL OF ST. JOHN AT BRUGES)

Composed in 1849, first printed in the *Germ*, no. 4 (April 1850), collected by Rossetti's brother in 1886 and thereafter. The sonnet references Memling's *The Mystic Marriage of St. Catherine*, the central panel of the so-called *St. John's Triptych* in the Hospital of St. John, now the Hans Memling Museum. The sonnet reconstructs the key spiritual event in the life of the Dominican tertiary and mystic St. Catherine of Siena (ca. 1347–80), her so-called Spiritual Espousal to Christ. In his characteristic way, Rossetti reads the painting for a contemporary and aesthetic significance. The Virgin and the "damsel at her knees read[ing] after her" from the "spread book" comprise a pair of figural forms signifying a future that clearly includes the interests and ideas of Rossetti.

A TRIP TO PARIS AND BELGIUM

This poetic sequence was first editorially constructed by Rossetti's brother, William Michael, who printed part of the series in his posthumous collected edition (1886) and augmented it in 1895 and 1911. Here the full series is given. The poems are verse epistles to William Michael written during Rossetti's art-research trip with Holman Hunt in the fall of 1849. He himself printed only a few, separately. The series is a significant Pre-Raphaelite document, having been written by Rossetti to and for the members back in England. Rossetti aligns the trip with the PRB's "revolutionary" cultural program. The text mentions in passing various PRB members and associates, including James Collinson, Millais, Frederic Stevens, and Thomas Woolner. The letters carrying these poems also carried a number of Rossetti's early "Sonnets for Pictures," specifically the sonnets on Giorgione and Ingres. One of this sequence's most interesting aspects is its deliberately apolitical focus, a fact underscored in the title supplied by Rossetti's brother. Rossetti and Hunt are drawn to Paris for its artistic, not its political, importance, and Belgium is regarded as the more significant destination, in particular the lesser towns of Bruges and Ghent. Rossetti took a skeptical view of the recent political upheavals in Paris and across Europe (see "On Refusal of Aid between Nations"), and his English jingoism in these poems is undisguised.

The poems are also important for the way they use poetic style as an argumentative vehicle. The sharply observed details comprise a running index of an aesthetic program that is specifically opposed to Rubens, Correggio, and others who were "Non noi pittori," as Rossetti says. This stylistic argument rhymes with Rossetti's mordant apolitical views, for his vision of cultural and social change was tied to a prior "revolution of imagination." We see this clearly throughout the sequence, not least in "Boulogne to Amiens and Paris" (47–48) when Rossetti's travel notebook—including this very sequence—is called an "émissaire de la perfide." The remark is completely ironical since the authorities would scarcely find anything explicitly political in Rossetti's travel notes. Yet from Rossetti's point of view, his personal and aesthetic stance toward his trip is subversive exactly because it casts a cold eye on the public sphere and what he saw as its futile, even hypocritical, agents.

The texts here are all taken from the manuscripts of the letters, where those are available. In cases where the manuscripts are unavailable, the texts are those provided in William Michael Rossetti's *D. G. Rossetti's Family Letters with a Memoir* (2 vols., 1895).

Boulogne to Amiens and Paris (3 to 11 p.m.; 3rd class)
title. The "3rd class" notation sets an important context and helps to explain how Rossetti might be (mis)perceived (see lines 47ff. and headnote to the sequence).

The Can-Can at Valentino's
William Michael Rossetti expurgated this text at lines 8 and 13–14 when he first printed it in 1895 in his *Memoir*.

To the P.R.B.
14. Sordello: the hero of Browning's poem *Sordello,* much admired by Rossetti.

Last Visit to the Louvre. The Cry of the P.R.B. after a Careful Examination of the Canvases of Rubens, Correggio, et hoc genus omne
1. Non Noi Pittori: Not our painters.

THE ORCHARD PIT

Rossetti sketched this marvelous long prose outline at Penkill in the fall of 1869, when he also drafted some lines for the poem he wanted to write. But the project never went further, and this text was published by Rossetti's brother posthumously (1886).

THE DOOM OF THE SIRENS. A LYRICAL TRAGEDY

As with "The Orchard Pit," Rossetti sketched this dark lyrical drama in the fall of 1869 but never completed the work. First published in the 1886 collected edition. At one point Rossetti imagined it as an opera.

DENNIS SHAND

Composed in 1850, Rossetti withdrew it from publication in the 1870 *Poems* because it dealt "trivially with a base amour (it was written very early), and is therefore really reprehensible to some extent." It was not published until 1911. The key to the poem's success is the way it manages to preserve its tension to the end. For in the concluding dialogue between Lady Joan and Earl Simon, one cannot be entirely sure if her deception controls the scene, or if he is aware of the adultery and has his own treachery in train through the cup which he keeps insisting that she and Dennis Shand should be the first to drink from. The drama of that sequence is maintained brilliantly, first, because the ballad takes such a neutral stance towards the three characters; and second, because the narrative lacunae are so strategically placed. Worth noting is the fact that the crucial stanza 17 was a late manuscript addition.

43. girdle-fee: that is, literally, pin money. The overtones in this case are sharply erotic. Pin money is ordinarily associated with a woman's allowance, but in this case Lady Joan is saying that she supplies her page and lover with a girdle-fee.

MACCRACKEN (PARODY ON TENNYSON'S "KRAKEN")

Composed in 1853 and circulated in Rossetti's correspondence, it was first printed in 1895 and collected thereafter. The poem is a wicked satire on the PRB patron and art collector Francis Mac-Cracken via a parody of Tennyson's "Kraken."

LIMERICKS

Rossetti wrote a series of these "nonsense rhymes," as he called them, mostly between 1869 and 1871. His brother first collected a group of them in his 1911 edition. The following is an ordered list of the limericks' subjects. Val: Valentine Cameron Prinsep (1838–1904), later PRB-influenced painter; Wells: Henry Tanworth Wells (1828–1903), minor painter; Hughes: Arthur Hughes (1832–1915), another late-PRB artist; Burges: William Burges (1827–81), architectural designer; Georgie: Lady Burne-Jones (Georgiana) (1840–1920); Edward Burne-Jones (1833–98); Chapman: George W. Chapman, minor painter of the period; Whistler: James McNeill Whistler (1834–1903); Ellis: F. S. Ellis, Rossetti's publisher; Howell: Charles Augustus Howell (1840?–90), PRB promoter and dealer; Inchbold: John William Inchbold, landscape painter; Brown: Ford Madox Brown (1821–93); Nolly: Oliver Madox Brown (1855–74), Madox Brown's second son; Agnew: Thomas Agnew and Sons; Huffer: Francis Hueffer, Madox Ford's father, a music critic; Scott, Scotus: William Bell Scott (1811–90), painter and poet; O'Shaughnessy: Arthur O'Shaughnessy (1844–81), poet; Knewstub: J. W. Knewstub, minor painter and Rossetti's studio assistant; Buchanan: Robert Buchanan.

Rossetti's brother noted that the limerick associating Georgiana Burne-Jones with "orgy" was pure "nonsense," deliberately outrageous.

PARTED LOVE!

Composed in 1869 as a parody of the *HL* sonnet "Parted Love," a love sonnet for Jane Morris that was written just before this text. First printed by William Michael in 1892 and collected thereafter under the title "The Wombat." The epigram recapitulates the sonnet's lament of separation from the beloved in a parodic vein. In the case of the epigram, Rossetti has in view his latest pet animal, a wombat, which arrived at his house in London while he was sojourning in Scotland at Penkill Castle.

The textual disjunction of sonnet and epigram is refigured in a new way in the drawing that accompanies this epigram. The drawing depicts Jane Morris leading a wombat on a leash. She and the wombat are both supplied with aureoles as signs of their sacred and beloved status. The drawing thus represents an unusual literalization of Rossetti's central subject, the relation of soul's beauty to body's beauty. But rarely does Rossetti, especially in the last fifteen years of his life, resort to a comical treatment of this subject.

AT LAST

Composed either in 1869 or in 1871 in the orbit of the *HL* sonnets, and Rossetti may have intended at one time to include it in the sequence. The poem was not, however, published until 1949, in Oswald Doughty's biography of Rossetti.

14. Genesis 1:3 and John 1:1–5.

FIRST FIRE

Composed in 1871, first printed in 1922 by T. J. Wise in *The Ashley Catalogue* (vol. 9, 115–16). Originally intended for *HL* as the companion piece to "Last Fire," Rossetti held the poem back almost certainly because of Buchanan's attack on "Nuptial Sleep." "First Fire" is perhaps an even more forthright treatment of erotic love than the latter.